The Right to Sanitation in India

The Right to Sanitation in India

Critical Perspectives

edited by

Philippe Cullet, Sujith Koonan, and Lovleen Bhullar

OXFORD

UNIVERSITY PRESS

OXFORD
UNIVERSITY PRESS

Oxford University Press is a department of the University of Oxford.
It furthers the University's objective of excellence in research, scholarship,
and education by publishing worldwide. Oxford is a registered trademark of
Oxford University Press in the UK and in certain other countries.

Published in India by
Oxford University Press
2/11 Ground Floor, Ansari Road, Daryaganj, New Delhi 110 002, India

ISBN-13: 978-0-19-948985-5
ISBN-10: 0-19-948985-8

Typeset in Adobe Garamond Pro 11/13
by Tranistics Data Technologies Pvt. Ltd, Kolkata 700 091
Printed in India by Replika Press Pvt. Ltd

Contents

Tables and Boxes

Tables

Boxes

Abbreviations

AfricaSan	African Conference on Sanitation
AMRUT	Atal Mission for Rejuvenation and Urban Transformation
ANC	African National Congress
APL	above poverty line
ATP	Aadi Tamilar Pervai
BGML	Bharat Gold Mines Limited
BIS	Bureau of Indian Standards
BPL	below poverty line
BWSSB	Bangalore Water Supply and Sewerage Board
CAG	Comptroller and Auditor General
CBO	community-based organization
CDP	Community Development Programme
CEDAW	Convention on the Elimination of All Forms of Discrimination against Women, 1979
CERD	Committee on the Elimination of Racial Discrimination
CESCR	Committee on Economic, Social and Cultural Rights
CLTS	community-led total sanitation
CPCB	Central Pollution Control Board

CPHEEO	Central Public Health and Environmental Engineering Organisation
CPR	Centre for Policy Research
CPWD	Central Public Works Department
CRC	Convention on the Rights of the Child
CRSP	Central Rural Sanitation Programme
CSIR	Council for Scientific and Industrial Research
DDWS	Department of Drinking Water Supply
DFID	Department for International Development
DHS	Department of Human Settlements (South Africa)
DPME	Department of Performance Monitoring and Evaluation (South Africa)
DWA	Department of Water Affairs (South Africa)
DWAF	Department of Water Affairs and Forestry (South Africa)
EHP	Emergency Housing Programme (South Africa)
ELRS	Environmental Law Research Society
FBSan	Free Basic Sanitation Implementation Strategy (South Africa)
FBW	Free Basic Water (South Africa)
FYP	Five-Year Plan
GLAAS	Global Analysis and Assessment of Sanitation and Drinking Water
GoM	Government of Maharashtra
GRIHA	Green Rating for Integrated Habitat Assessment
HIMUDA	Himachal Pradesh Housing and Urban Development Authority
HUDCO	Housing and Urban Development Corporation
IAS	Indian Administrative Service
IAY	Indira Awas Yojna
ICCPR	International Covenant on Civil and Political Rights, 1966
ICDS	Integrated Child Development Services
ICESCR	International Covenant on Economic, Social and Cultural Rights
IDP	internally displaced person
IEC	information, education, and communication
IHHL	individual household latrine

ILCS	Integrated Low Cost Sanitation Scheme
ILO	International Labour Organization
JNNURM	Jawaharlal Nehru National Urban Renewal Mission
KUWSDB	Karnataka Urban Water Supply and Drainage Board
LATINOSAN	Latin American Conference on Sanitation
MCGM	Municipal Corporation of Greater Mumbai
MDGs	Millennium Development Goals
MHM	menstrual hygiene management
MLA	member of the legislative assembly
MGNREGA	Mahatma Gandhi National Rural Employment Guarantee Act, 2005
MP	Member of Parliament
NABARD	National Bank for Agriculture and Rural Development
NAC	National Advisory Council
NBA	Nirmal Bharat Abhiyan
NCERT	National Council of Educational Research and Training
NCSK	National Commission for Safai Karamcharis
NEP	new economic policy
NGP	Nirmal Gram Puruskar
NHRC	National Human Rights Commission
NITI Aayog	National Institution for Transforming India
NRHM	National Rural Health Mission
NSLRS	National Scheme for Liberation and Rehabilitation of Scavengers and their Dependants
NUSP	National Urban Sanitation Policy
O&M	operation and maintenance
ODF	open defecation free
PCC	Pollution Control Committee
PDS	Public Distribution System
PHED	Public Health Engineering Department
PIL	public interest litigation
PPP	public–private partnership
PRIs	Panchayati Raj institutions

PSP	private sector participation
PUDR	People's Union for Democratic Rights
RTI	right to information
SAARC	South Asian Association for Regional Cooperation
SACOSAN	South Asian Conference on Sanitation
SAICE	South African Institution of Civil Engineering
SAP	structural adjustment programme
SBM	Swachh Bharat Mission
SBM-G	Swachh Bharat Mission (Gramin)
SBM-U	Swachh Bharat Mission (Urban)
SC	scheduled caste
SDGs	Sustainable Development Goals
SHG	self-help group
SKA	Safai Karmachari Andolan
SP	Superintendent of Police
SPCB	State Pollution Control Board
SSP	Slum Sanitation Programme
ST	scheduled tribe
TAHDCO	Tamil Nadu Adi Dravidar Housing and Development Corporation Limited
TPP	Twenty Point Programme
TSC	Total Sanitation Campaign
UDHR	Universal Declaration of Human Rights, 1948
UISP	Upgrading of Informal Settlements Programme (South Africa)
UNDP	United Nations Development Programme
UNECE	United Nations Economic Commission for Europe
UNICEF	United Nations Children's Fund
UP	Uttar Pradesh
VERC	Village Education Resource Centre
VIP	ventilated improved pit
WHO	World Health Organization
WSP	Water and Sanitation Programme

Foreword

Usha Ramanathan

The century turned, and another human right gained recognition. In its early years, sanitation found honourable mention in *General Comment No. 15* of the United Nations Committee on Economic, Social and Cultural Rights (CESCR), along with the right to water, which underlined that '[o]ver one billion persons lack access to a basic water supply, while several billion do not have access to adequate sanitation, which is the primary cause of water contamination and diseases linked to water'.[1] At that point, sanitation was largely seen through the worry of faeces contaminating water. In the decade that followed, the human right to sanitation found itself in the interstices of the right to health, the right to adequate housing, and the right to an adequate standard of living, alongside the right to water.

There are few who would doubt the value of safe, accessible, and hygienic sanitation. There has been too much silence around sanitation,

---

[1] UN Committee on Economic, Social and Cultural Rights, *General Comment No. 15: The Right to Water* (Arts 11 and 12 of the Covenant) UN Doc. E/C.12/2002/11 (2002), para 1.

and for far too long. Progressive recognition of this right in the international arena has acted as a prompt for states to place sanitation squarely on their agenda. In India, the recognition of the importance of sanitation started earlier, in 1999, with the Total Sanitation Campaign (TSC)—renamed the Nirmal Bharat Abhiyan (NBA)—with the goal of ending open defecation by 2017. In 2014, when a new government was formed at the Centre after the general election, among its early interventions in public policy was the Swachh Bharat Mission (SBM) (Clean India Campaign). The pressure has been building up since then, with the prime minister personally putting his heft behind the campaign with reward and punishment pursuing statistics around an acronym minted in the 2000s: ODF (Open Defecation Free).

It should be axiomatic that one human right ought not to be realized by violating other human rights. Yet, the Indian experience tells us that that is not as obvious as it may seem.

The first public shock about the calamitous effect of prejudice in the context of sanitation is recorded in a 1996 report of the People's Union for Democratic Rights (PUDR)-Delhi.[2] Dilip, a 19-year-old man visiting Delhi to witness the Republic Day celebrations in January 1995, was 'beaten, kicked and forced to run around and squat by constables of Delhi Police. Dilip collapsed and died on the spot.'[3] The provocation: that he was from a nearby slum and appeared to have used the park to defecate. In the ensuing conflict that erupted when the police attempted to remove Dilip's body, and irate slum dwellers resisted, the police fired, immediately killing three, one more person died subsequently, 16 were injured, and 123 arrested.

In interviews to the press, the Additional Commissioner of Police defended the firing as an 'inevitable and necessary intervention in a conflict between the "haves" (the residents of Ashok Vihar [a residential colony]) and the "have-nots" (the jhuggi dwellers)—sooner or later this had to happen'.[4] The police position on this episode was summed up in the report as follows:

---

[2] People's Union for Democratic Rights, *A Tale of Two Cities: Custodial Death and Police Firing in Ashok Vihar* (2nd edition, 1996); available at http://pudr.org/sites/default/files/pdfs/1996%20A%20tale%20of%20two%20cities-CD-ASHOK%20VIHAR.pdf.

[3] People's Union for Democratic Rights (n 2), 2.

[4] People's Union for Democratic Rights (n 2), 3.

(1) Slums have grown in Delhi.
(2) It is not possible to provide amenities to slum dwellers.
(3) Therefore, tensions are a necessary result.
(4) The police is not responsible for such a situation.
(5) But they are forced to intervene to preserve law and order.[5]

The PUDR report sets out a telling statistic:

the Slum Wing provides one tap for every hundred jhuggis and one toilet seat for every 25 jhuggis. It admits that one toilet seat ought to be provided for every 7 jhuggis. However, in Shaheed Sukhdev Nagar there are no toilets, for roughly 5,000 families. The Slum Wing cites a combination of factors 'as cause [including a] lack of space, and the' reluctance of the railways.[6]

This incident is teeming with multiple violations of human rights— to dignity and safety while doing what must be done; police brutality; arrest and detention; and the taking away of life itself.

Recent years have seen a return to this attitude of intolerance, accompanied by public shaming, exclusion, and punishment. The focus has moved away from dignity to shame, and from provision to punishment. Consider these representative incidents:

- On 17 June 2017, newspapers reported that a man had been beaten to death by municipal council employees when 'he tried to stop them from clicking photographs of women defecating in the open. He was allegedly kicked, punched and beaten with a stick. He died later at a hospital.'[7] This happened when the officials were on their morning tour of the area.
- The cruelty takes different forms. In October 2017, an IAS officer in Maharashtra reportedly 'garlanded and felicitated' two women labourers while they were returning from defecating in the open.

[5] People's Union for Democratic Rights (n 2), 3.
[6] People's Union for Democratic Rights (n 2), 7–8.
[7] HT Correspondent, 'Rajasthan Officials "Photograph Women Defecating in Public", Lynch Man who Objected', *Hindustan Times* (17 June 2017); available at www.hindustantimes.com/india-news/ man-objects-to-civic-officials-taking-photos-of-women-defecating-in-open-is-lynched-to-death/story-bjv71wviSpLGlXtT7SAWuL.html.

He then sent the pictures to the media. The state government ignored demands for action against the officer.[8]

- The state has acquired a reputation for adopting extreme measures in its keenness to end open defecation. Earlier in the year, the state government of Maharashtra set up what were called 'Good Morning Squads' to spot, and crack down on those defecating in the open. As a squad member explained to the reporter: 'it is necessary to create fear among people relieving themselves in the open. But we normally have to just shout or whistle to get people to run away'.[9]

- Public shaming, punishing, threatening, and inducing fear have become part of state practice in ridding itself of what it sees as the shame of open defecation. Others imitate these tactics. So, a TV channel started the following campaign:[10]

> Name and Shame Campaign
> #EndOpenDefecation
> Blow the Whistle on Open Defecation
> Send in pictures at …

See also, TMM Staff, 'Hyd Corporator's Insensitive Selfie, Posts a Pic of Lorry Driver Defecating in Open', *The News Minute* (23 January 2018); available at www.thenewsminute.com/article/hyd-corporators-insensitive-selfie-posts-pic-lorry-driver-defecating-open-75233.

[8] Express News Service, 'Solapur Open Defecation Row: IAS Officer Denies "Garlanding" Women to Shame Them', *The Indian Express* (9 October 2017); available at http://indianexpress.com/article/india/maharashtra-open-defecation-solapur-ias-officer-denies-garlanding-women-to-shame-them-4881085; HuffPost Staff, 'Two Women in Maharashtra were "Garlanded" and Photographed for Defecating in the Open', *Huffington Post* (8 October 2017); available at www.huffingtonpost.in/2017/10/08/two-women-in-maharashtra-were-garlanded-and-photographed-for-defecating-in-the-open_a_23236271/.

[9] *Hindustan Times*, '"Good Morning" Squads to Tackle Open Defecation in Maharashtra', *Hindustan Times* (20 May 2017); available at www.hindustantimes.com/mumbai-news/now-good-morning-squads-to-tackle-open-defecation-in-maharashtra/story-w0GMUH9FTMKRAbiN5n5FwL.html.

[10] CNN-News18, 'The Name and Shame Campaign: Time to End Open Defecation' (2 October 2017); available at www.news18.com/news/india/the-name-and-shame-campaign-time-to-end-open-defecation-1533911.html.

- A shift has been made from the human right to sanitation to the state's sense of shame, and ambition to make open defecation history. The lawless lengths which may be reached is evident from newspaper reports which list ways in which punishment is meted out, such as in the case of the state of Rajasthan where:
  - Six villagers were arrested in Bhilwara for defecating in the open;
  - Subsidized grains were denied under the public distribution system (PDS) to families without toilets in Jhalawar District;
  - In Jahazpur sub-division of Bhilwara District, power supply was disconnected in a village where only 19 per cent of households had toilets; and
  - In Karauli, women teachers were asked to mark attendance from the field by clicking selfies while they prevented villagers, men and women, from defecating in the open.[11]

[11] Manoj Ahuja, 'Power Cuts, Ration Cuts, Selfies with People Pooping in Open: Rajasthan Races against ODF Deadline', *Hindustan Times* (2 October 2017); available at www.hindustantimes.com/jaipur/power-cut-ration-cut-arrests-selfies-with-people-pooping-in-open-rajasthan-races-against-odf-deadline/story-3y6Cwcia6gjdIRnEcZ-c4uN.html. See also Vibha Sharma, 'South MCD to Penalise People Defecating in Open', *Hindustan Times* (20 June 2017); available at www.hindustantimes.com/delhi-news/south-mcd-to-penalise-people-defecating-in-open/story-CQnZqz9gkIQhoZ6DCW3CuL.html; Aishwarya Krishnan, 'Twinkle Khanna Trolls Man Openly Defecating & Promotes Akshay Kumar's Toilet Ek Prem Katha with This Hilarious Picture', *IndiaBuzz* (19 August 2017); available at www.india.com/buzz/twinkle-khanna-trolls-man-openly-defecating-promotes-akshay-kumars-toilet-ek-prem-katha-with-this-hilarious-picture-2413424/; FP Staff, 'Ranchi Authorities Publicly Shame Open Defecators: State Sponsored Vigilantism could be a Dangerous Idea', *First Post* (25 September 2017); available at www.firstpost.com/india/ranchi-authorities-publicly-shame-open-defecators-state-sponsored-vigilantism-can-be-a-dangerous-idea-4079243.html; Kelly Kislaya, 'Ranchi Civic Body Disrobes Those Defecating in the Open', *The Times of India* (25 September 2017); available at https://timesofindia.indiatimes.com/city/ranchi/ranchi-civic-body-disrobes-those-defecating-in-the-open/articleshow/60820903.cms.

- In Puducherry, Lt Governor Kiran Bedi tweeted that subsidized rice in the PDS would be given only in villages certified to be ODF.[12] Public outrage caused her to backtrack swiftly, while making a pitch for 'cleanliness'.[13]

This idea of the 'clean' has shifted the focus from the concerns of those below the poverty line to the priorities and prejudices of those wielding power. Law supports none of these actions. Quite to the contrary, the National Food Security Act, 2013 creates statutory entitlements to food, which are thwarted by the imposition of these unsanctioned penalties. Even arrest and detention have been taken out of the idea of the rule of law.

* * *

Illiteracy, indebtedness, and lack of sanitation facilities are among the challenges that rural India struggles with. In the beginning, there was the Central Rural Sanitation Programme (CRSP), run by the state, but with very little community participation. Then, there was the TSC, which was intended to be demand driven and people centred. This was followed by the SBM, which shifted the onus to the individual, with the state providing a grant to be used in building toilets, and demanding immediate compliance.

Sometimes, legislatures have exerted their muscle and enacted disqualifications and exclusions; and the Supreme Court of India has not found that to be a problem. In 2015, the state of Haryana amended its law on contesting elections to the panchayat, disqualifying

- those with educational qualifications lower than that prescribed,
- those with arrears of debt to a cooperative,

---

[12] Press Trust of India, Puducherry, 'Only Defecation-Free Puducherry Villages to Get Free Rice, Says Kiran Bedi', *Hindustan Times* (29 April 2018); available at www.hindustantimes.com/india-news/kiran-bedi-says-no-free-rice-for-puducherry-villages-if-not-defecation-free/story-XAT-8zub1x9eTWDeobqO64O.html.

[13] The Quint, 'Kiran Bedi Retracts Linking of Free Rice to Clean Villages', *The Quint* (28 April 2018); available at www.thequint.com/news/india/kiran-bedi-says-no-free-rice-to-village-with-open-defecation-garbage.

- those with arrears in payment for electricity, and
- those without functional toilets.[14]

These are examples of the state being disciplinarian and paternalistic. The amendment was challenged in the Supreme Court of India for adopting arbitrary bases, which had the effect of denying the right to contest to many with socio-economic vulnerability. The intolerance and impatience of the legislature was, however, endorsed by a two-judge bench. Statistics showed that large numbers of people— women, scheduled castes (SCs), scheduled tribes (STs)—would stand disqualified by these amendments. For instance, of the SC population of 21 lakh in Haryana, 11 lakh were men, and 10 lakh women. Of these, 6.3 lakh men and 3.1 lakh women were recorded as being educated. Assuming that all of them were educated to the level demanded by the amendments, at least 68 per cent women and 41 per cent men belonging to the SCs would be rendered ineligible to contest. Yet the Court was unwilling to see that these exclusions were arbitrary.[15]

In a statement that caused much consternation because of the bias that it revealed, the judge explained why he was sympathetic to these disqualifications: 'It is only education which gives a human being the power to discriminate between right and wrong, good and bad. Therefore, prescription of an educational qualification is not irrelevant for better administration of the panchayat.'[16]

It was argued that denying a person the right to contest panchayat elections, and so to become a participant in decisions affecting their lives, because they do not have a functional toilet in their homes, would exclude a large number of the rural poor. This is an unhealthy practice, the Court said, referring to open defecation, and the state has evolved schemes to provide financial assistance to those needing help in building toilets. Poverty is one of the reasons for not having toilets, but open defecation is not practiced only by the poor in rural

[14] The Haryana Panchayati Raj Act, 1994 as amended by the Haryana Panchayati Raj (Amendment) Act, 2015, s 175.

[15] *Rajbala* v *State of Haryana* Writ Petition (Civil) No. 671 of 2015 (Supreme Court of India, 2015) ('*Rajbala*').

[16] *Rajbala* (n 15), para 85.

India. 'If people still do not have a toilet, it is not because of their poverty but because of their lacking the requisite will', the Court said, upholding the amendments.[17]

Illiteracy, debt, and open defecation, all three indicate systemic failure. Yet, the Court readily endorsed the shifting of responsibility to large numbers of the rural poor, who have, over decades, been excluded from basic services, and who would now be cast in the mould of 'status offenders'.[18]

* * *

Such manifest prejudice against those in poverty is not entirely new. In 2000, the Supreme Court of India was dealing with a public interest litigation (PIL) about solid waste disposal in the four metropolitan cities of Mumbai, Chennai, Kolkata, and Delhi. In the midst of a diatribe against municipal authorities, the municipal employees tasked with cleaning the city, and the industrial and domestic waste being emptied into the river Yamuna, the Court directed its wrath at slums and slum dwellers.[19] 'When a large number of inhabitants live in unauthorised colonies with no proper means of dealing with the domestic effluents, or in slums with no care for hygiene, the problem becomes more complex',[20] the Court said. This was a prelude to launching an attack on the proliferation of slums: 'The number of slums has multiplied in the last few years by geometric

---

[17] *Rajbala* (n 15), para 95.

[18] *Rajbala* (n 15). In this case, the judges refused to test the legislation for arbitrariness under Article 14 of the Constitution of India, holding that 'it is not permissible for this court to declare a state legislation unconstitutional on the grounds that it is arbitrary'. This was expressly overruled in *Shayarabano* v *Union of India* Writ Petition (Civil) No. 118 of 2016 (Supreme Court of India, 2017). The *Rajbala* judgment will have to be revisited, and the legislation tested for arbitrariness. For a treatment of 'status offenders', see Usha Ramanathan, 'Ostensible Poverty, Beggary and the Law' (2008) XLIII(44) *Economic & Political Weekly*, 33.

[19] *Almitra Patel* v *Union of India* Writ Petition (Civil) No. 888 of 1996 (Supreme Court of India, Judgment dated 15 February 2000) ('*Almitra Patel*').

[20] *Almitra Patel* (n 19), 4.

proportions'; for usurping 'public land ... for private use free of cost'. 'Instead of Slum Clearance', the Court raged, 'there is Slum Creation in Delhi', resulting in increase in density in the city. The authorities must realize, the Court said, that there is a limit to which the population of a city can be increased. Then, in a twist of logic that certainly did not draw from the report of a committee that the Court had set up to study the problem of solid waste disposal, the Court pronounced: 'It is the garbage and solid waste generated by these slums which require to be dealt with most expeditiously and on the basis of priority'. Amidst these expostulations about slums, the Court made a statement that acquired notoriety: 'Rewarding an encroacher on public land with free alternative site is like giving a reward to a pickpocket'.[21]

This was a likening of poverty with criminality, which spoke volumes about judicial bias. What followed heightened the understanding of the Court's disdain for those in poverty, and its concern that slums and garbage could disrupt the lives of the rest of the denizens. Land for landfill sites was proving hard to find because of the cost of land. 'One of the reasons for the sites not being available,' the Court said,

was that land-owning agencies like the Delhi Development Authority or the government of the National Capital Territory of Delhi are demanding market value of the land of more than Rs. 40 lakhs per acre ... Keeping Delhi clean is a governmental function ... It is the duty of all concerned to see that landfill sites are provided in the interest of public health. Providing of landfill sites is not a commercial venture, which is being undertaken by the MCD. It is as much the duty of the MCD as that of other authorities ... to see that sufficient sites for landfills to meet the requirement of Delhi for next twenty years are provided. Not providing the same because the MCD is unable to pay an exorbitant amount is un-understandable. Landfill site has to be provided and it is wholly immaterial which Governmental agency or the local authority has to pay the price for it.[22]

---

[21] *Almitra Patel* (n 19), 4.
[22] *Almitra Patel* (n 19), 5.

This judgment marks a definitive shift in reimagining the 'public' in 'public interest', even as it lays blame and the city's shame on those too poor to be legal.

* * *

Years before sanitation got its place as a human right, untouchability, caste-based discrimination, and dispensability attributed to a community of persons had fomented a movement. Manual scavenging—a term with a meaning and a practice specific, ironically, to the modern Indian condition[23]—is a predominantly caste-based occupation, where human excreta is removed manually.

In 1950, Article 17 of the Constitution of India declared untouchability to be an offence.[24] It was only in 1993 that a law was enacted outlawing manual scavenging and dry latrines.[25] The law remained a statement of acknowledgement rather than of intent till, in 2003, a movement for the implementation of the 1993 law, and for the eradication of the practice, took the case to court. It was over a decade later that the Supreme Court of India expressly ruled that manual scavenging is a practice in untouchability, and cannot be constitutionally tolerated.[26] While the case was still in court, and spurred on by movements against manual scavenging around the country, Parliament enacted a further law in 2013 to prohibit manual scavenging, specifically recognizing the everyday risk and danger, and alarmingly frequent deaths, of sewer workers, in sewer lines and septic tanks.[27] In 2015, the escalating

[23] On the definition of manual scavenging, see Wilson (Chapter 10) and Khanna (Chapter 11) in this volume.

[24] Constitution of India, Art. 17 reads 'Abolition of Untouchability: Untouchability is abolished and its practice in any form is forbidden The enforcement of any disability arising out of untouchability shall be an offence punishable in accordance with law'.

[25] The Employment of Manual Scavengers and Construction of Dry Latrines (Prohibition) Act, 1993.

[26] Safai Karamchari Andolan & Others v Union of India & Others (2014) 11 SCC 224 (Supreme Court of India, 2014).

[27] The Prohibition of Employment as Manual Scavengers and Their Rehabilitation Act, 2013.

numbers of deaths of manual scavengers in sewer lines and septic tanks[28] was reflected in an amendment to the Scheduled Castes and Scheduled Tribes (Prevention of Atrocities) Act, 1989, asserting the caste basis of the practice, and that manual scavenging constitutes an 'atrocity'.

Despite these developments in law and judicial pronouncements, and the severity of the violations being publicly acknowledged, there is no evidence that this is a matter addressed while pursuing sanitation and ODF campaigns. In November 2017, the mission statement of the Special Rapporteur on the Human Rights to Safe Drinking Water and Sanitation set out categorically:

Discrimination against manual scavengers is another concern. ... From a human rights perspective, whether individuals are engaged in manual cleaning of open pits, septic tanks or sewer lines, with or without protective gear, in direct contact with excreta—as per the definition in the Act—is not a relevant factor to ascertaining that manual scavenging is a caste-based discrimination.

... I heard from several family members, during meetings in Delhi and Lucknow, a number of relatives (husbands, brothers, and sons) that died during the hard work of emptying latrines or cleaning sewer lines.

... In taking steps forward in the realisation of the right to sanitation, India may involuntarily contribute to violating the fundamental principle of non-discrimination. Particularly given the generations-old practice of imposing sanitary tasks onto the lower castes, the growth in number of toilets raises concerns that manual scavenging will continue to be practiced in a caste-based, discriminatory fashion.

Even in the case of Clean India Mission's preferred technology for excreta disposal—the twin-pit latrine—it is nevertheless questionable that manual scavenging as a discriminatory practice will be eliminated ... [and] some studies have indicated that the construction of single pit latrines is actually on the rise across several

---

[28] In just one year, 2017, the Safai Karmachari Andolan (SKA) recorded 132 deaths of persons sent into sewers.

Indian states, which will require even more unsafe work from manual scavengers.[29]

These are early years yet when the literature exploring the contours of the human right to sanitation is just beginning to be produced. There is so much to understand: Who is asking for it, what are the costs and who is having to pay for them, what the law is, what courts say, and what aspirations are found among people and among states. This volume marks a moment in the evolution of this human right, as it travels across issues, continents and countries, and concerns. It is empathetic to the importance of the right, as well as to the problems forced by notions of shame; pollution; cleanliness; and experience with exclusion, discrimination, violence, and coercion. This is a good time to take stock of what the right is, and how it can be achieved without putting other rights at risk.

[29] United Nations, 'End of Mission Statement by the Special Rapporteur on the Human Rights to Safe Drinking Water and Sanitation Mr Léo Heller', (10 November 2017); available at www.ohchr.org/EN/NewsEvents/Pages/DisplayNews.aspx?NewsID=22375&LangID=E.

Acknowledgements

The editors would like to acknowledge all the people who have contributed to the progressive development of this volume.

We would like to thank Jessy Thomas for translating Bezwada Wilson's interview, and for her extensive contribution to the copy-editing of this volume. We would also like to acknowledge the contribution of Arunoday Majumder in shaping Bezwada Wilson's interview into its chapter form. Finally, we would like to thank Preeti Mohan for preparing and presenting a paper at the workshop in Delhi, which laid the foundation of the chapter on sanitation and state planning. We also thank all the participants of the workshops organized in Delhi and London.

Philippe Cullet gratefully acknowledges the financial support of the Leverhulme Trust through an international academic fellowship, and the institutional support of the Centre for Policy Research (CPR), New Delhi, India and SOAS University of London, UK. Lovleen Bhullar and Sujith Koonan would also like to acknowledge the institutional support of the Environmental Law Research Society (ELRS), New Delhi.

New Delhi, 16 July 2017

Introduction

Philippe Cullet, Sujith Koonan, and *Lovleen Bhullar*

The right to sanitation has been progressively integrated into the international human rights law framework since the beginning of the century. In India, the recognition of the right itself is not a matter for debate since courts have repeatedly affirmed its existence as a right deriving from the fundamental right to life.[1] Key issues arise in the context of the conceptualization and realization of the right and relate to the existence of a law and policy framework for the realization of the right to sanitation for all, the scope of the right, its links with other rights such as health and gender equality, as well as issues of specific relevance in the Indian context, such as manual scavenging and more generally caste-based discrimination and exploitation linked to sanitation work. This book represents the first effort to conceptually engage with the various dimensions of the right to sanitation in India.

India faces a number of sanitation-related issues. While some of these challenges may be common with other countries, for example,

---

[1] For example, *Virendra Gaur v State of Haryana* (1995) 2 SCC 577 (Supreme Court of India, 1994).

South Africa, and/or form part of the debates at the international level, in various ways the situation in India is either different in terms of the scale of the issues, such as open defecation, or idiosyncratic, as in the case of manual scavenging and, more broadly, the caste-related issues linked to sanitation. This book analyses the right to sanitation in India in the broader international and comparative setting. In a context where sanitation challenges are more severe in India than in many other countries, this book is the first step towards a better understanding of the right to sanitation and its multiple dimensions. This contribution is necessary not only to deepen the context for understanding sanitation in India, but also to provide a point of comparison vis-à-vis other countries and to expand the scope of the debate at the international level.

One of the main contributions of this book is to foster an understanding of the right to sanitation as being much broader than the way in which it is currently recognized in mainstream debates.[2] Whereas sanitation interventions often focus on infrastructure development (toilets and sewerage), some of the central questions that arise from a rights perspective are linked to dignity. These may be related, for instance, to issues of privacy arising in the context of open defecation or discrimination against people engaged in sanitation work. This book also highlights a number of other dimensions that have not received sufficient attention from a sanitation perspective, such as environmental dimensions, including water pollution, wastewater treatment, and wastewater reuse that are usually addressed from the water or environmental perspective.

Situation in India and Challenges

The sanitation situation is particularly worrisome in India. Only six years ago, there were 81.4 crore people without access to sanitation,

---

[2] It follows and builds on a mapping exercise of the law and policy framework brought together in an edited compilation of sanitation-related instruments: Philippe Cullet and Lovleen Bhullar (eds), *Sanitation Law and Policy in India: An Introduction to Basic Instruments* (Oxford University Press, 2015).

out of which 62.6 crore people practised open defecation, accounting for 59 per cent of the worldwide figures.[3] Even worse, these figures do not represent the actual use of toilets. This was, for instance, confirmed in the national Baseline Survey of 2012, which found toilet coverage of rural households at 38.76 per cent, with only 79.42 per cent of these toilets being functional.[4]

With regard to toilet construction—the main indicator used to identify access to sanitation—there has been a significant increase in the number of structures built over the past few years. Since the launch of the SBM in October 2014, coverage of individual toilets in rural areas has increased from 38.7 per cent to 80.79 per cent.[5] As of April 2018, 14 states have been declared open defecation free (ODF). In urban areas, 31 lakh individual toilets and 1.15 lakh community and public toilets have been built.[6] In the states of Gujarat and Andhra Pradesh, all the cities are now ODF.[7]

As this book elucidates, toilet construction represents a limited entry point for the realization of the right to sanitation, and various other dimensions of sanitation need to be considered as well. First, there is the issue of toilet destruction. This is very specific to dry latrines. They should all have been replaced decades ago in furtherance of the constitutional prohibition on untouchability, one of the manifestations of which is manual scavenging. Therefore, any remaining dry latrines need to be urgently destroyed. Census 2011

---

[3] WHO/UNICEF, Progress on Drinking Water: 2012 Update (WHO/UNICEF Joint Monitoring Programme for Water Supply and Sanitation, 2012), 19, 21.

[4] Swachh Bharat Mission (Gramin), Baseline Survey 2012, All India Abstract Report; available at http://sbm.gov.in/BLS2012/State.aspx.

[5] Government of India, Ministry of Drinking Water and Sanitation, Swachh Bharat Mission (Gramin): All India; available at http://sbm.gov.in/sbmreport/Home.aspx; 5 April 2018.

[6] Swachh Bharat Mission website; available at http://swachhbharatmission.gov.in, 5 April 2018.

[7] Note that this is disputed. For example, Sagar, 'Down the Drain: How the Swachh Bharat Mission is Heading for Failure' *Caravan* (May 2017) 31, 34.

found that 7.94 lakh dry latrines were still in use countrywide.[8] The number has reduced since then but it has not reached zero yet.[9]

Second, there is the related issue of manual scavenging. For a long time, it was not addressed as part of sanitation. There are good reasons to address manual scavenging separately since it is intrinsically linked to untouchability and broader social issues. At the same time, manual scavenging represents a system of management of human excreta where certain human beings are in direct contact with human excreta, and thus it is an unavoidable debate in the sanitation sector. Census 2011 identified approximately 13 lakh scavengers, of whom 95 per cent were Dalits and 98 per cent were women.[10] However, these figures may not be accurate. The continuance of the practice has been discovered in places where it is declared to have been eradicated.[11]

Third, the health challenge linked to sanitation is acknowledged but not always clearly integrated into the debate around the right to sanitation. The negative health consequences of inadequate sanitation particularly affect children who are widely exposed to infections transmitted through faeces. This, in turn, is one of the causes of stunting that affects 48 per cent of children under five years of age.[12]

Fourth, there is an immense environmental challenge linked to sanitation that spans liquid and solid waste management. Untreated or partly treated domestic sewage is the known cause of most water

---

[8] Answer to Lok Sabha Starred Question No: 395 'Manual Scavenging', answered on 5 August 2014.

[9] For example, Sarika Malhotra, 'Swachh Bharat: Undocumented Manual Scavengers Nix Govt's Success Story', *Hindustan Times* (12 April 2017); available at http://www.hindustantimes.com/india-news/swachh-bharat-undocumented-manual-scavengers-nix-government-s-success-story/story-2lJjCi91xllbEwMw0spvyI.html.

[10] R. Ilangovan, 'Manual Scavenging: Death in the Gutter', *Frontline* (31 May 2013), 37.

[11] Malhotra (n 9).

[12] Robert Chambers and Gregor von Medeazza, 'Sanitation and Stunting in India: Undernutrition's Blind Spot', (2013) XLVIII(25) *Economic & Political Weekly* 15.

pollution.[13] Only a limited number of people are connected to sewerage infrastructure, and that too mostly in the biggest metropolitan cities, with Delhi and Mumbai having around 40 per cent of the country's installed capacity.[14] People who do not practise open defecation mostly use pit latrines that may result in leaching of human waste into the ground and contamination of groundwater, which is an important source of drinking water. Pit latrines may also generate septage, the disposal of which remains an unresolved issue in most parts of the country, and which is consequently mostly dumped untreated in open areas or into water bodies.

On the whole, the sanitation situation was for long seen as abysmal in terms of the number people going for open defecation. There has been much progress with toilet construction—though a lot more remains to be done—but access to toilets is only one of the several very significant sanitation challenges facing the country. Debates around the right to sanitation must consequently address these various dimensions.

Sanitation in the Law and Policy Framework

The recognition of the right to sanitation is unambiguous, but there is little by way of a statutory framework for the realization of the right in India. Instead, a complex framework consisting of laws, policies, and administrative directions at different levels governs sanitation interventions.

In a context where the national and international law frameworks influence each other, a first point to address is their interface. At the international level, sanitation has been viewed as an implicit component of the rights to adequate standard of living and to health.[15] A number of treaties and soft law instruments have also recognized the right to

[13] Sushmi Dey, '80% of India's Surface Water May Be Polluted, Report by International Body Says', *Times of India* (28 June 2015), 10.

[14] Report of the Working Group on Urban and Industrial Water Supply and Sanitation for the Twelfth Five-Year-Plan (2012–17)–Submitted to the Steering Group on Water Sector, Planning Commission (2011), 8.

[15] UN Committee on Economic, Social and Cultural Rights, *General Comment No. 15: The Right to Water* (Arts 11 and 12 of the Covenant), UN Doc. E/C.12/2002/11 (2002).

sanitation along with the right to water.[16] Further, in recent years, the right to sanitation has progressively been articulated as a distinct right.[17] Strictly speaking, the international law framework has exerted little influence in terms of the development of the right to sanitation in India, in part because India has a longer history of the recognition of the right to sanitation. Further, the conceptualization of the right at the international level is comparatively narrow and does not fully capture some of the idiosyncratic dimensions of the right to sanitation in India, such as caste and gender.

Indeed, regulatory developments at the national level are not influenced only by the adoption of international law norms and their implementation domestically. Among the many other mechanisms that influence the domestic regulatory framework, development funding and policy advice are quite important. This is the case, for instance, with the World Bank that has been influential in structuring the national-level policy framework for sanitation, which is being implemented in rural areas since the end of the last century.[18]

The question that arises is whether the law and policy developments at the international level are suitable for the specific situation of the countries in which they are implemented. It becomes apparent quickly that one of the core issues discussed at the international level in recent years—the need for a separate right to sanitation—is not necessarily what matters in India. The right to sanitation is derived from the fundamental right to life because this was the most obvious and strongest link in the Constitution of India. At the same time, the main issues that have arisen over the past couple of decades do not

---

[16] For example, Convention on the Rights of the Child (CRC), New York, 20 November 1989, 1577 UNTS 3, Art. 24 and Convention on the Elimination of All Forms of Discrimination against Women (CEDAW), New York, 18 December 1979, UN General Assembly Resolution 34/180, UN Doc. A/RES/34/180, Art. 14(2)(h).

[17] For example, Committee on Economic, Social and Cultural Rights, Statement on the Right to Sanitation, UN Doc. E/C.12/2010/1 (2010) and UN General Assembly Resolution, The Human Rights to Safe Drinking Water and Sanitation, 17 December 2015, UN Doc. A/RES/70/169.

[18] For example, World Bank, Swachh Bharat Mission Support Operation, Loan Number 8559-IN, Loan Agreement of 30 March 2016.

concern the nature of the right, rather its scope and its relationship with other rights. One of the central issues is that sanitation is understood narrowly, and health, environmental, gender, or caste-related issues are not considered as sanitation issues.

There are mainly two types of statutory provisions relating to sanitation in India, both focusing on sanitation-related infrastructure. A series of laws focus on access to toilets in specific contexts, and some of them recognize access to toilets as a right, for instance, in the context of schools.[19] Others provide an institutional framework and stipulate duties and functions concerning sanitation, for example, the laws governing local bodies in rural and urban areas.[20] However, these laws do not focus on issues of privacy, dignity, gender equality, or inequality linked to caste.

Sanitation is a much more complex field than what a focus on infrastructure implies. Infrastructure may be an important element contributing to the realization of the right to sanitation, but there is no reason why it should always take priority over other dimensions of the right. For instance, there is a need to place as much emphasis on the realization of the right to environment as the right to sanitation. This implies that construction of toilets cannot be prioritized over the allegedly much more cost-intensive need to ensure that human and animal excreta do not contaminate the environment. This also serves as a reminder that the right to sanitation should not only be concerned with human excreta specifically, but also with all types of excreta to the extent that it affects human health and the environment.

Another dimension that remains largely unaddressed in existing sanitation-related legal provisions is the conditions of work of sanitation workers. Finally, there is an even more urgent need for societal change that should lead to valuing sanitation work rather than devaluing the

---

[19] For example, The Right of Children to Free and Compulsory Education Act 2009, Section 19 and schedule. See also The Contract Labour (Regulation and Abolition) Act, 1970, Section 18 and The Building and Other Construction Workers (Regulation of Employment and Conditions of Service) Act, 1996, Section 33.

[20] For example, The Haryana Panchayati Raj Act, 1994, Section 21(18) and The Bihar Municipal Act, 2007, Section 45(a)(ii) and (iii).

people undertaking the tasks that foster the realization of the rights to life, environment, health, water, and sanitation of all.

While the legal framework follows a fragmented approach to sanitation as reflected in the case of different statutes addressing different issues pertaining to the realization of the right, there is an exclusive policy framework for sanitation interventions. As the basis for the disbursement of a significant portion of the funds to state governments, the policy framework predominantly regulates sanitation interventions, particularly in rural areas.

Overall, the law and policy framework raises a number of issues such as its narrow focus on sanitation infrastructure, lack of convergence between laws and policies, lack of cooperation between different institutions, and implications for the right to equality, particularly from a caste and gender perspective. There is an urgent need to foster an understanding of the multiple dimensions of these issues, which are discussed in detail in the different chapters of this book, beyond the 'silos' that have traditionally marked law- and policy-making and implementation.

Scope of the Book

This book is structured around an understanding of sanitation that encompasses its multiple dimensions and links with other sectors. As the first book-length treatment of the right to sanitation in India, it represents an entry point into the subject matter and covers key issues and challenges. This book provides the first analytical map of the field of sanitation law and policy in India as it relates to the right to sanitation. It covers the situation in India, but in a context where there is increasing cross-fertilization across legal orders; it also includes one chapter addressing another jurisdiction (South Africa) and another chapter on the international law and policy framework in order to put domestic developments into perspective.

The first part of this book analyses the right to sanitation in its domestic, international, and comparative perspective. In Chapter 1, De Albuquerque examines the significant developments at the international level in recent years that have given prominence and visibility to the right to sanitation. At the same time, this chapter serves as a reminder that debates on the recognition of the right at the international level started much later than in India and that its conceptual frame is in some ways different, which is not particularly surprising since India faces some distinctive sanitation-related challenges. In Chapter 2, Dugard provides an analytical overview of developments in South Africa, one of the countries that are comparable in many ways to India. The general framework in South Africa may not be more developed than that in India, but at a more specific level, administrative interventions and case law provide insights into the types of issues that the realization of the right to sanitation may raise in India. The next two chapters move to the situation in India. In Chapter 3, Cullet focuses on the development of the right to sanitation and the law and policy context for its realization, while in Chapter 4 Ruchi Shree examines the role and impact of the state in guiding sanitation law and policy since Independence. These two chapters confirm that sanitation has been a major concern for lawmakers and policymakers for a long time, progressively leading to the recognition of the right to sanitation through the fundamental right to life.

The second part of the book more specifically examines the different ways in which the right to sanitation is realized through law and policy interventions. One of the broad lessons arising from this part is that realization of the right may take place in limited ways irrespective of whether the specific legal instruments refer to the right or not. A structural challenge in the realization of the right is the fact that for decades, sanitation interventions have been conceived separately for rural areas and urban areas. For the first time, the SBM brings both aspects under one roof, but the legal instruments used for sanitation interventions remain, as before, entirely separate. Several chapters in this part directly discuss the emphasis of sanitation interventions on ending open defecation and building individual toilets, in line with the policy focus on access to individual household toilets as the main marker of a successful sanitation intervention. Concerning rural areas, in Chapter 5, Koonan analyses existing sanitation interventions, and the underlying policy framework that governs them. In Chapter 6, Mehta follows up by examining community-led total sanitation (CLTS), a framework to make sanitation interventions less dependent on state intervention and focused more on demand from communities. In Chapter 7, John offers a critical assessment of the connections between forms of governance and regulation, and their impact on the delivery of sanitation as a basic human right in urban areas. In Chapter 8, Desai, McFarlane, and Graham explore the relationship between the body and sanitation infrastructure in the context of the practice of open defecation in urban informal settlements in Mumbai. The overwhelming emphasis on individual toilets being de facto equated with the realization of the right, does not consider what happens to the untreated septage or wastewater, and leaves sanitation interventions devoid of an environmental context. In Chapter 9, Bhullar's contribution highlights the environmental dimensions of sanitation.

The third part moves on to examine some of the most serious challenges impeding the realization of the right to sanitation for all. The first two chapters deal with manual scavenging (Wilson and Khanna, Chapters 10 and 11 respectively), an issue that is not only central in its own right but particularly so in the context of a right to sanitation. The struggle to realize the rights of manual scavengers has been underway for many decades but they are yet to be fully implemented. Further, it has repeatedly proven difficult to link manual scavenging with debates on sanitation, for instance, where the call for building more toilets is not directly linked to considering the management of excreta or more generally septage. While manual scavenging will hopefully be eradicated soon, this will not signal the end of the questions that need to be posed from the perspective of a right to sanitation. Indeed, even if all the dry latrines in the country are destroyed, many sanitation workers are likely to be employed to maintain the sanitation infrastructure so that it does not cause harm to public health and the environment. This part thus also specifically examines the broader issue of the rights of sanitation workers (Sakthivel, Nirmalkumar, and Benjamin, Chapter 12), which has been taken up by courts on various occasions but remains at the centre of concerns, as highlighted by the reports of deaths of sanitation workers while at work. The final chapter focuses on the place of women in sanitation law and policy. It problematizes some of the gender dimensions of sanitation in the wider context of gender equality and the realization of women's right to sanitation (Koonan and Bhullar, Chapter 13).

PART I

CONCEPTUAL FRAMEWORK

1

Sanitation

The Last Taboo Becomes a Human Right

Catarina de Albuquerque

The Sanitation Crisis

The current sanitation crisis has dire implications for the lives and livelihoods of billions of people around the world; yet it remains one of the most neglected issues at the international and national levels. The WHO/UNICEF Joint Monitoring Programme Report 2017 has estimated that sanitation coverage in 2015 was 68 per cent, meaning that the remaining 32 per cent of the world's population either shares a toilet, has access to other types of unimproved sanitation, or even practices open defecation. Since 1990, almost 2.1 billion people have gained access to an improved sanitation facility. The world, however, missed the Millennium Development Goals' (MDGs') sanitation target by almost 700 million people.[1] The nearly 700 million

---

[1] The WHO/UNICEF Joint Monitoring Programme for Water Supply and Sanitation, *Progress on Sanitation and Drinking Water: 2015 Update and MDG Assessment* (UNICEF and World Health Organization, 2015), 5.

people who would have been served if the MDGs' target for sanitation had been met are equal to the number of unserved people in sub-Saharan Africa.

By 2015, there were 2.4 billion people who still did not use an improved sanitation facility. Of these, 638 million used public or shared sanitation facilities. Even though open defecation rates have been decreasing steadily since 1990, it is estimated that almost 946 million still practice open defecation worldwide, and two-thirds of them live in Southern Asia. The overwhelming majority (90 per cent) of those practicing open defecation live in rural areas. Between 1990 and 2015, open defecation declined in all regions, with the most dramatic reductions seen in the least developed countries (from 45 per cent in 1990 to 20 per cent in 2015), representing an important first step on the sanitation ladder.[2]

When it comes to meeting self-imposed national sanitation targets (as opposed to the globally agreed MDG target), most countries reported in 2011 that they were falling short: 83 per cent of countries reported falling significantly behind the trends required to meet national access targets for sanitation.[3]

It is undisputed today that lack of access to sanitation affects human dignity, and is at the origin of the non-realization of basic human rights; yet sanitation remains severely underfunded, politically under-prioritized, and neglected at all levels. The taboo surrounding sanitation is one of the biggest obstacles. For most people, sanitation is a highly private matter, and an uncomfortable topic for public discussion. As a result of the failure to prioritize sanitation, there is also a lack of effective national policies, diverse and fragmented responsibilities for sanitation across government ministries, and a general lack of understanding of the positive effects of investing in sanitation. It is important to bring this issue to the fore and tackle the

[2] WHO/UNICEF JMP (n 1), 12–13.
[3] World Health Organization and UN-Water, *UN-Water Global Analysis and Assessment of Sanitation and Drinking-Water (GLAAS) 2012 Report: The Challenge of Extending and Sustaining Services* (World Health Organization, 2012), 11.

taboo that surrounds it. Speaking honestly and openly about faeces and defecation may indeed change the lives of, and restore a sense of dignity to, hundreds of millions of people.

What Is Sanitation?

Even though there are numerous definitions of sanitation, they often do not adequately capture all the relevant human rights dimensions and principles. For example, the definition developed for the purpose of monitoring access to sanitation, particularly in the context of the MDGs, used the term 'improved sanitation', referring to types of technology and levels of services that are more likely to be sanitary than unimproved technologies. It considered excreta disposal systems as 'adequate' as long as they are private, and separate human excreta from human contact.

Hence, in 2009, the then United Nations Independent Expert on the human rights obligations related to access to safe drinking water and sanitation (Independent Expert) proposed a definition of sanitation which is drawn from elements related to sanitation as addressed in international human rights law. She defined sanitation as: 'a system for the collection, transport, treatment and disposal or reuse of human excreta and associated hygiene. States must ensure without discrimination that everyone has physical and economic access to sanitation, in all spheres of life, which is safe, hygienic, secure, socially and culturally acceptable, provides privacy and ensures dignity'.[4]

The United Nations Committee on Economic, Social and Cultural Rights (CESCR) later endorsed this definition in a statement on the Human Right to Sanitation issued in November 2010. The said statement asserts:

> In line with the definition of sanitation as proposed by the Independent Expert on water and sanitation as 'a system for the

[4] UN Human Rights Council, *Report of the Independent Expert on the Issue of Human Rights Obligations Related to Access to Safe Drinking Water and Sanitation, Catarina de Albuquerque*, 1 July 2009, UN Doc. A/HRC/12/24.

collection, transport, treatment and disposal or re-use of human excreta and associated hygiene', States must ensure that everyone, without discrimination, has physical and affordable access to sanitation, 'in all spheres of life, which is safe, hygienic, secure, socially and culturally acceptable, provides privacy and ensures dignity'. The Committee is of the view that the right to sanitation requires full recognition by States parties in compliance with the human rights principles related to non-discrimination, gender equality, participation and accountability.[5]

This definition and the consideration of sanitation as a human right entail other types of implications. It also poses added challenges, since human rights set the bar at a higher level than the existing development language and concepts. These issues will be discussed later on in this chapter.

The Interrelatedness of Sanitation and Other Human Rights

The process of discussing sanitation as a distinct human right at the national level and also at the United Nations level started with the acknowledgment of sanitation as an essential element for the realization of other human rights, including the rights to an adequate standard of living, adequate housing, health, education, water, work, life, physical security, the prohibition of inhuman or degrading treatment, gender equality, and the prohibition against discrimination.

The Right to an Adequate Standard of Living

Considering the profound impact that lack of sanitation has on the quality of life of an individual, sanitation was throughout time frequently understood to be indispensable for achieving an adequate standard of living. For example, Article 14, paragraph 2(h) of the Convention on the Elimination of All Forms of Discrimination against Women (CEDAW), addressing the specific situation of rural

---

[5] UN Committee on Economic, Social and Cultural Rights (CESCR), *Statement on the Right to Sanitation*, 2010, UN Doc. E/C.12/2010/1.

women, provides that states parties shall take all appropriate measures to ensure to women 'the right ... to enjoy adequate living conditions, particularly in relation to ... sanitation'.[6]

Article 11, paragraph 1 of the International Covenant on Economic, Social and Cultural Rights (ICESCR) provides for 'the right of everyone to an adequate standard of living for himself and his family, including adequate food, clothing and housing, and to the continuous improvement of living conditions'.[7] While this Article does not include sanitation explicitly, the CESCR, the treaty body responsible for monitoring state compliance with the ICESCR, clarified in 2002 that 'the use of the word "including" indicates that this catalogue of rights was not intended to be exhaustive'.[8] Furthermore, in its General Comment[9] No. 19 (2008) on the right to social security, the CESCR included sanitation in an extended list of elements of the right to an adequate standard of living.[10]

As will be explained further on, it was in line with this understanding that in 2010 the right to sanitation was recognized as a human right, and reaffirmed as an essential component of the right to an adequate standard of living enshrined in Article 11 of the ICESCR.[11]

The Right to Adequate Housing

The right to adequate housing has generally been understood to include access to sanitation facilities. Indeed, it is difficult to imagine

---

[6] *Convention on the Elimination of All Forms of Discrimination against Women (CEDAW)*, New York, 18 December 1979, UN General Assembly Resolution 34/180, UN Doc. A/RES/34/180.

[7] International Covenant on Economic, Social and Cultural Rights (ICESCR), New York, 19 December 1966, 993 UNTS 14531.

[8] CESCR, *General Comment No. 15: The Right to Water (Arts 11 and 12 of the Covenant)*, 2002, UN Doc. E/C.12/2002/11, para 3.

[9] General comments are authoritative interpretations of the ICESCR. They clarify the content of rights, and are used in the monitoring of states parties' compliance.

[10] See CESCR, *General Comment No. 19: The Right to Social Security (Art. 9 of the Covenant)*, 2008, UN Doc. E/C.12/GC/19, para 18.

[11] See CESCR (n 5), para 7.

characterizing a habitation as adequate if sanitation facilities are not available within the vicinity, or if they are inadequate or unsafe to use. The CESCR's *General Comment No. 4* (1991) on the right to adequate housing stipulates that an 'adequate house must contain certain facilities essential for health, security, comfort and nutrition. All beneficiaries of the right to adequate housing should have sustainable access to ... sanitation and washing facilities'.[12]

The Special Rapporteur on the right to adequate housing has emphasized that 'full realization of the right to adequate housing is closely interlinked with and contingent upon fulfilment of other rights and services, including access to safe drinking water and sanitation'.[13] Confirming this understanding, in 2010, the CESCR stated that the right to sanitation is integrally related to the right to housing enshrined in Article 11 of the ICESCR.[14]

The Right to Health

The links between access to sanitation and health are well documented. The WHO estimates that 88 per cent of diarrhoeal disease is caused by unsafe water and sanitation, leading to the death of about 1.8 million people annually, of whom 90 per cent are children under five, mostly in developing countries.[15] Where people have no access or limited access to sanitation, they can also develop kidney and liver problems, and constipation, as well as psychological trauma.

International treaties also specifically recognize the link between sanitation and the right to health. For example, Article 12 of the ICESCR, recognizing the right of everyone to the enjoyment of the

[12] CESCR, *General Comment No. 4: The Right to Adequate Housing (Art. 11 (1) of the Covenant)*, 1991, UN Doc. E/1992/23, Annex III, 114, para 8 (b).

[13] UN Commission on Human Rights, *Report of the Special Rapporteur on Adequate Housing as a Component of the Right to an Adequate Standard of Living*, 2002, UN Doc. E/CN.4/2002/59, para 56.

[14] CESCR (n 5), para 7.

[15] World Health Organization, *Water, Sanitation and Hygiene Links to Health: Facts and Figures* (World Health Organization, 2004).

highest attainable standard of physical and mental health, provides that states should take steps for 'the improvement of all aspects of environmental and industrial hygiene'.

In addition, in its *General Comment No. 14* (2000) on the right to the highest attainable standard of health, the CESCR explained that the right to health is 'an inclusive right extending not only to timely and appropriate health care but also to the underlying determinants of health, such as access to safe and potable water and adequate sanitation'.[16] The Special Rapporteur on the right to the highest attainable standard of physical and mental health reaffirmed that water and sanitation are underlying determinants of health, and provided detailed guidance on its implications for the realization of the right to health.[17]

Article 24 of the Convention on the Rights of the Child (CRC) explicitly refers to sanitation, requiring that states take appropriate measures 'to ensure that all segments of society, in particular parents and children, are informed, have access to education and are supported in the use of basic knowledge of child health and nutrition ... hygiene and environmental sanitation'.[18] The Committee on the Rights of the Child has further included sanitation under the right to health in its general comments and concluding observations to states' periodic reports.[19] In 2010, the CESCR unequivocally stated that the right to sanitation is integrally related to the right to health

---

[16] CESCR, *General Comment No. 14: The Right to the Highest Attainable Standard of Health (Art. 12 of the Covenant)*, 2000, UN Doc. E/C.12/2000/4, para 11.

[17] United Nations General Assembly, *Report of the Special Rapporteur on the Right of Everyone to the Enjoyment of the Highest Attainable Standard of Physical and Mental Health*, 2007, UN Doc. A/62/214, paras 45–102.

[18] Convention on the Rights of the Child (CRC), New York, 20 November 1989, 1577 UNTS 3.

[19] UN Committee on the Rights of the Child, *General Comment No. 11: Indigenous Children and Their Rights under the Convention [on the Rights of the Child]*, 2009, UN Doc. CRC/C/GC/11, para 25 and UN Committee on the Rights of the Child, *General Comment No. 7: Implementing Child Rights in Early Childhood*, 2006, UN Doc. CRC/C/GC/7/Rev.1, para 25.

as laid down in Article 12, paragraphs 1 and 2 (a), (b), and (c) of the ICESCR.[20]

The Right to Education

Lack of access to sanitation can also have serious negative impacts on the enjoyment of the right to education. Each year 443 million school days are lost due to sickness caused by poor water and sanitation conditions.[21] Diseases caused by lack of access to sanitation and drinking water also affect students' ability to learn. Furthermore, where schools do not have sanitation facilities, children's exposure to disease is exacerbated, and they may not attend school; where toilets are not sex-segregated, girls often drop out of school, notably at the age of menstruation. Girls, who are often discriminated against in the exercise of their human right to education, suffer further due to the inadequacy of sanitation facilities, which deny them privacy, especially during the menstruation period. The lack of private sanitary facilities for girls discourages parents from sending them to school, contributes to the drop out of girls at puberty, and contributes to fewer women teachers, who are needed to encourage girls to attend schools.

The Committee on the Rights of the Child has specifically referred to sanitation in educational settings in its *General Comment No. 4* (2003) on adolescent health and development, which states that:

> considering the importance of appropriate education for the current and future health and development of adolescents, as well as for their children, the Committee urges states parties ... to ... provide well-functioning school and recreational facilities which do not pose health risks to students, including water and sanitation.[22]

Furthermore, the Special Rapporteur on the right to education has recommended, with regard to school sanitation for girls, that states

[20] CESCR (n 5), para 7.

[21] United Nations Development Programme (UNDP), *Human Development Report 2006: Beyond Scarcity: Power, Poverty and the Global Water Crisis* (UNDP, 2006), 6.

[22] UN Committee on the Rights of the Child, *General Comment No. 4: Adolescent Health and Development in the Context of the Convention on the Rights of the Child*, 2003, UN Doc. CRC/GC/2003/4, para 13.

allocate resources to school infrastructure, specifying 'that infrastructure must be sited within communities and include a drinking water supply and separate, private, safe sanitation services for girls' as well as 'establish efficient mechanisms for supplying sanitary towels to adolescent girls who so wish, especially in rural areas, and ensure they can always have the use of the sanitation facilities they need'.[23]

The Right to Water

Sanitation has also been linked with the right to water, with the now-common reference to the rights to water and sanitation. The connection between water and sanitation is clear: Without proper sanitation, human excreta contaminates drinking water sources, affecting water quality and leading to disastrous health consequences. Water is further linked to sanitation because waterborne sewerage systems are common in many parts of the world.

In its *General Comment No. 15* (2002) on the right to water, the CESCR states that 'the water supply for each person must be sufficient and continuous for personal and domestic uses. These uses ordinarily include drinking, personal sanitation, washing of clothes, food preparation, personal and household hygiene'.[24] The Committee specifies that 'personal sanitation' means disposal of human excreta, and 'personal and household hygiene' means personal cleanliness and hygiene of the household environment. *General Comment No. 15* further notes that:

> ensuring that everyone has access to adequate sanitation is not only fundamental for human dignity and privacy, but is one of the principal mechanisms for protecting the quality of drinking water supplies and resources.... States parties have an obligation to progressively extend safe sanitation services, particularly to rural and deprived urban areas, taking into account the needs of women and children.[25]

---

[23] UN Commission on Human Rights, *Report Submitted by the Special Rapporteur on the Right to Education on Girls' Right to Education*, 2006, UN Doc. E/CN.4/2006/45, paras 129–30.

[24] *General Comment No. 15* (n 8), para 12 (a).

[25] *General Comment No. 15* (n 8), para 29.

In 2006, the Sub-Commission on the Promotion and Protection of Human Rights adopted guidelines on the realization of the right to drinking water and sanitation, treating the two issues together. Regarding sanitation, they specifically provide that 'everyone has the right to have access to adequate and safe sanitation that is conducive to the protection of public health and the environment'.[26] The guidelines further specify that sanitation must be physically accessible, culturally acceptable, safe, and affordable.

In 2010, the UN General Assembly[27] and the Human Rights Council[28] recognized water and sanitation as a single human right.

The Right to Work and the Right to Just and Favourable Working Conditions

The right to work can also be negatively affected by lack of access to sanitation. Workplaces which do not provide sanitation facilities, have prohibitively long waiting times for the use of facilities, or where employees are pressured not to interrupt work for toilet breaks, may prevent employees from keeping their jobs or raise serious concerns about their right to work in safe and healthy working conditions. Women are particularly affected, especially during menstruation and pregnancy.

In its *General Comment No. 14* on the right to the highest attainable standard of health, the CESCR specifies that, with regard to the right to healthy natural and workplace environments, '"[t]he improvement of all aspects of environmental and industrial hygiene" (Art. 12.2 (b)) comprises, inter alia … the requirement to ensure an adequate supply of safe and potable water and basic sanitation … [and it embraces] safe and hygienic working conditions'.[29]

---

[26] UN Sub-Commission on the Promotion and Protection of Human Rights, *Draft Guidelines for the Realization of the Right to Drinking Water and Sanitation*, 2005, UN Doc. E/CN.4/Sub.2/2005/25, para 1.2.

[27] UN General Assembly Resolution, *The Human Right to Water and Sanitation*, 28 July 2010, UN Doc. A/RES/64/292.

[28] UN Human Rights Council Resolution, *Human Rights and Access to Safe Drinking Water and Sanitation*, 30 September 2010, UN Doc. A/HRC/RES/15/9.

[29] *General Comment No. 14* (n 16), para 15.

The International Labour Organization (ILO) Convention concerning Hygiene in Commerce and Offices provides in Article 13 that 'sufficient and suitable washing facilities and sanitary conveniences shall be provided and properly maintained'.[30] The ILO Recommendation concerning Hygiene in Commerce and Offices provides further detailed guidance on sanitation in the workplace,[31] and the ILO Recommendation concerning the Protection of the Health of Workers in Places of Employment specifically refers to sanitation, explaining that:

> measures should be taken by the employer to ensure that the general conditions prevailing in places of employment are such as to provide adequate protection of the health of the workers concerned [including] sufficient and suitable sanitary conveniences and washing facilities ... provided in suitable places and properly maintained.[32]

The Right to Life

Considering the potentially fatal impact of poor sanitation on people's health, it can be seen as integrally linked to the right to life. Thus, in its *General Comment No. 6* (1982) on the right to life, the Human Rights Committee stated that the right to life should not be interpreted in a restrictive manner, and found that 'the Committee considers that it would be desirable for States parties to take all possible measures to reduce infant mortality and to increase life expectancy, especially in adopting measures to eliminate malnutrition and epidemics'.[33]

The Right to Physical Security

For many people, the simple act of 'relieving oneself' is a risky affair. Women and girls are especially vulnerable to attack when they walk

[30] ILO Convention No. 120 concerning Hygiene in Commerce and Offices, Geneva, 8 July 1964, 560 UNTS 201.

[31] ILO Recommendation No. 120 concerning Hygiene in Commerce and Offices (n 30), para 38.

[32] ILO Recommendation No. 97 concerning the Protection of the Health of Workers in Places of Employment, Geneva, 25 June 1953, para 2 (e).

[33] UN Human Rights Committee, *General Comment No. 6: Article 6— Right to Life*, 1982, UN Doc. HRI/GEN/1/Rev.9 (Vol. I), 176, para 5.

a long way to access sanitation facilities, or when they are forced to defecate in the open. In addition, women without access to sanitation often defecate under the cover of darkness in order to ensure a minimum level of privacy, but at considerable risk to their physical security.

Protection of physical integrity is at the core of human rights, and must also be taken into account when considering sanitation. The International Covenant on Civil and Political Rights (ICCPR) protects the right to security of every person,[34] and the Committee on the Elimination of Discrimination against Women argues that violence against women, in the absence of due diligence on the part of the state, is a form of discrimination based on sex and is thus a violation of human rights, including violence committed by private actors.[35] The CRC also provides that states must protect children from all forms of violence.[36] In the World Report on Violence against Children, it was specified that 'in locations such as shanty towns and refugee camps, particular emphasis [must be] placed on creating safe routes to communal water collection, and to bathing and toilet facilities'.[37]

Prohibition of Inhuman or Degrading Treatment

The lack of access to sanitation would also tantamount to inhuman or degrading treatment in certain circumstances, especially in the context of detention. In a 2005 report focused on water, sanitation, hygiene, and habitat in prisons, the International Committee of the Red Cross highlighted that 'waste water and refuse disposal is often the most intractable sanitation problem in places of detention.

[34] International Covenant on Civil and Political Rights, New York, 16 December 1966, 999 UNTS 171, Art. 9.

[35] UN Committee on the Elimination of Discrimination against Women (CEDAW), General Recommendations Nos. 19 and 20, adopted at the Eleventh Session, UN Doc. A/47/38(SUPP) (1992).

[36] Convention on the Rights of the Child (n 18), Art. 19.

[37] Paulo Sérgio Pinheiro, World Report on Violence against Children (United Nations Secretary-General's Report on Violence against Children, 2006), 324.

A large proportion of the diseases observed among the inmates of such establishments is transmitted by the faecal–oral route'.[38]

The Human Rights Committee and the Committee against Torture have regularly expressed concern about unsatisfactory conditions of detention, including poor sanitation, in their concluding observations to states' reports. The Special Rapporteur on torture has expressed concern about sanitation in his country missions,[39] as has the Working Group on Arbitrary Detention.[40]

Furthermore, paragraph 15 of the Standard Minimum Rules for the Treatment of Prisoners of 1955 provides that 'prisoners shall be required to keep their persons clean, and to this end they shall be provided with water and with such toilet articles as are necessary for health and cleanliness'.[41] The United Nations Rules for the Protection of Juveniles Deprived of Their Liberty of 1990 also refer to 'sanitary installations', specifying that they 'should be so located and of a sufficient standard to enable every juvenile to comply,

[38] International Committee of the Red Cross, *Water, Sanitation, Hygiene and Habitat in Prisons* (ICRC, 2005), 58.

[39] UN Human Rights Council, *Report of the Special Rapporteur on Torture and Other Cruel, Inhuman or Degrading Treatment or Punishment, Manfred Nowak: Addendum: Mission to Indonesia*, 2008, UN Doc. A/HRC/7/3/Add.7, para 68; UN Human Rights Council, *Report of the Special Rapporteur on Torture and Other Cruel, Inhuman or Degrading Treatment or Punishment, Manfred Nowak: Addendum: Mission to Togo*, 2008, UN Doc. A/HRC/7/3/Add.5, para 42; Appendix, paras 3, 31, 46–7, 70, and 95; UN Human Rights Council, *Report of the Special Rapporteur on Torture and Other Cruel, Inhuman or Degrading Treatment or Punishment, Manfred Nowak: Addendum: Mission to Nigeria*, 2007, UN Doc. A/HRC/7/3/Add.4, para 37, Appendix, paras 41, 95, 101, and 110.

[40] UN Human Rights Council, *Report of the Working Group on Arbitrary Detention: Addendum: Mission to Equatorial Guinea*, 2008, UN Doc. A/HRC/7/4/Add.3, para 83.

[41] Standard Minimum Rules for the Treatment of Prisoners, adopted by the First United Nations Congress on the Prevention of Crime and the Treatment of Offenders, Geneva, 1955 and approved by United Nations Economic and Social Council Resolution 663 C (XXIV), 31 July 1957.

as required, with their physical needs in privacy and in a clean and decent manner'.[42]

Equality of Women and Men

The disproportionate impact of lack of access to sanitation on girls and women has been well researched. Girls often drop out of school when menstruation begins since schools frequently lack 'girls only' or otherwise appropriate sanitation facilities. According to some, 'about 1 in 10 school age girls do not attend school during menstruation or drop out at puberty because of lack of clean and private sanitation facilities'.[43] When relatives become sick from sanitation-related diseases, women and girls often stay home to care for them, missing work and school. Furthermore, women and girls face security risks when they are forced to relieve themselves or to defecate in the open, or walk to toilets in the dark. Because of widespread discrimination against women, they are not included in the formulation of relevant policies, and therefore, their needs tend to be neglected.

Human rights law prohibits discrimination based on sex. Thus, all rights related to sanitation must be guaranteed without discrimination based on sex. As already mentioned earlier, CEDAW specifically refers to sanitation with regard to rural women; moreover, the Committee overseeing that treaty has regularly addressed the issue of sanitation in its concluding observations. The Special Rapporteurs on torture and on the right to education have also specifically referred to the sanitary needs of menstruating women.[44]

---

[42] UN General Assembly Resolution, *Rules for the Protection of Juveniles Deprived of their Liberty*, 14 December 1990, UN Doc. A/RES/45/113, para 34.

[43] Rose Lidonde, 'Scaling up School Sanitation and Hygiene Promotion and Gender Concerns', in Mariëlle Snell, Kathleen Shordt, and Annemarieke Mooijman (eds), *School Sanitation and Hygiene Education Symposium, The Way Forward: Construction Is Not Enough: Symposium Proceedings & Framework for Action* (IRC International Water and Sanitation Centre, 2004), 40.

[44] UN Human Rights Council, *Report of the Special Rapporteur on Torture and Other Cruel, Inhuman or Degrading Treatment or Punishment,*

Prohibition of Discrimination

More broadly, discrimination and exclusion play a significant role with regard to access to sanitation. It is often the poorest and the most marginalized groups who lack access to sanitation. According to the United Nations Development Programme (UNDP), the majority of people without access to sanitation live on less than USD 2 a day.[45]

Minority groups, migrants, indigenous peoples, refugees and internally displaced persons (IDPs), prisoners and detainees, and persons with disabilities among others, suffer discrimination, which may affect their access to sanitation. Sanitation workers face particular stigmatization for having a job which is perceived as 'unclean' or lowly. Toilets are associated with dirt, disease, and disgust, and an occupation in this field correlates with lower social status. Sanitation workers are often insulted and attacked when carrying out their work, and in some places are forced to work at night to conceal the nature of their tasks. Although sanitation workers in developed countries do not perform unhygienic work to the same extent, benefiting from protective gear and advanced sanitation systems, they also often face disrespect and rejection.[46] Such groups often have little influence on policy formulation and resource allocation at the national and local levels, making it difficult for them to improve their access to sanitation.

The ICCPR and the ICESCR, in common Article 2, provide that the rights contained in those Covenants should be enjoyed without discrimination. Article 26 of the ICCPR further provides for equal protection under the law, including 'effective protection against discrimination'. The treaty bodies have raised the issue of sanitation

Manfred Nowak, 2008, UN Doc. A/HRC/7/3, para 41; UN Commission on Human Rights, *Girls' Right to Education, Report submitted by the Special Rapporteur on the Right to Education, Mr V. Muñoz Villalobos*, 2006, UN Doc. E/CN.4/2006/45, paras 129–30.

[45] UNDP (n 21), 49.

[46] UN Human Rights Council, *Stigma and the Realization of the Human Rights to Water and Sanitation, Report of the Special Rapporteur on the Human Right to Safe Drinking Water and Sanitation, Catarina de Albuquerque*, 2012, UN Doc. A/HRC/21/42.

in the context of discussions on discriminatory treatment in their dialogues with states parties. The Special Rapporteur on torture has also specifically addressed sanitation with regard to persons with disabilities.[47]

* * *

The preceding analysis demonstrates that access to sanitation is indispensable, and has been recognized as such under international law, both by states and experts, for the enjoyment of numerous human rights. However, it does not provide a complete picture of the human rights dimensions of sanitation. Sanitation is not just about health, housing, education, work, gender equality, and the ability to survive. Sanitation, more than many other human rights issues, evokes the concept of human dignity; consider the vulnerability and shame that so many people experience every day when, again, they are forced to defecate in the open, in a bucket or a plastic bag. It is the indignity of this situation that causes the embarrassment. The Supreme Court of India eloquently described the indignity of lack of access to sanitation where the Court found that the failure of the municipality to provide basic public conveniences was driving 'the miserable slum-dwellers to ease in the streets, on the sly for a time, and openly thereafter, because under Nature's pressure, bashfulness becomes a luxury and dignity a difficult art'.[48] It is such infringements of human dignity that are not wholly captured when sanitation is considered only in the context of its links with other human rights.

The Recognition of a Self-Standing Right to Sanitation under International Human Rights Law

Both the Universal Declaration of Human Rights (UDHR) and the ICESCR, adopted by the United Nations General Assembly in 1948

[47] UN General Assembly, *Interim Report of the Special Rapporteur of the Human Rights Council on Torture and Other Cruel, Inhuman or Degrading Treatment or Punishment, Manfred Nowak*, 2008, UN Doc. A/63/175, paras 53 and 66.

[48] *Municipal Council, Ratlam* v *Shri Vardhichand & Others* (1980), 4 SCC 162 (Supreme Court of India, 1980).

and 1966, respectively, did not explicitly include the right to sanitation (or the right to water). They provide, however, for the right of everyone to an adequate standard of living,[49] which explicitly includes food, clothing, and housing. This omission has to be understood in the context of the world of that time, where the voices of those suffering from lack of access to sanitation were not represented at the negotiating table, and the situation was not as extreme as it is today. As the sanitation crisis became more pronounced in the second half of the twentieth century, with its attendant health and economic consequences, the human rights community took account of sanitation's growing importance.

International humanitarian law, namely the Geneva Convention (III) relative to the Treatment of Prisoners of War and the Geneva Convention (IV) relative to the Protection of Civilian Persons in Time of War of 1949, particularly refer to access to sanitation.[50] Article 29 of Geneva Convention III refers to the detaining power's obligation to ensure that prisoners of war 'have for their use, day and night, conveniences which conform to the rules of hygiene and are maintained in a constant state of cleanliness. In any camps in which women prisoners of war are accommodated, separate conveniences shall be provided for them'. Furthermore, the Convention establishes that 'apart from the baths and showers with which the camps shall be furnished, prisoners of war shall be provided with sufficient water and soap for their personal toilet and for washing their personal laundry; the necessary installations, facilities and time shall be granted them for that purpose'. Similar language is used in Geneva Convention IV when it refers to the conditions of places of internment.

As previously referred, some of the international human rights treaties make explicit reference to the importance of sanitation in realizing human rights, including CEDAW and the CRC.

---

[49] ICESCR (n 7), Art. 11(1); The Universal Declaration of Human Rights (UDHR), New York, 10 December 1948, Art. 25.

[50] Geneva Convention Relative to the Treatment of Prisoners of War, Geneva, 12 August 1949, 75 UNTS 135; Geneva Convention Relative to the Protection of Civilian Persons in Time of War, Geneva, 12 August 1949, 75 UNTS 287.

Furthermore, the past decade has witnessed remarkable development in international human rights law with respect to water and sanitation. *General Comment No. 15* of the CESCR found that the right to water is an implicit but essential component of the right to an adequate standard of living and the right to the highest attainable standard of health, enshrined in Articles 11 and 12 of the ICESCR, respectively. Even though sanitation was left out from the scope of *General Comment No. 15*, when the mandate of the Independent Expert was established, it comprised both sanitation and water, clearly indicating that the former is a human rights concern.

The declaration of 2008 as the International Year of Sanitation by the United Nations General Assembly put sanitation in the spotlight at the international level. In the same year, the Human Rights Council created the mandate of the Independent Expert on the issue of human rights obligations related to access to safe drinking water and sanitation. During the first year of her mandate, the Independent Expert gave priority attention to sanitation, and her first report to the Human Rights Council, in March 2009, was dedicated to the human rights obligations related to sanitation.[51] In that report she not only advanced a definition of sanitation that takes into account human rights, but also affirmed that sanitation should be recognized as a self-standing human right.

On 28 July 2010, the United Nations General Assembly called for a vote on a draft resolution on 'the Human Right to Water and Sanitation' introduced by Bolivia, and co-sponsored by 42 states,[52]

---

[51] *Report of the Independent Expert* (n 4). See also UN Human Rights Council, *Report of the Independent Expert on the Issue of Human Rights Obligations Related to Access to Safe Drinking Water and Sanitation, Catarina de Albuquerque*, 2009, UN Doc. A/HRC/10/6.

[52] Angola, Antigua and Barbuda, Azerbaijan, Bahrain, Bangladesh, Benin, the Plurinational State of Bolivia, Burkina Faso, Burundi, the Central African Republic, Congo, Cuba, Dominica, the Dominican Republic, Ecuador, El Salvador, Eritrea, Fiji, Georgia, Guinea, Haiti, Madagascar, Maldives, Mali, Mauritius, Nicaragua, Nigeria, Paraguay, Saint Vincent and the Grenadines, Samoa, Saint Lucia, Saudi Arabia, Serbia, Seychelles, Solomon Islands, Sri Lanka, Timor-Leste, Tuvalu, Uruguay, Vanuatu, the Bolivarian Republic of Venezuela, and Yemen.

which in its paragraph one recognizes 'the right to safe and clean drinking water and sanitation as a human right that is essential for the full enjoyment of life and all human rights'.[53] This resolution was voted upon, at the request of the United States, but was adopted with a significant number of abstentions (41),[54] leaving 122 votes in favour[55] and no votes against it.

[53] The Human Right to Water and Sanitation (n 27).

[54] The states abstaining were: Armenia, Australia, Austria, Bosnia and Herzegovina, Botswana, Bulgaria, Canada, Croatia, Cyprus, Czech Republic, Denmark, Estonia, Ethiopia, Greece, Guyana, Iceland, Ireland, Israel, Japan, Kazakhstan, Kenya, Latvia, Lesotho, Lithuania, Luxembourg, Malta, the Netherlands, New Zealand, Poland, Republic of Korea, Republic of Moldova, Romania, Slovakia, Sweden, Trinidad and Tobago, Turkey, Ukraine, United Kingdom of Great Britain and Northern Ireland, United Republic of Tanzania, United States of America, and Zambia.

[55] Voted in favour of the resolution: Afghanistan, Algeria, Andorra, Angola, Antigua and Barbuda, Argentina, Azerbaijan, Bahamas, Bahrain, Bangladesh, Barbados, Belarus, Belgium, Benin, Bhutan, the Plurinational State of Bolivia, Brazil, Brunei Darussalam, Burkina Faso, Burundi, Cambodia, Cape Verde, the Central African Republic, Chile, China, Colombia, Comoros, Congo, Costa Rica, Côte d'Ivoire, Cuba, Democratic People's Republic of Korea, Democratic Republic of the Congo, Djibouti, Dominica, the Dominican Republic, Ecuador, Egypt, El Salvador, Equatorial Guinea, Eritrea, Finland, France, Gabon, Georgia, Germany, Ghana, Grenada, Guatemala, Haiti, Honduras, Hungary, India, Indonesia, Iran (Islamic Republic of), Iraq, Italy, Jamaica, Jordan, Kuwait, Kyrgyzstan, Lao People's Democratic Republic, Lebanon, Liberia, Libyan Arab Jamahiriya, Liechtenstein, Madagascar, Malaysia, Maldives, Mali, Mauritius, Mexico, Monaco, Mongolia, Montenegro, Morocco, Myanmar, Nepal, Nicaragua, Niger, Nigeria, Norway, Oman, Pakistan, Panama, Paraguay, Peru, Portugal, Qatar, Russian Federation, Saint Lucia, Saint Vincent and the Grenadines, Samoa, San Marino, Saudi Arabia, Senegal, Serbia, Seychelles, Singapore, Slovenia, Solomon Islands, Somalia, South Africa, Spain, Sri Lanka, Sudan, Switzerland, Syrian Arab Republic, Tajikistan, Thailand, the former Yugoslav Republic of Macedonia, Timor-Leste, Togo, Tunisia, Tuvalu, United Arab Emirates, Uruguay, Vanuatu, the Bolivarian Republic of Venezuela, Vietnam, Yemen, and Zimbabwe.

Nevertheless, when analysing the interventions made by the representatives of many of the abstaining states, one can conclude that the most often invoked reason to justify their abstention (rather than a vote in favour) was the lack of transparency and inclusiveness in the negotiations of the resolution, rather than the resolution's specific recognition of the human right to water and sanitation.[56]

In the same year, another important event and a positive development materialized that led to the further reaffirmation of the human right to water and sanitation. On 30 September 2010, the United Nations Human Rights Council adopted, by consensus, Resolution 15/9, in which it not only '[r]ecalled General Assembly resolution 64/292 of 28 July 2010', but also '[a]ffirmed that the human right to safe drinking water and sanitation is derived from the right to an adequate standard of living and inextricably related to the right to the highest attainable standard of physical and mental health, as well as the right to life and human dignity'.[57]

Hence the Human Rights Council, the main United Nations body 'responsible for promoting universal respect for the protection of all human rights and fundamental freedoms for all, without distinction of any kind and in a fair and equal manner',[58] reaffirmed the human right to water and sanitation that had been recognized by the General Assembly two months prior, but this time by consensus without a vote. This was a significant, positive development in terms of the unequivocal recognition of the right to water and sanitation at the political level.

However, before the adoption of the Council resolution, some states made statements explaining their official position on the resolution before the vote. The representative of the United Kingdom (UK) stated that his country 'dissociates from consensus', while allowing the text to be adopted without a vote. The UK representative also affirmed his country's support for the human right to water,

---

[56] Some states referred to arguments of substance in order to justify their abstention in the vote on the resolution.

[57] UN Human Rights Council Resolution (n 28).

[58] UN General Assembly Resolution, *Human Rights Council*, 2006, UN Doc. A/RES/60/251.

but underlined the lack of clarity regarding a human right to sanitation, as well as the absence of an internationally agreed definition of a right to sanitation.[59]

In a statement issued shortly after the resolution's adoption, the Special Rapporteur Ms Catarina de Albuquerque furthermore declared that '[t]he right to water and sanitation is a human right, equal to all other human rights, which implies that it is justiciable and enforceable. Hence from today onwards we have an even greater responsibility to concentrate all our efforts in the implementation and full realisation of this essential right.'[60]

Moreover, in a statement issued in the aftermath of the approval of the resolution, Amnesty International equally declared that the said document 'effectively re-affirms that the rights to water and sanitation are implicitly contained in several human rights treaties, including the International Covenant on Economic, Social and Cultural Rights (ICESCR) to which 160 states are party, and the UN Convention on the Rights of the Child (CRC), which has reached nearly universal ratification, and are therefore legally binding rights'.[61]

Six months later, in March 2011, the two main co-sponsors of the water and sanitation resolution, Germany and Spain, presented a further draft resolution at the Human Rights Council with the objective of extending the mandate of the Independent Expert.[62] Instead of proposing a 'standard' extension of the mandate, however, the draft resolution included some significant changes to previous language adopted by the Council on this matter. Firstly, there was a

[59] UN General Assembly, *108th Plenary Meeting: Draft Resolution (A/64/L.63/Rev.1*)*, 2010, UN Doc. A/64/PV.108, 12.

[60] ReliefWeb, 'UN United to Make the Right to Water and Sanitation Legally Binding' (UN Office for the Coordination of Humanitarian Affairs, 2010); available at http://reliefweb.int/report/world/un-united-make-right-water-and-sanitation-legally-binding.

[61] Amnesty International, Public Statement, 'United Nations: Historic Re-affirmation that Rights to Water and Sanitation Are Legally Binding', 2010 (AI Index: IOR 40/018/2010).

[62] UN Human Rights Council Resolution, *The Human Right to Safe Drinking Water and Sanitation*, 2011, A/HRC/RES/16/2.

significant change in the title of the resolution, from 'Human Rights and access to water and sanitation' to 'the Human Right to Safe Drinking Water and Sanitation', fully endorsing the recognition of the right. Secondly, it welcomed

> the recognition of the human right to safe drinking water and sanitation by the General Assembly and the Human Rights Council, and the affirmation by the latter that the human right to safe drinking water and sanitation is derived from the right to an adequate standard of living and inextricably related to the right to the highest attainable standard of physical and mental health, as well as the right to life and human dignity.

Thirdly, while extending the mandate 'of the current mandate holder', it decided to rename it 'special rapporteur on the human right to safe drinking water and sanitation' for a period of three years. The resolution was co-sponsored by a significant number of states,[63] and adopted by consensus.

Hence, the authentic interpretation of the ICESCR by the CESCR, coupled with the series of resolutions adopted by both the United Nations General Assembly and the Human Rights Council recognizing and reaffirming the right to water and sanitation, put an end to a longstanding discussion over the recognition of water and sanitation as human rights. These developments have reinforced the realization of the right to sanitation as a legally binding obligation on all states parties to the ICESCR and other human rights treaties,[64] promoting the deepening and enrichment of international norms.

In addition to these international efforts, several regional fora have emerged in recent years to shore up political commitment to

---

[63] Albania, Andorra, Armenia, Benin, Bosnia and Herzegovina, Brazil, Bulgaria, Chile, Colombia, Costa Rica, Croatia, Cyprus, Estonia, Finland, France, Germany, Greece, Guatemala, Honduras, Hungary, Iceland, Ireland, Israel, Italy, Jordan, Lithuania, Luxembourg, Maldives, Monaco, Morocco, the Netherlands, Nicaragua, Norway, Palestine, Panama, Peru, Poland, Portugal, Romania, Serbia, Slovakia, Slovenia, Spain, Sweden, Switzerland, Uruguay, and Yemen.

[64] See CEDAW (n 6); CRC (n 18).

improving access to sanitation. The South Asian Conference on Sanitation (SACOSAN)[65] has met regularly since 2003 to exchange ideas and identify priorities in improving access to sanitation. At SACOSAN III, held in Delhi, India, in 2008, representatives from national water ministries, non-governmental organizations (NGOs), and academics agreed on the Delhi Declaration, which explicitly recognizes access to drinking water and sanitation as a human right, and emphasizes a participatory, flexible, and non-discriminatory effort towards achieving universal access to sanitation.[66] SACOSAN IV, held in Colombo, Sri Lanka, in April 2011, reiterated the importance of recognizing the right to sanitation, focusing on the theme of sanitation as it relates to quality of life. The equivalent 2011 African Conference on Sanitation (AfricaSan) picked up similar issues, agreeing to focus on equity and pro-poor outcomes, and that states should work harder towards meeting previously agreed commitments on sanitation. In May 2013, LATINOSAN III also reaffirmed the human right to sanitation in its Panama Declaration.[67]

Sanitation as a Distinct Right

The 2010 General Assembly resolution explicitly recognizing the human right to water and sanitation, and the Human Rights Council resolution of the same year clarifying that this right derives from the right to an adequate standard of living refer to a single human right. The title of the Special Rapporteur itself refers to the human right to water and sanitation. The first Special Rapporteur herself, however, was of the opinion that water and sanitation should be treated as two distinct human rights, both included within the right to an adequate

[65] SACOSAN is made up of Afghanistan, Bangladesh, Bhutan, India, the Maldives, Nepal, Pakistan, and Sri Lanka.

[66] The Delhi Declaration, Third South Asian Conference on Sanitation, New Delhi, 21 November 2008.

[67] Declaración de Panamá, Tercera Conferencia Latinoamericana y del Caribe de Saneamiento (LATINOSAN 2013), Ciudad de Panamá, Panamá, 31 May 2013.

standard of living, and with equal status. Amnesty International has taken the same approach.[68]

There were pragmatic reasons for this approach. All too often, when water and sanitation are mentioned together, the importance of sanitation is downgraded due to the political preference given to water. Naming water and sanitation as separate human rights provides an opportunity for governments, civil society, and other stakeholders to pay particular attention to defining specific standards for the right to sanitation, and subsequently for the realization of this right. Further, separating the right to sanitation from the right to water recognizes that not all sanitation options rely on water-borne systems.

Furthermore, as was stated earlier, more than many other human rights issues, sanitation evokes the concept of human dignity. The notion of dignity permeates all modern human rights instruments. The preambles to the ICESCR and the ICCPR explicitly recognize that all human rights derive from the inherent dignity of the human person. The UDHR contains several references to human dignity including Article 22, which states that 'everyone ... is entitled to realization ... of the economic, social and cultural rights indispensable for his dignity'.[69]

Dignity relates to the intrinsic worth of each human being, which should be recognized and respected by others. There are certain fundamental conditions upon which we must insist to have a 'minimum definition of what it means to be human in any morally tolerable form of society'.[70] It can be argued that 'degrading living conditions and deprivation of basic needs' fall below this minimum definition.[71] Dignity closely relates to self-respect, which is difficult to maintain when being forced to squat down in the open, with no respect for privacy, not having the opportunity to clean oneself after defecating, and facing the constant threat of assault at such a vulnerable

[68] Amnesty International, 'States Urged to Support Rights to Water and Sanitation' (29 July 2010); available at www.amnesty.org/en/latest/news/2010/07/estados-deben-apoyar-derecho-agua-saneamiento.

[69] UDHR (n 49).

[70] Jerome J Shestack, 'The Philosophical Foundations of Human Rights', (1998) 20 *Human Rights Quarterly* 201, 216.

[71] Oscar Schachter, 'Human Dignity as a Normative Concept', (1983) 77 *American Journal of International Law* 848, 852.

moment. Therefore, the Independent Expert believed that lack of access to sanitation constitutes demeaning living conditions; it is an affront to the intrinsic worth of human beings, and should not be tolerated in any society.[72]

Because dignity pervades the issue of sanitation, and sanitation cannot be entirely subsumed into any other existing human right, it should be considered a distinct human right. While it has been warned that a proliferation of rights runs the risk of undermining existing human rights,[73] standards must be adapted to address new (or only recently recognized) threats to the human person. The UN General Assembly, in its resolution 41/120, stated that standard-setting activities in the field of human rights should relate to standards that are, inter alia, 'of fundamental character and derive from the inherent dignity and worth of the human person' and '[are] sufficiently precise to give rise to identifiable and practicable rights and obligations'.[74] Due to the essential importance of sanitation for maintaining a life with human dignity, it could be argued that it is as important as other explicit components of the right to an adequate standard of living, such as food, clothing, and housing, and could be implied from that right.

Human Rights Obligations Related to Sanitation

Understanding the human rights obligations related to sanitation requires a working definition of sanitation in human rights terms, which is the one proposed by the Independent Expert, and endorsed by the CESCR. In addition to this definition, considering sanitation as a human right also implies that states are obliged to respect, protect, and fulfil human rights as they relate to sanitation. More concretely, states must, inter alia:[75]

- Refrain from measures which threaten or deny the existing access to sanitation of individuals or communities. States must also

---

[72] *Report of the Independent Expert* (n 4), para 57.

[73] *Report of the Independent Expert* (n 4), para 58.

[74] UN General Assembly Resolution, *Setting International Standards in the Field of Human Rights*, 1986, UN Doc. A/RES/41/120.

[75] *Report of the Independent Expert* (n 4).

ensure that the management of human excreta does not negatively impact human rights.

- Ensure that non-state actors[76] act in accordance with human rights obligations related to sanitation, including through the adoption of legislative and other measures to prevent the negative impact of non-state actors on the enjoyment of sanitation. When a private provider operates sanitation services, the state must establish an effective regulatory framework.

- Take steps applying the maximum of available resources to the progressive realization of economic, social, and cultural rights as they relate to sanitation. States must move as expeditiously and effectively as possible towards ensuring access to safe, affordable, and acceptable sanitation for all, which provides privacy and dignity. This requires deliberate, concrete, and targeted steps towards full realization, in particular with a view to creating an enabling environment for people to realize their rights related to sanitation. Hygiene promotion and education is a critical part of this obligation.

- Carefully consider and justify any retrogressive measures related to the human rights obligations regarding sanitation.

- Take the necessary measures directed towards the full realization of economic, social, and cultural rights as they relate to sanitation, inter alia, by according sufficient recognition of human rights obligations related to sanitation in the national political and legal systems, and by immediately developing and adopting a national sanitation strategy and plan of action.

- Provide effective judicial or other appropriate remedies at both the national and international levels in cases of violations of human rights obligations related to sanitation. Victims of violations should be entitled to adequate reparation, including restitution, compensation, satisfaction, and/or guarantees of non-repetition.

States are obliged to realize their human rights obligations related to sanitation in a non-discriminatory manner, and pay special attention

---

[76] Non-state actors include private individuals, private enterprises, civil society organizations, and any other entity, which is not an agent of the state.

to groups particularly vulnerable to exclusion and discrimination in relation to sanitation, including people living in poverty, sanitation workers, women, children, elderly persons, people with disabilities, people affected by health conditions, refugees and IDPs, and minority groups, among others.

Priority must be given to meeting the needs of these groups, and where necessary, positive measures should be adopted to redress existing discrimination, and to ensure their access to sanitation. States are obliged to eliminate both *de jure* and *de facto* discrimination on grounds of race, colour, sex, age, language, religion, political or other opinion, national or social origin, property, birth, physical or mental disability, health status, or any other civil, political, social, or other status.

States are also obliged to ensure that concerned individuals and communities are informed and have access to information about sanitation and hygiene, and are enabled to participate in all processes related to the planning, construction, maintenance, and monitoring of sanitation services. Full participation including representation of all concerned groups is key to ensuring that sanitation solutions answer the actual needs of communities, and are affordable, technically feasible, and culturally acceptable.

Participation is also crucial for achieving community ownership and dedication in order to bring about the required behavioural changes. All people must have full and equal access to information concerning sanitation and its effect on their health and environment. Information should be made available through various media, and should be translated into all relevant languages and dialects to ensure the greatest possible circulation.

It is also important to state clearly what is not required when considering sanitation in human rights terms.

- States are not obliged to provide everyone with access to a sewerage system. Human rights law does not aim to dictate specific technology options, but instead calls for context-specific solutions.
- States are not obliged to provide individual facilities in every home. This will also depend on the context—sometimes a safe and otherwise adequate facility in close proximity would suffice as an intermediate step towards full realization of related rights.

- States are not obliged to construct toilets; rather they must create an enabling environment. In fact, it is often argued that demand-led sanitation projects enjoy considerable success. Only in certain conditions, such as extreme poverty or natural disasters, when people, for reasons beyond their control, are genuinely unable to access sanitation through their own means, is the state obliged to actually provide sanitation services.
- States are not obliged to provide sanitation free of charge—those who are in a position to pay must contribute financially or in kind, for example, by offering labour for the construction of sanitation systems. Only when people are genuinely unable to pay for sanitation is the state obliged to provide sanitation services free of charge.
- States may decide to privatize sanitation services, but in that case, they must ensure—through adequate regulation, including effective and accessible complaints procedures—that private actors do not adopt approaches which result in human rights violations.
- States are not required to ensure the full implementation of their human rights obligations related to sanitation immediately. Rather, they must show that they are taking steps to the maximum of their available resources to ensure at least minimum essential levels of sanitation for all people, and they must ensure that they are not discriminating against certain groups in providing access.

Among professionals working on sanitation, it is commonly said that 'with rights come responsibilities', which alludes to the importance of individual behavioural change in ensuring the success of sanitation interventions. The state bears the primary human rights obligations related to sanitation, and is under an obligation to ensure that non-state actors, including individuals, do not jeopardize the enjoyment of any human rights. Where the state is complying with its duties to ensure access to sanitation facilities, which are safe, hygienic, secure, socially and culturally acceptable, provide privacy, and ensure dignity in a non-discriminatory manner, individuals have a responsibility to use such facilities. The state has a crucial role to play, and is obliged under human rights law to sensitize the population about the benefits of good sanitation and hygiene.

Content of Human Rights Obligations Related to Sanitation

In considering the content of human rights obligations, it is important to approach this framework with a degree of flexibility, recognizing that some elements may be understood under multiple categories depending on the perspective of the reader. In practice, the classification is of little importance. For example, whether we understand prohibitive waiting times for use of sanitation facilities as an issue of accessibility or one of availability, does not change the fact that states must ensure that excessive waiting times are avoided. Furthermore, this elaboration of the content of human rights obligations related to sanitation is intended to offer some examples, not to serve as an exhaustive list.

Availability

There must be a sufficient number of sanitation facilities (with associated services) within, or in the immediate vicinity of, each household, health or educational institution, public institutions and places, and workplaces. There must be a sufficient number of sanitation facilities to ensure that waiting times are not unreasonably long.

Although it is tempting to determine a specific minimum number of toilets needed to meet the requirement of availability, such determinations can be counterproductive in human rights terms. It is crucial that the assessment of the sanitation requirements of any community is informed by the context, as well as the characteristics of particular groups, which may have different sanitation needs. In this regard, participation is a vital aspect of meeting human rights obligations related to sanitation.

Quality

Sanitation facilities must be hygienically safe to use, which means that they must effectively prevent human, animal, and insect contact with human excreta. Sanitation facilities must further ensure access to safe water for hand washing as well as menstrual hygiene, and anal and genital cleansing, as well as mechanisms for the hygienic disposal of menstrual products. Regular cleaning, emptying of pits or other places that collect human excreta, and maintenance are essential for ensuring the sustainability of sanitation facilities and continued access.

Sanitation facilities must also be technically safe to use, which means that the superstructure is stable, and the floor is designed in a way that reduces the risk of accidents (for example, by slipping). People must be enabled to use them safely at night, whether through lighted paths, flashlights, or other measures. Furthermore, special attention should be paid to the safety needs of persons with disabilities, as well as the safety needs of children. Maintenance is crucial to guarantee technical safety.

Ensuring safe sanitation requires adequate hygiene promotion and education to encourage individuals to use toilets in a hygienic manner that respects the safety of others. Manual emptying of pit latrines is considered to be unsafe (as well as culturally unacceptable in many places, leading to stigmatization of those burdened with this task), meaning that mechanized alternatives that effectively prevent direct contact with human excreta should be used.

Physical Accessibility

Sanitation facilities must be physically accessible for everyone within, or in the immediate vicinity of, each household, health or educational institution, public institutions and places, and workplaces. Physical accessibility must be reliable, including access at all times of day and night. The location of sanitation facilities must ensure minimal risks to the physical security of users. This has particular implications for the path leading to the facility, which should be safe and convenient for all users, including older people and persons with disabilities, and it must be maintained in this state. Moreover, sanitation facilities should be constructed in a way that minimizes the risk of attack from animals or people, particularly for women and children.

Sanitation facilities should be designed so as to enable all users to physically access them, particularly those with special access needs, such as children, persons with disabilities, elderly persons, pregnant women, parents accompanying children, chronically ill people and those accompanying them. Considering the needs of these groups would have implications for the size of the entrance, the interior space, hand rails or other support mechanisms, the position of defecation, and other aspects.

Affordability

Access to sanitation facilities and services, including construction, emptying and maintenance of facilities, as well as treatment and disposal of faecal matter, must be available at a price that is affordable for all people without limiting their capacity to acquire other basic goods and services, including water, food, housing, health, and education guaranteed by other human rights. Water disconnections resulting from an inability to pay also impact waterborne sanitation, and this must be taken into consideration before disconnecting the water supply.

Various systems and structures can be put in place to ensure affordability, including income-support measures and measures that aim to reduce the cost of sanitation services. Subsidy schemes might be an option to ensure affordability. Governments could also consider setting targets, which represent a percentage of the household income. Experience suggests that in-kind contributions (such as labour) are also effective in sanitation projects. Technology choice can also have an impact on affordability (as well as sustainability). Human rights do not dictate which policy is best, but insist on a context-specific consideration of the situation.

Concerning the cost of sanitation, there may be differences depending on the area. For example, in urban areas, a connection to the sewerage system will almost always be the cheapest and most convenient option for the user. However, as with water connections, the price of a connection to the sewerage system will often be prohibitive for users living in poverty, and governments should develop policies to address this. In remote areas, where sewerage is normally not available, on-site sanitation is likely to be the preferable option. This may require subsidies for construction, emptying of receptacles for the collection of human waste, and associated maintenance. Assistance should also be provided to families who are unable to afford soap and cleaning products, or to women for sanitary products.

Acceptability

Sanitation facilities and services must be culturally acceptable. Personal sanitation is still a highly sensitive issue across regions and cultures, and differing perspectives about which sanitation solutions are acceptable must be taken into account regarding design, positioning, and conditions for use of sanitation facilities. In many cultures, to be acceptable, construction of toilets will need to ensure privacy. In most cultures, acceptability will require separate facilities for women and men in public places, and for girls and boys in schools. Women's toilets need to accommodate menstruation needs. Facilities will need to allow for culturally acceptable hygiene practices, such as hand washing and anal and genital cleansing.

The Special Rapporteur's understanding of the human right to sanitation was supported in November 2010 by the CESCR that stated in unequivocal terms that while the right to sanitation is an essential component of the right to an adequate standard of living (Article 11), and integrally related to the right to health (Article 12 paragraph 1 and 2 (a), (b), and (c)), the right to housing (Article 11), as well as the right to water (recognized in *General Comment No. 15*), it has distinct features which warrant its separate treatment from water in some respects.[77] The CESCR also stressed that the right to sanitation requires full recognition by states parties in compliance with the human rights principles related to non-discrimination, gender equality, participation, and accountability.[78]

* * *

As of today, there is universal support for the human right to sanitation including in the Sustainable Development Goals and 2030 Agenda for Sustainable Development[79]—a situation unimaginable some ten years ago. However, there is still a long way to go in order to ensure that everyone in the world has access to sanitation in

---

[77] CESCR (n 5), para 7.

[78] CESCR (n 5), para 8.

[79] UN General Assembly Resolution, *Transforming our World: The 2030 Agenda for Sustainable Development*, 2015, UN Doc. A/RES/70/1.

conditions of safety and dignity. Recognition of the right is simply an indispensable first step to make changes happen. Now it is up to governments, with the support of the international community and civil society, to transform this promise into concrete action for all.

One crucial dimension of transforming the human right to sanitation into a reality relates to its justiciability, and to holding public entities accountable for cases of non-compliance. In 1992, the CESCR rightly stated that we 'tolerate all too often breaches of economic, social and cultural rights which, if they occurred in relation to civil and political rights, would provoke expressions of horror and outrage and would lead to concerted calls for immediate remedial action'.[80] Even though recent decades have witnessed enormous progress in identifying violations, taking them more seriously and remedying them at the national as well as the international level, there is still a long way to go before violations of economic, social, and cultural rights provoke not only outrage, but also give rise to adequate preventive and remedial actions.

While it is generally recognized that a failure to comply with any human rights obligation constitutes a violation, key components of the right to sanitation are still too often viewed primarily as aspirational policy goals. Many situations of lack of enjoyment of the right to sanitation have not been clearly identified as violations; judicial or quasi-judicial mechanisms have not been resorted to; and such situations have not been addressed with the urgency and level of commitment that they require, particularly in the light of their potentially devastating effects on a large number of people. Where states have the necessary resources, it is unjustifiable that deprivations of access to even basic provision of water and sanitation persist.

Violations of the right to sanitation are often connected with systemic patterns of exclusion and unequal power relationships. Greater attention to violations of the right to sanitation and their structural causes can empower marginalized groups to secure effective remedies. Beyond remedying individual violations, identifying

---

[80] UN General Assembly, *World Conference on Human Rights, Preparatory Committee*, Contribution submitted by the Committee on Economic, Social and Cultural Rights, 1993, UN Doc. A/CONF.157/PC/62/Add.5, para 5.

patterns of violation will also help to prevent such violations, and will require governments to address their structural causes in policymaking and budgeting.

Violations of the human right to sanitation frequently correlate with broader deprivations and other violations, including of the human rights to life, health, food, housing, education, work, and a healthy environment. Lack of adequate sanitation in schools has huge implications for the rights to education and gender equality. It also puts the rights to privacy and human dignity at risk. These linkages become apparent in the case law dealing with water and sanitation, which frequently relies on the rights to life, to health, to housing, to a healthy environment, and to freedom from inhuman and degrading treatment.

To conclude, violations of the right to sanitation in general must receive more attention. Victims of violations of the right to sanitation are among the most stigmatized and marginalized in society, and there remain taboos preventing an open discussion about the indignities linked to unhygienic conditions. All actors should frame violations related to water and sanitation more explicitly as violations of the human rights to water and sanitation, in order to draw attention to the particularities of such violations and the deprivations and indignity they often cause.

2

Sanitation in South Africa

Policy, Practice, and Contestation

Jackie Dugard

In early June 2013, the residents of Khayelitsha, an informal settlement in Cape Town, made the news when, as part of a sustained protest against inadequate sanitation in the informal settlement, which had included two men dumping human waste on the steps of the Western Cape legislature, community members threw faeces at the bus that was carrying Western Cape premier, Helen Zille. Responding to these actions, a community member was quoted in the media as saying that this was a 'warning' of things to come, and 'we will return with thousands of these bucket toilets next week and empty them around the legislature building'—'we are ready to be arrested and will die for this'.[1]

---

[1] Anonymous, 'Faeces Thrown at Helen Zille's Bus', *City Press* (4 June 2013); available at http://www.news24.com/archives/city-press/faeces-thrown-at-helen-zilles-bus-20150429.

This event, as analysed in an opinion piece entitled 'The Politics of Shit and Why It Should Be Part of Public Protest', highlights the anguish and anger of people without decent sanitation, and underscores the mundane reality that improving access to sanitation is not always as prioritized as it should be.[2] Indeed, despite the critical importance of sanitation to poverty alleviation, healthcare, and human development (not to mention dignity), internationally, sanitation has traditionally been viewed as a lesser developmental priority and is somewhat the ugly stepsister of other rights or services. This is not only because in many places, sanitation is a taboo subject, but also because there are difficulties with defining what sanitation is and who bears the responsibility for providing it (the state, individuals, or communities).

Although perhaps not quite as much of a taboo as in other countries, in South Africa, too, sanitation has been relatively neglected in comparison with other rights and services. Indeed, the post-apartheid government has seemingly struggled to decide on which forms of sanitation services should be adopted, especially for publicly provided basic sanitation (usually communal toilets).[3] It has only been in the past few years that the government has signalled a shift away from waterborne sanitation, indicating that waterborne sanitation will be

---

[2] Gillian Schutte, 'The Politics of Shit and Why It Should be Part of Public Protest', *The South African Civil Society Information Service* (12 June 2013); available at http://sacsis.org.za/site/article/1691.

[3] In South Africa, as in many other countries, sanitation has a public and a private component. However, in South Africa, this divide is exacerbated by the apartheid legacy of non-provision of sanitation services to the largely rural African population meaning that there is a significant backlog in rural areas as well as in the mushrooming informal settlements around urban centres. In urban areas, household toilets (usually waterborne systems) are typically private, while bulk wastewater reticulation and treatment of sewage is public. In rural and informal areas, toilets are often communal—sometimes provided by the state (in the form of either chemical toilets or ventilated improved pit latrines), but often constructed by the community (rudimentary pit latrines or crude bucket systems)—or there are no toilets at all, so people practice open defecation, although open defecation is no longer very common as most households now have access to basic toilets.

pursued only in urban areas. This shift resulted, in May 2009, in sanitation services being moved from the Department of Water Affairs (DWA, previously known as the Department of Water Affairs and Forestry, DWAF) to the Department of Human Settlements (DHS, previously called the Department of Housing, although it has subsequently been moved away from the DHS again). However, there is still substantial non-clarity on what kind of sanitation services, if any, should be provided for the approximately 4 million people who live in informal settlements around the country,[4] and it is also unclear to what extent the government will subsidize rural on-site sanitation systems.

Thus, despite a raft of legislative and policy frameworks for basic sanitation services, including legislated basic standards for sanitation and a free basic sanitation policy, while approximately 95 per cent of households had basic access to water, almost 20 years after the advent of democracy, in 2010, approximately 21 per cent of households still had inadequate access to basic sanitation,[5] with an estimated 2.5 million households relying on rudimentary pit latrines, 728,000 households relying on the open fields, and 110,000 households still relying on the 'bucket system'.[6] And notwithstanding making significant inroads into eradicating the sanitation backlog, in 2010 the government acknowledged in its Millennium Development Goals (MDGs) Country Report that its erstwhile target of eliminating the full sanitation backlog by 2014 was 'too ambitious'.[7]

Inadequate sanitation, heightened by a growing impatience on the part of poor communities in the face of rising socio-economic inequality, has in recent years given rise to discrete litigation and

---

[4] South Africa's total population is around 55 million people in the year 2016, as per Statistics South Africa, *Mid-Year Population Estimates 2017*; available at https://www.statssa.gov.za/publications/P0302/P03022017.pdf.

[5] Government of the Republic of South Africa, *Millennium Development Goals: Country Report 2010* (2010), 94.

[6] Statistics South Africa, *General Household Survey 2010 (Statistical Release P0318 2011)* (2010), 126. There are an estimated 10 million households in South Africa. The 'bucket system' is a very basic toilet with a seat suspended over a bucket.

[7] Government of the Republic of South Africa (n 5), 94.

escalating community protest, including the throwing of shit at politicians as occurred in Cape Town in June 2013. But, even prior to this, it was clear that in the local government elections, in May 2011, sanitation was one of the key issues and a pivotal electioneering point used by both the major political parties against each other. This is largely because of the pre-election coverage in the media of two 'open toilet' scandals—one in Khayelitsha in Cape Town, which gave rise to the *Beja* litigation[8] described later, and one in Moqhaka local municipality in the Free State province—both relating to the rollout in poor communities by the respective local governments of communal toilets without any walls, doors, or any form of screens.

This chapter examines the realities of poor households' access to sanitation. It does so by first reviewing the domestic legal and policy frameworks, and then by pointing to the systemic implementation problems as analysed across established human-rights-related fault lines. It then goes on to analyse the growing resistance to inadequate sanitation-related conditions in the form of protest and public interest litigation (PIL).

Outlining the Right to Sanitation: Legal and Policy Frameworks

Historically under apartheid, sanitation services (along with all other services) were skewed in favour of the white minority, meaning that white residential areas were serviced by waterborne sanitation with flush toilets, while the bucket system or 'long drop' (a rudimentary pit latrine) dominated black residential areas. This meant that by 1994, 52 per cent of South African households did not have access to adequate sanitation,[9] and there was certainly no concept for the majority of the population of a right to sanitation.

Given that the apartheid system was underpinned and enforced by discriminatory law and policy, the immediate years following 1994

---

[8] *Ntombentsha Beja & Others* v *Premier of the Western Cape & Others (Beja)* 2011 (10) BCLR 1077 (WCC) (Western Cape High Court).
[9] Government of the Republic of South Africa (n 5), 94.

were dominated by wholesale projects to reform and democratize the frameworks governing socio-economic and political life. Sanitation was no exception. In recognition of the apartheid legacy of unequal and inadequate access to sanitation, post-apartheid legal and policy documents have sought to create a framework for the equitable provision of basic sanitation. These frameworks adopt a human rights approach to access to sanitation, establishing various state obligations in respect of the provision of basic sanitation to poor communities.

Although (as in the international human rights sphere[10]) there is no explicit right to sanitation in the Constitution of the Republic of South Africa, 1996 (Act No. 108 of 1996), it can be inferred from the right of access to housing in Section 26 and the right to a healthy environment in Section 24 of the Constitution. In relation to waterborne sanitation, Section 27(1)(b) of the Constitution guarantees everyone the right of access to sufficient water. Although the national and provincial spheres of government have a role to play in formulating sanitation-related policies, Part B of Schedule 4 of the Constitution mandates local government as responsible for sanitation services, defined as 'domestic waste-water and sewage disposal', and Section 153(a) of the Constitution provides that local government must 'structure and manage its administration and budgeting and

---

[10] It can be argued that the formulation of the socio-economic rights-related clauses of the South African Constitution (including the rights of access to adequate housing and to sufficient water) has been influenced by applicable international human rights law including the International Covenant on Economic, Social and Cultural Rights (ICESCR), which South Africa ratified in 2015. Notwithstanding this ratification, as clarified by the Constitutional Court in the cases of *Government of the Republic of South Africa* v *Grootboom & Others* 2001 (1) SA 46 (CC) and *Treatment Action Campaign* v *Minister of Health (No. 2)* 2002 (5) SA 721 (CC), South Africa pursues a reasonableness standard of review (testing in each case whether applicable government programmes and policies are reasonable) rather than the minimum core content approach to socio-economic rights as pursued under the ICESCR. As discussed later in this chapter, this has meant that the content of socio-economic rights remains overwhelmingly unclear and is largely determined through legislation rather than interpretation of the constitutional or international human rights provisions.

planning processes to give priority to the basic needs of the community and to promote the social and economic development of the community'.[11]

Like many human rights instruments, and especially so regarding inferred rights, the South African Constitution does not provide much detail about any of the socio-economic rights. Rather, the details—and much of the content from a rights-based perspective—are located in legislation and policies designed to give meaning to each of the constitutional rights. There is no overarching legislation regarding sanitation per se, but—somewhat uncomfortably—the Water Services Act (108 of 1997) is the primary national law relating to water and sanitation services. The linking of sanitation services to water at the national level is a hangover from the initial post-apartheid institutional arrangement, in terms of which, between 1994 and 2009, sanitation was housed in the DWAF.[12]

One of the main objects of the Water Services Act, as set out in Section 2(a), is to provide for 'the right of access to basic water supply and the right to basic sanitation necessary to secure sufficient water and an environment not harmful to human health or well-being'. Section 2(i) of the Act defines basic sanitation as:

[11] It is striking that there was no national regulator for sanitation (or water services) until 2010 and that the existing regulatory mechanism is still in its infancy and relatively toothless, meaning that the implementation of sanitation-related laws, policies, and programmes is left to individual municipalities largely without national regulation or sanction.

[12] National institutional structures for sanitation and water services have been under review. In September 2013, the Minister of Water Affairs announced that there were plans to merge the Water Services Act and the National Water Act (which deals with the management and protection of water resources). It was also acknowledged that moving sanitation services away from Water Affairs (and the legislation that governs sanitation) has had unanticipated negative consequences—including disrupting systems and processes begun under Water Affairs and institutionally severing sanitation from the legislation that governs its delivery (the Water Services Act). In May 2014, the review resulted in sanitation services being moved away from the DHS back to the DWA, which was renamed the Department of Water and Sanitation. At the time of writing, it was not possible to evaluate the

'the prescribed minimum standards of services necessary for the safe, hygienic and adequate collection, removal, disposal or purification of human excreta, domestic wastewater and sewage from households, including informal households'. As such, the Act suggests that the definition of basic sanitation goes beyond a toilet, but subsequent legislation enacted to further concretize the definition of basic sanitation suggests otherwise. On 8 June 2011, the Regulations Relating to Compulsory National Standards and Measures to Conserve Water (Compulsory National Standards) were published in terms of Section 9 of the Water Services Act. Regulation 2 provides that the minimum standard for basic sanitation is:

(a) The provision of appropriate education; and
(b) A toilet which is safe, reliable, environmentally sound, easy to keep clean, provides privacy and protection against the weather, well ventilated, keeps smells to a minimum, and prevents the entry and exit of flies and other disease-carrying pests.

Providing guidance about which kinds of toilets are inappropriate under the definition of basic sanitation, the DWAF's National Sanitation Policy, 1996, lists as inadequate methods of sanitation, traditional unimproved pits and bucket toilets, and comments that chemical toilets are inappropriate except in emergency situations.[13]

Specifying what kinds of toilets are appropriate, one further piece of relevant legislation, the Housing Act (107 of 1997), inter alia, lays the basis for financing national housing projects for low-income groups, which includes the rollout of sanitation infrastructure

---

(re)relocation of sanitation. Suffice it to say that, on the negative side, the move is likely, once again, to have caused institutional turmoil and has the adverse consequence of lumping all sanitation—whether waterborne or not—with water services. However, in light of the facts that *(a)* the relevant legislation is institutionally linked to Water Affairs and *(b)* much sanitation expertise is still located in Water Affairs, there are significant arguments for the move back to Water Affairs under the consolidated Department of Water and Sanitation.

[13] National Sanitation Task Team, Republic of South Africa, *National Sanitation Policy* (October 1996), 20.

through the National Housing Subsidy Scheme (which provides subsidies to developers to build low-income housing). Housing projects undertaken in terms of the National Housing Subsidy must meet minimum standards regarding sanitation, for which the basic level is a ventilated improved pit (VIP) latrine or alternative system agreed to between the community, municipality, and provincial government.

Regarding informal settlements, the in situ upgrading of such settlements is provided for in the Upgrading of Informal Settlements Programme (UISP), instituted in terms of Section 3(4)(g) of the Housing Act, and contained in Part 3 Volume 4 of the National Housing Code. The UISP establishes that '[w]here interim municipal engineering services are to be provided, they should as far as possible be undertaken on the basis that such interim services constitute the first phase of permanent services'.[14] According to the DWAF's National Sanitation Strategy, adopted in 2005, '[In informal settlements] solutions such as communal facilities and chemical toilets should not be used where the system is expected to have a duration of more than one month.'[15]

And dealing with emergency situations, the Emergency Housing Programme (EHP), which is also located in Part 3 Volume 4 of the National Housing Code, establishes a framework for assistance for people who find themselves in emergency housing situations because of floods, landslides, evictions, and so on. It extends financial assistance, in the form of rapid grants, to municipalities to enable them to provide shelter and basic services (including sanitation) to households on a temporary basis. In respect of emergency basic sanitation, the EHP stipulates that, where possible, VIP toilets must be provided on the basis of one VIP per five families.[16] However, it is clear from the National Sanitation Policy, 1996, that chemical toilets, while formally considered inappropriate for the vast majority of situations

[14] DHS, *National Housing Code*, 2009, Volume 4, Part 3, 'Upgrading Informal Settlement', 37.

[15] DWAF, *Final Draft National Sanitation Strategy*, 2005, 56.

[16] DHS (n 14), Volume 4, Part 3, 'Emergency Housing Programme', 38.

(including informal settlements[17]), are considered acceptable in emergency situations.[18]

Finally, in order to address the economic access component of the right to basic sanitation, in March 2009, the DWA published the Free Basic Sanitation Implementation Strategy (FBSan). This policy acknowledges that there is 'a right of access to a basic level of sanitation service', and that municipalities have an obligation to ensure that poor households are not denied access to basic services due to their inability to pay for such services.[19] The FBSan policy is, however, deliberately vague, stating that free basic sanitation is a controversial issue over which there is no universal agreement and, therefore, it affords maximum discretion to municipalities in terms of deciding how and even whether to implement the strategy. Thus, beyond recommending in cases of waterborne sanitation that an additional amount of free basic water (between 3 and 4 additional kilolitres per household per month) should be allocated to poor households above the usual free basic water (FBW) amount—the nationally prescribed FBW standard is 6 kilolitres of water to be provided to poor households per month, which amounts to 25 litres per person per day in a household of eight—the strategy provides very little in the way of concrete recommendations, and it skirts the issue of appropriate forms of basic sanitation for informal settlements, as well as any attempt to quantify the maximum number of people to share communal sanitation facilities.

Sanitation Practice Dissected across Human Rights-Related Fault Lines

The South African socio-political terrain is a curious mix of very progressive and pro-poor laws and policies, on the one hand, and very little adherence to laws and policies by government officials and

---

[17] According to the DWAF's *Final Draft National Sanitation Strategy*, 2005, 'informal settlements must not be treated as emergency situations for the purpose of this strategy but should be provided with viable and sustainable solutions'. See DWAF (n 15), 49.

[18] National Sanitation Task Team (n 13), 20.

[19] DWAF, *Free Basic Sanitation Implementation Strategy*, 2009, i.

agencies, on the other, creating a stark mismatch between rights on paper and the realities of daily lives, which is exacerbated by a creeping malaise of formal political spaces,[20] meaning that many of the struggles to realize sanitation (and other) rights occur on the streets or in courts as detailed in the section titled 'Filling in the Gaps to Realize the Right: Protest and Litigation' later.

Undoubtedly, great advances have been made in line with the rights-based frameworks set out above to extend basic sanitation services to poor households. However, a number of systemic problems remain that have compromised both the extent and adequacy of access to basic sanitation across the internationally recognized dimensions of the right.

Availability

Notwithstanding the statistical advances regarding the rollout of sanitation services since 1994, there are still significant backlogs

---

[20] There is an evolving political crisis in South Africa that is most acutely felt at the local-government level (responsible for service delivery including sanitation), in terms of which, corruption, incompetence, incapacity, and political unwillingness have become widespread, resulting in numerous municipalities being placed under administration. See Jackie Dugard, 'Urban Basic Services: Rights, Reality and Resistance', in Malcolm Langford, Ben Cousins, Jackie Dugard, and Tshepo Madlingozi (eds), *Socio-economic Rights in South Africa: Symbols or Substance?* (Cambridge University Press 2013), 275–6. Such malaise is aided by both the list system of proportional political representation (meaning that there is only a limited role for direct constituency-based accountability) and the party-political dominance of local vehicles for public participation such as ward committees and Integrated Development Plans, meaning that residents are all but excluded from formal local participation outside of elections. See Laurence Piper and Roger Deacon, 'Too Dependent to Participate: Ward Committees and Local Democratisation in South Africa' (2009) 35(4) *Local Government Studies*, 415. Although the escalating political crisis has started to erode the African National Congress' (ANC) dominance of party politics, especially at the local-government level, historical loyalty and identity politics, along with the absence of a credible alternative pro-poor party, mean that the ANC remains popular, especially at the national level.

in basic sanitation service delivery. According to a March 2012 intergovernmental report on the status of sanitation services in South Africa, approximately 11 per cent of households in South Africa still have to be provided with sanitation services, and 26 per cent (or 3.2 million households) are 'at risk of service failure and/or are experiencing service delivery breakdowns'.[21] And, according to the 2011 Census, 57 per cent of households have access to a flush toilet connected to a sewerage system; 3.1 per cent have access to a flush toilet connected to a septic tank; 8.8 per cent have access to a VIP; 19.3 per cent have access to a pit latrine without any ventilation or improvement; 2.5 per cent have access to a chemical toilet; 2.1 per cent use a bucket; 2.1 per cent use 'other' forms of toilets; and 5.2 per cent have no access to any formal form of sanitation.[22]

Rural areas remain an ongoing concern, with many households still using rudimentary bucket systems and some still practising open defecation,[23] underscoring the need for clear policy and practice regarding rural sanitation options. Yet, one of the greatest challenges facing South Africa is the provision of basic sanitation to informal settlements, where in many cases authorities do not want to provide bulk infrastructure because they would like to relocate the residents. However, as highlighted in the *Nokotyana* litigation,[24] examined in the section titled 'Filling in the Gaps to Realize the Right: Protest and Litigation' below, such proposed relocations are often contested by the informal settlement communities, and can take many years to be resolved. As acknowledged by the government, 64 per cent of informal settlement households (584,378 households, representing approximately 2 million people) live with interim services that are 'at risk of service failure and/or are experiencing service delivery

[21] DPME, DWA, and DHS, *Sanitation Services-Quality of Sanitation in South Africa: Report on the Status of Sanitation Services in South Africa* (2012), 3.

[22] Statistics South Africa, *Census 2011: Methodology and Highlights of Key Results* (2012), 13.

[23] DHS, *Ministerial Sanitation Task Team Report* (2012), 16.

[24] *Johnson Matotoba Nokotyana & Others* v *Ekurhuleni Metropolitan Municipality & Others* 2010 (4) BCLR 312 (CC) (Constitutional Court) ('*Nokotyana*').

breakdowns', indicating that the 'provision of adequate services to dwellings in (transient) informal settlements requires a strategy that takes into consideration permanency and land use objectives together with other considerations of topography, geo-hydrology, proximity to bulk services, etc.'[25] Of particular concern is the fact that there is not a clear regulated standard for the number of households that must share government-provided communal toilet facilities in informal settlements.

Beyond informal settlements, aggregated statistics on the rollout of sanitation across the country obscure both the quality of the services (as discussed below), as well as the problem of geographic areas with unusually low access to basic sanitation, such as the former homeland areas. Thus, the March 2012 Department of Performance Monitoring and Evaluation (DPME), DWA, and DHS report on sanitation found that the majority of households without adequate sanitation services are in KwaZulu-Natal, North West, and the Eastern Cape.[26] And a 2009 submission to the South African Human Rights Commission on access to water and sanitation highlighted that (based on 2001 census data) the 30 worst performing municipalities in terms of inadequate access to sanitation (and water) were in KwaZulu-Natal and the Eastern Cape, and, if you look at the sixty worst performing municipalities, these were all also in KwaZulu-Natal and the Eastern Cape, plus Limpopo.[27] The submission noted the striking coincidence between the worst performing municipalities and the geographic areas of the former independent homelands (especially the Transkei), indicating the continuation of apartheid-inherited patterns of underdevelopment.[28]

---

[25] DPME, DWA, and DHS (n 21), 15–16.

[26] DPME, DWA, and DHS (n 21), 17.

[27] Kate Tissington, P Berkowitz, and Jackie Dugard, *Submission to the South African Human Rights Commission on Access to Water and Sanitation in South Africa* (Centre for Applied Legal Studies, 9 February 2009), 5–6.

[28] Tissington, Berkowitz, and Dugard, 2009 (n 27), 6.

Another dimension of the (un)availability of sanitation facilities that is sometimes overlooked in the general statistics is the issue of toilet facilities at schools. The chronic under-provision of adequate toilet facilities at schools is currently confronted by the litigation mounted by Equal Education that in November 2013 secured a commitment by the national Department of Education to finally adopt Minimum Norms and Standards for school facilities including toilets.[29] This is a serious issue since it fundamentally compromises the rights of children, as well as disabled persons in particular, who are less able to make alternative arrangements, and girl children, many of whom are forced by the unavailability of toilets to drop out of school or stay at home, especially during their menstrual cycles.

In respect of households with waterborne sanitation services, there have not been any studies examining the sufficiency of the recommended FBSan allocation (15 litres per person per day over and above the FBW allocation) or the extent to which municipalities are pursuing this allocation, which is not considered to be a legal requirement. This impacts economic access because, obviously, where the FBSan amount is insufficient, for instance, in multi-dwelling households, households have to use some of the FBW allocation for waterborne sanitation, and/or pay for additional water, according to the rising Block tariffs in the relevant municipality, which may or may not be appropriately pro-poor.

One further specific problem impeding access to waterborne sanitation services by many of the poorest households is the common practice by municipalities of targeting Free Basic Services (including FBSan) through the municipal indigency policy.[30] Again, there are

[29] For further details on the campaign, see Equal Education, https://equaleducation.org.za; and Equal Education Law Centre, http://eelawcentre.org.za.

[30] In order to satisfy the legislative and policy imperatives to provide access to basic services for poor communities, most municipalities in South Africa pursue targeted indigency policies with varying qualifying criteria and free-basic-services-related benefits. A few of the bigger metropolitan municipalities pursue universal access to basic levels of free basic services alongside a targeted programme for additional benefits for qualifying

generalized problems related to municipal indigency policies, which serve to exclude the most vulnerable and poor households from any potential benefits including FBSan. Chief among these problems are an ad hoc definition of poverty for the purposes of qualifying for benefits. Some municipalities use a level of income equivalent to or just less than two state pensions, others use property/land value to determine whether a household qualifies, and still others use seemingly random income thresholds. In addition, the process around registering for benefits is typically very onerous, requiring numerous documents, and is perceived by potential recipients as stigmatizing.[31] This means that FBSan is not being accessed by those in most need, a fact highlighted in a report, which found that: 'FBSan services were benefiting the "haves" while the "have-nots" continued to live in squalid conditions with poor or no access to adequate sanitation services'.[32]

Accessibility (Physical and Economic) Including Gender and Disability Dimensions

Physical access to sanitation facilities remains a problem both in rural and informal settlement areas, where people often have to walk long

---

poorer households. Indigency policy targeting has been criticized for differing vastly and irrationally across municipalities, for being very onerous in general, and discouraging registration, especially among the poorest and most vulnerable households, including child-headed households. See for example, Kate Tissington, Marc Dettmann, Malcolm Langford, and Sonkita Conteh, *Water Services Fault Lines: An Assessment of South Africa's Water and Sanitation Provision across 15 Municipalities* (Centre for Applied Legal Studies, 2008), 34–40; Kate Tissington, *Targeting the Poor? An Analysis of Free Basic Services (FBS) and Municipal Indigent Policies* (Socio-Economic Rights Institute of South Africa, 2013).

[31] Kate Tissington, *Basic Sanitation in South Africa: A Guide to Legislation, Policy and Practice* (Socio-Economic Rights Institute of South Africa, 2011), 65.

[32] Nozibele Mjoli, Gillian Sykes, and Tracy Jooste, 'Towards the Realization of Free Basic Sanitation: Evaluation, Review and Recommendations', *Water Research Commission Research Report*, WRC Report No. TT 422/09 2009, 25, 56.

distances to relieve themselves. Inadequate physical access has both a gender and disability dimension as having to walk distances to sanitation facilities exposes women to safety concerns, making them vulnerable to attack by wild animals and people. Disabled persons also suffer when sanitation facilities are not conveniently located or are in other ways physically inaccessible to them. Critically, unlike with water services, where minimum basic standards include being located within 200 metres of a water supply, there are no standards for the proximity of sanitation facilities (nor for the number of households that have to share communal sanitation facilities) and no reliable figures for people's physical access to sanitation.

Economic access is equally difficult to assess. This is because there are no in-depth studies on what poor households spend on sanitation services. In part, this is because many poor households rely on government-provided sanitation services for which there is no household cost, or households dig latrines which represent a once-off cost in terms mainly of household labour. What is apparent from litigation such as *Nokotyana* is that where informal settlements have to rely on chemical toilets (which are at best meant to be temporary measures, but often are left as semi-permanent facilities), the chemicals are relatively expensive and unaffordable for the majority of households.

Quality, Sustainability, and Acceptability, Including Participation and Information Dimensions

Over the past decade, there has been an almost slavish focus in South Africa on constructing toilets, and achieving the political and MDG-driven imperative to meet targets, regardless of the acceptability, quality, suitability, or outcomes of the projects. Moreover, the target-driven approach has meant that the rollout of basic sanitation has often occurred with insufficient or no community participation, as evident in the sanitation projects around the country that have resulted in unenclosed toilets (such as in Makhaza) that no one can use. Further research is necessary to understand how sanitation projects could be more genuinely participatory, but in the meantime, it is clear that, as acknowledged by the government, 'the continuous chasing of targets (however

noble)' has come at 'a price of a lack of focus on the far more challenging requirements of the on-going sustainable operation and
maintenance of services'.[33]

These unintended negative consequences have been confirmed by
numerous reports. According to the 2009 Water Dialogues-South
Africa report, the preoccupation with numbers and targets has
meant that there is insufficient focus on the quality, maintenance,
and sustainability of the services.[34] The South African Institution
of Civil Engineering (SAICE) notes that users are 'often not receiving the full benefit because of high failure rates'.[35] A 2004/2005
DWAF sanitation sustainability audit commissioned to assess the
quality and sustainability of sanitation infrastructure found that
28 per cent of toilets that had been rolled out by government were
'already dysfunctional or had a high sustainability risk indicating a
high probability of failure within the short to medium term'.[36] And
a 2007 report by the Council for Scientific and Industrial Research
(CSIR) (commissioned by the DWAF), which involved an audit
of 2,410 sanitation projects in the Municipal Infrastructure Grant
(MIG) database that had moved beyond the planning phase, found
the following:

- Up to 25 per cent of on-site toilets were inadequately designed for
  ventilation;
- Up to 68 per cent of on-site top structures were constructed such
  that they could not be moved when the pits are full;
- Up to 28 per cent of the facilities had doors that could not be
  closed or locked;
- Some flush toilets did not have cisterns (23 per cent) or pedestals
  (18 per cent);
- Up to 61 per cent had no hand-washing facility near the toilet; and

[33] DPME, DWA, and DHS (n 21), 9.

[34] M. Galvin, *Straight Talk to Strengthen Delivery in the Water Services
Sector: The Water Dialogues—South Africa Synthesis Report 2009*, 2.

[35] The South African Institution of Civil Engineering (SAICE), *SAICE
Infrastructure Report Card for South Africa 2011* (2011), 16.

[36] DPME, DWA, and DHS (n 21), 9.

- On 60 per cent of the facilities, municipalities were only doing reactive maintenance and no proactive maintenance; while 40 per cent of municipalities were found not to have adequate maintenance capacity.[37]

An equally damning 2009 Water Research Commission[38] report on basic sanitation services highlighted that across South Africa, 'there was no single type of sanitation that fared uniformly well'.[39] Common problems identified by the report include:[40]

- Generally, sanitation facilities are not compliant with appropriate technical design standards and are built in a manner susceptible to quick failure and extreme maintenance difficulties;
- Insufficient attention to safety and access-related issues results in facilities not being used; and
- Municipalities are not paying sufficient attention to the maintenance of existing infrastructure, which is becoming degraded.

Regarding maintenance specifically, during the 2012 survey of sanitation services undertaken by the Ministerial Sanitation Task Team, members noted that around the country, municipalities were not emptying VIPs, resulting in unhealthy and unhygienic conditions for the users.[41] In some rural areas, the failure to empty pits relates to municipalities chasing targets through funds that are specifically for the construction of new toilets but not for their maintenance, resulting in many poor households that have several toilet structures on their properties, including ones with full

---

[37] Cited in DPME, DWA, and DHS (n 21), 10.

[38] The Water Research Commission is a semi-autonomous research institution established in terms of legislation from 1971, to provide strategic research related to water resource and services management in South Africa.

[39] David Still, Nick Walker, and Derek Hazelton, *Basic Sanitation Services in South Africa: Learning from the Past, Planning for the Future*, Water Research Commission Research Report, TT 414-09 2009, v.

[40] Cited in SAICE (n 35), 16.

[41] DHS (n 23), 16.

pits that need to be emptied.[42] Additional problems occur wherever there is waterborne sanitation, in that almost all wastewater treatment infrastructure, especially municipal treatment plants, have been poorly maintained and are in 'urgent need of maintenance and replacement', with many verging on being dysfunctional.[43] According to the DWA's Green Drop assessment report on the performance of wastewater treatment and management, of the 821 systems assessed in 2011, only 40 received Green Drop certification[44] from the DWA, and 317 wastewater treatment plants required urgent attention, with a further 143 being categorized as having a high risk of failure.[45]

The target-driven approach to sanitation additionally blinds implementers to relevant social issues and human rights-related determinants of sanitation such as access for people with disabilities, people living with HIV/AIDS, women, girls attending school; and cultural and religious practices; and so on. It also results in unsustainable and/or unsuitable systems being rolled out. For example, in the Free State province, the government's push to eradicate the bucket system throughout the province led to it being 'remedied' through the installation of waterborne systems even in relatively isolated and marginalized communities that had no or limited bulk sewer networks or wastewater treatment works, resulting in 'the provision of sanitation infrastructure that, in some cases, was not the optimal technical solution', and meaning extreme pressure on existing wastewater treatment works, and negative consequences 'in respect of long-term service affordability, functionality and sustainability'.[46] Elsewhere across the country, municipalities have

---

[42] Carol Paton, 'It's Still the Pits', *Financial Mail* (20 August 2010).

[43] SAICE (n 35), 16.

[44] The Green Drop system certifies that wastewater systems and processes are operating well.

[45] Department of Water Affairs, *Statement by the Minister of Water and Environmental Affairs Mrs Edna Molewa at the release of the Blue Drop and Green Drop Assessment Reports* (30 June 2011); available at www.gov.za/statement-minister-water-and-environmental-affairs-mrs-edna-molewa-release-blue-drop-and-green-drop.

[46] DPME, DWA, and DHS (n 21), 9.

provided flush toilets 'where there were inadequate water supplies for flushing'.[47]

Finally, the focus on targets has resulted in poor consultation with local communities over sanitation options. This oversight has been compounded by a widespread failure to provide appropriate hygiene- and sanitation-related education and readily available information, including on cleaning and emptying facilities. This has resulted in widespread misuse and neglect of facilities by communities,[48] which undermines the quality and long-term sustainability of services. The top-down approach has also led to unacceptable options being foisted on communities. This is apparent, for example, in the outcry over unenclosed toilets in Cape Town and the Free State, and the unpopularity of dry sanitation systems[49] in some provinces includ- ing the Free State,[50] as well as the rejection by poor communities in Cape Town of the 'porta-flush toilet', a portable hand-worked toilet that has a seat, a container for waste, and a chemical flushing system, which households do not like as they often leak, are not emptied regularly enough by the municipality and smell bad,[51] effectively making them function as 'little more than fancy bucket toilets'.[52] As recognized by the Ministerial Sanitation Task Team, to ensure the quality, acceptability, and sustainability of sanitation services, it is

---

[47] DPME, DWA, and DHS (n 21), 26.

[48] SAICE (n 35), 16.

[49] There is some debate as to whether dry sanitation options are suit- able, especially in the more humid climate of KwaZulu-Natal. Beyond this, some of the dry toilets that have been implemented are not appropriate for women, as they attempt to separate the faecal matter and urine into two dif- ferent compartments which is not possible with women's physiology.

[50] DPME, DWA, and DHS (n 21), 9.

[51] Mary-Anne Gontsana, 'Portable Flush Toilets: What Are They and Why the Fuss?' *Daily Maverick* (13 June 2013); available at www.dailymav- erick.co.za/article/2013-06-12-portable-flush-toilets-what-are-they-and- why-the-fuss/#.V-g7U865eFI.

[52] Peter Cunliffe-Jones (ed), 'Claim that No-one in Cape Town Has to Use "Bucket Toilets" Is Wrong', *Africa Check* (7 June 2013); available at www.africacheck.org/reports/claim-that-no-one-in-cape-town-has-to-use- bucket-toilets-is-wrong.

necessary for households and communities to be centrally involved in sanitation planning and implementation.[53]

For the first decade following the transition to democracy, there was a level of patience among poor communities regarding the above fault lines. However, enduring failure to deliver adequate basic sanitation services is increasingly giving way to frustration, which has manifested in vocal demands for improved delivery expressed through protest and litigation.

Filling in the Gaps to Realize the Right: Protest and Litigation

Media exposure of the unenclosed toilets in Makhaza informal settlement in Khalelitsha, Cape Town, and Rammulotsi township in Moqhaka local municipality in the Free State province, as well as of the explosion of local protests about inadequate service delivery across the country, has heightened public awareness about, and frustration over, the systemic and multilayered problems around access to basic sanitation outlined above. Growing dissatisfaction at the level of poor communities with inadequate access to basic services including sanitation has in recent years given rise to two forms of community activism—protest and litigation—which, in turn, have begun to give content to and to realize the right to basic sanitation.

Protest

Since 2004, South Africa has experienced a movement of local protest amounting to a rebellion of the poor. This has been widespread and intense, reaching insurrectionary proportions in some instances. On the surface, the protests have been about service delivery against uncaring, self-serving, and corrupt leaders of municipalities.[54]

---

[53] DHS (n 23), 69.

[54] Peter Alexander, 'Rebellion of the Poor: South Africa's Service Delivery Protests: A Preliminary Analysis' (2010), 37(2) *Review of African Political Economy*, 25.

In urban areas across the country, there is evidently growing dissatisfaction with inadequate access to basic services, as well as more generalized anger about the slow pace of transformation in South Africa, which has among the highest levels of socio-economic inequality in the world. Much grassroots discontent has manifested in 'service delivery' protests, which began to hit the media headlines in 2004 and have continued unabated ever since, reaching a height in 2009,[55] when there were an estimated 19.8 protests per month across the country.[56] The protests occur mainly in urban township or informal settlement areas and include marches, gatherings, and the handing over of petitions or memoranda, usually to government officials.

The protests clearly relate, in broad terms, to rising inequality and unemployment, as well as the exclusion of poor people from formal political spaces.[57] As commented by Richard Pithouse, the protests are best understood as being about 'the material benefits of full social

---

[55] Although it is possible to trace current protests back to the apartheid era, most commentators on contemporary local protests view 2004 as marking the beginning of a new wave of protests. See for example, Susan Booysen, 'With the Ballot and the Brick: The Politics of Attaining Service Delivery' (2007) 7(1) *Progress in Development Studies*, 21. It is likely that the onset, in 2004, of the current wave of protests relates to the consolidation of the powers of local government and the first round of local government elections in December 2000, as well as the poor communities' growing dissatisfaction, over the subsequent months and years, with the failures of the government to translate the constitutional vision into reality. Regarding the highpoint in 2009, there is evidence that protests have escalated since the election of President Jacob Zuma in April 2009—this is probably related to the raised, and then dashed, expectations from his presidency. It is also possible, however, that we have not yet experienced the true highpoint of protest in South Africa.

[56] Hirsh Jain, 'Community Protests in South Africa: Trends, Analysis and Explanations' (Local Government Working Paper Series No. 1, Community Law Centre, University of the Western Cape 2010) cited from Langford et al. (eds) (n 20), 285.

[57] There is growing evidence that the vehicles for local participation such as ward committees and integrated development planning forums have been 'hijacked' by party politics to the exclusion of poor residents.

inclusion ... as well as the right to be taken seriously when thinking and speaking through community organisations'.[58] Typically, local protests are the culmination of years of attempts by poor communities to engage officials, and it is evident from various studies that communities usually only erupt into protest following protracted indifference from government officials to community concerns.[59]

Notwithstanding the underlying issues, protesters have typically framed their actions as relating to inadequate access to service delivery at the local-government level. This is perhaps unsurprising as local government is the sphere of government that is most directly and most intimately involved in the lives of poor people (local government is responsible for water, electricity, sanitation and refuse services, as well, increasingly, as emergency, temporary, and social housing provision). As such, one of the few studies to have investigated the reasons behind such protests (between 2007 and 2010) found that the main reasons articulated by protestors were access to housing (36 per cent), access to water (18 per cent), access to electricity (18 per cent), poor service delivery in general (15 per cent), sanitation (13 per cent), and general corruption (11 per cent).[60]

While local protests do raise the profile of issues and draw public and government attention to deficits in delivery, they have in recent years resulted in serious casualties. For example, the protest by Maqheleng Concerned Citizens (a residents' association in Maqheleng township in the Setsoto municipality, Ficksburg, in the Free State province) about inadequate sanitation and water services

---

See for example, Laurence Piper and Lubna Nadvi, 'Popular Mobilisation, Party Dominance and Participatory Governance in South Africa', in Lisa Thompson and Chris Tapscott (eds), *Citizens and Social Movements: Perspectives from the Global South* (Zed Books, 2010), 212.

[58] Richard Pithouse, 'The University of Abahlali base Mjondolo', Indymedia UK (1 December 2007); available at www.indymedia.org.uk/en/2007/12/386876.html.

[59] Luke Sinwell et al., *Service Delivery Protests: Findings from Quick Response Research on Four 'Hotspots': Piet Retief, Balfour, Thokoza, Diepsloot* (Centre for Sociological Research, University of Johannesburg, 2010).

[60] Jain, 'Community Protests in South Africa', 29–30 cited from Langford et al. (eds) (n 20), 299.

on 13 April 2011 resulted in a community leader, Andries Tatane, being shot dead by the police. Paying tribute to his colleague and friend, Andries Tatane, the chairperson of Maqheleng Concerned Citizens was quoted in the media as saying:

> Tatane sacrificed his life to free us from the shackles of the Setsoto municipality. If our rights for clean water had been respected, we wouldn't be here. If our rights for a clean environment that is free of stinking sewage had been respected, we wouldn't be here. When will this substandard life come to an end, just when? Maybe the day Tatane died marked a turning point in the history of Ficksburg, Maqheleng.[61]

Litigation

In South Africa, socio-economic rights are explicitly justiciable, and as of 2016, 20 socio-economic rights-related cases have been decided by the Constitutional Court since its establishment in 1996. These include judgments on the rights of access to housing, water, social security, and electricity. And, on 19 November 2009, the South African Constitutional Court handed down judgment in its first and only sanitation-related case to date in the matter of *Johnson Matotoba Nokotyana & Others* v *Ekurhuleni Metropolitan Municipality & Others (Nokotyana)*.[62]

The *Nokotyana* case was an application by the residents of Harry Gwala informal settlement in Ekurhuleni municipality (close to Johannesburg) for an order against the municipality to install, inter alia, temporary basic sanitation facilities pending a decision by the local government on whether the settlement would be upgraded to a formal township.[63] Many of the residents had been living in

---

[61] Sipho Masondo, 'Tatane Showered with Praise' *The Times* (South Africa), (20 April 2011).

[62] *Nokotyana* (n 24).

[63] The Constitutional Court hearing was an appeal against a judgment of the South Gauteng High Court which dismissed the application for the government to provide temporary sanitation services and high-mast lighting but did order the provision of refuse collection and communal taps for the settlement.

the settlement since 1993, and had been attempting since then to get the municipality to pursue an in situ upgrading of the settlement. In the meantime, they were living in squalid conditions with only six communal taps for the entire settlement of approximately 1,500 households, no electric lighting or refuse collection, and only rudimentary communal pit latrines without adequate privacy built by the residents.

In August 2006, following years of fraught engagement with the municipality, including the municipality's attempt to evict the residents unlawfully without a court order, the Ekurhuleni municipality finally submitted a proposal on upgrading to the relevant provincial government official (the Member of the Executive Committee for Local Government and Housing, Gauteng). However, three years later, no decision had been taken, prompting the residents to take the matter to court.

In the Constitutional Court, the applicants based their claim for sanitation services primarily on Section 26 (right of access to adequate housing) of the Constitution (arguing that sanitation was a component of the right to adequate housing), the constitutional right to human dignity,[64] and the EHP and UISP of the National Housing Code. In April 2009, in the run-up to the Constitutional Court hearing, the municipality adopted a policy in terms of which it offered the residents of Harry Gwala informal settlement one chemical toilet per ten families. The residents rejected this offer, arguing for one VIP per household. Ultimately—despite ordering the Member of the Executive Committee to take a final decision on Ekurhuleni municipality's application in terms of Chapter 13 of the National Housing Code to upgrade the status of Harry Gwala settlement, within fourteen months of the Court order—the Court dismissed the appeal, rejecting the applicants' request for temporary sanitation (and lighting) on the grounds that neither the EHP nor UISP applied to informal settlements where no decision on upgrading had been taken, meaning that the residents were living in limbo until a decision on upgrading

---

[64] Section 10 of the Constitution provides that everyone has the right to have their dignity respected and protected.

was taken, and therefore, were effectively excluded from access to basic sanitation.[65]

The *Nokotyana* judgment has been criticized for being overly formalistic and deferential to the government, and for not giving due weight to the multiple violations of rights entailed in living for years in an informal settlement without adequate service, as well as for failing to develop the normative right of access to housing to include a right to sanitation.[66] It has also been criticized for misinterpreting the National Housing Code—particularly the UISP—so as to exclude an obligation to provide interim services in informal settlements where no decision has yet been taken regarding upgrading.[67] The Constitutional Court's approach and order in *Nokotyana* stands in sharp contrast with a subsequent case on access to basic sanitation services in an informal settlement heard by the Cape High Court—*Ntombentsha Beja & Others* v *Premier of the Western Cape & Others (Beja)*.[68]

In April 2011, the Western Cape High Court delivered its decision in the *Beja* case, which was an application by the residents of Makhaza informal settlement in Khayelitsha, Cape Town, to declare unconstitutional the 1,316 unenclosed waterborne toilets that the municipality had constructed as part of an upgrading project undertaken in terms of Chapter 13 of the National Housing Code (the UISP). The municipality referred to these toilets as 'loos with a view', and argued that the toilets had been constructed pursuant to an agreement with the community, in terms of which the municipality would provide one toilet per household and residents would provide an enclosure for each toilet, rather than the ratio the municipality argued it was obliged to provide, of one toilet per five households. The community (supported by the local ANC Youth

[65] The Court also rejected the applicants' attempt to rely on the rights to housing and dignity in the Constitution.

[66] David Bilchitz, 'Is the Constitutional Court Wasting Away the Rights of the Poor? *Nokotyana* v *Ekurhuleni Metropolitan Municipality*' (2010) 127 (3) *South African Law Journal* 597.

[67] Marie Huchzermeyer, *Cities with Slums: From Informal Settlement Eradication to a Right to the City in Africa* (UCT Press 2011), 224.

[68] *Beja* (n 8).

League branch[69]) complained about the toilets to the South African Human Rights Commission, which investigated the complaint and released a report in June 2010, finding that the municipality had violated the residents' right to human dignity.[70] On the basis of this finding, the residents went to court, filing an application in the Western Cape High Court in September 2010.

On 29 November 2010, following an inspection of the site, Judge Erasmus made an interim order for the municipality to enclose the toilets. Final judgment was handed down on 29 April 2011, finding in favour of the applicants, and providing detailed commentary regarding the level of agreement/consultation with the community on providing unenclosed toilets, the veracity of the municipality's argument that it was only obliged to provide toilets in the ratio of one toilet per five households, and whether or not the provision of unenclosed toilets violated constitutional rights.

Regarding the so-called consultation with the community, the Court found that the municipality could not prove that any agreement existed, and that, more generally, the consultation process was highly flawed. For example, the sanitation situation was only discussed at one meeting, for which the municipality provided four-days notice, and the circulated agenda contained no item on sanitation.[71] Moreover, the minutes of the meeting record that only 60 people out of a community of approximately 6,000 attended the meeting, and as it turned out, the toilets were only constructed two years after the meeting.[72]

More substantively, the judgment found that the municipality had failed to take into account people with disabilities, as well as the safety and security of vulnerable members of the community including women, who were exposed to the potential risk of gender-based

---

[69] In Cape Town, the ANC is not the ruling party, namely it is an opposition party in the municipality.

[70] South African Human Rights Commission, 'Report on the Matter of African National Congress Youth League Dullah Omar Region o.b.o Ward 95 Makhaza Residents and City of Cape Town', Case reference no: WC/2010/0029 (June 2010).

[71] *Beja* (n 8), para 80.

[72] *Beja* (n 8), paras 81 and 83.

violence. Pointing out that, in arguing that it had an obligation to provide only one toilet per five households, the municipality had wrongly conflated the EHP with non-emergency housing as provided by the municipality in the UISP project in Makhaza, the Judge denounced the toilets as not meeting the required standards, and noted that in any event, none of the toilets was in working order. For these reasons, the Judge ruled that there was a violation in terms of Sections 10 (human dignity), 12 (freedom and security of the person), 14 (privacy), 24 (environment), 26 (housing), and 27 (healthcare) of the Constitution.[73] He further held that the provision of unenclosed toilets is inconsistent with Regulation 2 of the Compulsory National Standards.[74] He therefore declared the municipality's conduct to be in violation of the residents' constitutional rights, and ordered the municipality to enclose all 1,316 toilets.

Although South Africa follows a system of judicial hierarchy and precedent in terms of which all lower courts are bound by the rulings of all higher courts, because the Constitutional Court essentially opted to avoid any specific pronouncements on sanitation-related rights in the *Nokotyana* case, until another sanitation-related case comes before the Constitutional Court, *Beja* stands as the strongest authority on local government obligations in respect of sanitation.

* * *

As recognized by the court in the *Beja* case, sanitation is intimately connected with a range of other rights such as privacy, dignity, freedom and security of the person, environment, healthcare, and housing. Moreover, access to adequate sanitation is fundamental to any efforts to reduce poverty, eradicate gender inequality, and promote economic and human development as well as environmental sustainability.

Responding to the desire to improve their lives and living conditions, protests such as the one in Khayelitsha involving the throwing of faeces at politicians, along with highly publicized court cases such as *Beja*, have drawn attention to the enduring problem of inadequate

---

[73] *Beja* (n 8), para 149.

[74] *Beja* (n 8), para 150.

toilets and lack of basic sanitation across the country. This has not only had an empowering and mobilizing impact vis-à-vis disadvantaged communities, as evidenced by communities becoming increasingly vocal and assertive in their demands for basic sanitation, but it has also begun to have an effect on government. In July 2011, the DHS announced that rising dissatisfaction with sanitation provision represents 'a renewed community interest and participation in the politics of development as opposed to the politics of politics', requiring 'a comprehensive solution'.[75]

This acknowledgment highlights that, although in South Africa, sanitation has until recently been relatively neglected and there are enduring problems related to the implementation of sanitation programmes, through the protest and litigation outlined above, the critical importance of sanitation to well-being and human development, as well as government's obligations in respect of advancing access to basic sanitation, are beginning to sink into public discourse and government priorities. In the final analysis, while the South African experience highlights that law and policy on their own do not translate smoothly into access to public goods and services, it also demonstrates that rights, law, and policies can act as catalysing and mobilizing agents for social change by constituting tools for empowering communities, and for holding government accountable for established obligations.

[75] DHS, 'Media Statement Issued by the Department of Human Settlements 14 July 2011 on the Toilet Saga' (14 July 2011) cited from Tissington (n 31), 16.

3

The Right to Sanitation

Multiple Dimensions and Challenges

Philippe Cullet

Access to sanitation remains an immense challenge in India. This is true in terms of the huge effort that is required to make the whole country open defecation free (ODF), the most common indicator of the realization of the right to sanitation. Indeed, as recently as 2016, 52.1 per cent of the rural population still practiced open defecation.[1] There is even more to be done in terms of the other dimensions of sanitation, including insufficient sewerage networks and limited capacity to treat wastewater and manage septage. In fact, it has been estimated that only 37 per cent of sewage generated flows through treatment plants.[2] It is then unsurprising to find that 75–80 per cent

[1] Government of India, National Sample Survey Office, *Swachhta Status Report* (2016).

[2] Lok Sabha, Unstarred Question No. 1478, Capacity of Sewage Treatment Plants, to be answered on 8 December 2015; available at http://164.100.47. 190/loksabhaquestions/annex/6/AU1478.pdf.

of water pollution is caused by domestic sewage, and 21 per cent of communicable diseases are water-related.[3] There are other crucial sanitation challenges that need to be tackled urgently. Among these, the realization of the constitutional imperative to eradicate manual scavenging stands out, since this should have ensued soon after the Constitution was adopted in 1950 but is yet to be fully achieved.[4]

Sanitation is thus a broad field. This has indeed been the official understanding since at least the beginning of this century with sanitation being seen as 'a comprehensive concept, which includes liquid and solid waste disposal, food hygiene, personal, domestic as well as environmental hygiene'.[5] A more recent definition views sanitation as including personal hygiene, home sanitation, safe water, garbage disposal, excreta disposal, and wastewater disposal.[6] These definitions are helpful in linking hygiene and sanitation, and recognizing the individual and public dimensions of sanitation as well as the link between liquid and solid waste management and between the environment and sanitation. At the same time, they fail, for instance, to specifically include manual scavenging in the ambit of sanitation, and do not highlight the particular gender issues that arise.[7]

In the 2017 version of the SBM (Gramin) (SBM-G) guidelines, a definition has been reintroduced, but it is surprisingly less comprehensive than earlier, limiting itself to 'safe disposal of human excreta,

---

[3] Sushmi Dey, '80% of India's Surface Water may be Polluted, Report by International Body Says', *The Times of India* (28 June 2015), 10; and Answer to 'Lok Sabha Unstarred Question No. 2428 to be Answered on 16.03.2017: Contamination of Drinking Water'; available at http://re.indiaenvironmentportal.org.in/files/file/Contamination%20of%20Drinking%20Water.pdf.

[4] See Wilson (Chapter 10) in this volume.

[5] Government of India, Ministry of Rural Development, Department of Drinking Water Supply, *Central Rural Sanitation Programme–Total Sanitation Campaign: Guidelines 2001*, s 1.

[6] Government of India, Ministry of Drinking Water and Sanitation, *Nirmal Bharat Abhiyan: Guidelines 2012*, s 1(2).

[7] Note that for urban areas, there is no definition of sanitation, but eradication of manual scavenging is the second objective of the Guidelines for Swachh Bharat Mission (Urban), 2017, s 2.1.2.

right use of toilet and avoiding open defecation as well as management of solid and liquid waste'.[8] Even this restricted definition remains of limited relevance since there is no definition of sanitation in any law. This lack of definition is problematic from two different perspectives. On the one hand, the scope of what falls under sanitation has reduced in the current framework, and the understanding of sanitation is different in rural and urban areas. This is reflected in the fact that both liquid and solid waste are included in the Guidelines for SBM-G, 2017, but the Guidelines for SBM (Urban) (SBM-U), 2017, only include solid waste management.[9] On the other hand, regardless of the broad understanding of sanitation that has held sway for a number of years, sanitation interventions have been centred overwhelmingly on ensuring that toilets are built in each house.[10] This narrow application of the concept of sanitation explains why the measure of access to sanitation or the realization of the right to sanitation is often limited to access to individual toilets. This unfortunately obscures other issues that are no less crucial to the realization of the right to sanitation for each individual and the community.

From a legal perspective, the starting point for analysis is the recognition of the right to sanitation by the higher judiciary (the Supreme Court of India and high courts). However, this remains incomplete insofar as its content has not been spelt out in any detail in the case law. Laws addressing sanitation are even less helpful since they fail to provide an overall context for sanitation interventions. There is thus an immense task at hand that requires bringing together the different sanitation-related components of the legal framework,

---

[8] Guidelines for Swachh Bharat Mission (Gramin) (SBM-G), 2017, s 1.

[9] Guidelines for Swachh Bharat Mission (Urban) (SBM-U), 2017, s 2.3.

[10] For example, two-thirds of the points given to gram panchayats towards selecting them for the Nirmal Gram Puraskar (NGP), an award for Panchayati Raj institutions (PRIs) contributing significantly towards ensuring full sanitation coverage in their areas of operation, focus on toilets. The last third includes access to drinking water, information, education, and communication (IEC) activities, and solid and liquid waste management. See Nirmal Gram Puraskar Guidelines, 2012, para 4.

such as access to toilets in schools or the workplace, with the recognition of the right to sanitation.

This chapter starts by analysing the judicial recognition of the right to sanitation, and existing sanitation-related laws and administrative directions. It uncovers the fragmented and limited nature of the existing measures, and the significant role played by administrative directions in the sanitation sector. The next section goes on to analyse the implementation of the right in practice, and critically examines some of the main issues arising in the context of ongoing sanitation interventions. The last section examines some of the issues that are insufficiently addressed in the current implementation framework. This includes the need to move beyond the focus on individual toilets, the need to consider sanitation in the broader context to which it belongs, the need to give more importance to environmental dimensions, and the need to focus on issues of dignity and equality, starting with the question of manual scavenging.

Right to Sanitation and Implementation Framework

The right to sanitation is well enshrined in the case law in India. Interestingly, this happened much earlier than the developments at the international level discussed by de Albuquerque (Chapter 1) in this volume. The recognition of the right by the higher judiciary was conceptually ground-breaking, but it is only when the right is enshrined in legislation and delegated instruments that it can become a reality for rights-holders. As this section shows, there has been no direct recognition of the right in statutory provisions, and the limited extent to which its realization has been undertaken has been through administrative directions that make no mention of the right.

Judicial Recognition of the Right to Sanitation

The Constitution of India, like other constitutions drafted before the 1990s, includes no specific right to sanitation. It is the higher judiciary that progressively considered issues related to sanitation and recognized its existence as a derivative right. As early as 1980, the Supreme Court addressed the issue of sanitation directly in the

Ratlam case, triggered by the lack of sufficient investments in public toilets and sewerage facilities.[11] Justice Krishna Iyer came down heavily on the municipality for not providing basic facilities and trying to wriggle out of its statutory obligations. He highlighted that the municipality was not able to plead that it was incapable of meeting its obligations because of an absence of financial resources. The judgment established in clear terms that the state is bound to allocate resources in such a way that it fulfils the basic functions for which it has been set up.

In the same year, the high court of Rajasthan was called upon to respond to a petition from residents of Mandal in Bhilwara District, complaining about the health hazards of domestic wastewater that was accumulating in the common *chowk*.[12] The petitioners specifically prayed 'for a direction to the Municipal Board for removal and discharge of filthy and dirty water and the construction of proper drainage or sewers for the discharge of such water'.[13] The court highlighted that municipal boards have mandatory statutory obligations with regard to the construction and maintenance of drains and sewers, as well as with regard to the cleanliness of public streets. It then pointed out that the municipal board had no discretion in the matter and could not refuse to discharge obligations imposed upon it.[14]

These early cases did not discuss sanitation in terms of a fundamental right, rather in terms of the duties of the state in respect of sanitation. These judicial pronouncements are particularly important in a context where it is now often the duties of individuals and communities that are emphasized more than those of the state. They also confirm the importance of the continuum between rights of individuals and duties of the state, since the realization of the former depends in large part on actions taken by the latter. This has become one of the most contentious points in ongoing sanitation

---

[11] *Municipal Council, Ratlam* v *Vardhichand* AIR 1980 SC 1622 (Supreme Court of India, 1980).

[12] *Rampal* v *State of Rajasthan* AIR 1981 Raj 121 (High Court of Rajasthan, 1980) (hereafter *Rampal*).

[13] *Rampal* (n 12), para 1.

[14] *Rampal* (n 12), para 5.

interventions that emphasize the need to create 'demand' from individuals for toilets rather than emphasizing their rights. Further, ongoing interventions seek to restrict the role of the state to that of a facilitator. This unfortunately takes the debate away from questions surrounding the responsibility of the state to build, maintain, and operate the public infrastructure necessary to ensure the realization of access to safe sanitation and hygiene.[15]

Following early cases focusing on municipal duties, the judiciary started linking the right to life with sanitation in the late 1980s. In a case concerning 'insanitation' in Jaipur, the High Court of Rajasthan asserted that '[m]aintenance of health, preservation of the [*sic*] sanitation and environment falls within the purview of Article 21 of the Constitution as it adversely affects the life of the citizen and it amounts to slow poisoning and reducing the life of the citizen because of the hazards created'.[16] A few years later, the High Court of Madhya Pradesh went a step ahead in *Dr K.C. Malhotra* v *State of Madhya Pradesh*, wherein it was alleged that the municipal corporation of Gwalior and the Public Health Engineering Department had failed in their duty to avoid the spread of an epidemic of cholera, resulting in the death of twelve children in 1991, and further deaths in 1992.[17] The High Court, rebutting the Municipal Corporation's assertion that it did as much as it could, made a specific point about the need for the right to be realized for everyone, regardless of class, and stated that while 'inhabitants of the locality may be of backward class or weaker sections of the society or community at large [they] have got a fundamental right under Article 21 of the Constitution entitling them to live as human beings'.[18] This implied in that specific case having a separate sewage line from which filthy water could flow out, covering the *nalla*, and the provision of proper lavatories for public conservancy which should be regularly cleaned. The High

---

[15] For further details, see the section titled 'Beyond Individual Toilets: Emphasising the Collective Dimensions of the Right' later at p. 99.

[16] *L.K. Koolwal* v *State of Rajasthan* AIR 1988 Raj 2 (High Court of Rajasthan, 19 September 1986), para 3.

[17] *Dr KC Malhotra* v *State of Madhya Pradesh* AIR 1994 MP 48 (Madhya Pradesh High Court, 1993) (*K.C. Malhotra*).

[18] *K.C. Malhotra* (n 17), para 14.

Court further made the link between Article 21 and Article 47 of the Constitution, thus recognizing the intrinsic relationship between Part III (Fundamental Rights) and Part IV (Directive Principles of State Policy) of the Constitution.[19]

The Supreme Court has also derived the right to sanitation from the right to life. In *Virendra Gaur* v *State of Haryana*, the Supreme Court was debating Haryana's Town Planning Scheme in a case concerning the Municipal Committee of Thanesar's proposed land-use change for an area earmarked for open spaces. In this context, the Court asserted that the 'right to life with human dignity' encompasses sanitation with pollution-free water and air, and the broader protection of the environment.[20]

Courts have also addressed various issues that are central to a broad understanding of sanitation, but have not necessarily been directly linked to the right recognized in the abovementioned cases. One of the most central issues that courts have had to address in recent years has been the question of the enforcement of the fundamental right guaranteed under Article 17 of the Constitution. The *Safai Karmachari Andolan* case is discussed in detail by Khanna in Chapter 11 in this volume,[21] and the broader campaign around the eradication of manual scavenging is discussed by Wilson in Chapter 10 in this volume. Courts have also separately addressed the work conditions of sanitation workers, even though this has not been done specifically in the context of the right to sanitation. This is explored in more detail by Sakhtivel, Nirmalkumar, and Benjamin in Chapter 12 this volume.

The cases discussed in this section confirm that the right to sanitation has been recognized for more than two decades. In addition, courts have addressed a variety of sanitation-related issues. Yet, the overall picture is one of a limited contribution made by courts.

---

[19] The former are enforceable (Constitution of India, Art. 32), while the latter are not (Constitution of India, Art. 37).

[20] *Virendra Gaur* v *State of Haryana* 1995 2 SCC 577 (Supreme Court of India, 1994), para 7.

[21] *Safai Karmachari Andolan & Others* v *Union of India* & Others 2014 11 SCC 224 (Supreme Court of India, 2014).

Indeed, they have neither provided a detailed account of the scope of the right to sanitation, nor effectively linked the various sanitation-related issues addressed in different cases in a single narrative. As a result, manual scavenging or the rights of sanitation workers are usually considered as distinct and largely self-contained issues, rather than as part of the broader consideration of all sanitation-related issues. Similarly, gender and environment concerns that abound in the sanitation sector are not given the central place they deserve in the sanitation-related case law. The overall impact of the courts is thus limited to the specific decisions taken, and to giving a general framework for understanding sanitation from a rights-based perspective.

Limited Legal Framework for Implementing the Right to Sanitation

The adoption of laws to make fundamental rights a reality is necessary to ensure that the state machinery has the requisite specific guidance to work from, something that the judiciary cannot effectively provide. At present, there is no legislation that directly refers to the right to sanitation. This is not to say that the legal framework does not contribute to the realization of the right to sanitation. In fact, it includes various measures without which the right cannot be realized. Yet, since implementation measures are not formulated in a rights framework, there is a dichotomy between the scheme set out by the higher judiciary and the measures implemented.

There is not only no legislation that directly mentions the right to sanitation, but there is also no general sanitation legislation.[22] Thus, there is no legislative instrument that sets out a broad framework of principles guiding the sanitation sector overall.[23] Statutory provisions that exist are found in state laws in accordance with the

---

[22] For an overall analysis of the statutory framework concerning sanitation, see Philippe Cullet and Lovleen Bhullar (eds), *Sanitation Law and Policy in India: An Introduction to Basic Instruments* (Oxford University Press, 2015).

[23] To date, the only instrument that could have linked sanitation and health and defined the right to sanitation in legislation was the proposed National Health Bill, 2009.

constitutional mandate that makes sanitation a state subject,[24] and in accordance with the devolution of powers and responsibilities regarding sanitation to local authorities.[25]

States have on the whole sought to give effect to the decentralization mandate through amendments to state legislation. Regarding urban areas, most municipal acts contain a chapter dealing with water supply and sanitation, which makes all sanitation-related tasks a responsibility of the concerned local bodies.[26] These laws tend to focus on the provision of infrastructure rather than the implementation of the right to sanitation per se. This is the case, for instance, with the Bihar Municipal Act, 2007, that has little to say about individual sanitation, but devotes a whole chapter to drainage and sewerage. The emphasis is thus on one important aspect of sanitation, that is, measures to be taken for disposal of sewage. The Act recognizes, for instance, that municipalities have a duty to construct and maintain drains and sewers.[27] With regard to treatment, storage, disinfection, and disposal of sewage, the obligation is less stringent, and the Act provides only that municipalities 'may' construct, operate, maintain, develop, and manage works within or outside the municipal area.[28] The Act also provides that the municipality must levy a sewerage charge on the owners of premises for connection of such premises to sewerage mains.[29] The measures provided by a municipal act like the Bihar Municipal Act, 2007, are important, but on the whole limited in terms of a comprehensive understanding of sanitation.

In the case of rural areas, most panchayat acts assign certain duties to panchayats. Thus, in Haryana, gram panchayats have a duty to plan for rural sanitation. Under this broad head, the Act includes a variety of functions from the maintenance of 'general sanitation' to the cleaning up of drains, the construction and maintenance of

---

[24] Constitution of India, Seventh Schedule, List II, Entry 6.

[25] Constitution of India, Arts 243G and 243W.

[26] For example, The Himachal Pradesh Municipal Corporation Act, 1994, s 43(a), that concerns obligatory functions of the corporation.

[27] The Bihar Municipal Act, 2007, s 193.

[28] The Bihar Municipal Act, 2007, s 194.

[29] The Bihar Municipal Act, 2007, s 216.

public latrines, the maintenance of cremation and burial grounds, as well as the management of washing and bathing *ghats*.[30] In certain cases, a specific responsibility to build toilets is included, as in the case of Karnataka, where the panchayat is given a duty to build sanitary latrines for not less than 10 per cent of the households every year.[31] Panchayats can also take health-related measures. They have the power to regulate the 'conditions of sanitation' to remove and prevent the spread of epidemics.[32] At the Block level, the *panchayat samiti* is tasked with the implementation of rural sanitation schemes, as well as carrying out environmental sanitation, health campaigns, and educating the public.[33] In some states, rural sanitation is envisioned as having a link to water supply. Thus, in Uttar Pradesh (UP), the *zila parishad* or *kshettra samiti* has the power to prohibit landowners from keeping toilets or drains within 50 feet from a source of drinking water for public use.[34]

Overall, existing local laws make important contributions to the regulation of sanitation in a general sense. They remain, however, limited in their focus that looks mostly at local bodies' responsibilities regarding sewage disposal rather than at sanitation as an overall issue. Further, while the right to sanitation is framed around the rights of individuals, local laws tend to focus on trunk infrastructure that may affect individual rights, but without directly making the link with individual concerns and rights.

Various other legal instruments are relevant and related to sanitation. These include the Water (Prevention and Control of Pollution) Act, 1974, giving powers to state pollution control boards to take appropriate action in respect of sewage treatment and disposal, and secondary instruments such as the Solid Waste Management Rules, 2016, and the Uniform Protocol on Water Quality Monitoring Order, 2005, adopted under the Environment (Protection) Act, 1986.[35] The

---

[30] The Haryana Panchayati Raj Act, 1994, s 21.

[31] The Karnataka Panchayat Raj Act, 1993, s 58(1A)(i).

[32] The Karnataka Panchayat Raj Act, 1993, s 25.

[33] The Karnataka Panchayat Raj Act, 1993, s 75.

[34] The Uttar Pradesh Kshettra Samitis and Zila Parishads Adhiniyam, 1961, s 195.

[35] This is explored in more detail by Bhullar (Chapter 9) in this volume.

direct link between sanitation and water pollution is not negated, but the laws that exist fail to make the link in such a way that they would be considered jointly. The contribution of these laws to the realization of the right to sanitation thus remains at best fortuitous, and the absence of a link does not ensure effective comprehensive thinking around water pollution and sanitation.

There are also various acts whose entry point into sanitation is access to toilets. These include the Right of Children to Free and Compulsory Education Act, 2009, that makes it a duty of the government to provide separate toilets for boys and girls in every school building.[36] In one case, the Supreme Court not only found that the lack of toilet facilities in schools violates the right to education, but also directed all schools, whether state-owned or privately owned, aided or unaided, minority or non-minority, to provide toilet facilities for boys and girls.[37] Another example is the Rights of Persons with Disabilities Act, 2016, that calls, for instance, for the provision of appropriate and accessible sanitation facilities.[38] There are also various statutes that address sanitation needs in the workplace. For instance, the Factories Act, 1948, makes it mandatory to provide sufficient latrines, conveniently situated and accessible at all times.[39]

Other sanitation-related legislation includes the two manual scavenging acts.[40] They are essentially about sanitation since manual scavenging concerns the removal of human excreta. Yet, they address the topic from a different angle. The essential purpose of these acts is the eradication of a sanitation practice that violates the prohibition of untouchability enshrined in Article 17 of the Constitution. Further, manual scavengers fighting for the eradication of manual scavenging are not looking towards being offered employment elsewhere in

[36] The Right of Children to Free and Compulsory Education Act, 2009, s 19 and schedule.

[37] *Environment & Consumer Protection Foundation* v *Delhi Administration & Others* 2012 (9) SCALE 692 (Supreme Court of India, 2012), para 4.

[38] The Rights of Persons with Disabilities Act, 2016, s 24(3)(e).

[39] The Factories Act, 1948, s 19(1).

[40] The Employment of Manual Scavengers and Construction of Dry Latrines (Prohibition) Act, 1993, and The Prohibition of Employment as Manual Scavengers and their Rehabilitation Act, 2013.

the sanitation sector, but towards other livelihoods allowing them to escape the burden of caste-imposed occupations. At the same time, the broader understanding of manual scavenging in the most recent legislation confirms that we cannot look at its eradication separately from the plight of sanitation workers.[41] Eradicating manual scavenging will not signal the end of sanitation work, and lessons learnt from the campaign for the eradication of the former will have to be kept in mind in addressing the latter, whether in terms of basic principles of dignity or in practical terms concerning conditions of work.[42]

Role of the Executive in Access to Sanitation

The analysis of the legislative framework shows that there is no statutory instrument directly taking forward the realization of the right to sanitation and there are significant gaps in terms of the coverage of sanitation's diverse dimensions. In a context where there has been increasing policy emphasis on sanitation since the 1980s, gaps in the legal framework have progressively been filled by the executive. This has taken the form of policies, guidelines, and administrative directions. Since 2014, sanitation has been at the very centre of the policy agenda of the union government and has therefore acquired increased visibility, as confirmed, for instance, by the fact that all new bank notes introduced since 2016 include the logo of the SBM.

The Union government's initiatives in the field of sanitation are particularly significant because sanitation is a state subject. This implies that constitutionally, states would be expected to take the lead in terms of policy and lawmaking in this sector. Yet, in a context where states have not made full use of their powers, the Union Government has been, for instance, increasingly active in prodding states to end open defecation.[43] At present, the sanitation initiatives

---

[41] The Prohibition of Employment as Manual Scavengers and their Rehabilitation Act, 2013, s 2(1)(g).

[42] See Wilson (Chapter 10) in this volume.

[43] As discussed in more detail by Khanna (Chapter 11) in this volume, states have not come under similar pressure in terms of ensuring the implementation of the constitutional and statutory provisions seeking the eradication of manual scavenging.

of the Centre are regrouped under the overall umbrella of the SBM. Yet, as in the past, there are different policy frameworks for rural and urban areas. For rural areas, the Guidelines for SBM-G, 2014, updated the framework known since 2012 as Nirmal Bharat Abhiyan Guidelines, which itself was an update of the Total Sanitation Campaign (TSC), kick-started in 1999. While each iteration of the policy framework has brought new elements, the central paradigm has remained unchanged since the late 1990s. The shift from a 'supply-led' to a 'demand-led' policy paradigm initiated in the late 1990s, thus remains the crux of the policy framework, that seeks to create 'demand' for toilets through motivation that should lead individuals to build and use individual household latrines (IHHLs).

The rationale for shifting to a demand paradigm is that the government should not provide subsidies for building toilets. In this context, the main role of the government is supposed to be of a facilitator, whose primary function is to foster collective behavioural change through a community-led approach brought about by information, education, and communication (IEC) support. Yet, in practice, the success and failure of the policy framework has been judged by the number of toilets built.[44] In a context where many people would not be able to afford the costs involved, erstwhile 'subsidies' were replaced by 'incentives' that have de facto become the central element of the sanitation interventions of the government. This incentive has not only been maintained over time, but its amount has been increased and its coverage extended.[45] The more the toilet-building challenge appeared daunting, the more the incentive was increased, from Rs 1,200 in 2007 to Rs 4,600 in 2012, and Rs 12,000 since 2014.[46] Similarly, while an incentive was offered at first only to below poverty line (BPL)

[44] For example, Ministry of Drinking Water and Sanitation, Annual Report 2014–15 (2015), in which the section 'Annual Progress Report—Physical' only lists toilets built.

[45] Note, however, that the revised SBM guidelines advocate that households should be motivated to make 'self-investment for construction'. Guidelines for SBM-G (n 8), s 5.2.8.

[46] Respectively, Total Sanitation Campaign Guidelines, 2007, s 9(e); Nirmal Bharat Abhiyan Guidelines (n 6), s 5(4)2; and Guidelines for SBM-G (n 8), s 5(4)8.

households, this was progressively expanded to cover a number of above poverty line (APL) households.[47] There has been a corresponding increase in the budgetary allocation for sanitation in rural areas from Rs 2,500 crores in 2012–13 to Rs 13,948 crores in 2017–18.[48]

The IEC effort and incentives have been overwhelmingly directed at the building of IHHLs, even though the policy definition of sanitation is broader. Indeed, the policy framework has emphasized community toilets as 'an important component' of sanitation interventions for more than a decade.[49] This has not been implemented effectively, however, and only related activities have been taken up beyond IHHLs, such as ensuring availability of toilets in schools, where there has been visible progress in recent years.

As far as urban areas are concerned, two different trends can be noticed. On the one hand, the case law discussed in the section titled 'Judicial Recognition of the Right to Sanitation' earlier, is overwhelmingly focused on urban areas, and the understanding of sanitation offered by the judiciary is thus relevant mostly to cities. On the other hand, government initiatives have logically focused first on rural areas, since it is in these areas that the overwhelming number of open defecators is found. In the context of fast urbanization and the growing recognition that urban sewage contributes an increasing share of overall water pollution, urban areas have progressively been given more attention.[50] Appropriately, the National Urban Sanitation Policy (NUSP), 2008, defined sanitation as safe management of human excreta and was also explicit in making the links not only with public health and the environment, but also with solid waste management and generation of industrial and other hazardous wastes.[51] This has been taken up further within the context of SBM-U, the first objective of which is unsurprisingly the elimination of open defecation,

---

[47]   Introduced by the Nirmal Bharat Abhiyan Guidelines (n 6), s 5(4)1, for APL households that are 'SCs/STs, small and marginal farmers, landless labourers with homestead, physically handicapped and women headed households'.

[48]   Accountability Initiative, Swachh Bharat Mission-Gramin (SBM-G), GoI, 2017–18 (Centre for Policy Research, Budget Briefs 10/3, 2018).

[49]   Total Sanitation Campaign Guidelines, 2004, s 9(e).

[50]   For more details, see John (Chapter 7) in this volume.

[51]   National Urban Sanitation Policy, 2008, s 1.

and its first component IHHLs.[52] It includes other objectives, such as the eradication of manual scavenging, but worryingly does not focus on liquid waste management at all, even though solid waste management is among its objectives. This does not mean that liquid waste management is totally absent, since sewerage and septage are two of the main mission components of the Atal Mission for Rejuvenation and Urban Transformation (AMRUT).[53]

Overall, the policy interventions of the Union Government have done a lot to give sanitation more visibility at all levels. This can be identified, for instance, in the increasing sense of urgency in achieving the goal of having the whole country ODF. Thus, for rural areas, SBM-G has sought to give a boost to the campaign by increasing the incentive amount to build IHHLs, and by bringing forward the date for achieving *nirmal Bharat/swachh* Bharat from 2022 to 2019.[54] In urban areas, the different initiatives taken show an increasing awareness of the problems that need to be addressed, even if realization remains largely in the offing. What the repeated iterations of the policy framework have not done is to foster the integration of the judicial recognition of the right to sanitation with the measures implemented on the ground. As a result, while the policy framework has focused mostly on IHHLs and hence individual needs, there has been no effort to frame this in terms of individual rights.[55]

The Right in Practice: Swachh Bharat Mission and Beyond

The previous section highlighted the fact that the right to sanitation is well established at a generic level, but that there is neither reference to the right in existing law and policy instruments nor is there legislation addressing the various dimensions of sanitation in a comprehensive manner. The limited coverage of sanitation in

[52] Guidelines for SBM-U (n 9), s 2.1.1 and 2.3.1.

[53] Atal Mission for Rejuvenation and Urban Transformation (AMRUT), Mission Statement & Guidelines, 2015, para 3.1.

[54] Respectively Nirmal Bharat Abhiyan Guidelines (n 6), s 2.1 and Guidelines for SBM-G (n 8), s 4.

[55] The only exception is Kerala's Malinya Mukta Keralam Action Plan, 2007.

legislation is compensated in part by the more extensive administrative directions, particularly for rural areas. Consequently, this section analyses the ways in which the right to sanitation is indirectly and partially implemented through the sanitation interventions based on the administrative directions of the government. This section emphasizes four critical issues arising from an assessment of the ongoing implementation of the SBM in rural areas. Yet, the different points highlighted here do not correspond to a specific policy instrument but reflect a policy orientation that was initiated in the late 1990s, and has been pursued for the better part of the last two decades.

Emphasis on Behaviour Change and Demand-Led Paradigm

Since the introduction of the TSC in the late 1990s, sanitation interventions have been based on a paradigm that sees the state as a facilitator rather than a provider. This was meant to avoid the perceived wastage involved in state provision of infrastructure that may not be used or maintained by people. The shift was thus meant to ensure that sanitation interventions would not result in building toilets where people had not requested them. Rather, the role of the state was to be one of persuading people of the usefulness of building an individual toilet at home, and stopping open defecation.

The intervention of the state has since then been centred around 'creating' demand through behaviour change interventions focused on IEC. This is meant to 'trigger' people into understanding that open defecation is to be avoided, thereby leading them to desire a toilet at home and to use it.

The practice of behaviour change has been much less neutral than the previous two paragraphs may suggest. One of the most direct ways in which people have been 'triggered' to stop going for open defecation has been by getting a group of people (sometimes under the name of *nigrani* or surveillance committee) to whistle people away from their defecation spots early in the morning. The trigger starts with a form of pressure,[56] even though this is conceptualized

---

[56] For example, Ajay T.G., 'How "Swachh Bharat" Is Being Forced upon Chhattisgarh Villagers', *The Wire* (15 December 2016); available at https://thewire.in/government/open-defecation-swachh-bharat.

as a 'community-led' mechanism. More worrying from a sanitation point of view is the fact that these whistling squads only have their whistles as a device of persuasion. Indeed, no temporary toilets are provided, either to show people how to use them or to persuade them of the positive consequences of using a toilet.

Another issue that has arisen is that behaviour change is meant to be adapted to local conditions to reflect the specific needs and situations of a given community. However, in practice, whistling squads have been the major tool used by the administration in various parts of the country.[57] This is unexpected since this strategy is meant to better reflect people's aspirations and needs and be built on people's participation.

Focus on Open Defecation Free and (Individual Household) Latrines

The construction of IHHLs that has been at the centre of attention, serves as a measure of the success of the interventions undertaken. Nearly everyone seems to share the idea that eliminating open defecation through the building of toilets is a positive step. This may be because individuals have been influenced by the IEC campaign or by neighbours (for instance, richer people, people having lived for some years in urban environments) or because open defecation is an inconvenience to them, for instance, because of the distance involved, the difficulties in going out during the day, or personal infirmity. Yet, in some parts of western Rajasthan, for instance, where the climate is mostly dry and hot, and where population density is low, everyone is not necessarily convinced by the health and/or environmental rationale for ending open defecation. Further, in different Districts of different states, women do not necessarily resent open defecation where it does not put them at risk because this provides them an opportunity to go for a walk—with other women—away from the men. Such reservations are shared by some officials, as witnessed by the controversy created by a senior IAS officer's criticism of the way

---

[57] Cf. Ministry of Drinking Water and Sanitation, 'ODF Sustainability Guidelines', 2016, para 11.

the ODF campaign is being taken forward, and the notice served on her by the government.[58]

The goal of ending open defecation is an important step in the realization of the right to sanitation. The crores of toilets built over the past couple of decades are thus relevant in an assessment of the progress towards realizing the right. At the same time, other elements need to be considered:

Firstly, proposing a single solution to realize the right everywhere seems inappropriate. In some places, building toilets for all may not be the best short-term solution, for instance, where there is insufficient water to cater to a more water-intensive sanitation practice than open defecation. Further, where the success of policy interventions is measured by the number of toilets built, this indicates that sanitation has been essentially reduced to a target-driven single factor issue. This does not provide the basis for addressing the multiple overlapping dimensions of sanitation.

Secondly, the goal of ending open defecation has been pursued mostly through infrastructure building. Progressively, as it became clear that many toilets were either unusable or were not being used, increasing emphasis was put simultaneously on building and using toilets. This is true for IHHLs, as well as for other toilets in other places, such as school toilets. In the latter case, the Supreme Court had an occasion to confirm that 'a toilet in structure only is not a toilet in reality'.[59] While this is an accepted position, the focus on use remains largely perfunctory since monitoring of IHHLs is limited to at the most a few months.

Thirdly, the focus on toilets leads in practice to human excreta being the only focus of sanitation interventions. In many parts of the country, one noticeable aspect of the external appearance of villages

---

[58] Deepali Rastogi, 'Some Washroom Wisdom', *The Hindu* (1 April 2017); available at www.thehindu.com/opinion/open-page/some-washroom-wisdom/article17759025.ece; Anonymous, 'MP Govt Issues Notice to IAS Officer over Article', *The Indian Express* (12 April 2017), 10.

[59] *JK Raju* v *State of Andhra Pradesh & Anr* Conmt Pet. (C) No. 532/2013 in Writ Petition (Civil) No. 631/2004 (Supreme Court of India, Order dated 27 January 2015).

is the significant number of buffaloes and cows in and around them, and the significant amount of dung found on the ground. While there are good reasons to separate the consideration of human and animal excreta, for instance, because the issue of manual scavenging only relates to human excreta, the two also need to be addressed simultaneously since animal excreta can also affect human health.[60] Thus, if the realization of the rights to sanitation and health is the ultimate goal to be pursued, an exclusive focus on human excreta will not lead to the desired results. This is addressed in part by the SBM guidelines insofar as they recognize that water sources must be clear of human and animal excreta,[61] but this needs to be considered in much broader terms if the health benefits of ending open defecation are to be fully realized.

Gender Narratives and Shortcomings

Women must be at the centre of sanitation interventions because they disproportionately suffer from insufficient access to sanitation and they have specific sanitation needs. This is necessary to foster gender equity and equality together with the right to sanitation. The reality of sanitation interventions has been until now in part at odds with these ideals.[62]

On the surface, women are indeed at the centre of sanitation interventions, as witnessed in their visibility in the radio and audio-visual campaign materials, such as in a long-running advertisement featuring actor Vidya Balan as the national brand ambassador advising women not to marry into families that do not have a toilet

---

[60] See for example, Alexander Schriewer et al., 'Human and Animal Fecal Contamination of Community Water Sources, Stored Drinking Water and Hands in Rural India Measured with Validated Microbial Source Tracking Assays' (2015) 93(3) *The American Journal of Tropical Medicine and Hygiene* 509.

[61] Guidelines for SBM-G (n 8), s 9.2.

[62] For further details, see Koonan and Bhullar (Chapter 13) in this volume.

at home.[63] This is linked to the broader message of the campaign that has used the dignity of women as a way to create 'demand' among men for toilets at home. In other words, the patriarchal framework that sees women enjoined to avoid the gaze of the outsider by covering themselves (*purdah*) is used to convince men that it is not appropriate to let women go out in the open to defecate. Women thus become the object of the campaign rather than the holders of sanitation-related entitlements. While this strategy was seen for a number of years as being a necessary evil meant to achieve the desired sanitation goals,[64] even though it was recognized that this was not helping the cause of women's rights more broadly, the shortcoming of this approach has been identified in new guidelines that acknowledge that it carries the risk of 'reinforcing of gender stereotypes'.[65]

Another issue that has become increasingly apparent is that toilet construction and use cannot be assumed to be gender neutral. As long as construction is planned and undertaken by men, the likelihood is that the sanitation needs of women will not be (fully) considered. This can lead, for instance, to a situation where a toilet is built in the part of the compound where men tend to congregate during the day, automatically leading women to refrain from using the toilet during the day. This goes against the very idea of building toilets that are supposed to ensure that women do not have to wait for the cover of darkness to step out of the house for their sanitation needs.

A related point is that toilets built at home may end up being a burden on women. This is particularly the case regarding water in all situations where water is fetched from outside of the house. Since this is nearly always a task undertaken by women, and since water-based

[63] For example, IANS, 'Vidya Balan Campaigns for Sanitation in UP, Bihar', *The Indian Express* (26 August 2015); available at http://indianexpress.com/article/entertainment/bollywood/vidya-balan-campaigns-for-sanitation-in-up-bihar.

[64] Cf. Swagata Yadavar and Shritama Bose, 'Not so Poopular', *The Week* (5 June 2016); available at www.theweek.in/theweek/cover/swachh-bharat-mission-fails-to-live-up-to-its-promo-campaign.html.

[65] SBM-G, Guidelines on Gender and Sanitation, 2017, para 4.

sanitation at home requires more water than open defecation, the additional task falls on women.

Finally, ongoing sanitation interventions fail to give priority to women's sanitation needs. There has been much progress in terms of making menstrual hygiene visible in policy debates and on the ground. Yet, a comprehensive approach towards menstrual hygiene management (MHM) remains lacking, such as one that ensures widespread availability of sanitary products to all women, the provision of environment-friendly disposal facilities, and extensive awareness campaigns. Similarly, in the context of school toilets, there has been significant improvement in the provision of toilets overall, but the link between availability of toilets and girls' education is not always made sufficiently directly. Indeed, in a number of cases, the absence of functional toilets is a factor contributing to girls dropping out of school, something that is not known to happen for boys. There are thus special issues that need to be addressed more vigorously, since the absence of sanitation facilities may end up affecting also the realization of the right to education, with lifelong implications for the concerned women.

From Right-Holders to Duty-Bearing Beneficiaries

Sanitation interventions are in principle based on the recognition of the right to sanitation that opposes the entitlements of right-holders against the duties of the state as the duty bearer. The state has indeed shown a growing commitment to the realization of at least one component of the right by becoming increasingly involved in the building of toilets, particularly in rural areas.

Yet, the clear distinction between rights and duties has become increasingly blurred. Firstly, individuals who are the right-holders are not recognized as such in the administrative directions. This has been the case for a number of years, and from the time of the Centrally Sponsored Rural Sanitation Programme up to the SBM, right-holders have been called 'beneficiaries'.[66] This did not change

---

[66] For example, General Guidelines for Implementation of Centrally Sponsored Rural Sanitation Programme, 1993, s 4.2.2.2 and Guidelines for SBM-G (n 8), s 5.2.9.

with the shift to a demand-led policy paradigm. Right-holders were seen as beneficiaries of the state's largesse when the state conceived itself as a welfare state, and they are still seen as beneficiaries when the state consciously withdraws from provision and seeks to promote 'ownership' of infrastructure by people/local communities.[67]

Secondly, where right-holders are called beneficiaries, their rights are not necessarily seen as entitlements. In the worst case scenario, there is not only no entitlement, but also the introduction of duties related to sanitation. In the current context where the emphasis is on building toilets, the duty imposed is often to have a toilet. One instance is Districts where BPL-card-holders are denied their ration unless they can show that they have built a toilet at home.[68] This is legally problematic, as confirmed in an order stating that '[d]enial of a ration card to a BPL person is virtually a denial of his or her right to food and thereby the right to life under Article 21 of the Constitution'.[69] Indeed, in a case where it was proposed to cut electricity to households without toilets in Bhilwara District, the order was quickly rescinded.[70]

Another instance is the case of a 2015 amendment to the Haryana Panchayati Raj Act, 1994, which introduced a new provision on disqualification for election to the three tiers of panchayats that now include a minimum educational qualification requirement and the need to submit a declaration to the effect of having a functional toilet at their place of residence.[71] This was challenged but the Supreme Court dismissed the challenge by indicating among other things that

---

[67] For example, Guidelines for SBM-G (n 8), s 6.4.8.

[68] For example, Milind Ghatwai, 'Sheopur Adm Gives Rations only to Villagers with Toilets', *The Indian Express* (25 January 2017), 2. For the disputed case of Ajmer District, see KumKum Dasgupta, 'With Stiff Target for Building Toilets under Swachh Bharat Abhiyan, States are Flouting Citizens' Rights', *Hindustan Times* (4 April 2017), 11.

[69] *Premlata w/o Ram Sagar & Others* v *Govt. of NCT Delhi* Writ Petition (Civil) 7687/2010 (High Court of Delhi, Order dated 13 May 2011).

[70] Mohammed Iqbal, 'No Power if you go in the Open, SDO Tells Villagers', *The Hindu* (22 August 2017) 1.

[71] The Haryana Panchayati Raj Act, 1994, as amended by the Haryana Panchayati Raj (Amendment) Act, 2015, s 175.

it is the duty of a candidate to set an example.[72] There was no reference to the right to sanitation in this decision, and as a result, the building of a toilet is simply seen as a duty of the would-be candidate in the context of their political rights. Here, lack of access to sanitation becomes a ground for denying other fundamental rights rather than being an entitlement flowing from a fundamental right.

Thirdly, where right-holders are considered as beneficiaries, this makes it difficult to hold the state accountable for non-performance of its duties. In fact, the problem is that the state does not understand itself as having duties linked to a right since its interventions are not framed around a rights-based framework. In practice, this means, for instance, that if a local body fails to fulfil its responsibilities with regard to the provision of sanitation as envisaged in the legislation, there is usually no specific avenue for recourse, besides approaching courts on grounds of violation of fundamental rights. This shortcoming has been the object of various campaigns, and some progress has been made in recent years, for instance, with the adoption of laws guaranteeing the delivery of public services.[73] Yet, this positive step can only make a material difference to the extent that sanitation is considered as a public service. In Kerala, this is limited to connection to sewerage and its change of ownership.[74] In Delhi, the only services related to water and sanitation are connection, disconnection, and mutation of water connections.[75] There is thus a long way to go before the various components of the right to sanitation are effectively included in services for the delivery of which the state is held accountable.

Finally, in certain contexts, the realization of the right is undertaken through putting pressure on the right-holders. This goes against

[72] *Rajbala* v *State of Haryana* 2016 2 SCC 445 (Supreme Court of India, 2015).

[73] See for example, The Kerala State Right to Service Act, 2012; The Uttar Pradesh Janhit Guarantee Adhiniyam, 2011; The Rajasthan Guaranteed Delivery of Public Services Act, 2011.

[74] Kerala Water Authority, Notification of 8 April 2013, No KWA/JB/E1/9387/2012.

[75] Government of NCT of Delhi, Circular No. 6(39)/IT/2011/2319–2388 – The Delhi (Right of Citizen to Time Bound Delivery of Services) Act, 2011, 5 April 2016.

the idea of 'demand' wherein people request something additional, such as a toilet, and the idea that a fundamental right is an entitlement that individuals hold and that the state is enjoined to contribute to realizing. This is particularly visible in situations where people are fined for defecating in the open, something that was called for in the context of a village-level award for achieving ODF status (Nirmal Gram Puraskar) which specifically mentioned that one of the criteria for the award was for the panchayat to pass a resolution 'banning' open defecation, and to introduce a suitable system of penalty.[76] There have been few reports of panchayats where this was enforced,[77] but even where this is not the case, the threat is used as a way to put pressure on people.[78] Further, the updated SBM guidelines specifically suggest that gram panchayats may impose 'fines on defaulters'.[79]

Overall, fining people for defecating in the open goes against the idea that people have entitlements linked to sanitation. In fact, such interventions may have the effect of undermining the realization of the right to sanitation. This is particularly problematic because the rights framework calls for focusing sanitation interventions on the poorest and most marginalized, while a system of fines and penalty is likely to affect largely the very people who may not have the funds to build their own toilets or even worse, not have a house they call their own. Further, in practice, coercive strategies are not the way to effect long-term behaviour change. As mentioned by villagers having been 'triggered', they had gone to another spot to defecate during the whistling campaign, and went back to their usual spots afterwards.[80]

---

[76] Nirmal Gram Puraskar Guidelines, 2012, 2.

[77] Nilika Mehrotra and S.M. Patnaik, 'Culture versus Coercion: Other Side of Nirmal Gram Yojana' (2008) XLIII(43) *Economic & Political Weekly* 25, 26.

[78] PTI, 'Family Fined Rs 75,000 for Open Defecation in Madhya Pradesh', *The Indian Express* (19 September 2017); available at http://indianexpress.com/article/india/family-fined-rs-75000-for-open-defecation-in-madhya-pradesh-4851102, and Rakesh Kalshian, 'The New Gift Economy' *Down to Earth* (28 February 2018), 29.

[79] Guidelines for SBM-G (n 8), s 5.3.3.

[80] For example, Khyora Katari, Kalyanpur Block, Kanpur Nagar District, Uttar Pradesh, as discussed during a visit in April 2016.

Rethinking the Content of the Right to Sanitation

The preceding sections show that the right to sanitation is well established judicially, lacks effective translation in the law and policy framework, and sanitation interventions on the ground fail to bridge the gap. This section takes up four issues that need to be addressed: The first is to ensure that the right to sanitation is understood and implemented in terms of its broader connotation, rather than essentially focused on toilets. The second is to read the right to sanitation as a separate right that is at the same time intrinsically linked to other fundamental rights. The third is the need to effectively incorporate the liquid and solid waste management dimension and other environmental aspects into the understanding of sanitation. The fourth is that the right should be centred around dignity in such a way that law and policy measures focused on sanitation start by considering impacts on people affected by sanitation interventions, such as manual scavengers, sanitation workers, and women.

Beyond Individual Toilets: Emphasizing the Collective Dimensions of the Right

The right to sanitation was first recognized by the courts in terms of its collective dimensions in the urban context, but interventions on the ground over the past three decades, particularly in rural areas, have focused essentially on its individual and private dimension of household latrines. The focus on the individual dimension is not necessarily surprising since this is what liberal rights emphasize. Yet, it is inappropriate because sanitation is one of the rights that cannot be reduced to its individual component alone.

Firstly, the worthy goal of ending open defecation does not have to imply building only individual toilets at home. Community toilets are indeed part of the menu of options proposed by the policy framework, but are framed as an exception.[81] In practice, they are

---

[81] Guidelines for SBM-G (n 8), s 6.8.1, stating that '[o]rdinarily, such complexes shall be constructed only when there is lack of land in the village for construction of household toilets'.

not even an exception but rather simply absent. The reason given is nearly always that community toilets will fail because nobody will be there to clean them. This is indeed an issue with current sanitation interventions that only focus on building infrastructure. Within the home, it is assumed that cleanliness will be ensured by the women of the house or, if wealthy enough, by calling someone to clean the toilet. In a collective context, no provision is made for paying a sanitation worker or for general maintenance and repairs, making it look like an imperfect option at the community level. Yet, in a context where many (no reliable number seems to be available) toilets built earlier became unusable quickly or within a few years, there are good reasons to consider other options. Community toilets can be conceived not only for a whole neighbourhood, but could also be facilities shared by two or a few houses. The current overwhelming emphasis on individual toilet construction does not give space enough for the various alternative models that may emerge otherwise.

Secondly, open defecation can only be eliminated if toilets are provided in all places where they may be needed. This includes access to toilets not only at home but also in various public places, including bus stands and market places, and in all workplaces.[82] This is particularly important for women in a context where it is socially acceptable for men to pee in public but not for women to do the same. Access to toilets in public places remains deficient in most places, but the general issue has been noticed and given specific policy attention in some contexts, in particular with regard to schools. Indeed, the lack of toilets leading girls to drop out of school led the government to take this up on a priority basis.[83] However, here too, building toilets is only a first step towards effective access to sanitation since they need to be regularly cleaned. Where no provision is made for the same, different strategies are used to cope with this gap, including getting school children to clean the toilets or locking them up for use only by selected people, such as teachers. Some states have

---

[82] In the revised Guidelines for SBM-G (n 8), s 5.3.3.

[83] For example, Government of India, Ministry of Human Resource Development, Swachh Bharat: Swachh Vidyalaya (2015).

taken initiatives that should help, such as a minimal monthly provision for cleanliness in schools in Rajasthan (enough, for instance, to buy soap, but too little to cover the cost of someone coming to clean regularly). In UP, a *safai karmi* is in principle in place in all villages, but this has not led to expected results.[84] Cleanliness of community or public toilets, as well as cleanliness of common areas is thus clearly a challenge, but this is not to say that the goal cannot be progressively achieved.

Thirdly, sanitation interventions need to take into account the fact that defecation has not always been associated with being a private individual activity. Indeed, many people in rural areas, particularly women, link defecation with an opportunity to leave their house for a while, and have discussions that cannot be overheard by men. This is not to say that open defecation is better than access to toilets, but to recognize that there is a collective dimension to the simple act of defecation. As noted earlier, this is particularly significant and problematic in rural areas where building a toilet at home may end up becoming another reason to stop women from interacting with the outside world.

Overall, the picture that emerges is one that is much more complex than the impression given by the focus of current sanitation interventions on IHHLs. There are unavoidable collective dimensions to the right that must be addressed simultaneously with the individual dimension to ensure realization of the right. This includes recognizing that IHHLs may not necessarily be the preferred solution when all aspects of sanitation are considered, including individual preferences, cost, maintenance, access to water, and disposal of septage. This also requires addressing the social dimensions of sanitation, and the need to plan transitions with the preferences of right-holders, in particular, women, in mind. Further, the public toilet dimension of sanitation needs to be addressed, not only in terms of building the required number of toilets, but also in planning this together with septage management or the provision of a sewerage system.

[84] See further the section titled 'Ensuring Dignity and Equality in Sanitation: Manual Scavengers, Sanitation Workers, and Beyond', 106.

Disentangling Sanitation from Water while Ensuring Convergence with Other Rights

Sanitation and water are intrinsically linked. This can be traced back many decades ago when the first major sanitation policy initiative was launched in 1954 as the National Water Supply and Sanitation Programme up to the present day where rural sanitation is institutionally linked to water in the Ministry of Drinking Water and Sanitation. The link between water and sanitation is indeed an essential one, and will remain so for the foreseeable future. At the same time, it is not possible to collapse the two into one subject matter because each sector, and consequently each right, has its own set of specific characteristics. In India, the need to address both as linked but distinct areas, starts from the fact that one of the key sanitation challenges concerns the eradication of manual scavenging that is linked to dry toilets. Yet, even when manual scavenging has been completely eradicated, sanitation will not be concerned only with water. Indeed, solid waste management cannot be separated from liquid waste management, as confirmed by the fact that manual scavengers are also often tasked with the removal of carcasses in villages. Further, while the overwhelming majority of toilets will remain water-based for the foreseeable future, there are an increasing number of new waterless toilets that are not 'dry toilets', and the future of defecation is thus not necessarily only linked to water.

The need to conceive the right to sanitation separately from water is not a call for severing the obvious and strong links with water. Rather, this acts as a starting point for recognizing the convergence between sanitation and several other rights in a manner that does not prioritize the links with one over the others. This is also necessary to emphasize that the realization of the right to sanitation is a precondition for the realization of other rights, such as the right to life, the right to water, the right to health, and the right to environment.

The need for convergence is in fact first apparent at the level of the link with water. Indeed, while the rights to water and sanitation have been too closely linked at a macro level, at the implementation level, the same does not necessarily obtain. Thus, where the construction of toilets is taken up without reference to water availability in a given locality, the result may be a drain on the limited water available for domestic uses or an additional burden imposed on women in rural areas who have to fetch more water from the distant sources from where they bring water daily. Lack of convergence can also lead to situations like the case of Udaipur city, where lakes earmarked as sources of drinking water are still used as sewage receptacles, or on a larger scale, the case of the city of Delhi dumping significant amounts of raw sewage into the Yamuna river that remains a source of drinking water (and irrigation) for downstream communities.

Another example of the need for convergence can be identified in the case of health. The link between health and sanitation was made early on and provided the driving force behind government efforts for at least a century-and-a-half to make massive investments in sewerage in urban areas. In India, this included the physical restructuring of cities, through the introduction of separate civil lines and cantonment areas.[85] The contribution of sewerage networks and other sanitation interventions has been immense and one of the key reasons behind rapidly falling infant and child mortality, as well as overall reduced exposure to multiple waterborne diseases linked to insanitary conditions. At the same time, poor water quality linked to the absence of basic sanitation and hygiene continues to be a leading cause of hospitalization in rural areas.[86] The close links between sanitation and health ensure that the realization of the two rights is inseparable. Yet, even if the health rationale has been and remains central in sanitation interventions, the law and policy framework is at best vague in linking the two areas. This is, for instance, the case with behaviour change interventions that focus on the honour of the family to stop open defecation rather than the health rationale. In fact, there is an urgent need to discuss the health rationale in much more detail because the deleterious impacts of open defecation are

[85] Susan E. Chaplin, *The Politics of Sanitation in India: Cities, Services and the State* (Orient BlackSwan, 2011), 37.

[86] Santosh Mehrotra, 'Public Health System in UP: What Can Be Done?' (2008) XLIII(49) *Economic & Political Weekly* 46, 47, mentioning that at the time of his study, 92 per cent of hospitalization cases in rural UP were on account of infectious and parasitic diseases, especially diarrhoea and gastroenteritis.

not necessarily accepted by everyone, such as in some arid parts of Rajasthan, where the health risks are perceived as minimal, and much less important than access to sufficient water.

In the case of the right to environment, the links are obvious in a context where inadequate sanitation has multiple negative impacts on the environment, but there is very limited recognition that the realization of the two rights is intrinsically linked. The link that is usually made is at the level of water pollution that is seen as an environmental issue. This is a first step, but an insufficient one since the two rights are largely considered in their own specific silos. The realization of the right to sanitation needs to be understood much more directly as a condition for the realization of the right to environment, thereby confirming that the two need to be considered in tandem.

Mainstreaming the Environment in Sanitation: Ensuring Liquid and Solid Waste Management

The impacts of insanitary conditions on the environment are direct and severe.[87] These are well-known and are a core policymaking issue in a context where waterborne diseases are a major burden on most communities. The links between sanitation and the environment encompass, for instance, a large segment of water pollution, since most grey and black water is mixed, making it a single issue in terms of environmental contamination. Yet, there is significant disconnect between sanitation and the environment, both at the regulatory level and on the ground. The sanitation framework is still largely silent on the broader environmental consequences of the different sanitation options.

The main consideration of the link between the environment and sanitation is found mostly in environmental law. Water pollution was in fact one of the first aspects of environmental law that was addressed through legislation, with the adoption of the Water (Prevention and Control of Pollution) Act, 1974. This Act generally provides the legal framework for sewage treatment, and the prevention and control of water pollution resulting from the disposal of untreated or partly

---

[87] For further analysis, see Bhullar (Chapter 9) in this volume.

treated sewage. There have also been a number of other initiatives over time towards linking sanitation and the environment. These include legal instruments dealing with water quality, such as the Water Quality Assessment Authority Order, 2001. In urban areas, attempts to separate grey water and ensure its recycling have commenced, such as in the case of the Nashik Grey Water Recycling and Water Incentive Byelaws, 2009. Building standards have also moved towards fostering water efficiency use and better wastewater treatment in new constructions and renovation projects.[88]

Overall, various links between the environment and sanitation are enshrined in the legal framework. However, they are limited since they mostly arise in the context of environmental law, the first entry point of which into the matter is preventing and controlling pollution. This indirectly addresses some sanitation concerns, but does not provide the basis for comprehensive regulation of the environmental aspects of sanitation. This fails, for instance, to provide a foundation for addressing the negative consequences on the environment and human health of building crores of toilets in rural areas. These consequences include groundwater contamination when toilets are built with unlined pits, and environmental and/or water contamination where septage is simply dumped anywhere. In other words, the focus on toilet construction and the mostly absent liquid waste management framework can be environmentally unfriendly, but this is not addressed on the sanitation side.

Another issue arising in the context of the link between sanitation and the environment is the question of solid waste. While only liquid waste is usually associated with sanitation, both solid and liquid waste must be addressed simultaneously. This is acknowledged in part at the policy level, since SBM-G provides a framework for addressing both, though SBM-U does not. In a context where the use of bio-composting toilets is likely to become more widespread in the

---

[88] For example, Government of India, Ministry of New and Renewable Energy, *Green Rating for Integrated Habitat Assessment (GRIHA) Manual* (2010); and Leadership in Energy & Environmental Design, Green Building Rating System for New Constructions and Major Renovations, Confederation of Indian Industry, 2011.

future, it is essential to effectively link the consideration of solid and liquid waste since both are generated here.[89]

Ensuring Dignity and Equality in Sanitation: Manual Scavengers, Sanitation Workers, and Beyond

The right to sanitation has been realized mostly through a focus on construction, in particular, individual household toilet construction. This may be a necessary step towards ending open defecation, but it does not address the intricate issues of dignity, equality, and equity that should be prioritized. This is not a controversial point from a rights perspective since the Supreme Court has confirmed that the Constitution 'has its own internal morality based on dignity and equality of all human beings'.[90] Yet, in the context of sanitation, this ideal remains to be realized and needs to be given much more emphasis.

At a general level, sanitation interventions should focus on vulnerable groups and people, including women, children, the elderly, disabled persons, landless people, migrant workers, and scheduled castes and scheduled tribes. At present, for some categories such as the elderly, there is insufficient attention to their specific needs, while in the case of women, current sanitation interventions have, as mentioned earlier, not contributed enough to fostering gender equality.

Dignity needs to be given a much more central place in debates concerning the realization of the right to sanitation. Dignity-related issues arise at various levels, starting with concerns related to privacy in the context of open defecation, and the specific problems that women face when they are forced to relieve themselves under the cover of darkness.[91] Beyond issues arising in daily sanitation routines, some people are particularly affected, such as manual scavengers and sanitation workers. As discussed in the chapters by Khanna

---

[89] Cf. Environment Agency (United Kingdom), 'Treating Solid Waste from Composting Toilets at the Depot from Where They Have Been Hired Out', Regulatory Position Statement 114 (2015).

[90] *National Legal Services Authority* v *Union of India & Others* (2014) 5 SCC 438 (Supreme Court of India, 2014), para 123.

[91] Koonan and Bhullar (Chapter 13) in this volume.

(Chapter 11) and Wilson (Chapter 10) in this volume, the very occupation of manual scavenging is deeply degrading, and dignity can
only be recovered by eradicating it. This will hopefully be achieved
at a not-too-distant point in the future, after the long and arduous
campaigns of the Safai Karmachari Andolan (SKA) and other movements. Yet, the eradication of manual scavenging itself will be no
guarantee that the dignity of manual scavengers has been restored.
There has been some progress in this area since the 2013 legislation
has broadened the definition of manual scavenging to include sanitation workers, thus making a direct link between sanitation workers
and manual scavengers.[92] This is an important step given the fact
that sanitation work is often carried out either by former manual
scavengers who have failed to move to other occupations, or other
people of low-caste backgrounds. Indeed, sanitation workers often
face conditions of work and social exclusion that are no better than
those of manual scavengers.

The need to give more attention to the plight of sanitation workers is highlighted by conditions on the ground, such as frequent
deaths inside the sewers.[93] Over the years, courts have taken up the
conditions of work of sanitation workers on some occasions.[94] Yet,
this remains limited in the absence of a statutory framework that
specifically ensures that they are treated on par with other workers,
and work only in conditions of dignity. This requires going beyond
the necessity to provide them with appropriate tools and protective clothing, to address the broader social and legal consequences
of engaging in sanitation work. As a starting point, discriminatory
provisions need to be removed from the statute book. This includes
the recognition of sanitation workers as a special category of workers
on whom special restrictions are imposed. This is found, for instance,

[92] On sanitation workers, see Sakthivel, Nirmalkumar, and Benjamin
(Chapter 12) in this volume.

[93] See, for example, Abhishek Angad, 'Cleaning Lajpat Nagar Sewer, 3
Labourers Die of Suffocation', *The Indian Express* (7 August 2017), 5.

[94] For example, *Praveen Rashtrapal* v *Chief Officer, Kadi Municipality*
(2006) 3 GLR 1809 (High Court of Gujarat, 2006), and *A Narayanan* v
The Chief Secretary, Government of Tamil Nadu and Others Writ Petition
No. 24403 of 2008 (High Court of Madras, Order of 20 November 2008).

in the Delhi Municipal Corporation Act, 1957, that defines sweeping as an 'essential service', and introduces specific restrictions on the right of sweepers to resign from employment, including sweepers employed for doing house scavenging.[95]

Another issue that needs to be addressed more effectively is the link between caste and sanitation work. The example of UP, where the post of safai karmi or village sweeper was introduced nearly a decade ago, is instructive. Firstly, this scheme is innovative in opening up the jobs to anyone, and thus breaks the vicious cycle of caste-based recruitment.[96] Secondly, in a context of increasingly limited government job opportunities, people belonging to castes that would have traditionally never considered such jobs, have applied for them, thus contributing to breaking the link between caste and occupation.[97] Thirdly, there are none or very few people from the *valmiki* community who hold these posts.[98] The example of this scheme thus seems to confirm that there is scope for evolution. At the same time, visits to different parts of UP give a different impression on the ground, where in village after village, the appointed person is not doing the work they are paid for, something that is reflected, for instance, in the poor condition of open drains. The arrangement that seems to be often found is that the person drawing the salary will pay someone who is from a community traditionally engaged in cleaning work to do essential work at a much-discounted rate. This calls into question both the impact of this scheme in breaking the link with caste, and the low number of appointments from the valmiki community. Indeed, while rehabilitation of manual scavengers is one of the community's own goals, the capture of available jobs that are then sub-contracted to them is not the appropriate way forward.

[95] The Delhi Municipal Corporation Act, 1957, ss 387, 388.

[96] Pradeep S. Salve, Dhananjay W. Bansod, and Hemangi Kadlak, 'Safai Karamcharis in a Vicious Cycle: A Study in the Perspective of Caste' (2017) LII(13) *Economic & Political Weekly* 37.

[97] Tulika Tripathi, 'Safai Karmi Scheme of Uttar Pradesh: Caste Dominance Continues' (2012) XLVII(37) *Economic & Political Weekly* 26.

[98] Tulika Tripathi, 'Safai Karmis of Uttar Pradesh: Caste, Power and Politics' (2015) L(6) *Economic & Political Weekly*; available at www.epw.in/node/130621/pdf.

Overall, the right to sanitation raises a range of concerns related to dignity. These have been most often discussed in respect of manual scavenging, but for many years debated as a distinct issue from sanitation. In the context of sanitation debates centred on access to toilets, there has been increasing focus on different groups that may require special measures, as visible in the recent SBM Guidelines on Gender Issues in Sanitation that include specific mention of elderly women and transgenders.[99] Yet, a great deal more needs to be done to ensure the realization of the right to sanitation for all.

* * *

Significant progress has been made since the 1980s in ensuring that sanitation is not the taboo it used to be. It can now be discussed as a separate issue from the village level to the national level. Simultaneously, substantial steps have been taken to foster the realization of the right to sanitation, even though this has generally been done without reference to a rights framework. This indirect implementation of judicial strictures is a positive step even though the right that is implemented in practice is largely limited to equating the right to sanitation with access to individual household toilets.

The launching of the SBM has been a further positive step in giving visibility to sanitation, and linking urban and rural issues at least at a broad level. At the same time, a lot remains to be achieved beyond the SBM. Firstly, the visibility of the SBM has gone more towards the superficial cleaning of inhabited areas and toilet construction than towards the more complex issues involved in realizing all aspects of the right to sanitation. Secondly, the limited focus of existing sanitation interventions on individual toilets has not allowed for comprehensive treatment of the collective dimensions of sanitation that are an integral part of the right. Thirdly, convergence remains a distant goal that must be pursued vigorously. This includes the environmental dimensions, health dimensions, and sanitation work dimensions, that are present but not effectively integrated.

---

[99] SBM (Gramin), Guidelines on Gender Issues in Sanitation, Annexure to Letter S-11018/2/2017-SBM, 3 April 2017.

As long as the social dimensions of sanitation remain at the periphery of a massive effort focused on construction, it is unlikely that the right will be effectively realized for everyone. This is true in terms of the deep caste fault lines that run through the sanitation sector and the insufficient attention given to gender issues. This is also true regarding attempts to impose sanitation-related duties on right-holders, as in the case of exclusion of candidates not having a functional toilet at home in panchayat elections. The right to sanitation is and must be recognized at all levels as a universal right. Achieving this is a challenge that will take time but success will be rewarding. Indeed, realizing the right to sanitation is a precondition for the realization of a number of other fundamental rights and is intrinsically linked to them. The steps that may be taken in years to come to ensure full realization of the right to sanitation for each person will thus reverberate much beyond the sanitation sector.

4

Sanitation and State Planning

An Analysis of Five-Year Plans

Ruchi Shree

'Sanitation is more important than independence.'

—Mahatma Gandhi

'The day every one of us gets a toilet to use, I shall know that our country has reached the pinnacle of progress.'

—Jawaharlal Nehru

'Building toilets is a priority over temples.'

—Narendra Modi[1]

[1] The sources of the three quotes are: *Navjivan*, 2 November 1919, cited in Shubhangi Rathi, 'The Importance of Gandhian Thoughts about Cleanliness' (n.d.); available at www.mkgandhi.org/articles/gandhian-thoughts-about-cleanliness.html; Benny George, 'Sanitation Programmes: A Glass Half-full', (2009) XLIV(8) *Economic & Political Weekly* 65; 'Sanitation in India: The Final Frontier', *The Economist* (19 July 2014);

The centrality of planning in sanitation, as in all social and economic enterprises in India since Independence, is key to understanding the evolution of policy formulation. The Planning Commission of India (the Planning Commission) was set up in March 1950 with the mandate to 'affect decisively the future welfare of the people in every sphere of national life', and to have 'planned development as a means of raising the country's standard of living'.[2] The Planning Commission was set up to 'act in close understanding and consultation with the Ministries of the Central Government and the Governments of the States'.[3] Although the constituting resolution envisaged a recommendatory role for the Planning Commission, the ambit, scope and mandate of planning, and the Five-Year Plans (FYPs) prepared by it grew gradually and progressively, and the successive plan documents reflected the linkages between poverty, poor health, and sanitation.

The key objective of this chapter is to examine the nature of state planning for sanitation in the Indian context. To accomplish this task, the FYPs have been categorized into three time frames: 1951–66 (First–Third plan), 1969–90 (Fourth–Seventh plan), and 1991–2017 (Eighth–Twelfth plan). In the course of analysing each plan in these three successive time frames, the chapter will dwell upon the following key factors as addressed in each plan—first, the main focus of the FYPs vis-à-vis sanitation; second, tracing the possible linkages between planning and the policies designed; and third, identifying the significant elements of the plans around the issue of sanitation. The chapter deals with several aspects concerning sanitation, that is, institutional transformation, gender sensitization, the increasing role of the private sector, and the devolution of power in post-liberalization India. The chapter also attempts to underscore some of the challenges facing planning for sanitation, including

---

available at www.economist.com/news/asia/21607837-fixing-dreadful-sanitation-india-requires-not-just-building-lavatories-also-changing.

[2] Government of India, Cabinet Secretariat, 'Government of India's Resolution Setting up the Planning Commission', Resolution (Planning) No. 1-P(C)/50 (15 March 1950).

[3] Government of India (n 2), para 6.

manual scavenging, decentralization, caste, and gender.[4] It is in this context that the chapter also analyses the role of the Indian state[5] and government policies concerning sanitation in the period after Independence.

Sanitation in the Five-Year Plans

India, on the path of development through planning for its people, adopted the Plan resolution on 15 March 1950. Among the various key objectives mentioned in the resolution, the most relevant ones for the present chapter were stated in the resolution setting up the Planning Commission.[6] The resolution dealt with poverty alleviation and health issues in detail. The problem of sanitation was discussed within the larger framework of water, health, and poverty.

As per the mandate of the Indian Constitution, sanitation is a subject in the State List.[7] But when it comes to policy formulation and major programmes, the Centre has historically played a very significant role in terms of highlighting the issue and designing policies on sanitation. At the federal level, rural sanitation falls under the Ministry of Drinking Water and Sanitation while urban sanitation is the responsibility of the Ministry of Urban Development. Through the 73rd and 74th constitutional amendments, the responsibility for providing sanitation was devolved to local governments. Overall, the issue of sanitation has so far been dealt with within the larger framework of planning initiated at the Centre, with broader policies

---

[4] Water supply and sanitation have been clubbed together under a common head in most of the Plan documents. The facts and figures on which this chapter has relied reflect the same, as it is difficult to find separate figures of expenditure for the sanitation sector in these documents.

[5] In this context, the 'state' refers to a broader concept, which includes the government, the legislature, opposition parties, and so on. In a democratic state like India, to attract the attention of voters, most of the political parties give ample space to welfare measures in their election manifestos.

[6] Government of India (n 2), para 1.

[7] Constitution of India, Seventh Schedule, List II, Entry 6.

and programmes set in coordination between the ministries and the Planning Commission (now the NITI Aayog).[8]

Through the FYPs, the Centre took steps in terms of guiding much of the investment on the issue of sanitation. The Centre also assisted in setting up the institutional mechanisms to lend money to the states to initiate policies on sanitation. For instance, a 2002 Planning Commission report mentions the role of the Centre in promoting various organizations to deal with the issue of training and research, and in promoting water quality monitoring and human resources development programmes.[9] The FYPs, historically, reflected the priorities of the Indian state, and also provided guidelines for the policies to be made by the Central Government as well as state governments. The Centre allocated funds through various plan heads, and also ensured that the funds were provided in state budgets. Indeed, progressively larger allocations were made for sanitation in successive FYPs.

The overview of FYPs vis-à-vis policymaking on sanitation presents a mixed trend. It was almost after four decades of independence that the Central Rural Sanitation Programme (CRSP) was launched in 1986, which was restructured after more than a decade into the Total Sanitation Campaign (TSC) in 1999. The major shift from the CRSP to the TSC can be seen as a paradigm shift towards a community-led and citizen-centric approach from the earlier state-agencies-led approach. Later, the TSC was further revamped into the Nirmal Bharat Abhiyan (NBA) in 2012, and then relaunched

---

[8] With the changed socio-economic and political environment, the planned development model in India has undergone momentous changes. Despite the fact that access to basic sanitation is one of the most crucial elements of human development, the programmes and policies around sanitation in India have evolved only gradually. With the neoliberal turn in the Indian economy and polity, the supply driven approach to sanitation has been replaced by demand-based low-cost sanitation since the 2000s. Another noteworthy change is that the NITI Aayog replaced the Planning Commission in India in 2015, and is to act more like a facilitator and mediator rather than an allocator.

[9] Planning Commission, *India: Assessment 2002: Water Supply and Sanitation* (Planning Commission of India, 2002), 23.

as the Swachh Bharat Mission (SBM) in 2014. Without going into the details of these programmes, this chapter intends to focus on the interlinkages between planning and sanitation in the abovementioned three phases to underline the changing role of the state in postcolonial India.

Planning for Sanitation around Health and Housing: First to Third Plan (1951–66)

The first phase of planned development in India can be broadly identified with the Nehruvian vision of heavy industry-based economic growth, which was expected to ultimately translate into 'public good'.[10] This growth model recognized the key problems that India was facing at the time of Independence. Soon after that, the First FYP was launched in 1951. The following objective was set for it:

> [T]he central objective of planning is to create conditions in which living standards are reasonably high and all citizens, men and women have full and equal opportunity for growth and service. We have not only to build up a big productive machine—though this is no doubt a necessary condition of development—we have at the same time to improve health, sanitation and education and create social conditions for vigorous cultural advance. Planning must mean coordinated development in all these fields.[11]

Such intent and focus of planning received immediate reflection in government policies in the initial years. The first National Water Supply and Sanitation Programme was formulated by the Central Government during the First FYP in 1954.[12] Water supply was identified as a key factor to ensure environmental hygiene and sanitation.

---

[10] For more details, see Sukhmoy Chakravarty, *Development Planning: The Indian Experience* (Oxford University Press, 1993).

[11] Planning Commission, 1st Five Year Plan, 'Chapter 2: Objectives, Techniques and Priorities in Planning' (1951), para 4.

[12] Water supply and sanitation remained part of housing and health in the first few FYPs.

Under this programme, an amount of Rs 12 crore was sanctioned as loans for urban water supply schemes, and Rs 6 crore as grants towards rural water supply schemes.[13] The Plan document attempted to link poor housing infrastructure in India with the issue of sanitation. It found that only 3 per cent of the population was served by a sewerage system, and thus there was an urgent need to widen the coverage in the coming years. Although no clear road map was mentioned in the Plan document, 'housing needs' occupied a significant place on the agenda.[14] The Plan took the position that the state had a duty to step in to fill the gaps wherever private enterprise is unable to fulfil the requirements to ensure housing and thus sanitation, especially in relation to lower-income groups.

The First FYP even remarked that most of the towns are growing haphazardly, which is leading to a large number of sub-standard houses and slums, ultimately contributing to poor sanitation in the cities.[15] In the above-mentioned context of provision for housing and sanitation, the First FYP also noted that the growth of slums is 'a disgrace to the country and it is a matter of regret that Governments, both Central and State, have so far paid little attention to this acute problem'.[16] The Plan further took on the local bodies—mainly municipalities of that time—for ignoring the rules and regulations related to sanitation, which had led to uncontrolled growth of slums in major cities.[17]

The First FYP document also mentioned the necessity of linking education, health, and hygiene to sanitation. It urged the improvement of public health through imparting elementary knowledge on sanitation. Overall, a large part of the investment in the First FYP was made in water supply, sewerage, and latrine construction, with

---

[13] There is a difference between loans and grants. While urban areas were given loans, which were to be returned, rural areas were getting grants, which were not to be paid back.

[14] Planning Commission, 1st FYP (n 11), 'Chapter 35: Housing', para 1.

[15] Planning Commission, 1st FYP (n 11), 'Chapter 35', para 3.

[16] Susan E. Chaplin, *The Politics of Sanitation in India: Cities, Services and the State* (Orient BlackSwan, 2011), 67.

[17] Planning Commission, 1st FYP (n 11), 'Chapter 35', para 3.

special emphasis on states like Bihar, where only 5 per cent of the population was using these essentials of sanitation. The First FYP also took up policy formulation and responsibilities as the topmost agenda. It categorically asked the states to look into the matter of sanitation with utmost care. Towards the end of the First FYP, the Central Government introduced the National Water Supply and Sanitation Programme, allotting funds for urban and rural sanitation separately.

The Second FYP (1956–61) was in many respects an extension and expansion of the First FYP. The allocation to sanitation under the head of housing, water supply, and sewerage was quadrupled, with a special emphasis on water supply. This time, a special provision of Rs 10 crore was made for urban areas which had established corporations.[18] The Plan mandated that state governments should allocate the funds for water supply and sanitation. Further, the Second FYP made special provisions for the welfare of Harijans as a focus area for sanitation.[19] While dealing with their housing and (incidentally) their sanitation needs, the emphasis was more on developing institutional mechanisms, which would study the prevailing conditions, and evolve better designs, lay-outs, and methods of construction, to ensure minimum standards of sanitation.[20] Provisions for better lighting, ventilation, and drainage were made compulsory in upcoming housing schemes for the poor, both in rural and urban areas.

The Second FYP proposed a substantive increase in the allotment of funds for both rural and urban sanitation schemes. In rural areas, the Plan underlined the crucial role of the active participation of the village community in ensuring proper implementation of policies centred on sanitation. The Plan also highlighted the need to take into consideration the growing urbanization in India, and its implications for sanitation and water supply.

[18] Planning Commission, 2nd Five Year Plan, 'Chapter 25: Health', section on 'Water Supply and Sanitation' (1956), para 47.

[19] Planning Commission, 2nd FYP (n 18), 'Chapter 26: Housing', paras 6 and 7.

[20] Planning Commission, 2nd FYP (n 18), 'Chapter 26', para 11.

In continuation of the Second FYP, the Third FYP emphasized the village-centric policy approach. In policy parlance, the Third FYP advocated that:

> an effort should be made to create greater awareness of rural sanitation problems and to introduce the use of sanitary latrines in schools and camps for groups of houses and, where possible, in individual houses. It would facilitate the introduction of latrines if the local sanitary inspectors are trained in casting the latrine sets. With the participation of the local people these latrines can be constructed at a fairly low cost.[21]

A central focus on health to tackle the issue of sanitation was conspicuously missing from the Second FYP, but was brought back in the Third FYP (1961–6). The broad objective was to ensure preventive healthcare services. This was not possible without paying due attention to the issue of sanitation. Complementing this, the rural water supply scheme was taken up as a priority under the broader umbrella of community development, local development works, and welfare of backward classes. This was further supplemented by the National Water Supply and Sanitation Programme to prevent diseases borne out of poor sanitation.

Learning lessons from the Second FYP in terms of the need for divergent focus on urban and rural challenges, sanitation in urban areas was dealt with differently this time. Programmes emphasizing sanitation schemes were supposed to be implemented in a phased manner now with tight technical scrutiny at every stage of implementation. In addition, the urgency and importance of providing drainage and sewerage, and arranging for safe disposal of sewage in towns and cities were identified as key concerns in the Third FYP. It stated that:

> these facilities are at present lagging behind the water supply facilities, and it is necessary that schemes of drainage and sewerage are considered simultaneously with those for water supply and are carried out

---

[21] Planning Commission, 3rd Five Year Plan, 'Chapter 32: Health and Family Planning', section titled 'Water Supply and Environmental Sanitation' (1961), para 10.

under a coordinated programme. This would insure against the risk of increased breeding of mosquitoes and deterioration in the sanitary conditions of the towns as a result of water supply schemes.[22]

Thus, the Third FYP prioritized a holistic approach to tackle the issue of sanitation as it dealt with drainage and water supply as complementary. The allocation for water supply and sanitation in the Third FYP increased to around Rs 100 crore, and the amount was divided between the Centre and the states.

In the first three FYPs, water supply and sanitation figured primarily in the chapter on health. Even the allocation of funds was under the allocation for the health sector. Thus, sanitation was mainly dealt with under the broader framework of 'infrastructure and development', and encompassed better water, health, and sewerage facilities for the poor, both in urban as well as rural areas.

Shift in Planning towards Sanitation as a Social Service: Fourth to Seventh Plan (1969–90)

In the second phase of planning, as in the first phase, the role of the state was central in delivering social services like sanitation to urban and rural citizens of the country. The key difference between the two phases was the major emphasis on 'stability' and 'self-reliance' in the second phase due to growing resentment against the state in the form of various social movements. In addition, social services (from the Sixth FYP onwards) including sanitation were now linked to poverty and unemployment.

The Fourth FYP[23] (1969–74) started with the main objectives of 'growth with stability' and 'progressive achievement of self-reliance'. These objectives were context specific and are relevant to the subject matter of this chapter. India had to reform and restructure its

---

[22] Planning Commission, 3rd FYP (n 21) 'Chapter 32', para 15.

[23] After the third FYP, successive years of drought, devaluation of the currency, rise in prices, and erosion of resources disrupted the planning process for some time. Another major reason for the Plan Holiday was the Indo-Pakistan War in 1965. As a result, three Annual Plans were formulated between 1966 and 1969.

expenditure agenda following the attacks on the country in 1962 and in 1965. India had hardly recovered when it was hit by severe drought. All these developments culminated in massive reduction in expenditure on social sectors such as sanitation. The preface to the Fourth FYP categorically mentioned:

> The attack on our territory in 1962 and again in 1965 forced us to modify the pattern of national expenditure. Before we could reconcile the competing claims of development and defence, drought struck us. Foreign credits became uncertain, recession followed. All these seriously restricted our freedom of choice. We had to divert our energies to fight drought and near famine and their aftermath.[24]

Regarding sanitation, the Plan revised the budget allocation, and argued for increased intervention through greater resources. The issue of water supply was given more importance, and it became part of a chapter titled 'Regional Development, Housing and Water Supply'.[25] Around Rs 400 crore was allocated for urban and rural water supply.[26] The Fourth FYP also emphasized village housing as integral to the sanitation issue. Performing a critical self-assessment of the previous plan, the Fourth FYP objectively examined the issue of sewerage in villages, and came up with following observation:

> It will be long before urban areas can afford full-fledged sewerage and sanitation systems. The problem of sanitation in towns other than those with sewerage schemes has so far been dealt with from the point of view of improving the conditions of those in unclean occupations; no reference was made to the problem of sanitation in the villages. The overall problems of sanitation require to be dealt

[24] Planning Commission, 4th Five Year Plan, 'Preface' (1969), para 2.

[25] Planning Commission, 4th FYP (n 24) 'Chapter 19: Regional Development, Housing and Water Supply', section IV 'Water Supply and Sanitation', para 19.24.

[26] One recurring feature of all the plan documents since the first plan was that none of them separately mentioned sanitation under budget allocation heads. Sanitation continued to be clubbed under water supply, drainage, and sewerage. So, one cannot estimate the exact resource allocation for the sanitation sector.

with on a long-term basis. The efforts made so far to improve the conditions of scavengers under existing arrangements have not had much success. It is necessary to think in terms of doing away with present arrangements by either adopting a proper system of underground sewerage of [*sic*] converting all dry latrines into some type of improved latrines.[27]

It is clear from the aforementioned self-assessment that the planned approach towards sanitation was undergoing some changes with growing emphasis on sewerage and long-term interventions, separating villages from the dominant urban-centric solution to the problem.

The Fifth FYP approach document endorsed sanitation as a priority issue by stating that: 'the elimination of abject poverty will not be attained as a corollary to certain acceleration in the rate of growth of the economy alone, but improvements in drinking water and environmental sanitation have direct correlation with levels of living'.[28] The Fifth FYP primarily aimed at removal of poverty, and the then prime minister, Indira Gandhi, announced her Twenty Point Programme (TPP) during this plan period. The basic objective of the TPP was to eradicate poverty and increase the standard of living of the poor. This time, sanitation was the central focus of the programme. Some of the key provisions directly linked to the issue of sanitation included improvement of slums, better housing facilities, and safe drinking water. One of the major priorities stated in the Fifth FYP was to 'develop new low cost housing designs and materials, rural sanitation and waste water management'.[29] Unfortunately, this plan was terminated before its term in 1978 amidst political turmoil, and two rolling annual plans were forwarded by the Janata Government.

The Sixth FYP (1980–5) recognized, at the outset, the importance of integrated services provided in villages, thus tackling the

[27] Planning Commission, 4th FYP (n 24), 'Chapter 19', para 19.25.

[28] Bakshi Dayanath Sinha and P.S.K. Menon, *Environmental Sanitation, Health and Panchayati Raj* (Concept Publishing House, 2000), 20.

[29] Planning Commission, 5th Five Year Plan, 'Chapter 5: Plan Outlays and Programmes of Development' (1974), para 5.194.

issue of sanitation through combining 'availability of shelter, safe water supply and facilities for hygienic sanitation as necessary in villages as much as in urban areas'.[30] The Sixth FYP, therefore, addressed the problems of spatial distribution of population, housing, water supply, and sanitation in an integrated manner. The Plan conducted a critical assessment of sanitation programmes pursued so far under the previous FYPs. It stated that 'although a national water supply programme was launched in 1954 during the very First Five Year Plan, and progressively larger allocations were made for water supply and sanitation in the succeeding Five Year Plans, the progress made so far in the provision of safe water supply and basic sanitation can hardly be called satisfactory'.[31] It also mentioned that during the first four FYPs, that is, in the period between 1951 and 1974, the total investment made by the Central and state governments for providing water supply and sanitation facilities was Rs 855 crore, and more than 65 per cent has been spent for urban areas. Thus, an urban bias can be noticed in resource allocation.

Here it is necessary to point out that the Sixth FYP categorized sanitation, which was so far part of the infrastructure and development sector, as a 'social service'. Categorization of sanitation as a social service had a far-reaching impact on the nature of funding, investment, and outlays in this sector. The Sixth FYP emphasized the role of private sector investments.[32]

The Seventh FYP (1985–1990) stated that despite a resource crunch, the Sixth FYP allocated a substantial outlay to the water supply and sanitation sector, and a high priority was given to the coverage of sanitation in such villages (named as problem villages) which still lacked sanitation facilities. Following the declaration of the International Drinking Water Supply and Sanitation Decade (1981–91), the Seventh FYP pledged to provide adequate drinking water to the entire population, and sanitation to 80 per cent of the

---

[30] Planning Commission, 6th Five Year Plan, 'Chapter 23: Housing, Urban Development and Water Supply', section on 'Water Supply and Sanitation' (1980), para 23.2.

[31] Planning Commission, 6th FYP (n 30) 'Chapter 23', para 23.36.

[32] Planning Commission, 6th FYP (n 30) 'Chapter 23', para 23.4.

urban population and to 25 per cent of the rural population.[33] 3.62 per cent of the total plan outlay was allocated to water and sanitation. It also included loan assistance from external agencies like the World Bank and bilateral agencies.[34]

The Plan also mentioned that the implementing agencies of the state governments for water supply and sanitation programmes should pay attention to the organizational and administrative structures at different levels to utilize Plan funds more efficiently. It further noted that the organizational structures vary not only in different states, but at times even within the same state.[35] For instance, while some states had set up a Water Supply and Sewerage Board, in some others, a multiplicity of agencies were dealing with sanitation, including Panchayati Raj institutions (PRIs), the Public Health Engineering Department (PHED), the community development department, and the Central Public Works Department (CPWD).

The second phase of plan development in India was different from the previous phase (1951–65). One, greater emphasis was laid on sanitation as a 'social service' thus recognizing, albeit tacitly, the need for a differential approach towards solving the sanitation problem, and refraining from clubbing the issue with infrastructure-development-based plans and projects. This further enhanced the prioritization of the issue of sanitation. Two, the second phase, towards the end, adopted a very critical approach towards sanitation programmes and policies, including budget allocation and utility. The critical approach in terms of policy implementation and budget allocation was probably an early sign of what was going to be on offer in the coming years in terms of planning. A new era of planning, completely different from the early vestiges of state-led development, was about to begin. The processes of liberalization, privatization, and globalization were soon going to transform the way in which the Indian state

[33] Planning Commission, 7th Five Year Plan, Volume 2, 'Chapter 12: Housing, Urban Development, Water Supply and Sanitation' (1985), para 12.46.

[34] Planning Commission, 7th FYP (n 33), Volume 2, 'Chapter 12', para 12.51.

[35] Planning Commission, 7th FYP (n 33), Volume 2, 'Chapter 12', para 12.50.

used to deal with issues akin to sanitation. The next section examines the major changes adopted by the Indian state vis-à-vis sanitation in the next phase (1991–2017).

Reorientation of Planning from Supply-Based to Demand-Driven Sanitation Services: Eighth to Twelfth Plan (1991–2017)

By the late 1980s, the major economies of the West had already moved to what is popularly called the 'open economy'. In the early 1990s, liberalization of the economy in India also commenced. One of the major changes was the state pulling out from social and economic activities, which were for long known to have a welfare impact on the people in general. The progressive withdrawal of the state as the sole actor in the social sector had a cascading impact on government interventions with regard to issues such as health facilities, drinking water and sewerage, and thus on sanitation. The new phase of planned development in India was about to witness three things, namely the 'reinvention of the government'; the increased role of private players; and an impact-assessment-based delivery mechanism in policymaking on sanitation.

The Eighth FYP could not take off in 1990 due to the fast changing political situation at the Centre, and the years 1990–1 and 1991–2 were treated as annual plans similar to the period 1966–9. The Eighth FYP was finally given effect to in 1992 after the adoption of the new economic policy (NEP) and the structural adjustment programme (SAP).[36] Recognizing the fiscal crises of the early 1990s, the preface to the Eighth FYP sought the roll back of public sector investment, and invited the private sector to pitch in. This was done, argued the Plan, to step up investment in the social sector including

---

[36] See Partha Chatterjee, 'Development Planning and the Indian State', in Zoya Hasan (ed), *Politics and the State in India* (Sage, 2000), 115; Prabhat Patnaik, 'The State in India's Economic Development', in Zoya Hasan (ed), *Politics and the State in India* (Sage, 2000), 142; Pranab Bardhan, 'The Political Economy of Reform in India', in Zoya Hasan (ed), *Politics and the State in India* (Sage, 2000), 158.

sanitation.[37] It also stated that the Eighth FYP will have to 'under-take re-examination and reorientation of the role of government as well as the process of planning'.[38]

The Eighth FYP, taking stock of the previous plans in terms of effectiveness in bridging the gap between state endeavour to provide effective sanitation and the actual delivery to the end beneficiaries, stated: 'Service deficiency is equally alarming. In 1985, only 28 per cent of urban population had access to proper sanitation'.[39] Taking a cue from the previous plans, the Eighth FYP pushed for linking housing with sanitation in terms of policies, both in rural and urban areas through the Indira Awas Yojna (IAY) and the Housing and Urban Development Corporation (HUDCO), respectively. The Plan proposed the Urban Low Cost Sanitation for Liberation of Scavengers scheme to be taken up by HUDCO. This centrally sponsored scheme, pushed by the Eighth FYP, was an important intervention for urban sanitation and 100 per cent liberation of scavengers on a 'whole town' coverage basis.

As mentioned earlier, private sector participation (PSP) received its first push in the Eighth FYP (1992–7) immediately after the adop-tion of the NEP in 1991, which emphasized that 'management'[40] and 'delivery of services' (including sanitation) should be effectively based on 'demand'. This new policy parlance laced with the idea of privatization was intended to 'reinvent the government' in an era of liberalization. Similarly, the major sectoral objectives of the Ninth FYP (1997–2002) clearly mentioned the need to promote PSP in the provision of public infrastructure.[41] The need for massive investment led to measures like alternative strategies, new technologies, low-cost

[37] Planning Commission, 8th Five Year Plan, Volume 1, 'Preface' (1992), para 4.

[38] Planning Commission, 8th FYP (n 37), Volume 1, 'Chapter 1', para 1.1.5.

[39] Planning Commission, 8th FYP (n 37), Volume 2, 'Chapter 14: Housing, Water Supply and Sanitation', para 14.2.4.

[40] Global Consultation on Safe Water and Sanitation, *New Delhi Statement*, 11 October 1990, UN Doc. A/C.2/45/3.

[41] Planning Commission, 9th Five Year Plan, Volume 1, 'Chapter 3: Public Sector Plan: Resources and Allocations' (1997), para 3.7.43.

solutions, and PSP. It also gave a few examples of trusts that had worked in villages.[42]

In congruence with the Ninth FYP, the Tenth FYP also stated that PSP should be encouraged. The Tenth FYP (2002–7) intended to treat water as an economic good rather than a free commodity—with responsibility for source regeneration on all user agencies.[43] This was bound to have far-reaching impacts on sanitation. It thereby became the basis for sanitation policies and schemes, which emphasized realization of costs from beneficiaries, stricter enforcement to ensure such collection, and also bringing about changes in attitudes and behaviour of the beneficiaries of such policies. The argument for PSP in FYPs translated into the setting up of sanitary marts in rural areas to provide cost-effective sanitation technology to rural households.[44] Thus, the shift in the nature of the plans provided more space to the private sector.

Following the trend set in the Ninth and Tenth FYPs, the Eleventh FYP (2007–12) also advocated PSP and public–private partnership (PPP). The Eleventh FYP suggested that India also needed to adopt strategies for efficient management of water resources and sanitation processes by pricing as well as recycling and reuse, and PPP was likely to help in attracting finance. Continuing with the strong pitch for private players, the Twelfth FYP (2012–17) explicitly mentioned the need for massive investment by the private sector to meet the cost of water treatment, sewage treatment, and so on. However, it also mentioned that private investment would not be the answer to the infrastructure challenge, and PPP will have to be conceptualized differently for the sanitation sector.[45]

In the early 1990s, liberalization also coincided with the 73rd and 74th constitutional amendments, and the increased recognition that

---

[42] Planning Commission, 9th FYP (n 41), Volume 1, 'Chapter 3', para 3.7.43.

[43] Planning Commission, 10th Five Year Plan, Volume 2, 'Chapter 6.2: Civic Amenities in Urban Areas' (2002), para 6.2.5.

[44] Planning Commission, 10th FYP (n 43), Volume 2, 'Chapter 5.5: Rural Water Supply and Sanitation', section titled 'Rural Sanitation', para 5.5.27.

[45] Planning Commission, Report of the Steering Committee on Water and Sanitation for Twelfth Five Year Plan (2012–17) (2012), 'Chapter 6: Urban and Industrial Water Supply and Sanitation'.

centralized, government-controlled, and supply-driven approaches need to be changed. From the Eighth FYP onwards, this recognition was clearly visible in the Plan documents, which shifted to more decentralized, people-centric, and demand-responsive approaches. Subsequent FYPs in the 1990s and 2000s largely adopted this approach, leading to revamping of the major sanitation policies in India. This major paradigm shift in thinking and policy, launched in 1999, led to the adoption of demand-responsive approaches based on 'empowerment' to ensure full 'participation' in decision-making processes and control and management by the communities. In addition, this led to a shift in the role of the government from direct service delivery to planning, policy formulation, monitoring and evaluation, and partial financial support. This had a cascading effect on policy formulation on sanitation.

The national policy on water and sanitation, which has generally shaped the approach to sanitation since the Eighth FYP, broadly follows the guiding principles of the New Delhi Statement.[46] The Ninth FYP was critical of the previous two phases, and sought to provide a clear mandate for change. The Plan identified the 'outlived assets' used for sanitation in an overpopulated country as the main reason behind the lacklustre performance of the government agencies. It also highlighted 'the lack of comprehensive urban planning in the past to promote regular upgradation'.[47]

The critical assessment of the previous FYPs led the Ninth FYP to register a note of caution. It stated that many goals of housing, potable water, and sanitation that were to be attained by 2001, may require the target point fixed 10–15 years before to be extended. This Plan also

---

[46] See Global Consultation on Safe Water and Sanitation (n 40). These principles include (*a*) protection of the environment and safeguarding of health through the integrated management of water resources and liquid and solid waste; (*b*) organization of reforms, promoting an integrated approach including changes in procedures, attitudes, and behaviour, and the full participation of women at all levels; (*c*) community management of services, backed by measures to strengthen local institutions in implementing and sustaining water and sanitation programmes; and (*d*) sound financial practices, achieved by better management of existing assets and extensive use of appropriate technologies.

[47] Planning Commission, 9th FYP (n 41), Volume 2, 'Chapter 3.7: Housing, Urban Development, Water Supply and Civic Amenities', para 3.7.2.

noted the need for filling the urban–rural gap. It observed: 'The Ninth Plan will take cognisance of this ground reality, particularly in respect of three critical components of human settlements development, namely, drinking water, sanitation and housing'.[48] It also identified sanitation as a crucial aspect of 'health for all'.[49] What is striking to note in the Ninth FYP is its continuing confidence in the state-led approach to the issue of sanitation as it reinforced the commitment to 'go all out to achieve the goal of expansion and improvement of sanitation facility along with other social infrastructure'.[50] This was despite the fact that in the post-liberalization phase, the previous FYPs were accused of poor fund management and delivery vis-à-vis sanitation.

One major palpable shift in the Ninth FYP was increased fund allocation. The allocation for urban water supply and sanitation that had remained largely unchanged from 1.28 per cent of the total funding in the First FYP to 1.38 per cent in the Eighth FYP (1992–7), increased in the Ninth FYP (1997–2002) to 2.17 per cent.[51] Thus, the social dimension of planning received renewed interest in the Ninth FYP, and this continued in successive FYPs. This Plan was about to cast its impression on the future of India's tryst with sanitation. In 1999, the Department of Drinking Water Supply (DDWS) for clean water and sanitation was formed under the Ministry of Rural Development. This was supposed to give a major boost to the focused approach to sanitation in rural India.

The Ninth FYP, despite its continued emphasis on the role of the state in sanitation, was unique in terms of openly inviting private players to take initiatives in the sector. The Plan mentioned categorically that '[p]rivate sector efforts in construction and maintenance of rural water supply and environmental sanitation should be encouraged and mobilised to the maximum extent'.[52] The Tenth FYP (2002–7)

[48] Planning Commission, 9th FYP (n 41), Volume 2, 'Chapter 3.7', para 3.7.6.

[49] Planning Commission, 9th FYP (n 41), Volume 2, 'Chapter 3.7', para 3.7.12.

[50] Planning Commission, 9th FYP (n 41), Volume 2, 'Chapter 3.7', para 3.7.12.

[51] Chaplin (n 16), 66.

[52] Planning Commission, 9th FYP (n 41), Volume 2, 'Chapter 3.7', para 3.7.43.

introduced new elements recognizing that economic growth could not be the only objective of the national plan, and thus set eleven key indicators of development, which mainly comprised social components including sanitation. The Plan outlay for sanitation and water supply in the Ninth FYP was Rs 11,700 crore, which was increased to Rs 18,749.2 crore in the Tenth FYP (2002–7). Unlike the Ninth FYP, this time, the major emphasis was on rural sanitation. The Plan recognized the close-knit link between sanitation, poverty, and health, and argued for a 'mission mode' to achieve the target on time.

This time the Plan charted out the main components of rural sanitation—safe handling of drinking water, safe disposal of human excreta, safe solid waste disposal, home sanitation and food hygiene, personal hygiene and sanitation in the community.[53] This was the first attempt by any Plan ever to draft such detailed components of rural sanitation. The Tenth FYP recognized the increased reach and scale of non-governmental agencies in comparison to state actors. On this ground, it invited non-governmental organizations (NGOs) and other existing social groups like self-help groups and cooperatives to take initiatives in the effective implementation of the sanitation programmes of the government. In this process of bringing in non-governmental players, the Plan gave a clarion call for sectoral reform. Funding to state governments through HUDCO and the National Bank for Agriculture and Rural Development (NABARD) was proposed so that the non-availability of funds was not an issue when it came to the implementation of sanitation policies and programmes. As mentioned before, the Plan proposed to increase private participation to encourage the setting up of building centres and sanitary marts in rural areas to bring cost-effective sanitation technology to rural households.[54]

The Eleventh FYP (2007–12) proposed a new orientation aimed at 'faster and more inclusive growth'. As a result, it attempted to match the level of social development and economic growth which India had registered in the previous two decades. Unlike the previous FYPs of the third phase, this time the Plan started on a positive note

[53] Planning Commission, 10th FYP (n 43), Volume 2, 'Chapter 5.5', para 5.5.27.

[54] Planning Commission, 10th FYP (n 43), Volume 2, 'Chapter 5.5', para 5.5.27.

by listing the achievements registered so far. It highlighted the programmes and policies initiated on the basis of previous plans, mainly the TSC and Nirmal Gram Yojana. This, however, did not prevent the Plan from noting the thin presence of toilet facilities in rural areas, a major concern within the larger issue of sanitation in India. The Plan gave the call for bringing drinking water, sanitation, and clean environment within the same ambit. As evident in previous plan documents, it is not that such linkages were not part of the plans. However, this time the section on sanitation began with this call on the top of the agenda. It hailed the achievement of the TSC in ensuring toilet coverage in villages. It went beyond one of the Millennium Development Goals (MDGs) of halving open defecation, and promised to cover the whole of India by the end of the Eleventh FYP.

The Eleventh FYP was innovative as it linked the implementation of sanitation policies to incentives. The Nirmal Gram Puraskar (NGP) was one such incentive, to be given to a village, Block, or District, which is 100 per cent sanitized, and open defecation free (ODF). In the case of urban areas, a substantive boost to funding came during this Plan with the launch of the Jawaharlal Nehru National Urban Renewal Mission (JNNURM) in 2005, as the amount increased to Rs 75,000 crore. Water supply and sanitation was accorded priority under the programme, and was supposed to receive 40 per cent of the Plan funds in this sector. This Plan also emphasized performance review of rural sanitation to keep a check on fund utilization and implementation of various sanitation programmes. Lack of priority to the JNNURM by many states leading to inadequate allocation of funds, absence of personal communication on sanitation at the village level, and inadequate capacity building at the grassroots are some of the key limitations highlighted in the Plan.[55]

In addition to continuing 'hardware' support to the states, the Plan advocated behavioural changes in the government vis-à-vis sanitation. The change in behaviour, maintained the Plan, needed to

[55] Planning Commission, 11th Five Year Plan, Volume 2, 'Chapter 5: Drinking Water, Sanitation, and Clean Living Conditions' (2007), para 5.57.

be brought both within the communities, as well as institutions like the state and panchayats. It also highlighted 'the need for a regulatory regime in water supply and sanitation to enthuse confidence among the private players'.[56] The Eleventh FYP, in many ways, was a continuation of the larger policy shift in the previous FYPs of the third phase. Performance-based incentives, the role of private players in sanitation, thoughtful resource allocation, sectoral reforms, the increased role of communities both at implementation and audit levels, and bringing in non-governmental players for wider reach illustrated the tropes of liberalization and privatization in the sanitation sector.

The Twelfth and last FYP (2012–17) had a broad vision of 'faster, sustainable and more inclusive growth'. It identified lack of proper sanitation as 'the major weakness of our system and one that most adversely impacts women'.[57] In this regard, the Plan promised to make a gender impact assessment of the TSC. It also promised to ensure toilets with water in all schools and *anganwadis* in India. The Twelfth Plan further stated that: 'States will have to prepare projects which will integrate drinking water supply along with sanitation with components of solid and liquid waste management, water quality, aquifer management, O&M and water security through re-charging. This cohesive and holistic approach will pave the way to achieve the dream of Nirmal Bharat.'[58]

Within the ambit of PRIs, involvement of women on the issue of sanitation was given top priority. Institutional mechanisms to ensure their presence in committees on sanitation were guaranteed. Similarly, through the Integrated Child Development Services (ICDS), the National Rural Health Mission (NRHM) and the TSC, a wider network of policy formulation and implementation was envisaged in this Plan.

---

[56] Planning Commission, 11th FYP (n 55), Volume 2, 'Chapter 5', paras 5.51 and 5.58.

[57] Planning Commission, 12th Five Year Plan, Volume 3: Social Sectors, 'Chapter 23: Women's Agency and Child Rights' (2012), para 23.35.

[58] Planning Commission Report of the Steering Commission (n 45), 'Chapter 4: Rural Domestic Water and Sanitation', 37.

In the third phase of planning, especially in the last two plans, the Central Government took initiatives to incentivize the achievement of ODF status by villages through the NGP. No such award was introduced in urban areas, although, due to large slum areas, open defecation remained a major challenge in urban areas too. The FYPs in the earlier two phases, as mentioned previously, were more or less identical in their emphasis on the crucial role of the public sector in dealing with the issue of sanitation. In the first phase, sanitation was under the ambit of infrastructure, and in the second phase, it was classified as a 'social service'. However, with the launch of the Ninth FYP in 1997, the emphasis on the public sector reduced substantially vis-à-vis the role of the private sector. Despite these changes, the prime mover of planned development in India continued to be 'growth with social justice and equality'.

Planning and Sanitation: Critical Evaluation

The previous sections have analysed the FYP documents to capture the essence of planning in the context of sanitation. After highlighting the nature of the shift in policymaking, and the growing role of the private sector, this section intends to engage with some of the major challenges that confront the goal of sanitation for all in India. Given the fact that a call for the recognition of sanitation as a basic human right has come to find increased currency in the past decade, there are numerous issues, such as access, affordability, safety, and privacy, which are being debated internationally as well as in domestic fora.

In the Indian context, the rural–urban dichotomy, rehabilitation of slum dwellers, decentralization without devolution of power, and the status of individuals engaged in tasks such as manual scavenging have emerged as major challenges. Despite the fact that successive governments have made national and international commitments to provide sanitation to all, the realization of this goal remains a distant dream. This section focuses on three broad areas, namely, the changing nature of government intervention through community development programmes for sanitation, decentralization, and challenges arising out of caste and gender identities.

Changing Nature of Government Intervention

From the 1990s onwards, government intervention strategies vis-à-vis sanitation have undergone substantial changes in terms of involvement of the stakeholders. This is most clearly visible in the role of communities in tackling the problem of sanitation. During the initial period of planning, the role of communities for various social sector initiatives including sanitation was envisioned through the Community Development Programme (CDP). The CDP was initiated in 1952 for rural reconstruction, and it was part and parcel of economic planning.[59] Since then, the nature of community involvement has changed in the sanitation sector. While during the early decades of Independence, the FYPs focused on the construction of toilets through the CDP, community awareness for behavioural change has become more important since the Tenth FYP.[60] This section flags some instances from the Plan documents to capture this changing orientation.

In the First FYP, 55 CDPs were taken up under the Indo-American Technical Aid Programme. It was suggested that villagers should use local material to make ventilated houses, manure-pits, and sanitary latrines.[61] The Second as well as the Third FYP mentioned that several villages have benefitted from CDPs, and improved their water supply and sanitation. The Fourth FYP stated that rural water supply schemes have been taken up under community development schemes.[62] During the Sixth FYP, the National Water Supply and Sanitation Programme of the Ministry of Health was launched to give a boost to community development.[63] The Seventh FYP referred to the presence of a community development department in some states for the implementation of water supply and sanitation programmes.[64]

---

[59] Baldev Raj Nayar, 'Community Development Programme: Its Political Impact' (1960) XII(38) *The Economic Weekly* 1401.

[60] Arghyam, Background Note of the Consultation on Behavioural Change Communication for Sanitation (2012).

[61] Planning Commission, 1st FYP (n 11), 'Chapter 35', para 34.

[62] Planning Commission, 4th FYP (n 24), 'Chapter 19', section IV on 'Water Supply and Sanitation', para 19.22.

[63] Planning Commission, 6th FYP (n 30), 'Chapter 23', para 23.41.

[64] Planning Commission, 7th FYP (n 33), Volume 2, 'Chapter 12', para 12.50.

The Tenth FYP further elaborated on the role of CDPs, and stated that the 'community has to be made conscious about water quality through health education and awareness campaigns and water testing kits shall be made available to a range of institutions, including schools and colleges and qualified NGOs in the area'.[65] The planmakers felt the need for change in the attitude of the community, and in the recent past, the FYPs have started stressing the necessity for behavioural change towards sanitation.[66] For instance, according to the Tenth FYP, 'school sanitation' was to be given the highest priority to spread awareness among children to make them a catalyst of social change.[67] The Plan documents in India thus reflect the emerging issues and challenges for the state to tackle the problem of sanitation. The change in approach is the result of increased pressure on successive governments to deliver in concrete terms on the sanitation front, and the skewed budget allocation to this sector. The major shifts in the last three decades are demand-driven planning for safe drinking water, community-led total sanitation (CLTS), and the thrust on PPP in planning.

Decentralization and Planning on Sanitation

Following the 73rd Amendment to the Constitution in 1992, PRIs were assigned numerous development activities as the third tier of government. With the institutionalization of PRIs during the Eighth FYP, the subsequent Plan documents made suggestions and guidelines for them. The Ninth FYP proposed that PRIs should be given the option to levy and collect user charges for drinking water and sanitation services so that at least O&M, if not further development

[65] Planning Commission, 10th FYP (n 43), Volume 2, 'Chapter 5.5', para 5.5.22.

[66] Planning Commission, India Assessment 2002 (n 9), 21.

[67] For details, see Planning Commission, 10th FYP (n 43), Volume 2, 'Chapter 5.5', section on Rural Sanitation, para 5.5.27. It also focused on the need for community awareness on sanitation issues. At present, many programmes involve some extent of community contribution and they are run under operation and maintenance (O&M) schemes. The introduction of the NGP under the TSC tried to further enhance the scope of community participation for the purpose of sanitation.

works too, may become a self-financing activity.[68] The Plan envisaged that such a move would not only empower PRIs, but also make devolution of power a reality. In 1999, the role of PRIs was further strengthened with the change of the CRSP into the TSC.[69]

The Tenth FYP (2002–7) underlined the lack of devolution of financial and administrative powers as limiting PRIs in realizing their potential. The Tenth FYP document mentioned that, under Article 243G of the Constitution, state legislatures may, by law, endow their panchayats with the powers and authority necessary to enable them to function as institutions of self-government. Further, such law may contain provisions for the devolution of powers and responsibilities with respect to (*a*) the preparation of plans for economic development and social justice, and (*b*) the implementation of schemes for economic development and social justice as may be entrusted to them, including those relating to matters in the 11th Schedule of the Constitution, which include drinking water and maintenance of community assets.[70]

The document further stated that: 'being institutions of local self-governance, PRIs should be strengthened and entrusted with all activities relating to water supply, sanitation, hygiene and nutrition. The single institution of the *gram panchayat* may handle various development functions, as this will increase the possibility of convergent planning and delivery of services.'[71]

PRIs are the third tier of governance in India, and are seen as the cornerstone of economic and social planning. But the Twelfth FYP (2012–17) argued that although the 73rd Amendment provides the needed policy and legislative framework to devolve the responsibility for rural water supply and sanitation to PRIs, the devolution of

[68] Planning Commission, 9th FYP (n 41), Volume 2, 'Chapter 3.7', para 3.7.40.

[69] While the CRSP was a supply driven programme, the TSC was a community-based programme, with the PRIs, the local government body, taking the lead. The TSC also constituted the NGP in 2003 as one of its components to incentivize villages and eventually to also give a boost to the sanitation programme.

[70] Planning Commission, 10th FYP (n 43), Volume 2, 'Chapter 5.5', para 5.5.8.

[71] Planning Commission, 10th FYP (n 43), Volume 2, 'Chapter 5.5', para 5.5.12.

management and financial management responsibility to the pan-chayats has been at best half-hearted.[72] The Plan document also stated that the sector-wise health plans prepared by the states should include elements like drinking water and sanitation along with AIDS control and health research.[73] It reflected the multi-sectoral approach under-taken in the decentralization and planning process in India. Thus, even after over two decades of their formation, PRIs in India have not been able to play the role envisaged at the time of their inception.

Caste and Gender

Caste and gender are two critical dimensions of planning and sanita-tion in India. In each case, a number of issues and challenges arise. This section highlights the issue of manual scavenging and the gender dimension in the Plan documents.

As a caste-based and hereditary profession, manual scavenging is the practice of manual cleaning of human excreta from service/dry latrines, which has been prevalent for a very long time in India. Although in the very First FYP, it was noted that there is a need to convert dry latrines into some form of improved latrines, the fact is that no such significant change has taken place at the grassroots level. Even today, about 1.3 million manual scavengers in India are involved in carrying human excreta.[74] Ninety per cent of sanitation workers die before the age of sixty because they contract various infectious diseases. They are also paid much below the minimum wage requirement.[75] Data from Census 2011 indicates the existence of 7.94 lakh latrines in India from which humans remove night soil.[76]

---

[72] Government of India, Twelfth Five Year Plan: 2012–17, Report of the Working Group on Rural Domestic Water and Sanitation (Ministry of Drinking Water and Sanitation 2012), 37.

[73] Planning Commission, 12th FYP (n 57), Volume 3, 'Chapter 20', 29 (Box 20.5).

[74] Bhasha Singh, 'Sanitation, Development and Social Change: Cleaning of Holy Minds' (2015) 59 *Yojana* 70.

[75] Singh (n 74), 70.

[76] Government of India, Ministry of Home Affairs, Office of the Registrar General of India and Census Commissioner, Census 2011, cited in Singh (n 74).

Needless to say manual scavenging is one of the major challenges faced by India when it comes to planning and sanitation.

In 1991, the Planning Commission decided that the Ministry of Urban Development would be in charge of conversion of dry latrines, and the Ministry of Welfare would look after the task of rehabilitation of scavengers.[77] It was in the Eighth FYP (1992–7) that the Centrally Sponsored Scheme of Urban Low Cost Sanitation for Liberation of Scavengers was made an important scheme for urban sanitation. The programme was first made operative through the Ministry of Home Affairs, and subsequently the Ministry of Social Justice and Empowerment implemented it. Since 1989–90, it is being operated through the Ministry of Urban Affairs and Employment. The Ninth FYP noted that the Eighth FYP provision was Rs 150 crore, which was only about 25 per cent of the required assistance to meet the objective of conversion of all existing dry latrines in urban areas of the country (numbering 50 lakh units) into low-cost pour-flush sanitary latrines, and 100 per cent liberation of scavengers on a 'whole town' coverage basis.[78] The fact remains that not much has been achieved, and the spirit of Article 17 of the Constitution has not fully touched the lives of manual scavengers. A review report for the Eleventh FYP found that:

> it is true that the previous 10 Five Year Plans had initiated some steps to alleviate their conditions and there are several schemes already in place. But their implementation leaves much to be desired, with the result the manual scavengers are neither released, liberated fully nor rehabilitated in the true sense of the term, they remain as mere initial steps.[79]

With regard to gender issues, various studies show that the education of children in India, especially the girl child, is significantly

---

[77] BN Srivastava, *Manual Scavenging in India: A Disgrace to the Country* (Concept Publishing Company, 1997), 60.

[78] Planning Commission, 9th FYP (n 41), Volume 2, 'Chapter 3.7', para 3.7.25.

[79] Government of India, Working Group on the Empowerment of Scheduled Castes (SCs) for the Eleventh Five-Year Plan (2007–12), Report of Sub Group on Safai Karmacharis Submitted to the Chairman of the Working Group on the Empowerment of Scheduled Castes (SCs) for the Eleventh Five-Year Plan (2007–12).

impacted by poor sanitation. Girls are often forced to miss school or they even have to drop out of education due to lack of sanitation facilities in schools.[80] Further, lack of sufficient provision of infrastructure discourages women from using public toilets. It was estimated in 2012 that approximately 30 per cent of women from the underprivileged section of society face violent sexual assaults as they go to secluded places or public toilets to meet their bodily needs.[81] The multidimensional link between gender and sanitation is captured by the remark that 'the need for toilets is not just a matter of modesty, privacy, health and hygiene. More urgently, it is a matter of women's safety'.[82]

With the objective of improving the quality of life of the rural population in general, and to provide privacy and dignity to women in particular, the CRSP was launched in 1986. It intended to supplement the efforts of the states. It had a provision of 70 per cent subsidy for exclusive sanitary marts for women, and the remaining 30 per cent was to be contributed by the panchayats/beneficiaries. The Ninth FYP stated that 'subsidy is extended to the Panchayats for exclusive sanitation complexes for women, in areas, where adequate space is not available for individual household latrines and other sanitation facilities in the villages/habitations'.[83] So, one may say that programmes and policies have been made to address the issue. However, not much has changed, and a large number of women and girls still do not have access to sanitation facilities in rural as well as urban areas.

There is a pressing need today to think of sanitation beyond merely access to latrines, especially when it comes to the gender aspect. The FYPs often seem to take more of a gender-neutral approach, and they have not addressed issues like menstrual hygiene management (MHM).

---

[80]   See Koonan and Bhullar, Chapter 13 in this volume.

[81]   Dasra—Catalyst for Social Change, *Squatting Rights: Access to Toilets in Urban India* (Dasra, 2012).

[82]   Arindam Chakrabarti, 'In India, No Toilets for Women', *The Hindu* (11 July 2015); available at www.thehindu.com/opinion/op-ed/in-india-no-toilets-for-women/article7408341.ece.

[83]   Planning Commission, 9th FYP (n 41), Volume 2, 'Chapter 3.7', para 3.7.30.

The Twelfth FYP mentioned that it would undertake a gender impact assessment of the TSC to assess whether it has reduced the workload of women, and improved their hygiene and reproductive health.[84] In this context, one may say that though FYPs reflect the gradually changing attitude towards the gender dimension of sanitation, much more is desirable in terms of these changes transforming the attitude towards sanitation.

* * *

The chapter traced the shifts in the nature of state planning for sanitation in post-Independence India. Planning as an exercise of efficient resource allocation has influenced and shaped the policy outcomes on sanitation in equal measure. The three phases of the evolution of planning in India reflect that with each successive Plan, the investment by the Centre as well as state governments for sanitation has continuously increased, but the country still remains far from realizing the dream of sanitation for all. The post-liberalization phase is marked by a new turn in the sanitation sector with the greater involvement of NGOs, private players, and community-level interventions along with a renewed interest from the state to take up the challenge of providing a healthy and dignified life to its citizens. With the NITI Aayog as the new *avatar* of the Planning Commission, the future of planning for sanitation is yet to be fully ascertained.

[84] Planning Commission, 12th FYP (n 57), 12th Five Year Plan, Volume 3, 'Chapter 20', 170.

PART II

REALIZING THE RIGHT TO SANITATION IN RURAL AND URBAN AREAS

5

Assessing the Realization of the Right to Sanitation in Rural Areas

Sujith Koonan

The rural sanitation scenario in India is far from adequate. While 12.6 per cent of the households in urban areas do not have access to any kind of toilet, the same figure for rural areas is 69.3 per cent.[1] According to the most recent report by the Government of India, the rural sanitation scenario has improved over the last few years from 38.7 per cent of the households in 2014 to 81.7 per cent as of April 2018.[2] However, the presence of toilets does not always necessarily signify public health benefits and environmental quality either due to the non-use of toilets or due to their unscientific design or

---

[1] Government of India, Census of India 2011, Availability and Type of Latrine Facility. For a discussion on various data on rural sanitation, see Arjun Kumar, 'Discrepancies in Sanitation Statistics of Rural India' (2015) L(2) *Economic & Political Weekly* 13, and Amandeep Singh and Nikhil George, 'Revisiting Discrepancies in Sanitation Statistics of Rural India' (2015) L(26) *Economic & Political Weekly* 96.

[2] Latest data available at http://sbm.gov.in/sbmdashboard/Default.aspx.

technology. For example, toilets with deep unlined pits may pollute groundwater due to the seepage of wastewater, and this is already a crisis in rural areas in certain states.[3]

Open defecation or inadequate sanitation facilities do not affect everyone in a similar way. They may affect women, children, and other vulnerable sections disproportionately. For instance, open defecation has been highlighted as an important reason for child stunting in India.[4] Similarly, studies have highlighted that women in rural areas face several health-, safety-, and dignity-related issues including physical and sexual violence due to inadequate or lack of sanitation facilities.[5]

While the absence of toilet facilities poses serious challenges for the realization of the right to sanitation in rural areas, presence of certain types of toilets, for instance, dry latrines, also poses challenges. Dry latrines and the related practice of manual scavenging are important issues in the context of the realization of the right to sanitation in rural areas.[6] On the one hand, the practice of manual scavenging exposes the link between sanitation and the caste system in India, because invariably people belonging to the lower castes, particularly Dalits (predominantly women), carry out manual scavenging. On the other hand, it exposes a practice where human beings are in direct contact with human excreta, a situation that sanitation interventions must eliminate completely.

The realization of the right to sanitation in rural areas essentially depends upon the extent to which the abovementioned issues, among other relevant issues, are addressed by the law and policy framework. While a number of these issues have been recognized under the relevant law and policy frameworks, a key question is to what extent they are addressed at the implementation level.

---

[3] P.U. Megha, P. Kavya, S. Murugan, and P.S. Harikumar, 'Sanitation Mapping of Groundwater Contamination in a Rural Village of India' (2015) 6 *Journal of Environmental Protection* 1, no. 34.

[4] Dean Spears, Arabinda Ghosh, and Oliver Cumming, 'Open Defecation and Childhood Stunting in India: An Ecological Analysis of New Data from 112 Districts' (2013) 8(9) *PLoS One*; available at http://journals.plos.org/plosone/article/file?id=10.1371/journal.pone.0073784&type=printable.

[5] See Koonan and Bhullar (Chapter 13) in this volume.

[6] See the chapters by Khanna (Chapter 11) and Wilson (Chapter 10) in this volume.

This chapter analyses the implementation of the law and policy frameworks related to the right to sanitation in rural areas. The chapter is divided into three parts. The first part explains the law and policy framework relevant to the realization of the right to sanitation in rural areas. A detailed analysis of the law and policy framework has been provided elsewhere in this volume.[7] Therefore, this part provides a brief account of the law and policy framework necessary to set the background for the remaining sections that focus on issues at the implementation level. Given the fact that the realization of the right to sanitation in rural areas is almost exclusively regulated by the policy framework (schemes, policies, and administrative directions),[8] the next two sections focus on the implementation of this framework. The second part examines the issue of focus on toilets, and its implications for the realization of the right to sanitation. The third part analyses the approach and strategies followed by implementing agencies at the local level from a rights perspective, with special emphasis on their implications for the right to sanitation.

Literature examining the implementation of the law and policy framework for rural sanitation in India from a right to sanitation perspective is virtually non-existent. Therefore, the analysis of issues related to implementation in this chapter is extensively based on primary documents and information collected through fieldwork conducted in rural areas in the states of Kerala, Rajasthan, and Uttar Pradesh (UP) during the period 2014–16.[9]

---

[7] See Cullet (Chapter 3) in this volume.

[8] The term 'policy framework' in this chapter is used broadly to denote various instruments including policies, schemes, programmes, and administrative directions adopted by the executive wing of the government.

[9] Fieldwork was conducted in selected Districts in three states—Kerala, Rajasthan, and Uttar Pradesh—during the period 2014–16. These states were selected on the basis of their relevance in terms of sanitation scenario and sanitation-related issues and challenges such as prevalence of open defecation, prevalence of manual scavenging, and environmental pollution. Following are the Districts where fieldwork was conducted: Kerala: Ernakulam, Kannur, Thiruvananthapuram, and Wayanad; Rajasthan: Bikaner, Churu, Jaipur, and Tonk; and UP: Chitrakoot, Kushinagar, Lucknow, and Pratapgarh.

Law and Policy Frameworks Governing
the Realization of the Right

The law and policy framework governing sanitation interventions in rural areas consists of constitutional provisions, statutes, and schemes, programmes, administrative directions, and so on, as explained earlier. The most important aspect of the legal framework is the recognition by the higher judiciary of the fundamental right to sanitation as a right deriving from the fundamental right to life.[10] In addition, there are different statutes addressing different aspects of sanitation in rural areas (some of these statutes are applicable to sanitation interventions in urban areas as well). For example, statutes prohibiting the practice of manual scavenging are relevant in the rural sanitation context, because dry latrines and their manual cleaning are still important challenges for the realization of the right to sanitation in rural areas.[11]

Similarly, there are environmental laws, which are relevant insofar as environmental dimensions (for example, wastewater disposal and water pollution due to toilets) of the right to sanitation are concerned.[12] Further there are many other statutes governing different aspects but having sanitation-related provisions, for example, the law related to the right to education, labour legislation, and legislation to protect the rights of differently abled people.[13] While these are central laws, some states have adopted laws to set up a centralized

[10] *Virendra Gaur* v *State of Haryana* 1995 (2) SCC 577 (Supreme Court of India, 1994); *L.K. Koolwal* v *State of Rajasthan* AIR 1988 Raj 2 (High Court of Rajasthan, 1986).

[11] See The Prohibition of Employment as Manual Scavengers and their Rehabilitation Act, 2013.

[12] For example, The Water (Prevention and Control of Pollution) Act, 1974, and The Environment (Protection) Act, 1986.

[13] For example, The Right of Children to Free and Compulsory Education Act, 2009; The Factories Act, 1948; The Building and Other Construction Workers (Regulation of Employment and Conditions of Service) Act, 1996; The Inter-State Migrant Workmen (Regulation of Employment and Conditions of Service) Act, 1979; and The Rights of Persons with Disabilities Act, 2016.

institutional mechanism to address certain aspects of both rural and urban sanitation. These laws generally mandate the agency established under the Act to 'control and manage' sanitation services and sewerage systems.[14]

While the abovementioned laws are applicable both in rural and urban contexts, there are laws specific to the rural sanitation context. Laws governing Panchayati Raj institutions (PRIs) are an important framework in this regard. Laws on PRIs generally contain provisions that make sanitation a responsibility of panchayats at the village, Block, and District level that includes the obligation to take all necessary action for the improvement of sanitation in their concerned jurisdictions.[15]

The statutory framework for the realization of the right to sanitation in rural areas is fragmented in nature with different statutes addressing different aspects of the right. The fragmented nature of the legal framework coupled with the lack of coordination between these statutes has made comprehensive conceptualization and implementation of the right difficult. At the same time, over the years, a separate policy framework has been developed to address rural-sanitation-related issues exclusively.

In the first couple of decades after Independence, sanitation, from a policy perspective, was treated as a part of other sectors such as health, housing, and water supply.[16] It gradually gained more

[14] For example, Legislature of the The Orissa Water Supply and Sewerage Board Act, 1991, and The U.P. Water Supply and Sewerage Act, 1975.

[15] There are some significant differences in the manner in which different PRI laws have articulated the responsibility of panchayats. While some laws have used unconditional language in listing the responsibilities (for example, The Kerala Panchayat Raj Act, 1994, s 166 and The Bihar Panchayat Raj Act, 2006, s 22), some others have used conditional language that makes the fulfilment of their responsibilities contingent upon various conditions, for instance, the availability of money (for instance, The Punjab Panchayati Raj Act, 1994, s 30 and The Haryana Panchayati Raj Act, 1994, s 21).

[16] Government of India, SACOSAN VI, India Country Paper, 2016, 5; available at https://www.endwaterpoverty.org/sites/default/files/oldfiles/SACOSAN_VI_declaration.pdf. See also Shree (Chapter 4) in this volume.

importance in terms of policy responses. From a rural sanitation point of view, the Central Rural Sanitation Programme (CRSP), adopted in 1986, was a landmark in terms of elevating rural sanitation to a sector with a separate policy framework. The CRSP focused on providing subsidies to individuals to build toilets. It reportedly did not yield the desired result.[17] This led to a paradigm shift in the rural sanitation policy framework by the Central Government by diverting policy attention mainly to motivation and education as opposed to providing subsidies to build sanitation infrastructure (mainly toilets). It marks a shift from the supply oriented approach to the demand-oriented approach to sanitation issues in rural areas.

The paradigm shift in the approach was reflected when the Government of India adopted the Total Sanitation Campaign (TSC) in 1999 with the goal of achieving universal rural sanitation coverage by 2012 through a demand-oriented approach. In 2012, the Nirmal Bharat Abhiyan (NBA) replaced the TSC, and in 2014, the Swachh Bharat Mission (SBM) replaced the NBA. The on-going SBM, although a single programme, addresses rural (SBM-Gramin) and urban sanitation (SBM-Urban) separately through different guidelines and different ministries.[18] Therefore, in the rural sanitation context, SBM-Gramin (SBM-G) has replaced the NBA. The SBM-G is currently the key policy framework that governs sanitation interventions, and is probably the most important framework relevant in the context of the realization of the right to sanitation in rural areas.

The SBM-G follows the demand-oriented approach as its predecessors. However, it has introduced a few significant changes when compared to the previous two flagship programmes on rural sanitation. First, it does not deal with all aspects of sanitation. Two key components—school sanitation and anganwadi sanitation—which were part of the erstwhile policy framework, have been taken

---

[17] Government of India, Total Sanitation Campaign Guidelines, 2011, 4.

[18] See Swachh Bharat Mission (Gramin) Guidelines (SBM-G Guidelines), 2017, and Swachh Bharat Mission (Urban) Guidelines (SBM-U Guidelines), 2017.

out of the purview of the SBM-G. The responsibility of school toilets is now vested with the Department of School Education & Literacy; and the Ministry of Women and Child Development is to take care of sanitation facilities in anganwadis.

Second, lack of sustainability has been a key criticism against the policy framework. The TSC and NBA had almost exclusively focused on toilet construction. There was little focus on, and virtually no mechanism to ensure, the sustainability of the toilets constructed. This has resulted in leaving a staggering number of toilets unused, and continued resort to open defecation by people, despite having a toilet at home. A number of reasons have been cited for this phenomenon including the unacceptable design of toilets, non-availability of water supply, people's reluctance to give up their habit (particularly, elderly people), and people's perception of open defecation as a better option in terms of health and aesthetic factors.[19] The SBM-G seeks to address the issue mainly by including a two-tier monitoring system, that is monitoring of both outputs (construction) and outcomes (usage).[20]

Third, the mechanism of funding or financial assistance from multiple sources as followed under the NBA no longer exists under the SBM-G. Under the NBA, financial assistance (Rs 5,400) was made available for the construction of toilets through schemes under the Mahatma Gandhi National Rural Employment Guarantee Act, 2005 (MGNREGA).[21] This money was in addition to the financial assistance available under the NBA (Rs 4,600). While the additional money available was a huge help particularly to poor people, there was unreasonable delay in getting the same.[22] The system of financial assistance from multiple sources was discontinued, and currently the financial

---

[19] Ashish Gupta et al., 'Revealed Preference for Open Defecation: Evidence from a New Survey in Rural North India' (2014) XLIX(38) *Economic & Political Weekly* 43.

[20] SBM-G Guidelines (n 18), Para 5.2.10.

[21] Ministry of Rural Development, Mahatma Gandhi National Rural Employment Guarantee Act Division, Guidelines (Revised) for Taking up Works Relating to Access to Sanitation Facilities, 2012.

[22] Interview with Mr Anandilal Vaishanav, District Coordinator, Nirmal Bharat Abhiyan, Tonk on 18 August 2014.

assistance has been increased, and is exclusively from the SBM-G (Rs 12,000).[23] While there is no formal link between the SBM-G and schemes under MGNREGA, the Ministry of Rural Development has committed separately to improve the rural sanitation scenario mainly by constructing toilets under MGNREGA.[24]

Sanitation interventions in rural areas since the adoption of the CRSP show mainly the following features. First, the erstwhile idea of 'subsidy' has been replaced by the idea of 'incentive'. As a result, the financial assistance sanctioned under the policy framework is available to individuals as 'incentive' for having constructed toilets, and not as 'subsidy' to construct toilets.[25] Second, great emphasis has been given to awareness creation programmes by including the same as a key component, namely information, education, and communication (IEC). Third, sanitation interventions in rural areas follow a decentralized participatory approach in their implementation. All these key features among others are problematic from a right to sanitation perspective, and the remaining parts of this chapter analyse them.

The rural sanitation sector in India shows a peculiar trend where laws are by and large fragmented, dormant, and inadequate. At the same time, the policy framework has been developed to address rural sanitation, and it has undergone significant transformations from time to time. Further, the policy framework is the source of the overwhelming majority of the fund to undertake various sanitation interventions at the local level. These factors cumulatively led to a situation where the policy framework occupies the dominant position insofar as the regulation of sanitation interventions in rural areas is concerned. Experience from the field reveals that the legal framework is almost completely invisible at the level of implementation. Implementing agencies are driven and regulated by the norms

---

[23] SBM-G Guidelines (n 18), para 5.2.8.

[24] Action Plan for Swachh Bharat Mission under MGNREGA (Mahatma Gandhi National Rural Employment Guarantee Act), MoRD Notification No. J-11017/41/2011-MGNREGA, 19 January 2015.

[25] However, this approach has been diluted under the SBM by relaxing the incentive norm, that is, by giving discretion to state governments to provide part of the financial assistance in advance. Thus, the SBM-G follows a mixed approach that combines both elements of subsidy and incentive.

and guidelines enshrined under the policy framework. The policy framework is, therefore, the most important framework insofar as the realization of the right to sanitation in rural areas is concerned. In this context, the next two sections of this chapter focus on analysing the policy framework.

The Race to Build Toilets: Exclusion, Exploitation, and Environmental Pollution

Over the last couple of decades, the policy framework for rural sanitation has been overwhelmingly focusing on toilets (more specifically, household toilets). This led to the undermining of many other key aspects of the right to sanitation in the rural context. Overall this approach resulted in a very narrow understanding of sanitation, with little effect for the realization of the right. In this context, this part examines the key focus of the policy framework at the level of implementation, and analyses it from a right to sanitation perspective.

Focus on Household Toilets and the Downplaying of Public Toilets

Toilets at the individual household level have been the foremost priority of sanitation interventions in rural areas. Access to sanitation in public places such as markets and bus stands has been an issue of low priority. The SBM-G Guidelines explicitly provide that community sanitary complexes can be considered in cases where individual household latrines are not possible. Similarly, it promotes public toilets in public places such as bus stands and markets.[26] However, at the implementation level, community sanitary complexes and public toilets are understood as a step that is supposed to be taken up after completing the target of toilets at the household level.

In rural areas in Rajasthan and UP, implementing agencies are yet to start focusing on public toilets. Wherever public toilets exist, for instance, in some villages in Kerala, most of them are non-functional

---

[26] SBM-G Guidelines (n 18), para 6.7.1.

or locked. Implementing agencies cite reasons such as lack of resources and facilities, mainly electricity and water supply, for not being able to provide and maintain basic sanitation facilities in public places. The lack of focus on public toilets is further clear from the fact that public toilets do not exist or function even in panchayats that have been declared open defecation free (ODF) and have received the Nirmal Gram Puraskar (NGP). This demonstrates the narrow approach of sanitation interventions in rural areas, where open defecation and urination while people are away from their homes are acceptable or tolerated for the time being, even in panchayats that have been declared ODF.

It seems irrational for sanitation interventions in rural areas to encourage people to use toilets at home on the one hand, and not to provide similar facilities in public places. While lack of toilets in individual houses has been a serious concern for the policy framework for rural sanitation, similar degree of interest has not been shown in the case of places where a large number of people gather for different purposes such as shopping, work, cultural events, and religious festivals. The policy framework for rural sanitation needs to internalize the fact that human beings move to different places for various purposes, possibly on a daily basis, and their right to sanitation must be respected in all places, not just in their homes.

The Exclusion of the Poor and the Marginalized from the Toilet Map

The focus on household toilets is also problematic from the point of view of the realization of the right to sanitation of the poor and the marginalized. First, the category 'household' has been taken as a single entity, and it overlooks the fact that there could be individuals within a household with different sanitation requirements. Second, the focus on 'households' systematically excludes the homeless or people living in buildings that are not technically considered as houses, for instance, labour camps or the so-called unauthorized dwellings on government land.

The universal design promoted by various rural sanitation programmes does not take into account the sanitation requirements of certain vulnerable groups of people, for instance, the differently abled or the elderly. For example, according to Census 2011, the state of UP houses the highest number of differently abled people (4,157,514), and a majority of them (31,66,615) live in rural areas. Even though the state of UP has recently started implementing sanitation interventions in rural areas, sanitation requirements of differently abled people have not yet been a focus. Sanitation interventions are, in fact, an opportunity for the government to fulfil its legal duty to ensure barrier-free access for differently abled people.[27] Implementing agencies are yet to understand the potential of linking sanitation interventions and legal duties of the state, for instance, the duties prescribed under the law on the rights of differently abled people.[28]

Migrant labourers constitute another vulnerable group from a rural sanitation point of view. While migration is a serious issue in urban areas, it is also relevant in the rural context, particularly in a state like Kerala where the urban–rural divide is not so significant in terms of employment opportunities. Migrant labourers are generally provided common accommodation covered with tin or plastic sheets with limited facilities. On the sanitation front, on an average, 3–5 toilets are available for 80–120 individuals.[29] It is also possible that their dwellings are not included in the list of 'households' to be served by sanitation interventions. For instance, a Block Development Officer in Kannur District of the state of Kerala admitted that migrant workers do not have adequate sanitation facilities, and yet the effort of the government has been to make them aware of the benefits of sanitation rather than providing the necessary facilities. This shows the insensitivity of the government to the rights of the migrant labourers including their right to sanitation. It also highlights the

[27] The Rights of Persons with Disabilities Act, 2016, s 40; The Rights of Persons with Disabilities Rules, 2017, rule 15.

[28] The Rights of Persons with Disabilities Act, s 40 and Rights of Persons with Disabilities Rules, rule 15.

[29] D. Narayana and C.S. Venkiteswaran, 'Domestic Migrant Labour in Kerala', A study conducted by the Gulati Institute of Finance and Taxation, submitted to Labour and Rehabilitation Department, Government of Kerala, 2013.

lack of interest in enforcing the relevant laws that protect the rights, including the right to sanitation, of workers in general, and migrant workers in particular.[30]

People belonging to the Scheduled Castes (SCs) and Scheduled Tribes (STs) are the other section of society generally missing from the toilet map. This is clear from the fact that basic sanitation facilities are inadequate or non-existent in areas predominantly inhabited by people belonging to the SCs and STs. In some cases, sanitation interventions do not reach places where people of SC and ST communities live. For instance, in Churu District of Rajasthan and Chitrakoot District of UP, some members of the SC communities stated that they had not received any financial assistance allotted under the policy framework.

A comparatively progressive state like Kerala in terms of its achievements in toilet coverage is not an exception when it comes to treating the people of the SC and ST communities. Basic sanitation facilities are inadequate in areas where predominantly SC and ST communities live.[31] The local level implementing agencies in Wayanad District cite the resistance of, for instance, the tribal people, to construct and use toilets as a major reason for the lack of basic sanitation facilities in tribal areas. Implementing agencies also cite language as a barrier to engage with the tribal population. The habit of the people and the language may be serious challenges, but these cannot be excuses for not taking or delaying initiatives. In fact, the challenges indicate the need for more attention to areas where people belonging to SC and ST communities live.

Women constitute another category whose sanitation needs and concerns have been undermined. This is partly due to the focus on building toilets without due regard to the question whether the

---

[30] For example, The Factories Act, 1948, s 19; The Building and Other Construction Workers (Regulation of Employment and Conditions of Service) Act, 1996, s 33; The Inter-State Migrant Workmen (Regulation of Employment and Conditions of Service) Act, 1979, s 16(d).

[31] Personal interview with Prof (Dr) Gangadharan, Kannur University, Kerala on 21 August 2015; fieldwork conducted in Wayanad District from 9 to 12 September 2014, a District in Kerala where the tribal population is significant.

toilets built are contributing to the realization of the right to sanitation of everyone. The gender-related issues in the context of the right to sanitation are discussed in detail elsewhere in this volume, and therefore this part stops at briefly highlighting the issue.[32]

Women have specific sanitation needs, for instance, menstrual hygiene management (MHM). They are arguably prone to several sanitation-related vulnerabilities, for instance, gender-based violence in the context of open defecation. However, the specific challenges faced by women have not yet been addressed in the implementation of sanitation interventions in rural areas. Issues such as MHM have progressively received the policymakers' attention.[33] However, it is yet to make a difference in terms of realization of the right to sanitation for women and girls in rural areas.

While the sanitation needs of women have not received adequate attention, the implementing agencies in rural areas have been using 'dignity' and 'prestige' of women to promote the construction of toilets. Thus, implementing agencies in Rajasthan and UP have been using gender stereotyped messages addressing men to invoke their male prestige to build toilets to protect the dignity of women. The principle of gender equality requires differential treatment for women and a special attention to their vulnerabilities caused by social and cultural practices. It appears that the implementation of sanitation interventions in rural areas has not respected this principle and, at the same time, it has violated the principle through action as well as inaction. In addition to being regressive from a gender equality point of view, this probably led to a situation where women use toilets wherever available, but men generally do not.

It is clear from the previous discussion that the race to achieve ODF status focuses only on the existence of at least one toilet in a house and it does not probe whether existing toilets are accessible to

---

[32] See Koonan and Bhullar (Chapter 13) in this volume.

[33] Menstrual Hygiene Management: National Guidelines, 2015. See also Scheme for Management of Menstrual Hygiene among Adolescent Girls in Rural India, Ministry of Health and Family Welfare, D.O. No. M/12015/103/2010-MCH, 4 March 2016; available at http://www.nhm.gov.in/images/pdf/programmes/mhs/Guidelines/Revised_Guidelines_for_Menstrual_Hygiene_Scheme.pdf.

everyone. Sanitation needs of the vulnerable and the marginalized are hardly taken into consideration. The exclusion of the marginalized and the vulnerable sections of society may be justifiable from a mission's point of view because it allows the achievement of targets in a phased manner. However, it cannot be justified from a human rights point of view because human rights law requires special attention on a priority basis to the needs of the most underprivileged. These concerns have not yet become influencing factors at the level of implementation in rural areas.

Some of the concerns mentioned earlier have been explicitly recognized as issues and challenges to be addressed. The latest version of the SBM-G Guidelines (as modified in October 2017), for instance, explicitly provides that 'toilets should be provided to be [*sic*] people staying on encroached lands under SBM(G), the same will be delinked from any form of tenure'.[34] Similarly, the issue of the use of gender stereotype messages by implementing agencies has been taken note of, and it provides that 'the SBM(G) messaging should ensure that it does not propagate, even inadvertently, any such gender bias'.[35] While these are indeed progressive steps and welcome responses, it is yet be seen how and to what extent these steps and responses influence implementing agencies at the local level, which often resort to 'construction overdrive' to achieve targets within a prescribed time limit.[36]

School Sanitation: The Gap between Statistics and the Ground Reality

School sanitation is an important component of the policy framework for rural sanitation. It was addressed under the general policy framework for rural sanitation (for example, the NBA) until the adoption of the SBM in 2014. The SBM-G brought a change and transferred the responsibility of school sanitation and anganwadi sanitation to the Department of School Education & Literacy and the Department

---

[34]   SBM-G Guidelines (n 18), para 6.2.7.

[35]   SBM-G Guidelines (n 18), Annexure XI.

[36]   Rashmi Varma, 'Cleaning a Dirty Patch', *Down to Earth* (16–30 April 2018) 18, 20.

of Women and Child Development, respectively. Nevertheless, the government continues to be fully responsible for school and anganwadi sanitation. For example, school toilets are generally being constructed under the Sarva Shiksha Abhiyan, a flagship programme of the Central Government on universal elementary education.[37]

This may be seen as a reflection of a duty-oriented approach, and an initiative to fulfil the duties of the state deriving from Article 21A of the Constitution, the Right of Children to Free and Compulsory Education Act, 2009, and the directives of the Supreme Court.[38] This interpretation is possible because the Swachh Bharat Swachh Vidyalaya (Clean India: Clean Schools) document explicitly recognizes these legal instruments, and highlights the legal obligations deriving from them.[39]

The initiatives of the government in this regard seem to have led to the improvement of sanitation facilities in schools. Thus, an estimate shows that 97.52 per cent of schools have girls' toilets and 97.02 per cent of schools have boys' toilets.[40] This is impressive when compared to the achievements in the context of household toilets and public toilets.

However, the fieldwork conducted in three states reveals a different scenario. Toilets in several schools in rural Rajasthan and UP are unusable. School staff and representatives of local bodies cite the lack of money for maintenance and lack of water supply as the key reasons for not being able to maintain the toilets in schools. In places where toilets are in a usable condition, several of them are locked. Teachers and staff explain that they lock it because students do not clean it after use. However, according to some students, those toilets in good condition are meant for the exclusive use of teachers and staff. In

---

[37] See Government of India, *Sarva Siksha Abhiyan: Framework for Implementation* (Ministry of Human Resource and Development, 2011).

[38] *Environment and Consumer Protection Foundation* v *Delhi Administration* Writ Petition (Civil) No. 631 of 2004 (Supreme Court of India, 3 October 2012).

[39] Government of India, Swachh Bharat Swachh Vidyalaya—A National Mission (Ministry of Human Resources Development, 2014) 7.

[40] National University of Educational Planning and Administration, *School Education in India: Flash Statistics 2015–16* (Department of School Education and Literacy, Ministry of Human Resource Development, 2016).

addition to that, adequacy of sanitation facilities is also a concern. Even though there are clear norms regarding the facilities to be made available in all schools,[41] none of them seem to have followed the same. Adequacy of toilets is an issue even in Kerala, where several schools have functioning toilets.

There seems to be a significant contrast between official statistics and the actual situation. It also points to the issue that sometimes the numbers and figures are misleading as they only signify the existence of the infrastructure and not the sanitation outcome or the realization of the right to sanitation. The gap between school sanitation norms and the actual situation further reveals that the presence of norms does not guarantee the realization of the right as it requires positive actions from the government, for instance, in terms of investments in infrastructure including water supply and regular funding for maintenance.

'Promoting' Manual Scavenging and Caste-Based Sanitation Work

In India, the link between caste and sanitation is deep and exploitative. It works mainly in two ways. First, the caste system treats people belonging to the lower castes as 'pollutants', and therefore 'untouchables'. Thus, the idea of cleanliness is not limited to physical conditions, but is a social construct too. Second, the caste system allocates all menial jobs to lower castes. Dalits, lowest in the caste hierarchy, are thus the worst victims of the link between caste and sanitation in India. They constitute the overwhelming majority of the people involved in the practice of manual scavenging and sanitation work, such as sweeping and sewage cleaning.[42] The policy framework for rural sanitation has been myopic to caste-based sanitation work in India. On the one hand, the policy framework has neglected the link, and on the other, it has positively used the caste system to achieve sanitation goals.

----

[41] Swachh Bharat Swachh Vidyalaya (n 39), 27.

[42] See Sakthivel, Nirmalkumar, and Benjamin (Chapter 12) in this volume.

The neglect of the link between caste and sanitation at the implementation level is evident from the fact that dry latrines and the related practice of manual scavenging have not been a major focus of sanitation interventions in rural areas. Considering the fact that manual scavenging is a serious issue in rural areas and the practice has been legally prohibited under the constitution and different statutes,[43] its elimination should have been an important goal of sanitation interventions in these areas. Sanitation interventions should have been implemented, on a priority basis, in places where the practice of manual scavenging persisted. For instance, a vast majority of the total number of dry latrines and manual scavengers in the country are reportedly in the state of UP.[44] This fact should have ideally driven the state government to implement sanitation interventions. Nevertheless, there was no serious effort to implement such interventions in rural areas until a couple of years ago. The presence of toilets may not per se address the root causes of manual scavenging. However, it could at least eliminate the visible physical conditions (for example, dry latrines) that make it possible or necessitate the practice of manual scavenging. The sanitation interventions could have thus contributed significantly to the implementation of the legal framework in this regard.

While the issue of manual scavenging has not been a key factor influencing the implementation of sanitation interventions in rural areas, the way in which sanitation interventions are being carried out at the local level is likely to entrench the practice of manual scavenging. For instance, the agencies implementing sanitation interventions almost exclusively focus on building toilets without providing any

[43] See chapters by Wilson (Chapter 10) and Khanna (Chapter 11) in this volume.

[44] According to an estimate, as many as 82 per cent of the 12,226 manual scavengers identified across India are in the state of UP. See Government of India, Ministry of Social Justice and Empowerment, Rajya Sabha, Unstarred Question No. 1402; available at http://164.100.47.234/question/annex/239/Au1402.pdf. See also Suresh Ediga, 'Manual Scavenging in India: 86% of All the Manual Scavengers in the Country are in Uttar Pradesh' (10 May 2015); available at https://factly.in/manual-scavenging-in-india-8-pc-manual-scavengers-are-in-uttar-pradesh/.

mechanism for the treatment and disposal of septage. This scenario may lead to manual emptying of millions of pits and septic tanks that are being built across the country, most probably by Dalits. Thus, the implementation of sanitation interventions is likely to 'promote' manual scavenging, instead of contributing to its eradication.

Further, implementing agencies 'use' the system of allocation of sanitation work on the basis of caste to achieve sanitation goals. This is evident from the fact that local bodies still employ Dalits to clean villages. Fieldwork in Rajasthan and UP reveals that upper-caste people and local bodies follow the perception that Dalits are sup-posed to carry out sanitation work. The caste-based allocation is to the extent that some village authorities in Rajasthan stated that they bring Dalits even from far-away places to clean public places such as markets and streets. Experience from UP further reveals the strong link between sanitation work and caste. In UP, there is a permanent sweeper post in all panchayats. Given the fact that it is a perma-nent government job, people from all castes have joined. However, invariably the higher-caste people refuse to undertake the work, and instead they pay a paltry sum to Dalits to do their job.[45] In some cases, the caste-oriented social system has even gone to the extent of forcing Dalit students to clean toilets at schools.[46]

The response of the policy framework for rural sanitation to the issue of the caste–sanitation link is problematic both from the point of view of its action and inaction. Although manual scavenging is a very important issue in rural areas, the implementing agencies have by and large neglected it. At the same time, implementing agencies have used the caste system to achieve sanitation goals, and thereby reinforced the historical link between sanitation and caste, which the anti-caste movements in India have been fighting against.[47]

---

[45] See also Tulika Tripathi, 'Safai Karmi Scheme of Uttar Pradesh: Caste Dominance Continues' (2012) XLVII(37) *Economic & Political Weekly* 26.

[46] P. Sudhakar, 'Teachers Held for Forcing Dalit Students to Clean Toilets', *The Hindu* (24 April 2015); available at www.thehindu.com/news/national/tamil-nadu/teachers-held-for-forcing-dalit-students-to-clean-toilets/article7136306.ece.

[47] For instance, the manual scavenging community has been fighting for eradication of manual scavenging for the last couple of decades. See Wilson (Chapter 10) in this volume.

By keeping the issue outside of its purview,[48] the policy framework for rural sanitation has missed an opportunity to give effect to the legal prohibition of manual scavenging and untouchability, as well as to contribute to the anti-manual scavenging movement led by the manual scavenging community in the last couple of decades.

Undermining Environmental Dimensions

The policy framework for rural sanitation follows, in principle, a broad definition of sanitation, which includes environmental dimensions among other things.[49] The inclusion of solid and liquid waste management, for instance, demonstrates the fact that environmental dimensions are addressed in the framework. However, this part is hardly implemented at the ground level. All other aspects of sanitation except toilets are regarded as secondary at the implementation level. This is, for instance, evident from the fact that hardly any mechanism exists in rural areas to manage solid and liquid waste. A common practice in rural areas in Rajasthan and UP is to let the wastewater flow to a nearby pond. Implementing agencies have not yet started addressing these issues. Similarly, lack of facilities to dispose safely used sanitary napkins and diapers leads to burying or burning them, which exemplifies the issue of environmental pollution due to lack of sanitation interventions.

While lack of sanitation is a source of environmental pollution in rural areas, various sanitation interventions also cause environmental pollution. One of the major issues in this regard is the tendency among people to dig deep unlined pits for their toilets to avoid the situation of emptying it frequently. Although implementing agencies are aware of the risk of water pollution due to such pits and septic tanks, they generally ignore the issue mainly because their major concern is to get the toilets constructed, and

[48] It is to be noted that the latest version of the SBM-G Guidelines underlines the duty of state governments to 'ensure complete survey of GPs [gram panchayats] on priority for presence of any insanitary toilets'. See SBM-G Guidelines (n 18), para 6.4.14.

[49] See Nirmal Bharat Abhiyan Guidelines, 2012, para 1(2).

not the long-term public health and environmental outcomes of sanitation interventions.

The undermining of environmental dimensions is also evident when sanitation interventions promote toilet construction, but at the same time, little focus is directed towards septage management. The septage crisis has already emerged in urban areas, and a policy instrument has been framed.[50] Given the speed at which toilets are being constructed in rural areas, septage management is going to be a serious sanitation issue in rural areas too, in the near future.[51] However, efforts to address the issue have not yet commenced. Environmental dimensions of sanitation have not yet become as important as the objective of elimination of open defecation. The neglect of the environmental dimensions of the right to sanitation may lead to the non-realization of not only the right to sanitation, but also other human rights, most importantly, the rights to water and environment.[52]

The Focus on 'Demand' and 'Incentives': Implications for Rights and Duties

Sanitation interventions in rural areas follow a demand-oriented approach. It focuses on employing different methods to create 'demand' so that the 'targets' or 'goals' can be achieved within the time frame prescribed under the policy framework. The focus on demand and incentives led to the absence of the language of rights and duties both at the policy and implementation levels. This part of the chapter analyses the basic approach of sanitation interventions in rural areas, and the ways in which they have been implemented, with a special emphasis on the right to sanitation.

[50] Ministry of Urban Development, National Urban Faecal Sludge & Septage Management (FSSM) Policy, 2017.

[51] One of the septage controversies in Kerala led to litigation before the High Court. See *R Sudha* v *Union of India and Others*, WP(C) No. 34496/2009 (High Court of Kerala, Order dated 10 March 2011).

[52] For details on environmental dimensions of the right to sanitation, see Bhullar (Chapter 9) in this volume.

Shifting of Responsibility from Government to Individuals

The policy framework for rural sanitation has been following a demand-oriented approach since the adoption of the TSC in 1999.[53] The role of the state has undergone significant transformation with this new approach when compared to the previous, supply-oriented, approach. Under the supply oriented approach, the state was expected to play a crucial role including in the provisioning of sanitation. However, the policy framework based on the demand-oriented approach led to the shifting of the responsibility of provisioning, particularly the provisioning of basic sanitation facilities such as toilets, to individuals. This is in sharp contrast with the basic principle of human rights law that entrusts the primary responsibility to the state.[54]

The changing role of the state as promoted by the policy framework has also influenced and shaped the understanding of sanitation (and, therefore, the right to sanitation) by implementing agencies at the state level and at the local level. Implementing agencies, by and large, believe their main role to be that of a facilitator, for instance, to encourage people to build and use toilets. Thus, the presumed ignorance of the people has been regarded as a major challenge to be addressed by the policy framework. A number of officials stated during the fieldwork that a major problem is the ignorance of the people. While implementing agencies in rural Rajasthan and rural UP mentioned the 'ignorance' of the rural population in general, implementing agencies in Kerala highlighted the 'ignorance' of certain groups, such as tribals and people living in coastal areas, as a key challenge.

These perceptions and strategies of awareness-creation programmes are not completely designed by implementing agencies at the local or state level. The role of international agencies in this regard is not insignificant. For instance, the World Bank and the Water Supply and Sanitation Collaborative Council of the United Nations play important and influential roles in the sanitation sector in Rajasthan

---

[53] Total Sanitation Campaign Guidelines, 2011, 1.4.

[54] UN Human Rights Council Resolution 18/1, 'The Human Right to Safe Drinking Water and Sanitation', 12 October 2011, UN Doc. A/HRC/18/1, para 5.

and UP, for instance, by giving training to government officials and non-governmental organizations (NGOs).

The awareness-creation programme per se is not problematic as it may be beneficial to enhance the awareness of people about the health and environmental outcomes of sanitation. However, this cannot be the key or primary strategy. Further, the strategy as it is being implemented is problematic because the underlying objective is apparently to shift the responsibility to individuals and to reduce the role of the state to that of a facilitator. This shift also indicates the transformation of the nature of human rights along the lines of a neoliberal logic wherein human rights are depicted as the responsibility of individuals, and they are expected to be realized through the medium of the market.[55]

Individuals as 'Targets' and Not as 'Right-Holders' and 'Participants'

The focus on demand generation and incentives treats people as 'targets' to be triggered, and in some cases, to be forced. This is essentially a top–down model that presumes the ignorance of the people. This approach is in sharp contrast with the rights-based approach. The role of the people in a framework based on human rights is that of a 'right-holder' with agency and autonomy. A right-holder is entitled to participate in the process towards the realization of the right. The participation in this regard could be through the elected representatives of the people or through democratic forums such as the *gram sabha*.[56] Participation of the people at both these levels is generally missing insofar as the implementation of the right to sanitation in rural areas is concerned.

[55] Paul O'Connell, 'The Death of Socio-economic Rights' (2011) 74(4) *Modern Law Review* 532; Joe Wills, 'The World Turned Upside Down? Neoliberalism, Socioeconomic Rights, and Hegemony' (2014) 27(1) *Leiden Journal of International Law* 11.

[56] A gram sabha is a body consisting of all persons eligible to cast their vote in a village. There could be a gram sabha for a village or for more than one village. For a legal definition, see for example, The Uttar Pradesh Panchayat Raj Act, 1947, s 2(g).

The implementation of sanitation interventions in rural areas reveals how the demand-oriented approach affects the procedural aspects of the right to sanitation, most importantly, the right to participate. Implementation of sanitation interventions in rural areas has generally been a government-driven programme without any meaningful participation of the right-holders. The lack of opportunity to participate may affect the poor and the marginalized disproportionately. For instance, women are not generally consulted while taking decisions, both at the panchayat level and at the household level. This may lead to decisions that do not take into consideration women's needs and concerns. For instance, the location of toilets is generally decided by men or the panchayat officials or the contractor appointed by the *pradhan* (village panchayat president). Thus, the decisions in many cases do not take into consideration whether it is convenient for women to access the toilet all the time. For instance, women may not prefer a toilet in the front part of the house, a place generally occupied by men.[57] Similarly, concerns and needs of the poor and lower-caste people may also be undermined due to the lack of opportunity to participate. This is generally confirmed from the fieldwork in Rajasthan and UP where many Dalit families were even unaware of the policy framework and the financial assistance they are entitled to.

The institution of the gram sabha is in principle, an opportunity for right-holders to participate in the process of governance, including in the decision-making process in the context of the implementation of the policy framework for rural sanitation. However, such meetings hardly take place in practice. The government officials generally claimed, during the fieldwork, that meetings at the panchayat level are conducted frequently, where every aspect of various social programmes including sanitation interventions is discussed. However, villagers in Rajasthan stated that such meetings hardly take place, and in most cases, the pradhan decides everything related to the implementation of all programmes including sanitation interventions. In reality, the

---

[57] See also Kathleen O'Reilly, 'Combining Sanitation and Women's Participation in Water Supply: An Example from Rajasthan' (2010) 20(1) *Development in Practice* 45.

caste and class factors seem to be deciding the power relations at the local level, and the right to participation is difficult to be realized for the poor and the marginalized.

Rights essentially involve the choices of right-holders. Any framework related to a right must respect the elements of choice and agency of right-holders. A right must not be imposed on right-holders, as the policy framework for rural sanitation is currently doing.

Shaming, Intimidating, and Penalizing the People: The Lack of Rights Consciousness

In addition to incentives and awareness-creation programmes, implementing agencies at the local level also use strategies of shaming and of forcing people to generate the 'demand'. This includes imposing fines on individuals for defecating in the open. For instance, in rural Rajasthan, the fine varies from place to place ranging from Rs 50 to 500. The imposition of fines is not really meant to be enforced in actual practice, but, as some officials in Rajasthan openly admitted, such a system is meant to have only a deterrent effect. The imposition of fines for open defecation was also an officially recognized policy as it was one of the mandatory conditions to be eligible to receive the NGP.[58]

The strategy of threat sometimes goes to the extent of denying or threatening to deny people's entitlements. For instance, a representative of a local body in rural Rajasthan supported the idea of blocking or denying entitlements related to the public distribution system or rural employment schemes. In some cases, the strategy went to the extent of threatening people with arrest and imprisonment for defecating in the open or for failing to construct toilets in their homes.[59] This shows that implementing agencies are willing to employ any strategy to achieve ODF status regardless of its implications for the rights of the people.

---

[58]   Nirmal Gram Puraskar Guidelines, 2012, para 3.

[59]   For instance, Arvind Chauhan, 'Jail Term for People Caught Defecating in Open' *The Times of India* (8 April 2016); available at http:// timesofindia.indiatimes.com/city/agra/Jail-term-for-people-caught-defecating-in-open/articleshow/51748088.cms.

Shaming is another strategy implementing agencies apply at the local level to achieve sanitation goals. For instance, the nigrani committees (monitoring committees) at the local level use the shaming strategy to prevent people from open defecation. Members of nigrani committees in various places stated that one of their strategies is to be physically present in or near the places used by people for open defecation or on the way to such places to prevent them doing so. In some cases, they blow whistles when they spot any incident of open defecation. The act of spotting people and blowing whistles may particularly be embarrassing for women in a context when men are predominantly members of the nigrani committees.

Some of the shaming and threatening narrations specifically target women, and are therefore of relevance from a gender perspective. For instance, in rural Rajasthan, implementing agencies tell women to be careful while defecating in the open as their privacy could be infringed by satellites. In some other cases, they remind women of the risks of sexual violence while resorting to open defecation. For instance, implementing agencies in UP stated that they show cuttings from newspapers reporting sexual harassment or rape of women in the context of open defecation.[60]

The strategy of shaming and intimidation is not limited to individuals. It also works at the institutional level. Institutions at the lower level are pressurized by the institutions above them. For instance, the District-level implementing agencies are pressurized by the state-level and national-level agencies. The pressure in this context is to achieve ODF status as early as possible. Village-level officials and office bearers of the gram panchayats are also pressurized. For instance, office bearers of a gram panchayat in Bikaner District of Rajasthan stated that differential seating arrangements on the basis of sanitation achievements are followed in some of the meetings in the office of the District collector. According to them, they have accelerated the construction of toilets to get rid of the shame of differential

---

[60] For a similar critique of the implementation of sanitation programmes in Madhya Pradesh, see M. Poornima, 'No "Maryada" for Women in MP Government's Sanitation Drive', *Hindustan Times* (24 December 2013); available at www.hindustantimes.com/india/no-maryada-for-women-in-mp-govt-s-sanitation-drive/story-SExznZ6YDuy6kzM1bhpwfN.html.

seating. This probably explains why implementing agencies are willing to apply the strategy of shaming, intimidation, and penalization to promote the construction of toilets.

The shaming and intimidation strategies expose the folly of the demand-oriented approach that is built upon the premise that people are generally willing and capable to take initiatives and they just need to be triggered. It appears that this premise does not capture the reality well. This probably explains the pressure tactics applied at the implementation level to achieve the goal. Further, shaming and intimidation strategies are fundamentally incompatible with the idea of human rights. In a context when the pressure element has moved even to the extent of denying various entitlements to the people, there is a need for the policy framework for rural sanitation to imbibe rights consciousness. An understanding that the realization of one right must not lead to the violation of another right or group of rights is also essential in order for the framework for rural sanitation to be a framework based on human rights.

The Missing Element of Sustainability

Lack of focus on sustainability is another major critique of the strategy of creation of demand and incentives. The incentive mechanism focuses mainly on the construction of toilets, not on its use or its contribution to the realization of the right to sanitation. The incapacity of the implementing agencies at the local level to monitor the sustainability is a serious issue in this regard, and the policy framework has not paid adequate attention to this issue. Thus, in UP, while a motivator gets Rs 75 for getting a household toilet constructed, there is hardly any system to monitor the actual use of toilets. Implementing agencies at the local level have also complained about inadequate money available for monitoring the sustainability of the sanitation infrastructure. The fact that a large number of toilets in rural Rajasthan and rural UP remain unusable or unused indicates limited or no impact of the incentive mechanism on the actual use of toilets, and thereby its contribution to the realization of the right to sanitation.

The experience of the NGP further illustrates the issue of lack of focus of the incentive mechanism on sustainability. The NGP was introduced as a mechanism of collective incentive for rural local bodies that achieve

ODF status.[61] The idea was to appreciate the concerned rural local bodies, and to encourage other rural local bodies to achieve the same. The NGP also focused on the construction aspect. This is clear from the fact that, in all three states where fieldwork was conducted, open defecation is practiced even in villages that had received the NGP.[62] For instance, in an NGP village in the Ernakulam District of Kerala, a few houses are using hanging toilets, which is just a structure to squat and the excreta is directly disposed into a canal. The failure of the NGP from a sustainability point of view is probably one reason why it was withdrawn in 2015,[63] and the new guidelines on the verification of ODF status focus on the sustainability element as well.[64]

The lack of focus on sustainability reflects the limited infra-structure focus of sanitation interventions in rural areas in India. It appears that the implementing agencies are focusing on 'building' sanitation infrastructure (in this case, toilets) and presume its use and the consequent public health and environmental outcomes. The experience from the field shows that the focus on infrastructure contributes in many cases only to the statistics and not to the realization of the right to sanitation.

* * *

An assessment of the implementation of sanitation interventions in rural areas shows that it has contributed very little to the realization of the right to sanitation. The only major contribution has been the promotion of toilets at the household level. This may be an important step as toilets and the underlying objective of elimination of open defecation are a vital element of the right to sanitation. However, the

---

[61] Nirmal Gram Puraskar Guidelines, 2012.

[62] See also Andrés Hueso and Brian Bell, 'An Untold Story of Policy Failure: The Total Sanitation Campaign in India' (2013) 6(15) *Water Policy* 1001.

[63] Discontinuation of Nirmal Gram Puraskar (NGP) Scheme, Ministry of Drinking Water and Sanitation, Doc No. S-11011/7/2015-SBM, 6 November 2015.

[64] Open Defecation Free (ODF) Sustainability Guidelines, Ministry of Drinking Water and Sanitation, Notification No. S11011/3/2015-SBM (Pt.1), 15 December 2016.

way in which sanitation interventions have promoted the element of toilets is far from satisfactory from a right to sanitation perspective.

On the one hand, sanitation interventions focus on getting toilets constructed and do not focus adequately on the actual use of toilets. As a result, a huge number of toilets constructed as part of the implementation of the policy framework remain unused or used for other purposes. On the other hand, the overwhelming focus on toilets at the household level has led to the undermining of a number of other key aspects of the right to sanitation. This includes the undermining of basic sanitation facilities in places other than individual houses such as public places and schools; the neglect of sanitation needs and concerns of some of the marginalized and vulnerable sections of society such as Dalits, women, and migrant labourers; passive and active promotion of caste-based allocation of sanitation work; and, last but not least, overlooking of the environmental dimensions of the right to sanitation. Thus, sanitation interventions in rural areas have been far from contributing to the realization of the right to sanitation.

The strategies adopted by sanitation interventions to promote toilet construction are also problematic from a right to sanitation perspective. The demand-oriented approach as followed by the policy framework marks a drastic deviation from the human–rights-based approach. Most importantly, the policy framework seeks to minimize the responsibility of the government, and shift the responsibility of provisioning of basic sanitation facilities to individuals. Further, the policy framework treats individuals as 'beneficiaries' of various sanitation interventions and not as right-holders in the context of the fundamental right to sanitation as recognized under the Constitution of India. Also, the demand-oriented approach and the related hurry to declare villages ODF have led implementing agencies to use strategies of threat and intimidation with severe implications for the human rights of individuals.

Overall, the implementation of sanitation interventions in rural areas has very little impact on the realization of the right to sanitation. On the one hand, the implementation of sanitation interventions has not been informed and influenced by the idea of the right to sanitation. On the other hand, various actions and inactions of implementing agencies have violated basic human rights of individuals including the right to sanitation.

6

Community-Led Total Sanitation and Its Potential to Realize the Right to Sanitation

Lyla Mehta

Out of the 2.5 billion people who lack access to improved sanitation around the world, 1.2 billion defecate in the open.[1] Poor sanitation and open defecation represent a silent epidemic leading to the death of some 1.5 million children annually, due to diarrhoea and other parasitic diseases.[2] Furthermore, open defecation has also been linked to issues concerning social and economic inequality and marginalization[3]—captured powerfully through the term 'second-class

---

[1] WHO/UNICEF Joint Monitoring Programme, *Progress on Drinking Water and Sanitation: 2014 Update* (WHO/UNICEF, 2014).

[2] WHO/UNICEF Joint Monitoring Programme (n 2).

[3] Sarah Jewitt, 'Geographies of Shit: Spatial and Temporal Variations in Attitudes towards Human Waste' (2011) 35(5) *Progress in Human Geography* 608.

shitizens'.[4] India leads the world in open defecation with about 60 crore people defecating in the open every day, either because they lack access to toilets or because they choose not to use toilets.[5]

In recent years, innovations such as community-led total sanitation (CLTS) have attracted significant attention as a way to address the global crisis of open defecation and poor sanitation. CLTS has led to thousands of low-cost toilets springing up all over rural areas of South Asia, Southeast Asia, Africa, and beyond. Usually built by villagers and barefoot innovators out of local materials such as bamboo, tin, and jute, the resulting 'open defecation free' (ODF) villages have often led to a noticeable increased sense of pride about toilet possession, and self-confidence about newly gained dignity, health benefits, and freedom from embarrassment, which was caused due to the lack of privacy, especially for women.[6]

CLTS differs from earlier approaches to sanitation, which prescribed high standards regarding toilets in order to reduce the costs of operation and maintenance (O&M).[7] Earlier approaches also involved upfront hardware subsidies in order to induce people to use the latrines or toilets.[8] However, the toilets were often not

---

[4] Art Cohen, 'Calling for an End to Second-Class Shitizenship' (2010) 42(2) *Review of Radical Political Economics* 269.

[5] Santosh Mehrotra, 'Swachh Bharat will Fail unless the Modi Government Totally Redesigns UPA's Sanitation Programme', *The Times of India* (6 October 2014); available at http://blogs.timesofindia.indiatimes.com/toi-edit-page/swachh-bharat-will-fail-unless-the-modi-government-totally-redesigns-upas-sanitation-programme.

[6] Lyla Mehta and Synne Movik (eds), *Shit Matters: The Potential of Community-Led Total Sanitation* (Practical Action Publishing, 2011).

[7] It must be noted that CLTS largely deals with the disposal of human waste and is now increasingly accompanied by hygiene programmes. It does not necessarily deal with the whole range of issues, for instance, solid waste management, though in some cases CLTS may be accompanied by solid waste management.

[8] This chapter uses the term 'toilet' instead of 'latrine' for low-cost and simple toilets built by local people. It also uses the term 'shit' in accordance with the current trend in sanitation to break the silence and taboo around sanitation and defecation.

used or they were used for other purposes such as storage. There were also problems of affordability. CLTS refrains from advocating toilet construction for individual households. Instead, the whole community is targeted with the aim of creation of ODF villages and communities. The core assumption is that even partial sanitation does not lead to minimizing the adverse effects of open defecation.[9]

CLTS is based on the principle that communities should be motivated to undertake an analysis of their defecation situation, and to resolve to stop open defecation by building and using toilets without the support of major external hardware subsidies. This then leads to intense local community action, and clean and shit-free villages. The rapid spread of CLTS within countries, across regions and continents has the makings of a development success story. This is because CLTS has contributed significantly towards meeting a host of Millennium Development Goals (MDGs), such as the one on water and sanitation (goal 7), and also through the knock-on impacts of improved sanitation on combating major diseases, particularly diarrhoea (goal 6); improving maternal health (goal 5); and reducing child mortality (goal 4). It also has a key role to play in the recently declared Agenda 2030 and the Sustainable Development Goals (SDGs).

This chapter tracks the origins of CLTS, and highlights its key tenets. It discusses how CLTS spread from Bangladesh to India, and the gaps between rhetoric and practice on the ground. The chapter then discusses India's CLTS story and its key challenges, before discussing its implications for the right to sanitation.

[9] The author is aware that this is a contested issue both on epidemiological and practical grounds. Epidemiologically, the links between improved sanitation and enhanced health outcomes, while recognized, are difficult to prove. It is now acknowledged that there are multiple factors such as poverty reduction, access to water, good nutrition, handwashing, and so on (along with improved sanitation) that lead to disease reduction. Practically, it is often impossible to define what constitutes an ODF community due to porous boundaries between communities and villages. It is, however, beyond the scope of this chapter to handle these issues further.

Community-Led Total Sanitation: Origins, Approach, and Spread

The charismatic Dr Kamal Kar, a development consultant from India, pioneered CLTS together with the Village Education Resource Centre (VERC), a partner of WaterAid Bangladesh, while evaluating a traditionally subsidized sanitation programme in Mosmoil, a village in the Rajshahi District of Bangladesh, in 2000. Dr Kar, who has years of experience in participatory approaches in a range of development projects, was successful in persuading the local non-governmental organization (NGO) to stop top-down toilet construction through upfront subsidy. He advocated change in institutional attitudes and the need to draw on intense local mobilization and facilitation to enable villagers to analyse their sanitation and waste situation and to bring about collective decision-making to stop open defecation.[10]

CLTS is based on the belief that in the past, many sanitation projects were unsuccessful because they assumed that the provision of subsidized toilets would result in improved sanitation and hygiene. It is now well known that merely building toilets does not guarantee their use. Instead, it is also important to focus on the behavioural issues at stake, as well as traditional cultural habits and practices. Earlier, more conventional approaches to sanitation prescribed high initial standards in order to reduce the costs of O&M later, and they involved hardware subsidies as an incentive for adoption of toilets. However, this often led to uneven adoption, problems with long-term sustainability, only partial use of facilities or their use for other purposes such as for storage or as animal shelters. As a result, open defecation, and with it the cycle of faecal–oral contamination continued, with negative impacts on human well-being.[11]

---

[10] For more details, see Kamal Kar, *Practical Guide to Triggering Community-Led Total Sanitation (CLTS)* (Institute of Development Studies, 2005); Kamal Kar and Katherine Pasteur, *Subsidy or Self-Respect? Community-Led Total Sanitation: An Update on Recent Developments* (Institute of Development Studies, Working Paper 257, 2005); Mehta and Movik (n 6); Kamal Kar and Robert Chambers, *Handbook on Community-Led Total Sanitation* (Plan UK, 2008).

[11] Kar (n 10); Kar and Pasteur (n 10).

The underlying assumption of CLTS is that once people are convinced about the need for sanitation, they will construct their own toilets according to the available resources. While authorities are discouraged from providing upfront subsidies to construct toilets, financial and institutional support is required for facilitation, monitoring, evaluation, and mobilization, and subsidies can be provided indirectly in the form of rewards and incentives. Thus, while it is often assumed that CLTS is a low- or no-cost enterprise, in effect, funding is required to ensure that CLTS is rolled out effectively, while ensuring quality. For instance, a recent study of 3,000 rural households in North India shows that people continue to defecate in the open even if they have access to a functioning toilet at home.[12] Many rural Indians (especially men) consider open defecation to be healthy and conducive to life in rural areas due to the exposure to fresh air, and find toilets close to the home to be polluting.

Thus, it is important to focus on the behavioural issues at stake as well as cultural habits and practices. Through the use of participatory methods, community members analyse their own sanitation profile, including the extent of open defecation, and the spread of faecal–oral contamination that detrimentally affects every one of them. This is believed to cause an upsurge of various emotions in the community, including the feeling of embarrassment and disgust. The community members are supposed to collectively realize the terrible impact of open defecation on their health. The realization that they are quite literally ingesting one another's "shit" mobilizes them into initiating collective local action to improve the sanitation situation in the community.[13]

The CLTS triggering process often starts with an informal talk with a few community members during a walk through the village (a 'transect walk'). The aim is to motivate people to carry out a more substantial sanitation analysis involving the whole community. There are many different ways of initiating a discussion on open defecation and village sanitation, for example, by visiting places where people

---

[12] Diane Coffey, 'Culture, Religion and Open Defecation in Rural North India' (19 August 2014); available at www.theigc.org/blog/culture-religion-and-open-defecation-in-rural-north-india.

[13] Kar (n 10); Kar and Pasteur (n 10).

defecate, and raising questions like: 'Whose shit is this?' 'Who defecated in the open this morning?', and so on. Throughout the facilitation process, local and crude words for 'shit' and 'shitting' are used rather than the polite terms often used when discussing these taboo subjects. Other methods include a transect walk as well as calculation of the shit produced in the village every day. The facilitator is not supposed to preach or tell people what to do. Ideally, a dialogue should ensue between the facilitator and the local people, and between different categories of villagers (rich/poor/women/men/different castes and ethnic groups). In most cases, an external facilitator, who of course may be a powerful and articulate person compared to the villagers, conducts this triggering. While the role of the community is central, CLTS does tend to draw on a rather idealized notion of community where it is assumed that all members, once convinced of CLTS, will unite together to achieve ODF status. This perspective may not pay adequate attention to intra-community dynamics such as class, caste, gender, and power relations. Also, the reality, particularly in multi-caste, highly differentiated Indian villages, can be far more complex.

Once the community and the individuals within it have started to take positive action against open defecation, the facilitators can aid the process by fuelling their enthusiasm, for example, by telling them that if they achieved 100 per cent total sanitation and stopped open defecation, many people from outside and neighbouring villages would come and visit their village, or their village would get a national award. In many countries, governments now provide incentives and rewards once the village becomes ODF, something this chapter will turn to later. Once a village has been successfully 'triggered', changes can take place quite rapidly, and can have a dramatic effect on individual and collective well-being. Whether the programme is sustainable in the long run is another matter.

Institutional Dynamics and the Politics of Scaling Up

While CLTS chimes well with debates on 'bottom-up' and grassroots/participatory approaches to development, clearly the state and various actors have played a key role in scaling it up. In many countries, the state is often needed for large-scale impacts and institutionalization.

Since its emergence in rural Bangladesh in early 2000, CLTS has spread remarkably fast across Asia and then subsequently to Africa, the Middle East, and Latin America. Its spread has been through both NGO and government processes, and its champions have been dynamic grassroots activists, state bureaucrats, and members from the NGO and donor communities. The Water and Sanitation Programme (WSP) initially played an important role in enabling its spread to neighbouring India, Indonesia, and parts of Africa, and UNICEF, arguably the largest player among the relevant aid agencies, also turned around its policies and practices in 2008 to support CLTS and similar community-based approaches to sanitation. Non-governmental organizations such as Plan and WaterAid have also played a crucial role. Today CLTS is being implemented in diverse ways in more than 60 countries, and has been officially adopted in the sanitation programmes of several countries around the world, especially in sub-Saharan Africa.[14] It must be noted though that CLTS is largely a rural movement except for a few scattered cases such as Kalyani and Nanded in India and Nairobi in Kenya.

The spread of CLTS in a little over a decade has been remarkable, and the result of several processes, individuals, and organizations. The charismatic presence of the pioneer Dr Kamal Kar, who has personally rolled out CLTS in most of the countries, is a key factor. Other key aspects include exposure visits between countries organized by the WSP and governments. These have served not only as learning opportunities, but have also convinced governments, NGOs and others to try CLTS, and provided the evidence that CLTS can work. The Department for International Development (DFID) played a key role in CLTS uptake and spread in South Asia, and UNICEF's contribution in its spread across Africa has been significant. International NGOs have also played an important role in sharing experiences with CLTS between their different regional and country programmes. Learning platforms, the CLTS website, and the

---

[14] Sophie Hickling and Jane Bevan, 'Scaling up CLTS in Sub-Saharan Africa', in *Participatory Learning and Action*, 61, 'Tales of Shit: Community-Led Total Sanitation in Africa' (IDS/Plan/IIED 2010), 51.

Kolkata-based CLTS Foundation[15] have also contributed in allowing for exchanges and learning across different contexts, organizations, and countries. Regional conferences on sanitation in Asia and Africa have served as platforms to launch CLTS, and have facilitated learning between donors, government officials, researchers, and practitioners.

Diversity versus Uniformity in Community-Led Total Sanitation

The pioneer of CLTS, Dr Kamal Kar, has put forward some non-negotiable principles of rural CLTS, for example, (1) no upfront subsidy for hardware; (2) no blueprint design, only people's design; (3) people first: they can do it; (4) facilitate, don't provide; and (5) go slow at first for faster later.[16] Universal principles also include that the community must lead the process, and that the entire community should be ODF. Still CLTS remains contextualized. Today, there remains a tremendous diversity in approaches around CLTS and the context varies a lot from country to country. There are also a range of interpretations around what is CLTS and what is not CLTS, with CLTS purists insisting that something that is executed in a top–down manner and that doles out subsidies for toilet construction at the outset cannot be considered to be CLTS. Many major agencies and government departments including in India say that they are engaged in CLTS, but CLTS proponents often dispute this. The major ideological battle is around the subsidy issue, especially in the Indian context, which has a very strong and entrenched subsidy regime to which this chapter will soon turn.

Myths and Reality of Community-Led Total Sanitation

There are questions surrounding the reality and practice of CLTS on the ground, for example, whether successes have led to the creation of myths about the extent to which the approach really generates

[15] See CLTS website, www.communityledtotalsanitation.org; CLTS Foundation website, www.cltsfoundation.org.
[16] Kamal Kar, 'Changing Behaviour: The Missing Link in Sanitation', (presentation from the World Water Week, Stockholm, 17–23 August 2008).

ODF communities. There are also questions regarding inclusion and attention to local-level poverty, and challenges regarding sustainability, monitoring, and evaluation.

Spread

CLTS has spread rapidly and differently around the world. It is most successful when champions are present at the village or state level, and when local facilitation and mobilization are of high quality and time-intensive, which is an indirect form of subsidization, since governments or NGOs need to invest in good facilitation and mobilization. Usually CLTS is successful in smaller and more homogenous communities that are cohesive, and when efforts are made to address the needs of the poor and the marginalized.[17] In the absence of these factors, CLTS may not take off. There are questions about how to best support champions and natural/spontaneous leaders, and what role NGOs and governments can play in supporting the spread of CLTS at the local level, without imposing constraints, turning it into a top–down process, or it being limited by the duration of NGO projects or government programmes.

Institutional Challenges

In large countries such as India and Indonesia[18] with state-driven sanitation programmes, the institutional context is key. Scaling up CLTS means that messages can be diluted and proper facilitation is compromised. To enable its spread, governments may introduce

[17] Lyla Mehta, 'Introduction: Why Shit Matters, Community-Led Total Sanitation and the Sanitation Challenge for the 21st Century', in Lyla Mehta and Synne Movik (eds), *Shit Matters: The Potential of Community-Led Total Sanitation* (Practical Action Publishing, 2011), 1.

[18] Nilanjana Mukherjee and Nina Shatifan, 'The CLTS Story in Indonesia: Empowering Communities, Transforming Institutions, Furthering Decentralization', in Lyla Mehta and Synne Movik (eds), *Shit Matters: The Potential of Community-Led Total Sanitation* (Practical Action Publishing, 2011), 145.

targets and a reward system, which could lead to a false sense of achievement (further discussed in the section on page 182). There is also often the pressure to disburse hardware subsidies, which may not lead to individual ownership of toilets. In Indonesia, Priyono has shown that when CLTS begins as something that is either donor- or NGO-driven, it is a challenge to transfer it into a regular government programme.[19] Donors or NGOs need to change their role from being an implementing agency to a supporting agency. This means champions within state agencies and institutions are necessary to promote CLTS.

It is important for CLTS to be located in an appropriate government institution. Often it is the Ministry of Health (for example, Indonesia, Ethiopia), but sanitation also needs buy in from other departments (for example, finance, water resources, public works, and so on). In the absence of buy in, sanitation will not be taken seriously and mainstreamed into development policies and programmes. This buy in could be in the form of developing a cadre of facilitators, developing campaigns around sanitation and CLTS, encouraging local governments to adopt CLTS, and so on.

The Poorest, Subsidies, and the Nature of Community

Despite examples that attest that CLTS can help to trigger solidarity, mutual help, and collective action, the question of what happens to the poorest households in a community is an important one. Whilst it is stated that the realization that everyone is ingesting each other's shit leads to inclusive collective action, the reality may often be different. Sanctions and fines as well as peer pressure to comply with the community's decision to be totally ODF could adversely affect the poorest, at least in the short term. This is because such measures can build on existing dynamics of marginality and disenfranchisement experienced by the extremely poor and marginalized groups in local communities.

---

[19] Edy Priyono, 'Institutional Dimensions of Scaling up CLTS in Indonesia', in Lyla Mehta and Synne Movik (eds), *Shit Matters: The Potential of Community-Led Total Sanitation* (Practical Action Publishing, 2011), 175.

CLTS is often criticized for pandering to neoliberal discourses that leave the state off the hook, or communitarian ones that glorify the ability of the community to fix their own problems and gloss over intra-community cleavages such as gender, caste, and so on. CLTS is also often considered to be 'anti-poor' by NGOs and many government officials because it is assumed that the rich will not be interested in cross-subsidizing the poor, and that the poor will invariably lose out. Based on my own research it can be said that while CLTS proponents are certainly not anti-poor, in some cases, marginalized people have been left out of CLTS programmes. This is because poverty has often prevented them from constructing new toilets and/or rebuilding toilets after they collapse.[20]

What about the community level? Do the rich really cross-subsidize the poor? Are the interests of the poor, women, and female-headed households really taken on board in CLTS? Research and observations in the field have been mixed. In villages in Bangladesh, I observed in 2007 that the rich have provided land, bamboo, labour, and so on to poorer households, widows, among others, in order to make the entire community ODF. But during the same visit I also observed that rich Muslim households in north-west Bangladesh had refused to grant the poorer and destitute groups of the village any land to build toilets because they considered the poorer Hindus to be dirty and unworthy of help.

It could also be argued that indirect forms of subsidy take place in CLTS all the time. The collective reward to a village at the end of the intervention could be seen as a form of subsidy, and in many cases different kinds of subsidies are provided to support the poorest. In many parts of India, CLTS-inspired programmes provide subsidies to below poverty level (BPL) households. These subsidies can be provided before or after the toilets are constructed. Non-governmental organizations in Bangladesh have also explicitly targeted the poorest of the poor, who are left out once most of the

[20] Anowarul Haq and Brigitta Bode, 'The Challenges of Facilitating CLTS', in Lyla Mehta and Synne Movik (eds), *Shit Matters: The Potential of Community-Led Total Sanitation* (Practical Action Publishing, 2011), 71.

village achieves ODF status. Mahbub[21] and Haq and Bode[22] also talk about the need to explicitly target the poor and some women in CLTS areas, who despite gaining from the positive benefits may need some concerted help.

In India, research has documented that exclusion based on subsidy takes place due to politics, caste, and patronage.[23] Groups that tend to have strong political connections can benefit whereas widows, tribals, and displaced people tend to be excluded, even from the BPL subsidy. Even though there are recent changes to provide incentives to above poverty line (APL) groups such as scheduled castes (SCs), tribals, and so on, there is no indication that politics will not dominate here too.[24]

Targets, Incentives, Behaviour Change, and Open Defecation Free Status

Incentives, rewards, and sanctions (both formal and informal) play a big role in galvanizing communities to achieve ODF status. In the drive to achieve targets, massive reward systems such as huge cash prizes to ODF communities can inflate the indication of success, and lead to capture by elites (as is often the case in India[25]). It is also unclear whether and for how long behaviour change is sustained, once the reward has been obtained.

100 per cent ODF is the aim of CLTS, but research seems to suggest that this is difficult to sustain.[26] In many cases, 100 per cent ODF may never have been achieved. Largely, monitoring and verification systems are weak in most countries. As discussed, behaviour change is

[21] Amina Mahbub, 'Exploring the Social Dynamics of CLTS in Bangladesh: The Inclusion of Children, Women and Vulnerable People', in Lyla Mehta and Synne Movik (eds), *Shit Matters: The Potential of Community-Led Total Sanitation* (Practical Action Publishing, 2011), 39.

[22] Haq and Bode (n 20).

[23] Andrés Hueso and Brian Bell, 'An Untold Story of Policy Failure: The Total Sanitation Campaign in India', (2013) 6, 15 *Water Policy* 1001.

[24] Hueso and Bell (n 23).

[25] Mehta and Movik (n 6).

[26] Mehta and Movik (n 6).

very difficult to sustain, and there are usually some defaulters. Even if there are some defaulters in villages, it is common to hear both men and women speak with confidence about the changes in their lives and villages (for example, a cleaner and smell-free environment; benefits for women such as privacy and security from the fear of violence and rape; pride in community mobilization). They are also pleased with the other positive spin offs that have arisen after CLTS has been implemented (for example, a water scheme as a reward either from the government or NGO, a new road, or electricity, and so on).

There are several reasons why behaviour change is difficult to sustain.

1. Poor facilitation, verification, and monitoring can contribute to a false sense of success.
2. There are many constraints faced by poor women and men in terms of resources, time, and capacity with respect to their daily hygiene and sanitation practices. In villages without much social cohesion and where special efforts have not been made to address the interests of the poor, behaviour change of the whole population may not be achieved.
3. There is a tendency to lose sight of the role of water in the context of both livelihood strategies and in acting as a constraint for toilet construction and use.
4. The sanctions and restrictions imposed on defaulters could intensify processes of social exclusion in local communities and further exclude poor people.

Problems with Toilet Counting, Moving up the Sanitation Ladder, and Cultural Preferences

Despite its emphasis on behaviour change, implementation of CLTS through government programmes and NGO projects means that success is often still measured in terms of the number of toilets constructed. Messages about behaviour change and empowerment can sometimes get lost in the process, and indicators for CLTS success frequently revert to easily measurable indicators like the number of toilets. Governments want and need to measure the progress that they have achieved. But effectively measuring and understanding behaviour change are both notoriously difficult. In India, various sanitation missions have tended to focus on building toilets rather than on education and collective action, as the chapter goes on to outline later.

Initially, people usually install easily affordable, low-cost toilets from locally available materials to instantly stop open defecation. However, over time, the idea is that they will move up the sanitation ladder from pit toilets to more sustainable and complex models. However, research in India suggests that this may not be taking place as quickly as may be desired by the implementing body.[27] In Haryana, the interviews conducted by the author in CLTS areas in 2008 revealed that CLTS facilitators had convinced many rural residents that even a simple and affordable toilet (that is, *kaccha* pit latrine) could encourage healthy and productive living. By contrast, some studies highlight that most rural Indians would find such toilets to be polluting, and would rather go straight for an expensive *pucca* toilet with a septic tank.[28]

Religion and caste may also play a role in determining toilet use in rural India. Muslims tend to be more open to owning and using affordable pit latrines that need to be emptied every few years, and 55 per cent of rural Muslims defecate in the open as opposed to 77 per cent of rural Hindus.[29] Other studies have also highlighted the importance of religious leaders, such as *imams* in Indonesia and Bangladesh, in promoting toilet use, and Islam's emphasis on cleanliness before prayer.[30] Hindu perceptions of toilet use are likely to be linked to strong notions of pollution and purity, which also

[27] Nisheeth Kumar and J.P. Shukla, 'CLTS in the Context of a Countrywide Programme in India: Public Good, Private Good?', in Lyla Mehta and Synne Movik (eds), *Shit Matters: The Potential of Community-Led Total Sanitation* (Practical Action Publishing, 2011), 131; A. Dyalchand, M. Khale, and S. Vasudevan, 'Institutional Arrangements and Social Norms Influencing Sanitation Behaviour in Rural India', in Lyla Mehta and Synne Movik (eds), *Shit Matters: The Potential of Community-Led Total Sanitation* (Practical Action Publishing, 2011), 101.

[28] Coffey (n 12).

[29] Coffey (n 12).

[30] Mehta (n 17).

support the unjust system of manual scavenging. It is, however, important not to generalize issues concerning religion and culture.

Appropriate and Safe Technology

In some cases, decentralized open defecation may even be better than concentrated fixed-point defecation. A high concentration of pit latrines near groundwater sources could contaminate water sources leading to various environmental problems. Another related issue is runoff and the flooding of pit latrines during the rainy season and the contamination of surface water and groundwater. Soil contamination could also take place, depending on soil quality. Indeed, research conducted by the Institute of Development Studies in India suggests that groundwater contamination is quite high in some CLTS villages.[31] Furthermore, many of the constructed toilets may actually be unsafe from a health point of view, and ultimately serve as fixed-point open defecation. Even though CLTS does not prescribe models, it may need to build in more technical advice on what constitutes a safe latrine, depending on local topography, and soil and water conditions.

Monitoring and Evaluation

Verification of success is usually arbitrary, and good monitoring systems are often not in place.[32] There also seems to be some slippage on the 100 per cent ODF status.[33] Better monitoring and follow-up systems are required to ensure the sustainability of CLTS. This can take place through facilitators, local government, or community leaders. Funding and institutional support is required for monitoring

[31] Manisha Khale and Ashok Dyalchand, 'The Impact of Rural Sanitation on Water Quality and Waterborne Diseases', in Lyla Mehta and Synne Movik (eds), *Shit Matters: The Potential of Community-Led Total Sanitation* (Practical Action Publishing, 2011), 115.

[32] Robert Chambers, 'Spread and Scale with CLTS: Past Lessons, Future Paths', in Lyla Mehta and Synne Movik (eds), *Shit Matters: The Potential of Community-Led Total Sanitation* (Practical Action Publishing, 2011), 245.

[33] Mehta (n 17).

and evaluation as well as for post-CLTS follow-up. This is why Dr Kamal Kar began to emphasize issues such as post-triggering, post-ODF follow-up, and also institutional triggering at the District and national levels.[34]

Gender

While it is true that there are extraordinary benefits to be derived for women in terms of dignity, privacy, safety, comfort, and well-being, it is not always clear whether women also end up taking on additional burdens. Unequal traditional division of labour may also be reinforced, with women being seen as responsible for the maintenance and cleaning of toilets. Also, CLTS may not adequately challenge unequal gender and power relations in a community, and indeed often builds its programmes on them. With CLTS making claims of community empowerment, it is crucial that gender and power relations are also scrutinized. While it is true that CLTS has mobilized women very effectively, even in highly gender-segregated areas, to assume leadership roles, this strong participation of women in CLTS processes, and improved well-being for them as a result of better sanitation, do not equal empowerment.[35]

The Indian Context

A Mixed Bag of Experiences

From Bangladesh, the approach first spread to India. CLTS has been promoted in and spread to, India by champions within the state governments and WSP India, with very little involvement of NGOs. The India Country Team Leader of WSP visited Bangladesh and learned about CLTS, and was impressed by the results. He then involved Dr Kamal Kar in discussions with the government of Maharashtra and eventually the government of Maharashtra was convinced to introduce CLTS with pilot projects in two Districts, Ahmednagar and Nanded, in 2002. The success in the pilot Districts

[34] Personal communication from Kamal Kar to the author (June 2015).
[35] Mehta (n 17).

led to the adoption of the CLTS approach by all other Districts in the state. Subsequently, other states showed a keen interest in adopting the CLTS approach. Himachal Pradesh and Haryana enthusiastically adopted the approach, largely due to the efforts of District administrators from the Indian Administrative Service (IAS), who personally got very involved in spreading CLTS in their Districts. (I focus briefly on Himachal Pradesh below.) These efforts took place with strong support from WSP India.

CLTS has played a major role in dramatically improving sanitation across the state of Himachal Pradesh. In 2004, toilet coverage was estimated at 28 per cent. After adopting a new strategy that was inspired by CLTS, sanitation coverage is said to have increased to 90 per cent.[36] This can be attributed to the state government's strong political will and the endorsement of a demand-led approach promoting community ownership and involvement, a rejection of upfront hardware subsidies, as well as encouraging partnerships with NGOs/CBOs (community-based organizations) and inter-government coordination, and emphasis on monitoring and evaluation.[37] The strong passion, motivation, and influence of Deepak Sanan, a senior IAS officer who served in various capacities including as secretary of rural development, no doubt played a key role. He also worked at WSP as the India Country Team Leader before returning to the state of Himachal Pradesh. Sanan believed strongly in CLTS, in decentralization, and empowering local governments as key in improving accountability in service delivery, and saw sanitation as an entry point to increase the participation of local authorities in service delivery.[38]

Mr Sanan, together with WSP, led a long-term effort to introduce a new sanitation policy in the state that was inspired by CLTS

[36] Deepak Sanan, Pradeep Chauhan, and Vinod Rana, 'Survey of Recent Sanitation Achievement in Himachal Pradesh: A Study by Institute of Development Studies' (India Water Portal, 23 June 2011).

[37] Hueso and Bell (n 23).

[38] Deepak Sanan, 'The CLTS Story in India: The Sanitation Story of the Millennium', in Lyla Mehta and Synne Movik (eds), *Shit Matters: The Potential of Community-Led Total Sanitation* (Practical Action Publishing, 2011), 85.

principles. Rather than upfront subsidies for toilet construction, the ODF community received a community reward linked to sanitation needs. Through workshops, training, and exposure visits, mid-level officers and champions emerged at all levels in the state, and they monitored and implemented the campaign.[39] Himachal Pradesh has also been successful in improving toilet coverage in schools and other public places. (However, it needs to be noted that coverage does not mean the toilets are used or are sustainable.)

Efforts to introduce CLTS have been made in states such as Madhya Pradesh, Rajasthan, Chhattisgarh, Odisha, Gujarat, Karnataka, and Andhra Pradesh, but so far scaling up of CLTS, in other than the three states mentioned earlier, is very slow. This is because there is considerable resistance to CLTS in India, not least because of its emphasis on avoiding upfront hardware subsidies in rural areas, and due to the other reasons discussed below.

Challenges to Community-Led Total Sanitation in India

Mr Deepak Sanan, who mainstreamed CLTS in Himachal Pradesh's sanitation programme, has written eloquently about the stumbling blocks that CLTS faces in the Indian context. This largely has to do with the intractability of the subsidy issue. Indeed, CLTS in India faces several challenges. There is widespread resistance to the no-hardware subsidy stance, since India has a long tradition of doling out subsidies through which political leaders and politicians get political mileage. This subsidy monster is difficult to tackle. Even donors such as UNICEF, which globally adopt a no-household-level hardware subsidy, work differently in India, and do not want to antagonize the Government of India due to their desire to continue their operations in the country.[40] Due to hostility at the national level, CLTS has relied on committed officials at state, District, and Block levels. In some areas, there have been islands of success, but this is usually linked to factors such as high community participation, high quality

---

[39] Andres Hueso, Alejandra Boni, and Alvaro Fernández-Baldor, 'Embracing the Complexity of Policy Processes in Sanitation: Insights from India', (2017) *Development Policy Review*, vol. 2, 36, 203.

[40] Sanan (n 38).

facilitation, and committed village leadership. But going to scale has been difficult due to the transfer of these bureaucrats, and the lack of widespread institutional buy in.

Until 2014, the context for CLTS in India was the Government of India's Total Sanitation Campaign (TSC), which was launched in 1999. It was renamed as Nirmal Bharat Abhiyan (NBA) in 2012, which, in turn, was replaced by the Swachh Bharat Mission (SBM) in 2014. The TSC/NBA/SBM claimed to emphasize a demand-driven, community-led, and people-centred approach, and to increase awareness and education, but in reality they remained construction focused and subsidy driven.[41]

The Nirmal Gram Puruskar (NGP) was given to rural local governments that achieved ODF status and also managed sanitation in public spaces, drainage, and solid waste issues to ensure total sanitation in relation to their environment.[42] However, the NGP turned out to be a 'perverse incentive' that often counteracted the CLTS efforts, as it led to another target-/toilet-driven top-down initiative rather than community-led processes. Moreover, verification and monitoring of ODF status are patchy, and overall sustainability is thus questionable. Whilst some villages have received the award for being 100 per cent ODF, the scheme has also led to false declarations and the 'massaging' of numbers. This gives a false sense of both success and sustainability.[43] Also the focus largely was on toilet construction, rather than any attempt at behaviour change,[44] let alone taking a more holistic approach to sanitation including addressing hygiene, behaviour change, manual scavenging, waste disposal, and so on. Little wonder then that in many NGP-winning villages, open defecation was rampant. While the Ministry of Rural Development reported that toilets had been built for 68 per cent of households, Census 2011 revealed that 60 million of the toilets constructed could not be located or found.[45] Since 1986, India has spent over $3 billion

[41] Hueso and Bell (n 23).

[42] Ministry of Drinking Water and Sanitation, Guidelines: Nirmal Gram Puraskar 2012 (MoDWS 2012).

[43] Mehta (n 17).

[44] Sanan (n 38).

[45] Mehrotra (n 5).

on constructing toilets across the country,[46] with very poor results. Corruption has been rampant, and there are millions and millions of missing toilets. Thus, there has been little benefit to people really needing and wanting toilets.

After 2010, the emphasis shifted to selecting a particular Block and making it ODF. Mandi District in Himachal Pradesh is a good example, where NGOs adopted CLTS triggering tools to implement a zero-subsidy and community-focused programme using street theatre and door-to-door visits, resulting in 100 per cent ODF villages in some gram panchayats.[47] By contrast, in Khandwa District in Madhya Pradesh, despite buy in from senior District officials, there was resistance from local-level bureaucrats, who felt that CLTS-inspired approaches would involve more work, and it would be difficult to mobilize communities.[48] Local politicians who were keen to receive and manage big funds, presumably due to patronage and corruption gains, also resisted CLTS. Hueso, Boni, and Fernández-Baldor's research reveals how CLTS discourses are used instrumentally with poor emphasis on community mobilization and top-down, subsidy-driven toilet construction. The result was a 7 per cent increase in rural sanitation coverage, which is modest but still higher than the state average.[49]

Another challenge to CLTS in India is the frequent transfer of officials, which threatens its continuity even in areas where it has been successful. For example, CLTS often takes off dramatically when it is promoted by local champions. This could be at the District or village level. When civil servants are transferred or promoted, it possibly affects the momentum of CLTS in the concerned areas. The challenge thus is to institutionalize the momentum created.

[46] Ajai Sreevatsan, 'Indian's Sanitation Campaigns Have Cost 40 Times Mars Mission Budget', *The Hindu* (8 October 2014); available at www.thehindu.com/news/national/costly-sanitation-campaigns-but-very-little-to-show-for-it/article6479587.ece.

[47] Hueso, Boni, and Fernández-Baldor (n 39).

[48] Hueso, Boni, and Fernández-Baldor (n 39).

[49] Hueso, Boni, and Fernández-Baldor (n 39).

There are more mobile phones than toilet users in India.[50] Very poor people in Indian villages also use mobile phones, even though no subsidies have encouraged the mobile phone boom across the country. Unlike neighbouring Bangladesh, India has not invested adequately in education, and in addressing cultural and gender issues. Neighbouring Nepal and Bangladesh, which are far poorer, are faring much better than India, and at far lower costs. Around 3 per cent of Bangladeshis practise open defecation as opposed to nearly 50 per cent in India.[51] This has been attributed to the more holistic approach in Bangladesh, which also focuses heavily on education and communication as opposed to merely enhancing toilet construction as in India. Other strategies include changing socio-cultural and religious norms as well as focusing on a combination of strategies including community mobilization, social marketing, private sector involvement, and different forms of incentives and accountability.[52] Local people are also motivated to choose the toilet technology for themselves, instead of leaving it to the local government (or gram panchayat).

It must be noted that Bangladesh was the birthplace of CLTS, and its policies and programmes have been inspired by CLTS. No such support exists for CLTS in India, even though Dr Kamal Kar is an Indian, and operates out of Kolkata, India. But even in Bangladesh, challenges such as waste containment, and the need to target the poorest continue to persist.[53]

On 15 August 2014, Prime Minister Narendra Modi announced the SBM to make India ODF by 2019. This endorsement from the highest level has increased attention to sanitation in India, a country

[50] Kamal Kar, 'Community-Led Total Sanitation (CLTS): Challenges of Nation-wide Scaling up and Sustainability', (IDS Seminar, 11 June 2015).

[51] Jocalyn Clark, 'Why Has Bangladesh Had Such Success Improving Sanitation but Not Neighboring India?', *The BMJ Opinion* (23 September 2014); available at http://blogs.bmj.com/bmj/2014/09/23/jocalyn-clark-why-has-bangladesh-had-such-success-in-improving-sanitation-but-not-neighboring-india.

[52] Clark (n 51).

[53] Haq and Bode (n 20); Mahbub (n 21).

where 50 per cent of the population continues open defecation, and where more than 600,000 people are engaged in manual scavenging despite legislation prohibiting the employment of manual scavengers.[54]

Despite all the huge fanfare and media attention, several analyses have shown how the SBM may not be more than old wine in a new bottle.[55] The TSC, which started in 1999 also aimed at a 'Nirmal Bharat' by 2012, and failed. Instead, there were 8 million more rural households defecating in the open than in 2001.[56] There is also a lack of coordination between the different ministries working on sanitation (the Ministry of Drinking Water and Sanitation for rural areas; the Ministry of Urban Development for urban areas; school sanitation falling under the purview of the Ministry of Human Resource Development; and the Ministry of Women and Child Development for anganwadi sanitation). While it has been claimed that there has been a massive increase in toilet construction, on-the-ground verification found that many of these so-called toilets do not actually exist.[57]

The Modi government plans to spend an additional $31 billion under the SBM.[58] It has also increased the incentives, and individual households will receive Rs 12,000.[59] This does not address the key problem. The mission continues with the supply-oriented hardware-driven approach, which has consistently failed in previous sanitation missions. It also does not consider issues such as post-implementation monitoring and audit, and the allocation for

[54] Harsh Mander, 'Saluting Bezwada Wilson, A Man Who Gets His Hands Dirty to Clean the Rot of Caste Oppression', *Scroll.in* (1 August 2016); available at https://scroll.in/article/812849/saluting-bezwada-wilson-a-man-who-gets-his-hands-dirty-to-clean-the-rot-of-caste-oppression.

[55] Mamata Dash, 'India on the Road to Cleanliness!' (WaterAid 28 May 2015); available at http://wateraidindia.in/blog/india-on-the-road-to-cleanliness.

[56] Mehrotra (n 5).

[57] Dash (n 55).

[58] Sreevatsan (n 46).

[59] Guidelines for Swachh Bharat Mission (Gramin), 2017, s 5.4.3.

education and behaviour change has been cut from 15 per cent under the past programme to 8 per cent.[60] Leaving such a small proportion of the budget for information, communication, and education (IEC) is very problematic.

In sum, national programmes have been unsuccessful in facilitating demand, and creating a community-driven approach. Thus, an enabling state environment is key, without pressure to produce quick results and receive awards. Champions (both state and non-state) are key. In the case of state champions, there is a danger that after their transfer, the momentum will die down, which calls for long-term institutional triggering. Finally, as discussed earlier in this chapter, many Indian villages are very differentiated and dominated by strong gender, caste, and class cleavages. The community is rarely unified— which also poses a challenge to collective action and equitable development programmes such as CLTS.

Community-Led Total Sanitation and the Right to Sanitation

It is indisputable that CLTS—through its focus on universal access— has played a key role in helping to realize the right to sanitation. It also builds nicely on the focus of human-rights-approaches to development that prioritize bottom-up and participatory interventions that avoid blueprint models. CLTS benefits do not just concern sanitation, but there are also positive spin offs on health, dignity and security of women, livelihoods, and nutrition. This highlights how CLTS can help realize other basic human rights.

CLTS interventions (when they work) are more effective than top-down, target-driven approaches of the government. While CLTS focuses on local community action, there is much room for government and donor actions to ensure people's basic right to sanitation via CLTS. This could include ensuring institutional sustainability, providing funding for dedicated staff and facilitators and health and extension workers, proper verification and monitoring systems, and also hard money for toilets in schools, market places,

[60] Sreevatsan (n 46).

and so on. There is certainly scope to draw on CLTS principles to ensure that community/public toilets in slums, peri-urban areas, and so on remain well maintained and sustainable.

The CLTS approach is still maturing and evolving, and there are several areas that need further attention. This chapter concludes with a few thoughts on this, especially in the context of the right to sanitation. One, wastewater and solid waste disposal and drainage issues need more attention. These are particularly relevant in crowded peri-urban or urban areas, where far more coproduction is required with municipal services. Two, CLTS proponents could also engage more critically with local community dynamics, and examine whether these can impede the equitable and sustainable implementation of the approach. Three, in the Indian context, CLTS's idealized notion of community may neglect issues of violation of human rights in sanitation practices. Manual scavenging is a good case in point, and CLTS increasingly needs to pay attention to who clears and collects the shit, how it is disposed and treated, and the possibilities of its reuse that could serve to enhance livelihood options (that is, agricultural production, energy generation, and so on). Finally, CLTS practitioners or those who use the label CLTS must avoid toilet counting exercises, and instead spend time, resources, and energy on post-defecation follow-up and sustainability issues, not just at the local level, but also increasingly at the institutional and ministerial level from District to national scales.

7

Right to Sanitation in Urban Areas

Legal Obligations and Institutional Challenges

Mathew John

The sanitation challenge in India, whether urban or rural, is more pressing today than it has ever been. According to a recent report by the Government of India, 88.8 per cent of the households in urban areas are reported to have sanitary toilets, and 7.5 per cent of the total urban population is estimated to defecate in the open.[1] In addition, an overwhelming majority of urban India either has no access to drainage or has to put up with open drainage of human waste, and at least a third of human waste generated in urban India is discharged untreated into water channels, largely because of poor sanitation networks and systems.[2] Expectedly this state of affairs has

[1] Government of India, Ministry of Statistics and Programme Implementation, National Sample Survey Office, Swachhta Status Report 2016 (Ministry of Statistics and Programme Implementation, 2016), i & ii.
[2] Government of India, Ministry of Urban Development, National Urban Sanitation Policy (Ministry of Urban Development, 2008), 6.

a knock-on effect on health, education, employment, and general well-being,[3] and there is therefore little question that the state of sanitation services in urban India is a stark indictment of conditions that do not permit a life that might be lived with dignity. It is against this background that articulating the problem in terms of a 'right to sanitation' is acquiring significance as a likely legal and policy response. Most significantly, against projections that more than half of India is likely to be living in urban areas by the middle of the twenty-first century, this state of affairs with patchy policy responses is only likely to mushroom into one of the most significant urban challenges in India.

Over the last three to four decades, there has been a global shift towards rights-based approaches to address governance challenges. This is primarily due to the promise that the language of rights holds out for demanding and enforcing greater accountability and responsiveness from government.[4] India in particular has made ambitious strides towards rights-based governance through court decisions, and more recently, through legislation recognizing enforceable rights in relation to education, employment, and food.[5] The normative horizon around sanitation too has been steadily taking shape over the last few decades, culminating in the express recognition of a right to sanitation by the United Nations.[6] However, these advances have not led to a statutorily recognized right to sanitation

---

[3] The problem posed by inadequate sanitation has been detailed in various studies. For instance, the World Bank's Water and Sanitation Program (WSP) estimated that India's lack of sanitation coverage cost the country the equivalent of 6.4 per cent of its 2006 gross domestic product. See Water and Sanitation Program, 'Economic Impacts of Inadequate Sanitation in India' (World Bank, 2011).

[4] For example, Andrea Cornwall and Celestine Nyamu-Musembi, 'Putting the "Rights Based Approach" to Development into Perspective', (2004) 25(8) *Third World Quarterly* 1415.

[5] Right of Children to Free and Compulsory Education Act, 2009; Mahatma Gandhi National Rural Employment Guarantee Act, 2005; National Food Security Act, 2013.

[6] For example, UN General Assembly Resolution, *The Human Rights to Safe Drinking Water and Sanitation,* 17 December 2015, UN Doc. A/RES/70/169.

in India or to widely accepted standards to measure and benchmark the state of sanitation services. As with other social and economic rights, the absence of a statutorily recognized 'right to sanitation' has much to do with complex sets of legal, policy, political, technical, social, and cultural concerns that are yet to be negotiated at the intersection of the state, markets, and communities. Even so, there is an elaborate though fragmented web of institutions, policies, and citizens' entitlements that address the provision of sanitation services, be they rural or urban. It is against this institutional background that this chapter will attempt to untangle what might be the basic elements of an entitlement or a right to sanitation in the urban context.

Any concern for the provision of sanitation services involves a whole host of specific challenges including water supply, toilets, drainage, sewage treatment, and so on. Each of these constitutes an important part of the sanitation problem. However, it is extremely unlikely that the sanitation problem can be either conceived or resolved by emphasizing any one of these challenges. For instance, the problem of manual scavenging continues to be closely tied up with the problem of delivery of sanitation services in India. However, this chapter does not directly touch upon this very serious problem that is both constitutionally and statutorily proscribed as it is discussed elsewhere in this volume (see Wilson [Chapter 10] and Khanna [Chapter 11] in this volume). Similarly, securing functioning toilets is undoubtedly at the heart of what must constitute the content of the right to sanitation in the urban context.[7] However, important as it is, functioning toilets also require drains, sewerage, and in most cases, access to reliable water supply. Further, even among those who seek to extend the reach of sanitation services, there could be serious differences in policy approaches on whether the state should emphasize toilets or other aspects of the sanitation problem when choosing to spend scarce resources. Thus, instead of

---

[7] For example, Orders of the Delhi High Court in *Dr B.L. Wadhera* v *Union of India & Others* CWP No. 841 of 1998. For an account of the governance of public toilets, see Sundar Burra, Sheela Patel, and Thomas Kerr, 'Community-Designed, Built and Managed Toilet Blocks in Indian Cities', (2003) 15(2) *Environment & Urbanization* 11.

picking up a slice of the broader problem and weighing competing policy alternatives, this chapter situates the right to sanitation to include the entire range of the services that the state could potentially owe its citizens.

The chapter sets itself the following tasks—first, it outlines salient aspects of the institutional framework through which sanitation is delivered in urban India, and the rights recognized by this institutional scheme. Second, it details the manner in which courts have adjudicated and elaborated the extent of state obligation to provide urban sanitation. And lastly, it identifies a set of constraints in the political economy of urban sanitation that will determine the realization of the provision of sanitation services in urban areas.

Providing Urban Sanitation: Elements of the Institutional Framework

In responding to social and economic claims demanding sanitation, it is important to recognize that insofar as the debate acquires the complexion of 'rights', it is always structured around positive obligations of states to provide their citizens with what are deemed to be basic entitlements.[8] Demarcating these entitlements confronts a range of difficult challenges such as the identification of right-holders, the duties that states owe to right-holders, and the technical details that ensure that the duties are faithfully discharged. This task is particularly complex in the Indian context as these obligations are fragmented across the institutional landscape of India's federal polity, and the pressures at different levels of the institutional system could pull in different directions. Therefore, in a normative field where there is no clearly organized hierarchy of statutory rights and

---

[8] There is an extremely rich debate on various dimensions of socio-economic rights such as its imposition of positive obligations on states, vagueness, cost implications, and so on, which will be touched upon, in passing, as encountered. However, for a detailed account of this debate, see Henry J. Steiner, Philip Alston, and Ryan Goodman, *International Human Rights in Context: Law, Politics, Morals: Text and Materials* (Oxford University Press, 2008), 280.

obligations, it is useful to explore the contours of state obligations through a broad outline of the institutional framework designed to provide urban sanitation.

Across the considerable unevenness in the institutional framework, there are broad structural strands of law and policy that tie together the provision of sanitation across India's cities. Executive power to act on matters relating to sanitation is constitutionally vested in the provincial state governments. In turn, state governments have tended to statutorily delegate sanitation functions in urban areas to institutions of urban local government. This delegation and decentralization of functions to urban local bodies has acquired greater urgency after the passage of the 74th Amendment to the Constitution that was designed to recognize, facilitate, and increase the role of urban local government.[9] On the other hand, the Central Government intervenes to shape sanitation policy primarily through schemes, for instance, the Swachh Bharat Mission (SBM), that incentivize policy goals by tying funding to pre-formatted programmes and reform objectives. Further, environmental statutes at the national level addressing environmental and water pollution also frame standards within which government bodies are expected to discharge their sanitation responsibilities.[10] Thus there are multiple institutional layers imposing multiple legal and policy pressures on governments to provide sanitation services in urban areas.

[9] It is debatable whether there has been meaningful devolution of powers to local government, but Entry 6 of List 2 of the Seventh Schedule vests 'public health and sanitation' as a power of the state governments while Article 243W permits state governments to vest municipalities with appropriate powers to function as institutions of self-government. Further Article 243ZF would suggest that municipal statutes be revisited and suitably amended such that they are in accordance with the decentralization mandate of the 74th Amendment.

[10] Water pollution is governed by The Water (Prevention and Control of Pollution) Act, 1974, and environmental pollution more generally by The Environment (Protection) Act, 1986. The latter allows the Central Government to act across a range of environmental problems by way of standards, rules, and regulations, while the former addresses water pollution through the Central Pollution Control Board and state pollution control boards.

Notwithstanding the multilayered influences on the provision of sanitation services, frontline services are most often discharged by local municipal bodies, though these services could also in some circumstances be discharged by water and sewage boards, cantonment boards, town improvement trusts, and other similar bodies. These services, as detailed in municipal and other related local government statutes, generally include water supply, sewerage, street cleaning, solid waste management, elimination of public nuisance, and the provision of community and public toilets.[11] Each of these services deserves individual consideration, but for the purpose of this chapter, the provision of urban sanitation services will be discussed more generally at the level of the existing or perceived obligations of municipal or local bodies to provide any or all of these services. That is, all these services will be viewed as a set of related government duties located along a continuum.

As can be gathered from Table 7A.1, municipal statutes impose both obligatory and discretionary duties on municipal and local bodies. In other words, some obligations are considered to be the core of municipal obligation while others might be fulfilled at its discretion. Most sanitation functions as outlined in Table 7A.1 are obligatory; however, despite the stated obligatory duty to provide sanitation services, the capacity and perhaps even the commitment of municipal bodies to address the challenge of the sanitation problem in contemporary India are grossly inadequate.[12] Further, and going beyond the gap between ideals and practice, Bhullar notes the conditional phrasing of municipal statutes which frame municipal obligations to provide sanitation services with qualifying phrases such as 'reasonable and adequate', or 'within financial means at its disposal'.[13] In other cases, state governments are permitted to exempt

[11] See Table 7A.1 which draws on a randomly chosen set of states to snapshot various sanitation functions that are vested in local bodies by municipal and other related statutes, as well as the extent to which these functions have been devolved to local bodies.

[12] For the state of sanitation services in India, see Ministry of Statistics and Programme Implementation (n 1).

[13] Lovleen Bhullar, 'Ensuring Safe Municipal Wastewater Disposal in Urban India: Is there a Legal Basis?', (2013) 25(2) *Journal of Environmental Law* 235.

municipalities from the performance of certain duties, and in one instance, the municipal statute itself prohibits the institution of suits for damages or specific performance against the municipality.[14] In addition, it is also important to keep in mind that the obligations of municipalities are restricted to municipal boundaries, leaving peri-urban areas affected by the spill-over effects of urban waste outside the framework of urban governance norms.[15] As a result, despite explicitly stated obligations, the gap between stated obligations and existing practice, the phrasing of these obligations, and the inability of urban institutions to respond to urban expansion, cast doubt on the robustness of existing urban institutional design, institutional performance, and institutional commitment to provide sanitation services. Even so, some manner of local government obligation is widely recognized.

The most obvious approach to understand the robustness of local governmental obligations regarding urban sanitation would be to study the design of local institutions, the manner in which they understand and interpret their obligations, and examine their practice and commitment to delivering sanitation services. Though invaluable, this approach to obligations in sanitation requires detailed empirical investigation of the working of local government, which is beyond the scope of this chapter. Therefore, the present discussion on the obligatory functions of local government is a rather more limited investigation of the prism of legality and the manner in which courts have interpreted legal obligations.

Outlining the Judicial Approach to Urban Sanitation

The Indian higher judiciary has been repeatedly petitioned to order governments and their agencies to perform obligatory duties in relation to sanitation arising from municipal statutes and pollution control statutes, and under Article 32 or Article 226 of the Constitution,

---

[14] Bhullar (n 13).

[15] Though the 74th Amendment does recognize the phenomenon of peri-urban areas, the obligations of government in relation to these areas are unclear. See for example, Annapurna Shaw, 'Peri-urban Interface of Indian Cities', (2005) XL(2) *Economic & Political Weekly* 129.

to fulfil the promise of fundamental rights. However, as the legal framework on rights in sanitation has been less than fully clear, it is important to notice the manner in which courts have interpreted statutory and constitutional obligations, and extended rights in sanitation services in urban areas. It must be emphasized again that this section does not address the obligation to provide any particular sanitation service or services, but is a comment on judicial interpretation of the obligation to provide urban sanitation services generally, as gathered in Table 7A.1.

The Ratlam Case and Its Implications for the Scope of Municipal Statutory Obligations

Municipal Council, Ratlam v *Shri Vardhichand and Others*[16] is a much-discussed decision of the Supreme Court that ruled on municipal obligations to redress the problem of overflowing sewage and insufficient drainage in a residential colony in the town of Ratlam in the state of Madhya Pradesh. This problem was set against the statutory background of the Madhya Pradesh Municipalities Act, 1961, which requires the state to make 'reasonable and adequate' provisions towards meeting obligatory services regarding sewage disposal and for the provision of drainage. Further, Section 268 of the Indian Penal Code, 1860, penalizes public nuisance, which is defined as acts or omissions which cause common injury, danger, or annoyance. However, as the penalty for the offence of public nuisance is a negligible fine, the respondent brought an action against the municipality seeking to enforce a duty imposed on executive magistrates to abate public nuisance, under Section 133 of the Code of Criminal Procedure, 1973.

Challenging the action of the executive magistrate under Section 133 of the Code of Criminal Procedure, the municipality contended

[16] *Municipal Court, Ratlam* v *Shri Vardhichand & Others* (1980) 4 SCC 162 (Supreme Court of India, 1980) ('*Ratlam*'). A discussion of this case is available in any standard textbook on environmental law in the section on the obligations of municipalities to abate public nuisance. See, for example, Shyam Divan and Armin Rosencranz, *Environmental Law and Policy in India: Cases, Materials and Statutes* (Oxford University Press, 2002), 114–20.

that the Madhya Pradesh Municipalities Act, 1961, imposed no mandatory obligation to meet its sanitary duties,[17] that citizens were free to choose where they lived, and that paucity of funds made it difficult to construct drains and provide for amenities. The Court, however, ruled against the municipality by holding that the executive magistrate was mandatorily obliged to abate and remove public nuisances as provided for in Section 133 of the Code of Criminal Procedure.[18] More importantly, the Court also held that removal of sewage was a basic and fundamental obligation that the municipality would have to discharge regardless of funds available at its disposal. In the words of Justice Krishna Iyer: '[D]ecency and dignity are non-negotiable facets of human rights and are a first charge on local self-governing bodies. Similarly, providing drainage systems not pompous and attractive, but in working condition and sufficient to meet the needs of the people cannot be evaded if the municipality is to justify its existence.'[19] Consequently, the executive magistrate was adjudged entirely justified in directing the municipality to fulfil its sanitation-related obligations, and it was held that paucity of municipal funds would be no excuse.

The Court asserted the 'primary' or 'obligatory' duty of the municipality to act against inadequate sanitation services in such cases where it constituted a public nuisance as defined in the Indian Penal Code. Though there was a mention that municipal obligations also drew on the guarantees of the fundamental rights and the directive principles of state policy in the Constitution, the judgment

[17] Section 123 of The Madhya Pradesh Municipalities Act, 1961, stipulates that the Municipality '(1) ... undertake and make *reasonable and adequate* provision for the following matters within the limits of the Municipality, namely ... (b) cleansing public streets, places and sewers, and all places, not being private property, which are open to the enjoyment of the public ... and abating all public nuisances, (c) disposing of night-soil and rubbish and preparation of compost manure from night-soil and rubbish' (emphasis added).

[18] *Ratlam* (n 16), 171. See also, *Citizens and Inhabitants of Municipal Ward No. 15* v *Municipal Corporation, Gwalior* AIR 1997 MP 33 (High Court of Madhya Pradesh, 1995).

[19] *Ratlam* (n 16), 171.

turned on the public nuisance caused by the failure of the municipal authority to perform what were adjudged to be its primary duties. Pursuing redress for the failure of the municipal authority to perform its sanitation functions on statutory grounds does not, however, seem to have found much traction in subsequent cases, and was taken over by the altogether more easily pursued remedies offered by public interest litigation (PIL).

Fundamental Rights and Municipal Obligations Regarding Sanitation

The *Ratlam* case was significant for the links that it drew between municipal obligations, sanitation, and public nuisance. However, petitioning a court on these grounds was considerably cumbersome as it required approaching executive authorities to abate a nuisance after which further grievance could be judicially appealed. On the other hand, petitioning courts directly through PILs for violation of fundamental rights would prove much simpler.[20] When the *Ratlam* case was decided, PIL had not yet caught on as an established form of adjudication in the Supreme Court and high courts. However, through this new form of adjudication of fundamental rights developed in the 1980s, the Supreme Court made innovations in judicial process that included relaxed rules of standing, admission of petitions solely on the basis of letters, and gathering of evidence in judicial proceedings by affidavits and commissions of enquiry. In addition, the Court also made innovations in substantive law that read numerous directive principles into the right to life guaranteed under Article 21 of the Constitution.[21] Collectively, these innovations made the Court more accessible to fundamental-rights-based

[20] However, for the continuing impact of the discourse of nuisance law even on PILs, see D. Asher Ghertner, 'Analysis of New Legal Discourse behind Delhi's Slum Demolitions', (2008) XLIII(20) *Economic & Political Weekly* 57.

[21] For a sense of these developments, see Lavanya Rajamani, 'Public Interest Environmental Litigation in India: Exploring Issues of Access, Participation, Equity, Effectiveness and Sustainability', (2007) 19(3) *Journal of Environmental Law* 293; Ashok H. Desai and S. Muralidhar, 'Public Interest Litigation: Potential and Problems', in B.N. Kirpal, Ashok H. Desai,

claims, and also vastly expanded the reach of the higher judiciary's supervision over a range of governance issues affecting social and economic rights, including rights in sanitation in general and urban sanitation in particular.

The higher judiciary in India has asserted rights in sanitation as a part of Article 21 of the Constitution in a number of cases, and has intervened through positive injunctions to fashion remedies permitting considerable judicial supervision of governmental obligations in urban sanitation.[22] Thus for instance, in *M.C. Mehta* v *Union of India & Others*, the Court passed a series of directions to all the municipal bodies along the course of the river Ganga to take measures to prevent the pollution of the river.[23] In *Janki Nathubhai Chhara & Others* v *Sardarnagar Municipality*, the Gujarat High Court coaxed and persuaded the municipality to build a sewerage and drainage system in a low-income neighbourhood to deal with monsoon flooding.[24] In *M.C. Mehta* v *State of Orissa & Others*, the Orissa High Court responded to a petition regarding the impact of sewage-related pollution on provisioning of clean drinking water in Cuttack by constituting a coordination committee of senior government officials to ensure provision of clean drinking water and improvement in sanitation.[25]

Gopal Subramanium, Rajeev Dhavan, and Raju Ramachandran (eds), *Supreme but Not Infallible: Essays in Honour of the Supreme Court of India* (Oxford University Press, 2004), 159; Upendra Baxi, 'Taking Suffering Seriously: Social Action Litigation in the Supreme Court of India', (1985) 4 *Third World Legal Studies* 107.

[22] On positive injunctions, see Mark Tushnet, 'Reflections on Judicial Enforcement of Social and Economic Rights in the Twenty-First Century', (2011) 4 *NUJS Law Review* 177.

[23] *M.C. Mehta* v *Union of India & Others* AIR 1988 SC 1115 (Supreme Court of India, 1988) ('*Mehta* (1988)').

[24] *Janki Nathubhai Chhara & Others* v *Sardarnagar Municipality* AIR 1986 Guj 49 (High Court of Gujarat, 1985).

[25] M.C. *Mehta* v *State of Orissa & Others AIR* 1992 Ori 225 (High Court of Orissa, 1992). See also *Dhanajirao Jivarao Jadhav* v *State of Maharashtra* 1998 (2) Mah LJ 462 (High Court of Bombay, 1997), and a contrasting decision in *Nanded City Development Committee* v *State of Maharashtra* 1994 (2) Bom C Rep 7 (High Court of Bombay, 1993).

In *L.K. Koolwal* v *State of Rajasthan & Others*, the High Court of Rajasthan held that ensuring street cleaning, removal of noxious substances, and the abatement of public nuisances were obligatory municipal functions that could not be evaded on grounds of limited resources.[26] And similarly, addressing issues of solid waste management in *Almitra Patel* v *Union of India*, the Supreme Court constituted a committee whose report formed the basis of the Municipal Solid Waste (Management and Handling) Rules, 2000, which were notified by the Ministry of Environment and Forests under the Environment (Protection) Act, 1986.[27]

In most of these cases, there has been a clear recognition of one or the other of the bouquet of rights in sanitation gathered in Table 7A.1, and often as part of the right to life under Article 21 of the Constitution. This has generally been accompanied by positive injunctions with varying intensities of judicial review of administrative action in the different cases brought before the courts. This sort of judicial intervention has often raised questions regarding the appropriate separation of governmental powers and the legitimacy and effectiveness of judicial intervention to remedy administrative shortcomings.[28] However, for our current purposes, it is important to note, through a few decided cases, the manner in which courts have intervened in the administration and governance of sanitation through PIL to affirm justiciable rights in sanitation.

---

[26] *L.K. Koolwal* v *State of Rajasthan & Others* AIR 1988 Raj 2 (High Court of Rajasthan, 1986) (*'Koolwal'*). See also *Dr K.C. Malhotra* v *State of Madhya Pradesh* AIR 1994 MP 48 (High Court of Madhya Pradesh, 1993).

[27] See *Almitra Patel* v *Union of India* Writ Petition No. 888 of 1996 (Supreme Court of India, Order dated 11 January 2000). In 2014, this case was shifted to the National Green Tribunal, which disposed the case finally in 2016. See *Almitra Patel & Others* v *Union of India & Others* Original Application No. 199 of 2014 (National Green Tribunal (Principal Bench), Order dated 22 December 2016). For a very similar case, see *Suo Motu* v *Ahmedabad Municipal Corporation* Special Civil Application No. 14128 of 2005 (High Court of Gujarat, Judgment dated 15 February 2006).

[28] Pratap Bhanu Mehta, 'The Rise of Judicial Sovereignty' (2007) 18 *Journal of Democracy* 70.

The judiciary and the obligation to provide sanitation

In the *Koolwal* case, the court had to decide the obligation of the Jaipur Municipality to remove dirt and filth from public streets, which the petitioner claimed, affected the right to a clean and healthy environment guaranteed by Article 21 of the Constitution.[29] The court interpreted the statutory scheme of the Rajasthan Municipalities Act, 1959, stating that the municipal body was expected to make 'reasonable provisions' to mean that it was obliged to ensure street cleaning and removal of public nuisance which were listed as 'primary duties' of the municipality. In doing so it also held that insufficient funds could not be offered as a plea for the non-performance of these primary duties. Consequently, the court fashioned a remedy for the problem by directing a court-appointed commissioner, the municipality, and the petitioner in the case to work together to ensure that the municipality removed the dirt and filth within a period of six months.

Similarly, the *M.C. Mehta* case dealt with a writ petition in public interest alleging violation of fundamental rights resulting from the pollution of the river Ganga as a consequence of untreated sewage, especially as it flowed past the city of Kanpur.[30] Here, too, the Court identified the Kanpur Nagarpalika's primary responsibility for safe disposal of sewage and additionally the responsibility of the pollution control boards under the Water (Prevention and Control of Pollution) Act, 1974, and the Environment (Protection) Act, 1986, to monitor, check compliance, and ensure prevention and abatement of water pollution.[31] The Court also noted the slow progress of sewage management work under the Ganga Action Plan initiated by the Central Government, which, the Court asserted, justified judicial intervention to enforce municipal obligation to prevent further pollution of the river. Consequently, the Court intervened in the case to fashion a series of directives that included construction of sewage works under the 'Ganga Action Plan' in a time-bound manner; submission of a timeframe by the Nagarpalika for installation of sewage

[29] *Koolwal* (n 26).
[30] *Mehta* (n 23).
[31] *Mehta* (n 23).

treatment works; prevention of waste accumulation from dairies which was flowing into the river; construction of a sewer system in labour colonies; construction of public urinals; preventing the practice of throwing corpses into the river; and the need for educational programmes in schools impressing upon students the need for protection of the environment.

Once again, just like in *Koolwal*, the Court's orders in *M.C. Mehta* asserted a strong role in the governance of sanitation for the courts while reiterating the primary obligation of the municipality to make 'reasonable and adequate provision' to provide sewerage and related services. Importantly, the Court seemed to tie together municipal obligations to provide sanitation services with the obligation to ensure that municipal sewage was treated according to statutorily specified pollution standards, before it was discharged into the river Ganga. In addition, these statutory obligations were tied together with constitutionally guaranteed fundamental rights. However, in each of these cases it is important to note that beyond declaring rights or government obligations regarding sanitation, the Court also took on the task of making substantive policy choices on matters regarding sanitation.[32] Judicial intervention in matters of policy is a much-discussed issue, and the next section picks up a particularly stark example of judicial intervention and the implications for its legitimacy even as the Court expanded the right to sanitation.

The legitimacy of the judiciary in the provision of sanitation services

The *Almitra Patel* case stemmed from a petition alleging that various deficiencies in the solid waste management system across the country violated the right to life under Article 21 of the Constitution. In this regard, it must be mentioned that some accounts of the provision

---

[32] Many of these cases dealing with the pollution of river Ganga have now been shifted to the National Green Tribunal established in 2010, which carries on the approach to environmental governance of sanitation and related issues established by the Supreme Court, though with the assistance of technical members.

of sanitation services consider solid waste management as falling beyond the purview of rights in sanitation. However, against the continuum of obligations as previously identified, this case will also be considered as illustrative of the broader set of municipal obligations to provide urban sanitation. In particular, the current discussion is concerned with the active policy role that the Supreme Court has asserted for itself, and its implications for the fairness and legitimacy of the obligations it determines regarding the provision of services in urban sanitation.

In the instant case, action was sought by the petitioner in relation to poorly managed open dumping of waste; the identification of facilities for waste processing and disposal; and better collection, transportation, treatment, and disposal of municipal solid waste. As in other public interest petitions raising complex issues of public administration, the Court responded to the petitioner by establishing a committee to guide the task of reforming solid waste management practices. Similarly, as in the *M.C. Mehta* case,[33] the problem of solid waste management was also understood to be a municipal responsibility involving a significant degree of environmental regulation and management. Accordingly, the Court acted on the report of the committee by pressing the Ministry of Environment and Forests to notify the Municipal Solid Waste (Management and Handling) Rules, 2000, under the Environment (Protection) Act.[34] Further, in its long oversight of the case,[35] the Court has passed numerous orders on various aspects of the solid waste disposal problem including municipal responsibilities relating to collection, transport, sorting,

[33] *Mehta* (n 23).

[34] The 2000 Rules have now been superseded by the Solid Waste Management Rules, 2016. Further, it is important to note that the Solid Waste Management Rules, 2016, cast mandatory duties on a range of authorities from central ministries, local and municipal bodies, to pollution control boards, who have the overall responsibility of monitoring the efficient disposal of solid waste.

[35] The oversight of cases over long periods has been made possible through judicial devices such as continuing mandamus. For a mention of this form, see Rajamani (n 21).

disposal, and recycling of solid waste.[36] Thus, the Court was not just establishing obligatory duties of municipal government regarding municipal solid waste, but was also deeply involved in defining the very policy choices to improve environmental management and regulation of municipal solid waste.

Following the notification of the Municipal Solid Waste (Management and Handling) Rules, 2000, the Court set its sights on implementation of targets specified in those rules regarding the establishment of waste processing and disposal facilities, improvement of landfill sites, and identification of landfill sites for the future. It sought to achieve these policy goals in the four metropolitan cities and Bengaluru. As with the cases discussed earlier, the *Almitra Patel* case posed no lack of certainty on the existence of governmental obligations but raised questions regarding the propriety, fairness, and legitimacy of the Supreme Court's intervention in solid waste management policy as it determined municipal obligations. Detailing the *Almitra Patel* case in a broader comment on public interest environmental litigation, Rajamani forcefully illustrates the problems that follow court interventions in multifaceted policy problems. That is, courts could lean in favour of specific policies, adopt debatable and dubious technologies, impose unrealistic policy objectives, and at the same time, be unable to fashion sustained administrative monitoring of policy problems.[37]

Apart from the obvious problem of ensuring that judicial decisions do not stray from the democratic processes of decision-making, it is useful to detail how the extension of judicial writ could be seen to be illegitimate in the *Almitra Patel* case. Speaking on the impact of urban slums on garbage removal in the city of Delhi, the Court in one of its orders stated that:

> Establishment or creating of slums, it seems, appears to be good business and is well organised. The number of slums has multiplied in the last few years by geometrical proportion. Large areas of public land, in this way, are usurped for private use free of cost. … The promise of

---

[36] See for example, the following orders of the Supreme Court in this case: AIR 1986 SC 983; 1998 (4) SCALE 9; 1999 (2) SCALE 685.

[37] Rajamani (n 21), 303–4.

free land, at the taxpayers cost, in place of a jhuggi, is a proposal which attracts more land grabbers. Rewarding an encroacher on public land with [*sic*] free alternate site is like giving a reward to a pickpocket. The department of slum clearance does not seem to have cleared any slum ... for decades. ... This in turn gives rise to domestic waste being strewn on open land in and around the slums. This can best be controlled at least, in the first instance, by preventing the growth of slums.[38]

These comments were accompanied by orders to government agencies in Delhi to take steps to prevent the encroachment of public land leading to the creation of slums.

The Court's hostility towards slums is barely concealed in these comments, and it is far from clear why the Court had to issue directions in relation to slums to address the solid waste problem. A cursory consideration of the substantive issues regarding solid waste management could suggest that the Court's pronouncement on slums betrays a poor, if not debatable, understanding of the significant role of slum dwellers in the recycling of waste,[39] their marginal footprint on the solid waste generated by a city,[40] and of the role slums play in providing appropriately priced housing for the overwhelming majority of citizens in most Indian cities.[41]

Summing Up on the Courts and the Right to Sanitation

The judicial decisions discussed in this section are by no means an exhaustive sweep of the courts' position on urban sanitation, but they

---

[38] *Almitra H. Patel* v *Union of India & Others* 2000(1) SCALE 568 (Supreme Court of India, 2000).

[39] Kaveri Gill, *Of Poverty and Plastic: Scavenging and Scrap Trading Entrepreneurs in India's Urban Informal Economy* (Oxford University Press, 2009).

[40] For instance, it is estimated that slum dwellers contribute to less than 5 per cent of the waste in cities. See Sunita Narain, *Excreta Matters: State of India's Environment: A Citizens Report* (Centre for Science and Environment, 2012), 7.

[41] For instance, only around 20 per cent of Delhi's residents live in planned colonies. Figures drawn from Gautam Bhan, '"This Is No Longer the City I Once Knew": Evictions, the Urban Poor and the Right to the City in Millennial Delhi', (2009) 21(1) *Environment & Urbanization* 127, 132.

nonetheless represent a clear judicial inclination to affirm municipal obligations to provide urban sanitation. In addition, the PIL cases in particular have demonstrated that the courts have also emerged as an additional pole in the governance of sanitation with little reluctance to take on complex public policy issues. Further, cases like *Almitra Patel* demonstrate how specific orders of the courts in their long oversight of particular sanitation-related issues could be seen to be less than fair and legitimate. Even so, the intervention of the courts via PIL has established them as a key administrative player in the discharge of obligations related to sanitation.

Each of the decisions discussed in this section involve instances where the courts were confronted with poor sanitation services resulting from various governance and policy failures. Despite the courts' best, and sometimes, overzealous defence of rights in sanitation, the state of sanitation services remains woefully inadequate, and the need for improved sanitation is only likely to get even more pressing. Therefore, as sanitation becomes an ever more urgent urban problem, policy design and administrative action to provide sanitation services is only likely to assume even more of the centre stage, and it is unlikely that piecemeal court-fashioned policy can replace the need for a comprehensive administrative response to the problem. Accordingly, assuming that municipal governments and urban local bodies will be at the forefront of delivering rights in urban sanitation, the following sections map an idiosyncratic selection of institutional challenges that they will be pressed to address in order to deliver services that the courts have declared to be their obligatory function, and part of the fundamental rights of individuals.

Institutional Challenges for the Extension of Sanitation Services in Urban India

Extending the reach and quality of urban sanitation services is arguably amongst the most pressing challenges for contemporary sanitation policy, especially from the perspective of the urban poor, who are the most excluded from the provision of urban sanitation services. There are of course infrastructural, technical, policy, economic, and other similar dimensions to the challenge of extending the reach of service provision, and making it more inclusive for all urban residents. However, the present section highlights only a subset of this broader set of issues, which are believed to be crucial to outlining, elaborating, and actualizing a right to sanitation in the urban context.

Rights in Land and the Challenge of Extending Access to Sanitation Services

In the idealized legal scheme for planned urban development, the extension of sanitation-related services to urban settlements is tied to their orderly absorption into the organized urban land market. This typically involves processes of preparation and transformation of urban land that include the conversion of a proposed settlement in land revenue records from rural to urban; the grant of development approval from the town and country planning authorities for plotting a colony with provision for services and amenities like roads, electricity, sanitation, and other such services; and the grant of building plan approval by the municipal bodies. Generally, it is after compliance with such requirements that legally valid applications can be made to the municipal government for the provision of sanitation-related services.

As a matter of fact, however, much urban land is either 'illegally' occupied by squatters in slums or by 'unauthorized' or 'irregular' residents whose settlements have not passed the compliance requirements imposed on them by the urban planning laws. In other words, illegal squatting or non-compliant development of colonies is the background condition that defines the occupation of land by a majority of urban residents in most parts of India. By extension, planned urbanization and provision of services has been able to include only a very small section of most urban settlements.[42] Consequently, if the provision of services is tied to full legality of tenure and the legal compliances demanded by planning norms, as it often is, then it will have severe adverse effects on a city's ability to provide sanitation-related services to the majority of urban residents.

---

[42] For instance, in the city of Delhi, just about 20 per cent of the city's population live in fully planned colonies with fully legal title to land. See Bhan (n 41), 132.

The exclusions produced by the processes of planned urban development emphasize the need to respond to irregularity and illegality at a policy and administrative level to be able to provide services to the largest section of urban residents.[43] An underexplored area of research in this regard is the complex forms of administrative practice which have evolved to permit regularization of settlements that have not followed planning norms by way of slum notifications and the phased granting of tenure to certain types of individual tenements over time.[44] Aiming to provide urban residents with a measure of security in land, regularization provides for a variety of rights falling short of full legal title that include the grant of *pattas*, no-eviction guarantees, declaration of a settlement as a slum under slum acts, and so on. Regularization is therefore a powerful tool by which calibrated administrative recognition of 'illegal' and 'irregular' urban tenements permits not only security of tenure, but also the possibility of extending the horizons of entitlement to services like sanitation in the interstices of planned urbanization.

For instance, in a case study in Bhopal tracing links between land tenure, planning permissions, and access to services, it has been noticed that the quality of tenure in land has a direct bearing on the quality of services available for residents. That is, municipal

[43] For example, Alternative Law Forum, *Of Master Plans, Laws and Illegalities in an Era of Transition* (Alternative Law Forum, 2003); Gautam Bhan, 'Planned Illegalities, Housing and the "Failure" of Planning in Delhi: 1947–2010', (2013) XLVIII(24) *Economic & Political Weekly* 58; Sharmila L. Murthy, 'Land Security and the Challenges of Realizing the Human Right to Water and Sanitation in the Slums of Mumbai, India', (2013) 14(2) *Health and Human Rights* 1; Geetanjoy Sahu and Ratoola Kundu, 'Selective Inclusions and Exclusions', (2014) XLIX(48) *Economic & Political Weekly* 69.

[44] Arkaja Singh, 'Legal Aspects of Tenure and Housing Finance in Informal Settlements: Law and Practice from Indian States', Scholarly Paper ID 2289149 (Social Science Research Network, 2012). See also Darshini Mahadevia, 'Tenure Security and Urban Social Protection Links: India', (2010) 41(4) *IDS Bulletin* 52; Geoffrey K. Payne, *Urban Land Tenure and Property Rights in Developing Countries: A Review* (Overseas Development Administration, 1996).

administrations have found legitimate administrative means of moving past tenure in land to extend water and sanitation services in notified slum settlements, and where individual residents have been able to incrementally wrest limited rights of recognition to their tenements.[45] This of course does not take away from the precarious relationship of the urban poor in relation to land,[46] but it does point to links between administrative recognition of land tenure status and the availability of sanitation services.[47] Consequently from the perspective of law and policy efforts that seek to extend rights in urban sanitation, it is of considerable significance to trace the manner in which land tenure status and planning laws impede the provision of urban services, and the extent to which these barriers to the provision of services might be dismantled.[48]

The State of Devolved Power: Increasing Municipal Accountability for the Provision of Sanitation Services

As already mentioned, municipalities have been at the forefront of the delivery of sanitation services either as institutions of self-government or as instrumentalities through which state governments deliver services. However, since the early 1990s, the obligation to provide sanitation-related services in urban areas has been framed by the 74th Amendment to the Constitution, under which sanitation-related

[45] Singh (n 44).

[46] A sobering example in this regard is the drive towards illegalizing slum residents in Delhi over the last decade. See Usha Ramanathan, 'Illegality and the Urban Poor', (2006) XLI(29) *Economic & Political Weekly* 3193.

[47] For a similar account in the city of Mumbai, see Murthy (n 43).

[48] To some extent this has been made possible by the Rajiv Awas Yojana, the slum policy of the Ministry of Housing and Urban Poverty Alleviation, which mandates compulsory coverage and provision of sanitation-related services even for those residing in slums. However, this is a policy that focuses on granting property rights to residents of slums rather than providing them with sanitation services. See The Draft Model Property Rights to Slum Dwellers Act, 2011.

functions have been or are expected to be devolved to municipal bodies. The 74th Amendment was founded on the expectation that municipal bodies would function as institutions of self-government with real functional and financial autonomy. However, devolution of powers to municipal government is a complex story. Punctuated by the occasional case of strong municipal bodies with considerable financial autonomy and operational wherewithal to effectively perform sanitation-related functions, most municipal bodies do not currently have either the power or the capacity to effectively function as institutions of self-government.[49] Nonetheless, the fate of rights in sanitation is tied to what seems like the slow but steady movement towards greater devolution of power to municipal bodies, as demonstrated, for instance, in the checklist of reforms under the Jawaharlal Nehru National Urban Renewal Mission (JNNURM), which ties funding for urban projects to devolution of powers to urban local bodies.[50]

Following the passage of the 74th Amendment, elected local bodies have been constituted as mandated by the amendment in almost all urban areas. Illustratively, even though Table 7A.1 is not representative of any broader trend, it does suggest that different functions are differently devolved, and some states devolve more functions than others. For instance, water supply and sewerage are functions that are less devolved than street cleaning and removal of solid waste. Similarly, a state like Maharashtra seems to devolve more power to local bodies than Rajasthan. This could be attributed to a range of factors from willingness of state governments to devolve powers and functions effectively, the perceived capacities of local governments to provide sanitation services, the historical strength of local governments to pitch for and take on these functions, as well as the strength of parastatal bodies in a given state.

[49] For an account of the devolution process in India, see National Institute of Urban Affairs, *Impact of the Constitution (74th Amendment) Act on the Working of Urban Local Bodies* (National Institute of Urban Affairs, 2005).

[50] See Government of India, Ministry of Urban Development, Jawaharlal Nehru National Urban Renewal Mission, 'Revised Guidelines (Sub-mission for Urban Infrastructure and Governance)' (Ministry of Urban Development, 2011).

The 12th Schedule inserted into the Constitution as part of the 74th Amendment lists the functions that state governments might devolve to municipal bodies to enable them to function as institutions of self-government. These functions include planning, land use, building construction, water supply, sanitation, solid waste management, slum improvement, urban poverty, as well as urban amenities. However, this list is merely illustrative, and there is no mandatory duty on governments to devolve these powers, and correspondingly, there are few administrative responsibilities that are passed on to urban local bodies. Similarly, with limited fiscal powers and no mandatory constitutional provisions for sharing of tax revenues, the municipality's effectiveness in matters relating to sanitation is likely to be severely limited.[51] Even so, the 74th Amendment is a normative beacon, which clearly signals that the road ahead cannot but involve a movement towards greater decentralization of powers in services such as sanitation to urban local government.

The move towards greater decentralization is a leap of faith in deepening democratic accountability by localizing governance. As already mentioned, there are numerous considerations ranging from the willingness of state governments to effectively devolve powers and functions, and the competence of urban local governments to take on complex tasks associated with sanitation, to the attempts of the Central Government to push for greater decentralization through reform conditions tied to its funding of urban projects. All these different influences will obviously pull in different directions, and will come to rest in different forms in different states. Even so, it is at their intersection that the move towards more self-assured local government capable of equitably and efficiently resolving challenges in sanitation will be located.

---

[51] For detailed accounts on this aspect of decentralization of powers to urban local bodies, see K.C. Sivaramakrishnan, *Courts, Panchayats and Nagarpalikas: Background and Review of the Case Law* (Academic Foundation, 2009); Sharmila L. Murthy and Maya J. Mahin, 'Constitutional Impediments to Decentralization in the World's Largest Federal Country', (2015) 26(1) *Duke Journal of Comparative & International Law* 79.

Regulatory Standards and the Performance of Sanitation Functions by Municipal Authorities

The scale of the sanitation problem might be rapidly overwhelming the capacity of the state to come to grips with the problem of sanitizing India's cities. Consider for instance, the statistic, that installed capacity to treat sewage generated by Indian cities is only 31 per cent, which often does not operate to full capacity, and further, that the bulk of the installed capacity to treat sewage is on the river Ganga as part of the Ganga Action Plan.[52] Consequently, in addition to the problems posed by the absence of rights in land and inadequate devolution, realizing the right to sanitation will to some extent depend on the ability to hold institutions, and especially municipal institutions, to established and evolving legal norms and pollution standards at different levels of the federal system.

An obvious source of standards to tie municipal bodies to environmental norms is the collection of environmental laws comprising the Environment (Protection) Act, 1986, the Water (Prevention and Control of Pollution) Act, 1974, and the Air (Prevention and Control of Pollution) Act, 1981. The regulatory scheme of these statutes is governed by very detailed standards established by the Central Government, which are primarily enforced by pollution control agencies at the state and the central level. These statutes require compliance from municipalities as well as a range of industrial, commercial, and other urban actors. However, the state of sanitation services in India suggests that there could be various aspects of the design and implementation of environmental legislation and associated institutions that require significant reform. A thorough evaluation of the failures of environmental legislation in relation to the sanitation challenge is a problem that awaits separate analysis, but the scale of the problem across services such as water supply, drainage, sewage treatment, and solid waste management also suggests the need for innovative policy interventions and better implementation of existing law and legal standards.

In this regard, the Ministry of Urban Development laid out a document in the form of the National Urban Sanitation Policy (NUSP)

---

[52] Bhullar (n 13), 236.

in 2008, elaborating its vision for a policy thrust towards improved urban sanitation. The NUSP conception of the sanitation problem covers the range of sanitation services currently performed by municipalities, and includes not just the management of human waste, but solutions that incorporate all aspects of environmental sanitation including tasks such as solid waste management, disposal of industrial and hazardous waste, as well as access to water.[53] Further, the NUSP roadmap for sanitized cities emphasizes governance goals such as greater social awareness about sanitation issues, elimination of open defecation, working beyond fragmented institutional responsibility, building an integrated state- and city-based approach to sanitation to reflect local requirements, generating appropriate technology choices, reaching the unserved and the poor, and building a culture of responsiveness to citizen demands. Significantly, the NUSP also ties the obligation to provide sanitation with a reform agenda seeking to generate data on the quality of sanitation services by way of measurable indices.[54]

Quite like the standards-based regulation in the environmental laws previously mentioned, the Ministry of Urban Development commenced the task of developing a set of benchmarked indicators for sanitation services from the year 2009. Tracking the quality of provision of sanitation services along 28 indicators, which is also called 'service level benchmarking', it covers service provision in water, sewage, solid waste management, and storm water drainage. The stated object of this benchmarking initiative is to identify a minimum set of standard performance parameters for the water and sanitation sector that are commonly understood and used by all stakeholders across the country, define a common minimum framework for monitoring and reporting on these indicators, and set out guidelines on how to operationalize this framework in a phased manner.[55]

---

[53] NUSP (n 2), 6.

[54] Government of India, Ministry of Urban Development, City Sanitation Plans (CSP) Self-Review Checklist: An Aid to Cities for Ensuring Quality while Finalizing the Draft CSP for Submission (Ministry of Urban Development, 2011).

[55] Government of India, Ministry of Urban Development, Improving Urban Services through Service Level Benchmarking (Ministry of Urban Development, 2010).

Benchmarked services are intended and designed to perform the extremely important task of monitoring the effectiveness of the enormous investments that have poured, and are likely to pour into the sanitation sector through schemes like the JNNURM and the SBM by emphasizing improvements in the quality of the policy track chosen, and services delivered by the government. Consequently, service level benchmarking is aimed to effect a more integrated and performance-oriented policy framework for sanitation services that is able to identify and rectify administrative failings swiftly and accurately, as well as to evaluate the effects of investments in the sanitation sector. However, while such benchmarking tools might have extremely important accountability and efficiency spinoffs, their implications for rights, especially at the citizen or user interface, cannot be taken for granted. As the Handbook on Service Level Benchmarking issued by the Ministry of Urban Development suggests, the parameters to measure and benchmark services are 'defined from a utility manager's perspective', and primarily emphasize efficiency of service.[56] However, as policy direction, incentives, resource allocation, and penalties are likely in the future to turn on benchmarking results, it is also important to emphasize other criteria that will improve the provision of services at the citizen interface, especially for the urban poor. In addition, these standards are also important for ecological and climate change outcomes, locally appropriate sanitation technologies, as well as standards in environmental law that must define the sanitation agenda and the right to sanitation in urban areas.[57]

The move towards benchmarking services is of course driven by the Central Government, whose influence over the provision of sanitation services by state and municipal governments is only indirect, exercised by making available tied funds. The effectiveness with which these efforts will impact the actual delivery of sanitation services awaits further investigation. However, from the perspective of a right in sanitation, this discussion on benchmarked indicators suggests some of the challenges that will be involved in delivering

[56] Government of India, Ministry of Urban Development, *Handbook on Service Level Benchmarking* (Ministry of Urban Development, 2011).

[57] These are also the objectives listed in the NUSP.

sanitation outcomes, and ensuring standards in institutional functioning, especially at the level of the citizen interface.

* * *

The primarily descriptive map of some of the issues that might bear on a right to sanitation in the urban context has emphasized three kinds of concerns. First, it noted the interlocking institutional layers within which the sanitation problem in urban India is located. Thus, any solution to the problem would necessarily imply the mobilization of institutional energies across the central, state, and local tiers of government. Second, despite ambiguities in the statutory framework on government obligations regarding urban sanitation, the courts have unambiguously asserted a range of sanitation services, from sewage disposal to solid waste management in urban contexts as obligations that government must necessarily discharge. These obligations could derive from obligations of municipal officials to abate nuisance as in the *Ratlam* case or they could derive from municipal obligations read with fundamental rights as in the *Koolwal, M.C. Mehta,* and *Almitra Patel* cases. However, across these cases, judicial recognition of government obligation to provide sanitation services has far from solved the practical challenge of delimiting the content of rights in sanitation, and the institutional framework within which these rights are to be delivered. In fact, as the *Almitra Patel* case demonstrates, overzealous involvement might both be illegitimate, perhaps even counterproductive, to extending the right to the widest section of the urban population. It was these concerns that motivated the last set of investigations on the institutional challenges around which any definitional detail of a right or rights in sanitation will take shape.

As mentioned at the very outset, the content of the right to sanitation such as water supply, toilets, manual scavenging, drainage, sewage treatment and so on, require more detailed disaggregation than is presently possible. Even so, it is only at the intersection of issues such as land tenure, local government, and enforceable standards that a robust institutional ecosystem for sanitation rights in urban India could emerge to define meaningful rights in sanitation as outlined in this chapter.

Annexure 7A

Table 7A.1   Sanitation Functions of Municipal and Local Bodies

No	Function		Himachal Pradesh	Madhya Pradesh
			(Himachal Pradesh Municipal Corporation Act, 1994)	(Madhya Pradesh Municipal Corporations Act, 1956)
	Basic Services			
1	Water Supply	Law	Function may be transferred by notification of state government. 'water supply for domestic, industrial and commercial purposes'.	Obligatory functions include 'the management and maintenance of all municipal water works and the construction and maintenance of new works and means for providing a sufficient supply of suitable water for public and private purposes'.
		Devolution	Shimla Municipal Corporation. However, function may be performed by Irrigation & Public Health Department, Government of Himachal Pradesh, in other towns.	Functions gradually transferred to municipal bodies from PHED. Some degree of financial responsibility and staffing control by state government, but operational control has been transferred.

Maharashtra	Odisha	Karnataka	Rajasthan
(Bombay Provincial Municipal Corporations Act, 1949)	(Orissa Municipal Corporations Act, 2003)	(Karnataka Municipal Corporations Act, 1973)	(Rajasthan Municipalities Act, 2009)
Obligatory functions include 'the management and maintenance of all municipal water works and the construction or acquisition of new works necessary for a sufficient supply of water for public and private purposes'.	Obligatory functions include 'the management and maintenance of all Corporation water works and the construction or acquisition of new works necessary for sufficient supply of water for public and private purposes'.	Obligatory functions include 'the management and maintenance of all municipal water works and the construction or acquisition of new works necessary for a sufficient supply of water for public and private purposes'.	Several provisions refer to water projects, mains, and water works which may be managed or maintained by the municipal body or state government, but no specific provision casts a duty for the maintenance and management of water supply systems.
Functions devolved to municipal body, in most urban bodies.	Public Health Unit under Housing and Urban Development Department.	Bangalore Water Supply and Sewerage Board (BWSSB) in Bengaluru; in other towns, distribution functions have been partially handed over from the Karnataka Urban Water Supply and Drainage Board (KUWSDB) to municipal bodies.	Function with PHED.

(*Cont'd*)

Table 7A.1 (*Cont'd*)

No	Function		Himachal Pradesh	Madhya Pradesh
			(Himachal Pradesh Municipal Corporation Act, 1994)	(Madhya Pradesh Municipal Corporations Act, 1956)
2	Sewerage	Law	Function may be transferred by notification of the state government. 'public health, sanitation, conservancy and solid waste management'.	Obligatory function: 'Disposing of night soil and rubbish'; 'cleaning public streets, places and sewers'.
		Devolution	Shimla Municipal Corporation. However, function may be performed by Irrigation & Public Health Department, Government of Himachal Pradesh, in other towns.	Functions gradually transferred to municipal bodies from PHED. Some degree of financial responsibility and staffing control by state government, but operational control has been transferred.
3	Street Cleaning	Law	Function may be transferred by notification of state government.	'Cleaning public streets' is an obligatory function.

Maharashtra	Odisha	Karnataka	Rajasthan
(Bombay Provincial Municipal Corporations Act, 1949)	(Orissa Municipal Corporations Act, 2003)	(Karnataka Municipal Corporations Act, 1973)	(Rajasthan Municipalities Act, 2009)
'The collection, removal, treatment and disposal of sewage, offensive matter and rubbish' is an obligatory function.	'The collection, removal, treatment and disposal of solid wastes, sewage, offensive matter and rubbish' is an obligatory municipal function.	'The collection, removal, treatment and disposal of sewage, offensive matter and rubbish' is an obligatory function.	Making reasonable and proper provision for public health, sanitation, conservation, solid waste management, drainage and sewerage, cleaning public streets, and so on, is an obligatory municipal function.
Functions devolved to municipal body, in most urban bodies.	Orissa Sewerage Board.	Bangalore Water Supply and Sewerage Board in Bengaluru; in other towns, collection and network functions have been partially handed over from KUWSDB to municipal bodies.	Functions performed by PHED.
'The watering, scavenging and cleansing of all public streets and places in the city and the removal of all sweepings therefrom' is an obligatory function.	'The watering, scavenging and cleaning of all public streets and places in the city and removal of all sweepings therefrom' is an obligatory function.	'The watering and cleansing of all public streets and public places in the city and the removal of all sweepings therefrom' is an obligatory function.	Making reasonable and proper provision for public health, sanitation, conservation, solid waste management, drainage and sewerage, cleaning public streets, and so on, is an obligatory municipal function.

(Cont'd)

Table 7A.1 (*Cont'd*)

No	Function		Himachal Pradesh	Madhya Pradesh
			(Himachal Pradesh Municipal Corporation Act, 1994)	(Madhya Pradesh Municipal Corporations Act, 1956)
3	Street Cleaning	Devolution	Municipal bodies in most towns. May be retained by Himachal Pradesh Housing and Urban Development Authority (HIMUDA) in some new development areas.	Municipal body.
4	Solid Waste Management	Law	Function may be transferred by notification of state government. 'public health, sanitation, conservancy and solid waste management'.	'Removal of night soil and rubbish' is an obligatory function.
		Devolution	Municipal body in most towns. May be retained by HIMUDA in some new development areas.	Municipal body.

Maharashtra	Odisha	Karnataka	Rajasthan
(Bombay Provincial Municipal Corporations Act, 1949)	(Orissa Municipal Corporations Act, 2003)	(Karnataka Municipal Corporations Act, 1973)	(Rajasthan Municipalities Act, 2009)
Municipal body.	Municipal body.	Municipal body.	Function split between municipal body and urban improvement trusts/development authorities in major towns.
'The collection, removal, treatment and disposal of sewage, offensive matter and rubbish' is an obligatory function.	'The collection, removal, treatment and disposal of solid wastes, sewage, offensive matter and rubbish' is an obligatory municipal function.	'The collection, removal, treatment and disposal of sewage, offensive matter and rubbish' is an obligatory function.	Making reasonable and proper provision for public health, sanitation, conservation, solid waste management, drainage and sewerage, cleaning public streets, and so on, is an obligatory municipal function. In addition, the municipality to be responsible for the implementation of rules made by the Central Government to regulate the management and handling of solid wastes.
Municipal body.	Municipal body.	Municipal body.	Function split between municipal body and urban improvement trusts/development authorities in major towns.

8

The Politics of Open Defecation

Informality, Body, and Infrastructure in Mumbai*

Renu Desai, Colin McFarlane, and *Stephen Graham*

How are bodies and infrastructure related in contexts of severe urban poverty and exploitation? Or more precisely, what kinds of relations become possible, and how are they experienced, in the shifting socio-material configurations of infrastructures in informal neigh-bourhoods? Despite the vital wealth of critical research on urban infrastructures and political ecologies, critical urban and geographical research lacks an understanding of the micropolitics through which infrastructures are differently made, unmade, and experienced. This is an important gap, because it is in this making and unmaking that much of urban life is increasingly lived and politicized, and especially so among the growing numbers of people—in both the global South and North—living in informal settlements.

Drawing on examples from fundamental infrastructures of sanitation in Mumbai, we explore in this chapter a multiplicity of

* An earlier version of this chapter was published in *Antipode* 47(1) in 2015, 98–120.

relationships between the body and infrastructure. Issues of access, routine, perception, and experience—in short, the lived worlds of urban infrastructure, come to the fore. Important here are practices of improvisation, too often neglected in accounts of urban infra-structure and political ecologies, which we examine in relation to different forms of open defecation. These practices of improvisation are coping mechanisms that often reproduce and deepen inequalities rather than articulate political claims such as the right to sanitation infrastructure. But these practices, we will argue, also enter into political claim-making for residents of informal neighbourhoods, whether in the form of demands for certain kinds of sanitation infrastructure, or in response to new forms of disciplining by the state, or in the ways in which residents can become divided around lines of class, religion, ethnicity, or caste in response to improvisatory practices pursued by different groups.

By way of context, we want to begin with a particular and impor-tant moment in Mumbai in 2006, when the city saw the legislation of the Cleanliness and Sanitation Bye-laws which introduced punitive measures against cooking, bathing, spitting, urinating, and defecat-ing in public spaces.[1] While the bye-laws—which regulate a variety of other activities like littering, waste segregation, and so on—are aimed at disciplining all urban residents and elevating their civic conscious-ness, many of the punitive measures are based on what Baviskar refers to as 'bourgeois environmentalism'.[2] This casts upper-class concerns around aesthetics, leisure, and health, which usually clash with the rights of the poor, under broader, seemingly class-neutral discourses of environment-friendly quality of life. In introducing disciplinary action against open defecation in a city in which around 25 per cent of residents have no or inadequate sanitation facilities,[3] the bye-laws

[1] Municipal Corporation of Greater Mumbai (MCGM), Greater Mumbai Cleanliness and Sanitation Bye-laws, 2006. Under the bye-laws, a person is liable to pay a fine of Rs 200 for urinating and Rs 100 for defecat-ing in a public place.

[2] Amita Baviskar, 'Between Violence and Desire: Space, Power and Identity in the Making of Metropolitan Delhi' (2003) 55(175) *International Social Science Journal* 89, 90.

[3] MW-YUVA, *Slum Sanitation Project: Final Report* (Municipal Corporation of Brihan-Mumbai, 2001), 10.

pitted the basic bodily need to empty one's bowels against the right to a clean and sanitary environment.[4]

These bye-laws, moreover, rest on particular conceptions of the relationship between the body and the sanitary/unsanitary city. Open defecation is prohibited under the bye-laws because it creates 'public nuisance'. This includes any act or thing which 'causes or is likely to cause injury, danger, annoyance or offence to the sense of sight, smelling or hearing or which is or may be dangerous to life or injurious to health or property and environment' in a public place.[5] Such a discourse of public nuisance casts practices of open defecation and the presence of human excreta in open spaces as offending to the city's visual and olfactory aesthetic. This, however, privileges the sensory experiences of the urban middle class and elites and erases the sensory experiences of the urban poor, many of whom have to contend with the offensiveness of using unbearably dirty public toilets and who might, at times, even turn to open defecation precisely because of this. The public nuisance discourse also ascribes open defecation as an individual's private bodily act which is in conflict with the city's public health and environment.[6] The significant role of infrastructures in mediating the relationship between private and public, the body and the city, and the body and bodily wastes is thus all but absent in this discourse.

The bye-laws do include a section on the obligatory duties of the municipal government to provide 'adequate community toilets' in 'slum localities'; however, there is no consideration of what constitutes adequate toilets. Government sanitation programmes, which are setting higher targets for toilet provision than ever before, are largely restricted to 'notified slums', that is, informal settlements entitled to basic services. 'Non-notified slums', in which 4.5 per cent

---

[4] We focus only on open defecation because most women from the informal settlements we studied did not resort to open space for urinating since bathing spaces inside their houses were usually used for this.

[5] MCGM (n 1), cl 3.30.

[6] Awadhendra Sharan, 'In the City, Out of Place: Environment and Modernity, Delhi 1860s to 1960s', (2006) XLI(47) *Economic & Political Weekly* 4905; see also Asher Ghertner, 'Analysis of New Legal Discourse Behind Delhi's Slum Demolitions', (2008) XLIII(20) *Economic & Political Weekly* 57.

of Mumbai's population lives, and pavement dwellers are not entitled to basic services.[7] But, while the right to sanitation is spatially differentiated, in practice, even 'notified slums' are often not provided with sanitation, quite frequently through a lack of political will. 'Notified slums' comprise of a wide array of toilet blocks with different levels of cleanliness, maintenance, and accessibility, leading residents to regularly or intermittently defecate in the open in many cases. Partly as a response to the lack of cleanliness and maintenance of toilets delivered under various sanitation programmes in Mumbai, slum sanitation approaches have changed, introducing partnerships between the state, non-governmental organizations (NGOs), and communities through the Slum Sanitation Programme (SSP). However, sanitation programme outcomes are still measured and publicized primarily in terms of numbers, taking a narrow conception of sanitation inadequacy. Moreover, even inadequate sanitation is often not perceived as a good enough reason for people to turn to open defecation. For instance, the CEO of a private security agency contracted to implement the bye-laws explained: 'It is not that there aren't toilets but perhaps there are inadequate toilets and long lines so people just go in the open. Even women'.[8] This implies that people are impatient, and if only they would wait in the toilet queues for their turn, Mumbai would be cleaner in this regard.

In this chapter, we seek to chart out radically different conceptions of the relationship between the body and the sanitary/unsanitary city by thinking through the body's relationship to infrastructures in the metabolic city, which creates profoundly unequal opportunities for fulfilling basic bodily needs. The chapter emerges from ethnographic fieldwork carried out in two informal settlements: Rafinagar, a 'non-notified' settlement which comprises an older and more established

[7] In 2001, 6.25 million people lived in 1959 'slum settlements', accounting for 54 per cent of the city's population. Of this, the city's 'non-notified slums' included 137 settlements with a population of 0.52 million. See MW-YUVA (n 3).

[8] The company name is kept anonymous. The interview took place on 27 April 2010. According to this individual, the most common actions for which people were fined by his agency were spitting, littering, urinating, and defecating.

Part 1 and a newer and still expanding Part 2 in eastern Mumbai, and Khotwadi, an established and 'notified' settlement in western Mumbai. The chapter begins with a discussion of debates around the body, sanitation, filth, and infrastructure, to lay out the intellectual context and framework. By 'infrastructure', we are referring both to material configurations—toilets, water connections, and so on, which of course are made and unmade through not just physical but also social, economic, political, and ecological processes—and social configurations, such as women coordinating with other women to make or unmake systems that enable everyday urban life. This latter use of infrastructure includes, for instance, routinized social arrangements for using particular open spaces at particular times for defecation, and they too are infrastructures because we take infrastructure to be, expansively, systems that enable urban life to collectively take place. If this leaves us with a rather open definition of infrastructure, then that is part of what we want to achieve with the chapter: to disrupt what and who we read and recognize as infrastructure by paying greater attention to the multiple ways in which systems have to be put in place to allow urban life to take place in precarious and marginalized neighbourhoods.

In the next section, we examine how open defecation emerges through everyday embodied experiences, practices, and perceptions that are forged in relation to the diverse materialities of sanitation infrastructures. We do so by tracing the micropolitics of provision, access, territoriality, and control of sanitation infrastructures; daily routines and rhythms, both of people (their physiological routines and rhythms as well as those of daily living in informal settlements) and infrastructures; and experiences of disgust and perceptions of dignity. Through a discussion of these embodied materialities of open defecation, we seek to show how the capacities of sanitation infrastructures to meet people's individual and collective needs—and thus prevent open defecation—are shaped by a multiplicity of relationships between the body and infrastructure. We also think through the body's relationship to open space in the metabolic city by interrogating practices of open defecation as embodied spatial and temporal improvisations that require considerable effort and produce particular risks.

This focus on the everyday embodied materialities of open defecation attends to the ways in which defecation and sanitation experiences, practices, and perceptions are differentiated by class, income, gender, age, and other social power relations, as well as how they are forged in relation to urban materialities of informality and infrastructure. We conclude by discussing how our analysis deepens understandings of the relationships between the body, infrastructure, and the city; how the nature of these relationships constitutes urban poverty and inequality; and how the objectives of sanitation policies and programmes need to be expanded to address these relationships.

Body, Infrastructure, and Open Defecation in the City

Defecation is a bodily process that is crucial to life itself. Yet, there has been scant research on open defecation despite its widespread prevalence in many cities in the global South. Perhaps one reason for this is that open defecation is perceived to be at complete odds with the modern city. Investigations by development practitioners, journalists, and scholars have of course directed attention to practices of open defecation. In this moment of a 'sanitation crisis' and urgency to meet the Millennium Development Goals (MDGs), their writings focus on the dire consequences of these practices for health, women's dignity and safety, the environment, the economy, and so forth, and call for appropriate sanitation interventions in terms of technology, cultural and social norms, and the differentiated needs of men, women, and children.[9] However, the relationships between open defecation, the body, and infrastructure in the city remain under-researched and under-theorized in these investigations. Debates

[9] For example, Meera Bapat and Indu Agarwal, 'Our Needs, Our Priorities: Women and Men from the Slums in Mumbai and Pune Talk about Their Needs for Water and Sanitation', (2003) 15(2) *Environment & Urbanization* 71; Sheridan Bartlett, 'Water, Sanitation and Urban Children: The Need to Go Beyond "Improved" Provision', (2003) 15(2) *Environment & Urbanization* 57; Maggie Black and Ben Fawcett, *The Last Taboo: Opening the Door on the Global Sanitation Crisis* (Earthscan, 2008); Rose George, *The Big Necessity: Adventures in the World of Human Waste* (Portobello Books, 2008); Sarah Jewitt, 'Geographies of Shit: Spatial and Temporal Variations in Attitudes towards Human Waste', (2011) 35(5) *Progress in Human Geography* 608.

around the body, sanitation, filth, and infrastructure are crucial for exploring these relationships.

Scholars have argued, for instance, that the exclusion of what is considered filth, particularly human excreta, and the distancing from bodily substances and odours has been central to the ways in which modern urban citizens define themselves.[10] Architecture, urban planning, public health initiatives, and the regulation of public spaces have played a key role in this quest to protect the human senses from contact with bodily wastes, normalizing practices through which bodily functions like defecation are carried out, and bodily wastes like shit are disposed. Thus, shit was increasingly relegated to the private sphere,[11] and then was increasingly brought under public management. Attitudes to filth and cleanliness, and the regulation of bodily functions and bodily wastes have thus been central to the shaping of the modern city. Yet, the bourgeois regulation of filth and cleanliness not only served to carry out vast urban improvements, but also served as justification for the surveillance and control of the poor, and the denigration of certain groups.[12]

Unsanitary conditions and disease were associated with poverty, crime, and immorality in 19th- and early 20th-century European and American cities, justifying sanitary reforms that penetrated the daily lives of the poor and working classes. In the colonies, unsanitary conditions and disease were associated with spaces of the 'native', particularly the inner cities, and with disloyalty and potential rebellion.[13]

---

[10] William A. Cohen, 'Introduction: Locating Filth', in William A. Cohen and Ryan Johnson (eds), *Filth: Dirt, Disgust, and Modern Life* (University of Minnesota Press, 2005). See also David S. Barnes, 'Confronting Sensory Crisis in the Great Stinks of London and Paris', in William A. Cohen and Ryan Johnson (eds), *Filth: Dirt, Disgust, and Modern Life* (University of Minnesota Press, 2005); Alain Corbin, *Foul and the Fragrant: Odor and the French Social Imagination* (M.L. Kochan trans., Harvard University Press, 1986); Dominique Laporte, *The History of Shit* (N. Benabid and R. El-Khoury trans., MIT Press, 2000).

[11] Laporte (n 10).

[12] Cohen (n 10).

[13] Dipesh Chakrabarty, 'Of Garbage, Modernity and the Citizen's Gaze', (1992) XXVII (10–11) *Economic & Political Weekly* 541.

Orientalist binaries separating clean and sanitary Europeans from unclean, colonial Others usually led to colonial interventions in sanitation that were imposed from above through demolition, policing, coercion, and punishment. These were often met with local resistance based on indigenous views of health and urban life.[14] Ultimately, with military and economic concerns taking precedence over social welfare in the colonies, colonial cities developed as fragmented and polarized landscapes. Spacious residential quarters with modern infrastructure networks were developed for Europeans and their Indian elite and upper middle-class collaborators. On the other hand, 'native' inner cities and poorer areas remained devoid of sanitary improvements.[15] Indian elites, even when involved in local government, also failed to prioritize city-wide sanitation provision.[16] After Independence, these cities became sites of new kinds of modernist projects, and these fragmentations and polarizations increasingly evolved into a formal/informal divide. Sanitation divides became more entrenched in cities like Mumbai, as the impetus for widespread sanitary reform dissipated with urban middle classes increasingly able to protect themselves from disease by monopolizing state-provided urban services and access to modern medicine.[17]

Chakrabarty argues that while the attempts by colonial governments and elites to regulate and create orderly public spaces were rooted in discourses of the 'natives' being indifferent to filth in public spaces and using these spaces in inappropriate ways, nationalist

[14] Jyoti Hosagrahar, *Indigenous Modernities: Negotiating Architecture and Urbanism* (Routledge, 2005); Colin McFarlane, 'Governing the Contaminated City: Infrastructure and Sanitation in Colonial and Post-colonial Bombay', (2008) 32(2) *International Journal of Urban and Regional Research* 415.

[15] Susan E. Chaplin, *The Politics of Sanitation in India: Cities, Services and the State* (Orient BlackSwan, 2011); William J. Glover, *Making Lahore Modern: Constructing and Imagining A Colonial City* (University of Minnesota Press, 2008); Hosagrahar (n 14).

[16] Chaplin (n 15).

[17] Susan Chaplin, 'Cities, Sewers and Poverty: India's Politics of Sanitation', (1999) 11(1) *Environment & Urbanization* 145.

projects of social reform also sought to create clean and orderly public spaces, albeit through transformed discourses that appealed to civic consciousness and citizen-like behaviour.[18] People's practices have, however, continually challenged the realization of such projects in Indian cities. With regard to practices of open defecation, for the Indian middle classes and elites, these have increasingly come to mark the presence of the rural and the non-modern in the contemporary Indian city. Those who defecate in the open are often cast as uncivilized folk who need to be coercively disciplined into using toilets. These othering discourses in the contemporary Indian city have a powerful echo of the colonial, which closes off alternate possibilities of understanding people's sanitation practices, as well as sustains and creates new fragmentations and polarizations in the urban landscape.

Chakrabarty[19]—and following him Kaviraj[20]—have brought a postcolonial reading to the presence of filth in public spaces in India. They contrast the conception of public space based on modernist desires, civic consciousness, and public order with the notion of the 'outside' held historically in India. This 'outside' was the opposite not of the 'private' but of the 'inside' and was viewed as a space that carried fears of miscegenation and dangers of offence, especially for people accustomed to living in a caste society. While care and attention to cleanliness might be lavished upon the home that was the 'inside', the street as the 'outside' was a space that lacked any association with obligation and 'did not constitute a different kind of valued space, a *civic* space with norms and rules of use of its own'.[21] This had consequences for behaviour in urban open spaces, and garbage when thrown 'outside' was understood to be thrown over a conceptual boundary. Kaviraj further argues that this historical conception of the inside/outside mapped onto the European modernist conception of private/public to produce a

---

[18] Chakrabarty (n 13).

[19] Chakrabarty (n 13).

[20] Sudipta Kaviraj, 'Filth and the Public Sphere: Concepts and Practices about Space in Calcutta', (1997) 10(1) *Public Culture* 83.

[21] Kaviraj (n 20), 98.

peculiar configuration of the modern, which moreover varied across classes as well.[22] For the poor and destitute, 'public' gradually came to mean that which is not private; spaces from which they cannot be excluded by somebody's right to property; an 'outside' that is a matter not of collective pride but of desperate uses, sanctioned by the state through 'a curious mixture of paternalism, obligation of the powerful to care for the destitute, and democracy'.[23] In this analysis, the use of public space in Indian cities and the presence of filth in them are understood as a reflection of the 'plebianisation of public space',[24] and the different conceptual maps of private/public among the rich and poor in Indian cities chart a very different practice of modernity. It is striking too that in the contemporary period, while the logics and imaginaries may well be different, there are legacies of this in the casting out of many sites, groups, and practices of the urban poor as unsanitary, and in need of punitive treatment.[25]

The postcolonial analyses described earlier are useful in alerting us to different notions of public and private, of filth in public spaces, and of what might be considered an 'appropriate' or 'inappropriate' use of public space. However, they also have serious limitations, particularly when they include shit in their discussion of filth and open defecation as one among many uses of public space by the poor. This fails to consider the nature of embodiment in practices of defecation that differentiates it from other 'private' uses of 'public' space by the poor. These analyses also suggest that the poor have

---

[22] We do not think that Chakrabarty and Kaviraj mean this as an argument about cultural specificity. It is widely known that people threw garbage and emptied chamber pots on the streets in Europe and America until the 18th–19th century. However, while notions of 'public space' linked to a bourgeois notion of 'civic consciousness' became hegemonic in shaping the use of streets and open urban spaces in Europe and America (with indoor plumbing, city-wide sanitation systems, and so on, playing a role in this), Chakrabarty and Kaviraj seek to show that this was not the case in Indian cities.

[23] Kaviraj (n 20), 104–5.

[24] Kaviraj (n 20), 108.

[25] Baviskar (n 2); Ghertner (n 6); McFarlane (n 14).

a fixed conceptual map of public/private, and a greater tolerance to filth, and while this is considered to be a consequence of their impoverished circumstances, there is nonetheless a tendency not to connect open defecation to the politics of urban informality, infrastructure, and political economy. In the process, they also essentialize notions of filth held by the poor, and ignore the efforts often made by them to create sanitary environments. We argue that to understand open defecation, a focused analysis of the relationships of the body to the diverse materialities of sanitation infrastructure in the unequal city is imperative.

Debates in urban political ecology are an important point of departure in exploring these relationships. Writings on urban metabolism[26] approach the city as a metabolic process involving circulations and flows mediated through biophysical and social networks of bodies, infrastructures, and political economies, in which uneven power relations are deeply implicated. They direct attention to the uneven, fragmented, and polarized urban environments—and the enabling and disabling environments[27]—that are produced through urban metabolic transformations, which refer to complex and contested processes of socio-environmental urban change. Here, power-laden processes structure relations of access to (and exclusion from access to) food, water, and so forth, linking individual bodies to urban social processes.[28] Everyday life in the city is thus understood as being constituted by entanglements of the social and technological across a variety of spatialities.[29]

---

[26] Matthew Gandy, 'Rethinking Urban Metabolism: Water, Space and the Modern City', (2004) 8(3) *City* 363; Nik Heynen, 'Justice of Eating in the City: The Political Ecology of Urban Hunger', in Nik Heynen, Maria Kaika, and Erik Swyngedouw (eds), *In the Nature of Cities: Urban Political Ecology and the Politics of Urban Metabolism* (Routledge, 2006); Erik Swyngedouw, *Social Power and the Urbanisation of Water: Flows of Power* (Oxford University Press, 2004).

[27] Heynen, Kaika, and Swyngedouw (n 26).

[28] Heynen (n 26); Swyngedouw (n 26).

[29] Gandy (n 26).

However, despite these important theorizations, there is still limited scholarship in urban political ecology that explores people's everyday experiences and practices in relation to infrastructure, and that deepens our understanding of the relationships between the body, infrastructure, and the city. Certainly, a growing corpus of literature offers a glimpse into the significance of the everyday in shaping experiences and practices around water and sanitation.[30] Recently, a feminist political ecology approach has been brought to urban political ecology to show how everyday embodied experiences, processes of social differentiation, and micropolitics over resources can complicate and deepen our analyses of water inequality in cities.[31] There is also a growing body of work, of which Truelove is an example,[32] examining the intersections between everyday life, political ecologies, and infrastructure in the city in South Asia. This includes, for example, important studies of the movement, internment, and experience of different sorts of urban waste,[33] the biophysical and political travels of water,[34] or the relationship between water and citizenship.[35] This literature has enriched our understanding

[30] Bapat and Agarwal (n 9); Black and Fawcett (n 9); Kathleen O'Reilly, 'Combining Sanitation and Women's Participation in Water Supply: An Example from Rajasthan', (2010) 20(1) *Development in Practice* 45; Ben Page, 'Naked Power: Women and the Social Production of Water in Anglophone Cameroon', in Anne Coles and Tina Wallace (eds), *Gender, Water and Development* (Berg, 2005), 57; Swyngedouw (n 26).

[31] Yaffa Truelove, '(Re-)Conceptualizing Water Inequality in Delhi, India through a Feminist Political Ecology Framework', (2011) 42(2) *Geoforum* 143.

[32] Truelove (n 31).

[33] Vinay Gidwani and Rajyashree N. Reddy, 'The Afterlives of "Waste": Notes from India for a Minor History of Capitalist Surplus', (2011) 43(5) *Antipode* 1625.

[34] Nikhil Anand, 'Pressure: The PoliTechnics of Water Supply in Mumbai', (2011) 26(4) *Cultural Anthropology* 542.

[35] Yaffa Truelove and Emma Mawdsley, 'Class and Criminality: Discourses of Water and Citizenship in Clean, Green Delhi', in Isabelle Clark-Deces (ed), *A Companion to the Anthropology of India* (Wiley-Blackwell, 2011), 407.

of the everyday experience and multiplicity of exploitative urban political ecologies in South Asia, and as such, has been very helpful in formulating our own approach and arguments here.[36] It is also part of an important wider effort to rethink urban political ecology from the urban global South.[37]

With some exceptions,[38] however, everyday sanitation practices and experiences in the making and unmaking of urban political ecologies and infrastructures, particularly open defecation, continue to command less empirical and analytical attention. We attend to this by examining the everyday embodied materialities of (open) defecation. By this, we refer to: (*i*) how open defecation emerges through everyday embodied experiences, practices, and perceptions forged in relation to complex materialities of informality and infrastructure, and (*ii*) the embodied spatialities and temporalities of open defecation. To examine the former, we focus on three processes (which take us beyond toilet seat numbers to understand sanitation adequacy): the micropolitics of provision, access, territoriality, and control of sanitation infrastructures; daily routines and rhythms, both of people (physiological routines and rhythms as well as those of daily living in informal settlements) and of infrastructures; and experiences of disgust and perceptions of dignity. There is a large literature on the centrality of patronage and vote-bank politics in the provision of tenure security and basic services (such as water and sanitation) to informal settlements.[39] However, we argue that there is a need to expand the

---

[36] See Colin McFarlane, Renu Desai, and Steve Graham, 'Informal Urban Sanitation: Everyday Life, Poverty and Comparison', (2014) 104(5) *Annals of the Association of American Geographers* 989.

[37] For example, Mary Lawhon, Henrik Ersnston, and Jonathan Silver, 'Provincializing Urban Political Ecology: Towards a Situated UPE through African Urbanism', (2014) 46(2) *Antipode* 497.

[38] For example, Truelove and Mawdsley (n 35).

[39] For example, Partha Chatterjee, *The Politics of the Governed: Reflections on Popular Politics in Most of the World* (Permanent Black, 2004); Joop de Wit, 'Decentralised Management of Solid Waste in Mumbai Slums: Informal Privatisation through Patronage', (2010) 33(12–13) *International Journal of Public Administration* 767.

analysis of sanitation politics. Understanding infrastructure as constituted by a range of social relations allows us to attend to the micropolitics of infrastructure provision, access, territoriality, and control within informal localities, how they structure people's everyday experiences and practices, and how they contribute to the emergence of open defecation. Here, the location of toilet blocks, the role of formal and informal caretakers as well as toilet users, the commodification or privatization of public sanitation, and social power relations such as age and gender, all play a role in shaping this micropolitics.

There is also a growing body of literature that examines the role of repair and maintenance in the working of infrastructures and the disruption and failure of infrastructure networks.[40] While this literature recognizes the significance of these processes for shaping everyday lives and possibilities in the city, there are few in-depth studies. In this chapter, we attend to the routines and rhythms of use, repair, maintenance, and breakdown of sanitation infrastructures in informal settlements and show how these shape people's experiences and practices, including open defecation, in crucial ways. Our emphasis on the embodiment of people's practices also leads us to attend to people's routines and rhythms as they intersect with the routines and rhythms of sanitation infrastructures.

A third set of processes that we examine involve experiences of disgust and perceptions of dignity amongst residents of informal settlements. Debates on disgust, filth, and cleanliness show how sensory responses such as disgust have played a key role in the distancing of filth, including human excreta. While many regard disgust as an 'evolved aversion to potential sources of disease' and thus automatic and unmediated by conscious thought,[41] others like Mary Douglas[42] have viewed it as culturally mutable.[43] Writings also show that there are distinct historical variations in disgust to shit, and in responses

[40] Steve Graham and Nigel Thrift, 'Out of Order: Understanding Repair and Maintenance', (2007) 24(3) *Theory, Culture and Society* 1.

[41] Barnes (n 10).

[42] Mary Douglas, *Purity and Danger: An Analysis of Concept of Pollution and Taboo* (Routledge, 2002).

[43] Barnes (n 10), 105.

to this disgust.[44] There are also cross-cultural variations, and Jewitt writes of faecophilic and faecophobic cultures, the former tolerating the handling of shit, and the latter—which includes India—finding it abhorrent and ritually polluting.[45] In India, the association of handling shit with so-called 'untouchable' castes, whose occupation was restricted to manual scavenging, that is, manually removing, carrying, and disposing of human excreta, links abhorrence and disgust around human faeces with cultural notions of pollution and purity, and a policing of social hierarchical boundaries.[46] These experiences and notions of disgust—and the imagined 'geographies of contamination'[47] they give rise to—have recently mobilized revanchist actions in Mumbai with the formulation of bye-laws that bring a police approach to open defecation and the city's cleanliness. However, tracing subaltern rather than middle-class and elite experiences of filth, reveals another geography of disgust and contamination.

Disgust has been taken seriously in sanitation programmes such as community-led total sanitation (CLTS), which deploys these emotions—indeed, produces them—to 'trigger' behavioural change from open defecation to toilet use.[48] However, contemporary sanitation literature unfortunately remains limited in its understanding of subaltern perceptions of cleanliness and filth, subaltern experiences of disgust, and the everyday practices that emerge through these. We seek to take a step towards addressing this lacuna. By contrast,

[44] Barnes (n 10). See also Laporte (n 10).

[45] Jewitt (n 9).

[46] Jewitt (n 9). On caste and manual scavenging, see Mari M. Thekaekara, *Endless Filth: The Saga of the Bhangis* (Zed Books, 2003).

[47] McFarlane (n 14).

[48] Community-Led total sanitation involves participatory mapping of neighborhoods in order to understand current practices of open defecation and sanitation more broadly, and then organizing communities into self-help groups to build and maintain toilets. A key strength of CLTS is, precisely, its concern with building sanitation solutions directly from everyday experience. See Lyla Mehta and Synne Movik (eds), *Shit Matters: The Potential of Community-Led Total Sanitation* (Practical Action Publishing, 2010).

the literature on sanitation provides ample evidence of the indignity experienced by women when they are forced to turn to open defecation. However, this has also foreclosed any in-depth analysis into perceptions of dignity vis-à-vis defecation: the differentiation of these perceptions by age and gender; the variation across rural and urban geographies; their link to conditions of visibility, privacy, and safety; and their link to experiences of sanitation infrastructures. As a result, we have scarce understanding about how perceptions of dignity shape practices of open defecation.

To examine the embodied spatialities and temporalities of open defecation, we propose 'improvisation' as a useful analytic. This notion of improvisation is inspired by AbdouMaliq Simone's writings on urban practices in African cities. For Simone, improvisation involves practices through which bodies, infrastructures, objects, and spaces, are brought into various combinations and configurations that become a platform for providing for life in the uncertain city, and generating stability. These practices facilitate 'the intersection of socialities so that an expanded space of economic and cultural operation becomes available for residents of limited means'.[49] Such improvisations are pursued around sanitation as well, for instance, when groups of residents without access to toilets come together to contribute time, money, material, and labour for the construction of makeshift hanging latrines, or when groups of residents introduce lock-and-key arrangements on a public toilet block to restrict access, and thus control the cleanliness of the toilets they use. However, such improvisations might not always be possible, or the improvisations by one group might restrict access to sanitation infrastructures for another group. In such situations, people may turn to open defecation to fulfil their bodily needs, and in this context, practices of open defecation themselves emerge as improvisations which involve devising the least vulnerable and the most convenient configurations of the body, time, and space. This not only reveals how people cope with lack of or limited sanitation, but also shows how particular practices of open defecation emerge, and the efforts and risks they entail.

[49] AbdouMaliq Simone, 'People as Infrastructure: Intersecting Fragments in Johannesburg', (2004) 16(3) *Public Culture* 407.

Embodied Materialities of (Open) Defecation

Micropolitics of Provision, Access, Territoriality, and Control

The experiences and practices of residents of Rafinagar and Khotwadi around fulfilling their bodily needs were shaped in significant ways by both the unevenness of sanitation provision in Mumbai, as well as the settlement-level micropolitics of toilet provision, access, territoriality, and control. In Rafinagar, six toilet blocks—three public and three private—had been constructed over the years, providing one toilet seat for every 263 persons. While the official acceptable standard is to provide one toilet seat for every 50 persons—a number that emerged as part of the city's SSP[50]—our toilet surveys found that each toilet seat was used by many more, between 80–115 persons in most cases. While inadequate toilet numbers certainly meant that open defecation in Rafinagar was inevitable, the micropolitics of toilet access, territoriality, and control was an important factor shaping people's experiences, and thus, the emergence of open defecation amongst certain residents and not others. Not only were all toilet blocks located in Rafinagar Part 1, but the distance of the three public toilet blocks from Part 2 and many parts of Part 1 too, the location of two of them in internal lanes, and the attempts by surrounding residents and/or informal caretakers to restrict access meant that these were territorialized and controlled in a way that effectively removed them from being truly public toilets. As a result, each block was accessible to residents from only a particular cluster of lanes in Part 1, and Part 2 residents as well as many Part 1 residents were effectively unable to access them at all.

By contrast, Khotwadi has 24 toilet blocks, with one toilet seat for every 55 persons. Given that this closely conforms to the official acceptable standard of one toilet seat for every 50 persons, one is apt to conclude that there should be no open defecation in Khotwadi on account of infrastructure. However, we observed a similar micropolitics of toilet territoriality and control in Khotwadi, with many of the blocks or some individual cubicles in

---

[50]   Colin McFarlane, 'Sanitation in Mumbai's Informal Settlements: State, "Slum" and Infrastructure', (2008) 40(1) *Environment and Planning* 88.

them territorialized and controlled by groups of residents, thus making them inaccessible to others. In the early morning hours, this led to longer queues at the other blocks, which were open to all. This, in turn, led many men from some of the neighbourhoods along the railway tracks to turn to open defecation along the tracks. This underlines the significance of understanding sanitation in terms of the micropolitics of toilet provision, access, territoriality, and control.

As a result of the territorialization and control of the public blocks in Rafinagar Part 1, the only blocks that Part 2 residents could use were the three private pay-per-use blocks. However, two of these were at a distance from Part 2, and were thus not quickly accessible to its residents. In fact, one of these blocks was not even accessible to Part 1 residents at times since the toilet block operator and caretaker had full control over the block, and thus kept the block closed on days when they could not obtain water (an issue that was linked to the wider water crisis in the area). Moreover, Part 2 residents also sometimes found the third, nearer, private toilet block difficult to access due to the long toilet queues. Taslima, a resident of Part 2, explained her experience: 'When there are long queues then people shout at each other, no? Then the residents who live [near the private toilet block] complain about the people who go from here. They say there is such a big *maidan* there, why are you coming here?'

Equally significantly, the private pay-per-use toilet blocks were accessible only to those who were willing and able to pay the Rs 1–2 that these toilet blocks charged per use. The per-use charges (and in one block, monthly passes) were a form of control that determined who was able to access the toilet, including how many times, and who was not. With many families in Rafinagar, particularly in Part 2, earning Rs 100–50 a day as ragpickers, this form of control over sanitation infrastructures led many to turn to open defecation, either on a daily basis or intermittently. Taslima explained that when possible she would use open space, because 'if I can save one rupee then my children can eat something more'. However, as discussed later, the spaces and routines of open defecation did not always allow Taslima to use open space. On such days, she took her six-year-old daughter with her to the private toilet since the caretaker allowed children of that age to use the block for free when they came with their mother. If her daughter wanted to defecate at any other time, Taslima made her sit on a newspaper outside their house. In fact, many families in Part 1 and Part 2 who did not have access to any of Rafinagar's public toilet blocks, and whose financial circumstances were straitened, allowed children to defecate in the open since spending a minimum of Rs 30 per month (Rs 1 per use) for each family member was just too expensive. One 14-year-old boy explained that he used open space because of 'tension around money'.

Everyday Routines and Rhythms

Practices of open defecation emerge through everyday routines and rhythms, both physiological routines, as well as routines and rhythms of daily life in informal settlements, as they intersect with sanitation infrastructures in these settlements. These routines mean that large numbers of residents in Rafinagar and Khotwadi sought the use of toilet blocks in the morning hours. In the context of inadequate toilet numbers, this led to long toilet queues in Rafinagar during these hours. As a result, users were also pressurized to hurry up so that others could use the toilet. Our toilet surveys at Rafinagar's public toilet blocks revealed that in one block, each of the men had an average of five minutes to answer nature's call, and in another block, each had an average of 3.75 minutes. Many men came with their water-pots to use a particular toilet block and then, on seeing long queues or after waiting for a few minutes, departed to use the open space outside the settlement. If they were willing and able to pay, they would first check the queues at one of the private pay-per-use toilet blocks. Many men could not afford to wait for long in toilet queues not only because of their body's physiological routines, but also because of their routines of urban living. For many of them, the latter not only involved getting to work on time, but also the time-consuming and cumbersome task of fetching water on their cycles from long distances between 7 and 10 am, especially after December 2009, when municipal raids on 'illegal' water supplies in the area led to a deepening water crisis.[51]

---

[51] Steve Graham, Renu Desai, and Colin McFarlane, 'Water Wars in Mumbai', (2013) 25(1) *Public Culture* 115.

In the women's sections in these blocks, our findings varied only marginally, and each user had an average of just below five minutes to answer nature's call. We found rare instances of women from Rafinagar Part 1 resorting to open defecation, partly because of the social norms of modesty in a patriarchal society. Women were more likely to cope with this situation by controlling their bodies and its excretions, working around domestic routines (which often involved searching for, waiting for, and filling water), and revisiting the toilet block when queues might have become shorter.[52]

However, there were women who turned to open defecation intermittently as a result of these routines and rhythms, and their intersection with sanitation infrastructures. Consider Naina, a young woman who used one of Rafinagar's private pay-per-use blocks, but also at times used the open space in the early mornings. Naina and her husband were among the more well-earning households in Rafinagar, and she thus had both a willingness and ability to pay for using the private toilet. She worked with a religious charity, running tuition classes at her home for children in the mornings. However, 'If the line is long, if it is urgent, if there is no time, then [one can] immediately go there', she had explained, vaguely waving towards the vast open space visible from her house. Her response captures how her practices of intermittent open defecation were shaped by the intersections of her body's physiological rhythms ('if it is urgent'), her domestic and work routines ('if there is no time'), and the nature of available sanitation infrastructures, in this case, the distance of the toilet block from her house and its inadequate toilet seats for meeting the collective rhythms and routines of the area's residents ('if the line is long').

Shakira, who had lived in Rafinagar Part 1 for more than 20 years, had explained that she often used to go to the nearby maidan when the toilet block she uses today used to be smaller. 'There would be a crowd there, people from all over the place used to come there. There would be ten people in the queue. We would get a stomach problem so we used to go to the maidan. The maidan was open, so sit down in comfort.'

---

[52] We did not trace other practices of defecation that women might resort to under such circumstances, such as defecating in plastic bags at home.

This notion of being able to defecate in comfort, without having to experience the bodily discomfort and pain of waiting in a queue to defecate, is clearly not the notion of luxurious comfort that is increasingly shaping residential toilet design in urban India.[53] Rather, this is the basic comfort of being able to satisfy rather than fight off the urge of one's physiological bodily routines and rhythms. Not being able to relieve oneself when one has the urge to defecate leads to abdominal pain and psychological stress, and regularly delaying defecation can also lead to chronic constipation.[54]

For Taslima in Rafinagar Part 2, her domestic routines—which involve being at home to take care of her young children while her husband goes to fetch water on his cycle between 7 and 10 am—led her to try and finish with her bodily needs early in the morning before her husband leaves. At this time, the private toilet, which was also far from her house, had long queues, and in any case, since she was hard-pressed to pay daily for the use of a private toilet, she usually turned to open defecation.

The routines and rhythms of the sanitation infrastructures are shaped by the frequency of cleaning, the time of the day when they are cleaned, the availability of adequate water for cleaning, and the frequency and adequacy of their maintenance (such as repairing broken doors, removal of choke-ups, maintenance of the septic tank/aqua privy, and so on) (all of which are in turn shaped by the practices and politics of municipal officials, municipal sanitation workers, local political leaders, toilet block caretakers, informal sanitation workers, and so on), leading to intermittent practices of open defecation. For instance, most of the public toilet blocks in Rafinagar choked up and became entirely unusable for a few days every few months. While most women then turned to private pay-per-use blocks, many men and even many children turned to open defecation during this time.

[53] Srinivas analyses how bathrooms in middle-class Hindu homes have become showplaces of conspicuous consumption and display. See Tulasi Srinivas, 'Flush with Success: Bathing, Defecation, Worship, and Social Change in South India', (2002) 5(4) *Space and Culture* 368.

[54] WHO-UNICEF, *Meeting the MDG Drinking Water and Sanitation Target: A Mid-term Assessment of Progress* (2004); available at www.unicef. org/wash/files/who_unicef_watsan_midterm_rev.pdf.

In Khotwadi, the routines and rhythms of cleaning and maintaining the toilets were generally more regular and frequent than in Rafinagar since most of the toilets were territorialized and controlled by resident groups or looked after by local political leaders or community-based organizations (CBOs). Serious disruptions in the workings of the toilets were therefore rare. In case of such disruptions, people temporarily resorted to other blocks since there are a larger number of toilet blocks in Khotwadi. As a result of this larger number of blocks, the physiological routines of the body as well as routines and rhythms of daily life were also generally fulfilled without having to resort to open defecation, except where the micropolitics of toilet provision, access, territoriality, and control made this impossible. As discussed earlier, this was the case only in the neighbourhoods near the railway tracks where men turned to open defecation.

Disgust and Dignity

Many women in both Rafinagar and Khotwadi talked about the toilets they regularly used, and how they got dirty, choked up, and often stank unbearably, making them difficult to use. For instance, one resident of Rafinagar explained that the informal cleaner had not come since some days, as a result of which she had to use half the water in her water-pot to throw on the worms breeding in the toilet so that they wouldn't climb onto her feet. Another resident explained that there were only four toilets for the women in the neighbourhood, leading to frequent blockages. Still another resident explained: 'When the toilet fills up, then it fills up to the top. There is no place to keep one's feet also, it becomes so dirty.' Many women talked about how toilets got dirty and smelly because of practices of other women, particularly those who left sanitary cloths in the toilet. One woman explained: 'It is shameful that women throw all this in the toilet. If we keep the toilet clean, then it will remain clean. These women should understand that sanitary cloths should not be left like this. They should be wrapped in plastic and thrown directly into the garbage bin.'

In Khotwadi, one resident asked the researcher to go into the toilet block and experience for herself that it was impossible to even stand there because of the smell. These narratives show that the filth and smell in most shared toilets provoked disgust amongst residents who had to occupy these spaces while answering nature's call.

For some, the visual and olfactory experiences of bodily wastes in overloaded, poorly ventilated, and infrequently cleaned toilets provoked disgust to the point of it being a potentially sickening experience. One resident expressed this when she explained that she would not be able to eat all day if she used the dirty public toilet block near her house in the morning, adding that she used a private toilet block a bit further away. Such options are not always available, however, and while it is certainly not clear how many men and women turn to open defecation because of dirty and smelly toilets, it is possible that rather than be disgusted by open defecation, some would actually turn to open defecation precisely because of disgust with the condition of shared toilets.

Jewitt argues that in rural areas, where there is plenty of open space and privacy, 'people often choose open defecation in preference to using a smelly, mosquito-infested toilet'.[55] Comparing her use of the maidan to the toilets in Rafinagar, Taslima explained that 'in the maidan you don't get a smell. The smell is bad in the toilet since it is closed'. While this reveals that when it came to smell, Taslima preferred the maidan to the existing toilets, she had to also factor in questions of privacy. Such choices then are of course more difficult in the city, which does not easily offer open space and privacy. But the narratives explored here show that for residents of informal settlements, everyday geographies of disgust, contamination, and the unsanitary city involve poorly-ventilated, irregularly-cleaned toilets that large numbers of people are forced to use without adequate access to water. While it is not entirely clear how often these experiences and geographies lead people to turn to open defecation, there is clearly a need for more sophisticated understandings in this direction.

Subaltern perceptions of dignity also play a role in shaping open defecation practices. Naina shared her views on cleanliness, and the role of personal responsibility in keeping oneself, one's house, and one's neighbourhood clean. In this context, the casual, matter-of-fact tone in which she mentioned her intermittent open defecation

---

[55] Jewitt (n 9).

practices suggested that she did not consider this to be an undignified or humiliating practice. Given writings on urban sanitation—which have repeatedly pointed to the impacts that open defecation have on women's privacy, dignity, and safety—as researchers, we have perhaps come to expect that women informants will talk about open defecation only in ways that fit into these narratives. These narratives certainly emerged in Rafinagar as well, as we will later discuss in this chapter. However, when Naina—and a number of other women in Rafinagar—mentioned open defecation in a casual, matter-of-fact tone, it was unsettling to us as researchers, and provoked questions.

Clearly, open defecation is not a humiliating practice in all contexts. The humiliation associated with open defecation is, indeed, a historical construct. Srinivas writes about how bathing and defecation in rural areas in India were social activities until the late 1940s (though certainly segregated by gender).[56] It was, in fact, considered to be quite appropriate to be sociable while bathing and defecating, and people 'made a separation between the corporeal self and the social self, [thus] while the physical body engaged in evacuation or purification, the social self continued interaction unabated'.[57] According to Srinivas, this 'communal bond of defecation' was lost as villagers began to build individual toilets in their backyards; the social individual and the corporeal body fused into one, and notions of privacy and shame became associated with open defecation.[58] While Srinivas seems to suggest that open defecation is uniformly seen as a shameful practice now, this is clearly questionable. Writings on rural sanitation, for instance, reveal that collective norms and behaviours can make open defecation acceptable.[59]

In the case of recent migrants to the city from rural areas, it is indeed possible then that not everyone perceives open defecation as a humiliating practice in and of itself. Indeed, being forced to use a disgustingly dirty toilet can be a challenge to one's dignity as well, and one might prefer open defecation on these grounds.

[56] Srinivas (n 53), 370.
[57] Srinivas (n 53), 371.
[58] Srinivas (n 53), 371.
[59] For example, Mehta and Movik (n 48); Jewitt (n 9).

Mukhopadhyay argues that toilet festivals organized by middle-class activists advocating improvements in sanitation in Mumbai's slums, link open defecation, humiliation, victimization, and a lack of dignity (and are approvingly described as such by Appadurai)[60] in ways that are not necessarily shared by slum dwellers themselves. Rather than impose urban elite notions of dignity and humiliation onto urban subalterns, he argues that there is a need to examine attitudes that shape sanitation norms, more so because the rendering of certain defecation practices as unacceptable and humiliating can foreclose options.[61] There is clearly a need for a better understanding of notions of dignity vis-à-vis open defecation. How do notions of dignity (and indignity) get linked to visibility, privacy, safety, disgust, and infrastructures, and how do they vary across age and gender?

Spatialities and Temporalities of Open Defecation

Although there were large areas of open space around Rafinagar, people did not '*just go in the open*' as presumed by the security agency's CEO quoted earlier. Rather, they spatially and temporally improvised so as to use the open space in ways deemed most proper and safe in the context of prevailing social relations and norms. Open spaces were thus differentiated for their use for open defecation by different groups. While young children living in Rafinagar Part 1 went on the road outside the settlement, other children and most men of Part 1 walked across the road to the garden or maidan, a vast open space located behind one of the private toilet blocks. In Rafinagar Part 2, most young children used the adjacent maidan (also known as *kabristan* since the municipal government had earmarked this land for a graveyard), beyond which rose the Deonar garbage dump, Mumbai's largest garbage disposal site. The youngest of the children were often made to sit on newspapers and plastic bags just outside the house because of fears (such as their getting bitten by

---

[60] Arjun Appadurai, 'The Capacity to Aspire: Culture and the Terms of Recognition', in Vijayendra Rao and Michael Walton (eds), *Culture and Public Action* (Stanford University Press, 2004), 59.

[61] Bhaskar Mukhopadhyay, 'Crossing the Howrah Bridge: Calcutta, Filth and Dwelling', (2006) 23(7–8) *Theory, Culture and Society* 221, 227.

aggressive stray dogs) associated with letting them defecate further away. Some men used the maidan/kabristan as well.

For men and women, the Deonar garbage dump with its heaps of garbage provided a particularly suitable topography for creating gendered separations for open defecation. Men often used open spaces at the lower edges of the dump, especially beside the water channel along the dump's western edge, while women walked up onto the garbage dump, finding spaces behind garbage heaps or in the ditches created by the dumping of garbage to shield themselves from prying eyes. These spatial improvisations thus involved cooperation between men and women. However, not everyone cooperated. There were many cases of women being harassed when they went to the garbage dump. Some residents recounted instances of young girls being raped. Salma explained the reasons for these cases of harassment: 'Our sons and husbands understand. That our mothers and sisters go. But [men] come from outside and harass us … They [drink] alcohol; they do *charas*, *ganja*, *solution* …[62] Many rapes have happened. Some parents don't bring it out in the open to protect their honour; they are scared.' She went on to explain that these were men from other parts of Shivaji Nagar, the larger area comprising of an official slum resettlement site, and various informal settlements. But it is possible that men from within Rafinagar also harassed women at the dump. Many residents mentioned alcohol and drug abuse amongst young men within Rafinagar, and women recounted instances of harassment by such men, including at one of the toilet blocks.[63]

Although using open spaces such as the maidan and kabristan that were visible to more people might have at least prevented sexual assault, securing some kind of privacy for performing bodily functions was more important for women, given the social norms of modesty in a patriarchal society. Most women tried to decrease the possibilities of assault by going to the garbage dump with other women and by going before 10–11 am after which garbage trucks

[62] *Charas* and *ganja* are made from the cannabis plant. 'Solution' refers to Erazex, a typewriter correction fluid inhaled to produce intoxication.

[63] Alcohol, tobacco addiction, and drug abuse, amongst young men in Rafinagar, were mentioned by participants of our focus group discussion with a male youth group.

began to ply the dump. Collaborations amongst women thus constituted social infrastructures necessary to safely fulfil sanitation needs. However, certain kinds of verbal and visual harassment were still not easily avoided. One woman resident explained that if one went alone, someone would 'cover your mouth and carry you off'; this, she added, would not happen if two women went together, although men might still pass comments and make obscene gestures. It would not be an exaggeration to say that at times some women took a chance on their safety in their search for privacy and to conform to social norms of modesty. Moreover, going on to the garbage dump to find privacy itself posed risks of being bitten by aggressive stray dogs, falling into deep ditches, and sinking into the garbage especially during the monsoons.

The spatial and temporal improvisations that constituted open defecation practices thus involved considerable effort, particularly by women. If these improvisations tried to minimize certain risks, then they also deepened other risks. Women who did not want to undertake the risks associated with going on to the garbage dump, used the maidan/kabristan, but only under the cover of darkness. However, as this involved controlling the body and its excretions, it made women vulnerable to various health-related risks.

Moreover, everyday life in informal settlements often involves coping with change in the unevenly developing city, over which residents have little control. Such changes can also profoundly disrupt practices of open defecation, requiring new improvisations that often created new risks and vulnerabilities. In November 2009, plans began for the scientific closure of the Deonar garbage dump. Receiving Mumbai's garbage since 1927, the garbage disposal site had been reaching the end of its life. Middle-class residents from surrounding areas had also protested against the air pollution caused by the vapours of decomposing garbage, and the fumes caused by garbage burning by ragpickers to extract metals. The municipal government thus handed the site to a private company for its closure. Salma explained how this had affected the use of this space for open defecation:

The vehicles start to run [on the dump] at 6–7 am. They run the entire day. Till seven in the evening. Even at night sometimes … . The road [on which the vehicles run] is high. Everything can be seen from above if someone is sitting below ... . If one is sitting then sometimes somebody will come and chase one away. If you've worn a *sari*, then it is okay. But it is difficult in a *salwar* [a kind of loose trouser], there is no time to tie it also ... . First the [garbage] trucks used to come 'time to time' [that is, at specific times]. Ever since it has become private, there is more harassment. No matter where you look there is a vehicle.

The garbage dump was also being levelled by the private company for its conversion into a sanitary landfill and development as a green belt, and Salma explained that this too created difficulties since there were no longer heaps of garbage and ditches where one could shield oneself. Other women mentioned that whereas earlier they could go onto the dump till 10–11 am, with the coming of the private company's bulldozers, security guards, and vehicles, they now had to go earlier in the morning, usually before 8 am. Amina now woke her 16 year-old daughter at 6 am daily to send her to the garbage dump so as to decrease chances of her being seen or harassed.

Taslima had begun to go to the dump before 6–7 am, but on many days she could not finish with her bodily needs this early. On such days she would walk over to a private toilet block around 10–11 am, after her husband returned from fetching water. She paid Rs 1 to use this toilet block. Both Taslima and her husband work alternately as rag-pickers on the garbage dump, earning Rs 100–50 per day between them for their family of six. As mentioned earlier, Taslima took her six-year-old daughter with her to the private toilet so that she would not have to pay separately for her as well. Their use of the private toilet was not about willingess-to-pay, as the World Bank and many development practitioners would like to portray it, but the inescapable need to fulfil the body's physiological needs in the context of the changing city around them, their domestic routines (some of which are shaped by the fragmentary and polarized geographies of water in Mumbai), the narrow toilet block options available to them, and their own deeply straitened financial circumstances. In a couple of years, the family will have to spend more on toilet access as their daughters grow up, even as they will have to explore other livelihood options with the garbage dump's closure. The private block had also begun to charge Rs 2 in the men's section, and so per-use charges were also likely to increase in the women's section in the future.

In mid-2010, the municipal government also began constructing a wall around the kabristan to develop the graveyard. This would narrow the open space that children could use for defecation as well as that women could use under the cover of darkness. Several people pointed to this emerging enclosure, emphasizing the urgency of building a toilet block in Rafinagar Part 2.

Elsewhere too, changes in the unevenly developing city often mean a narrowing of open spaces affording privacy, safety, and gendered separation. In Khotwadi, for instance, many men defecated along the railway tracks adjacent to the settlement, risking their limbs and lives every day in the process of fulfilling their bodily needs.

Practices of open defecation emerge then from deep sanitation inequalities in the city. They involve considerable effort through spatial and temporal improvisations, and while these seek to ensure maximum privacy, safety, and gendered separation, they also deepen urban inequalities in various ways, especially for women and children. Deepening inequalities also emerge from the effects of open defecation on health. Non-governmental organizations working in Rafinagar noted the high incidence of diarrhoea, dysentery, and worms.[64] In Rafinagar, open spaces used for defecation are some of the only open spaces for children to play (as with the garden, maidan, and kabristan), and are also spaces where many adults and children spend long hours working as rag-pickers (as with the Deonar garbage dump).

* * *

In this chapter, we have analysed how open defecation surfaces through everyday embodied experiences, practices, and perceptions that emerge in relation to the materialities of sanitation infrastructures in the deeply fragmented and unequal Indian city, by tracing the micropolitics of access, territoriality, and control of

---

[64] For more on health and open defecation, see Black and Fawcett (n 9); UN Millennium Project, *Health, Dignity and Development: What Will it Take?* (Report of the Millennium Task Force on Water and Sanitation, 2005).

sanitation infrastructures; people's daily routines and rhythms; and people's sensory experiences of disgust and perceptions of dignity and humiliation. By interrogating these embodied materialities, this chapter has sought to better articulate the multiplicity of relationships between the body and infrastructure in the metabolic city, and thus also expand our conception of the relationships between the body, infrastructure, and the sanitary/unsanitary city. The manner in which these embodied materialities create precarious conditions for the fulfilment of basic bodily needs, or deny the fulfilment of these needs (regularly or intermittently), is a crucial dimension of urban poverty and inequality.

We have also interrogated practices of open defecation as spatial and temporal improvisations. These improvisations produce and reinforce inequalities through their implications for health and women's safety. As the Rafinagar case shows, these improvisations are also disrupted in the unevenly developing city, forcing people to chart out new improvisations. These disruptions and the new improvisations that emerge often deepen vulnerabilities and inequalities in various ways. Our tracing of these improvisations and experiences is not to simply reveal how people cope with lack of or limited sanitation, but to emphasize the different ways in which they emerge and take shape.

Indeed, practices of improvisation around open defecation are essentially coping mechanisms, and often reproduce and deepen inequalities rather than articulate political claims such as the right to sanitation and water. In this sense, improvisation may appear to lack a politics. However, these improvisation practices and the difficulties and inequalities they produce are at times made visible in political claim-making. For instance, political demands for more toilets or for certain kinds of toilets or for toilets in particular localities could be strengthened by how persuasively and powerfully people narrate their everyday experiences, the efforts they make (that is, their improvisations) to fulfil their bodily needs in the absence of adequate sanitation, and the risks and vulnerabilities these produce. Moreover, improvisation can become political in different ways. This might be due to the state bye-laws further disciplining improvisatory responses, or when residents become divided around lines of class, religion, ethnicity, or caste in response to improvisatory practices pursued by different groups. While these improvisatory micropolitics of making and unmaking urban infrastructure have been largely neglected in debates on urban infrastructure and political ecology, we hope that we have shown that this constitutes a vital realm of urban life that demands more research focus, especially given that it is in these practices that more and more of urban life is lived.

Moreover, it is clear that simply invoking the right to sanitation—a right, remember, which is spatially differentiated by 'notified' and 'non-notified' slums—will not be enough. New social movements such as the Right to Pee movement in Mumbai, an amalgam of various NGOs and community groups,[65] is welcome, but as actors in this and other social movements in Mumbai know, the right to sanitation is secured through political will and not simply through legislation and enforcement (as important as these domains none-theless remain). Even in notified slums, the provision of sanitation is unreliable and inconsistent. Rights, then, can only be a part of the struggle, and in this context, the politics of improvisation has a role in foregrounding the nature of everyday challenges and possibilities.

This focus on people's everyday practices, experiences, and perceptions in relation to sanitation infrastructures and open defecation also problematizes the bourgeois urban aesthetic, which has recently mobilized a police approach to sanitation in Mumbai's public spaces, and the relationships between the body, infrastructure, and the urban environment that such approaches presume. Such an approach is part of a wider move across many Indian cities to reclaim the city from the poor and working classes for its middle classes and elites,[66] with many of these urban revanchist moves[67] pitting 'public' (read 'middle-class') concerns around the environment against the 'private'

---

[65] For example, Chhavi Sachdev, 'Women in India Agitate for their Right to Pee', *Public Radio International* (2014); available at www.pri.org/stories/2014-11-25/women-india-agitate-their-right-pee.

[66] See Baviskar (n 2); Ghertner (n 6); Sharan (n 6).

[67] Neil Smith, *The New Urban Frontier: Gentrification and the Revanchist City* (Routledge, 1996).

acts of the urban poor. While such approaches presume that the urban poor are unwilling to use sanitation infrastructures, are impatient and irresponsible in their use of them, and do not mind using open space because they lack any sense of disgust or dignity, our analysis challenges these presumptions.

The histories of colonialism and nationalism have continually produced an urban modernity in postcolonial cities wherein the relation between the body, infrastructure, and the city has continually been rendered uncertain, precarious, shifting, and disruptive for the majority of urban dwellers. This investigation of how open defecation emerges through the relations between the body and infrastructure in the fragmented and unequal Indian city, and how open defecation involves precarious spatial and temporal improvisations, shows that in the current moment of a globalizing urbanism in cities like Mumbai, the uncertainty and disruption that marks this relation continues to be deepened.

We hope that it is evident that this focus on open defecation, informality, the body, and infrastructure has implications for sanitation policy and practice. Many writings on urban sanitation have, of course, pointed to how open defecation is prevalent in cities because of inadequate toilets. The recent emphasis on community participation in urban sanitation programmes like the SSP in Mumbai has partly emerged from an awareness that not only must more toilets be built in the city, but that they must be functional and they must meet people's needs if they are to prevent open defecation. However, the outcomes of such programmes continue to be calculated in policy circles in terms of number of toilet seats built, even though in practice, the outcomes are uneven in terms of creating adequate—that is, clean, well-maintained, easily accessible, and affordable—toilets in the city.[68] To create adequate sanitation for truly fulfilling the bodily needs of urban dwellers, sanitation policy and practice will have to engage with people's practices,

---

[68] McFarlane (n 50); TARU and Water, Engineering and Development Centre (WEDC), *Study of the World Bank Financed Slum Sanitation Project in Mumbai* (Report to the Water and Sanitation Programme and the World Bank, 2005).

experiences, and perceptions in relation to sanitation infrastructures and (open) defecation. It is imperative that to bring an end to open defecation as well as to provide truly adequate sanitation for all, sanitation policies and programmes need to be broadened to address the multiplicity of relationships between the body and infrastructure that we have discussed.

9

The Environmental Dimension of the Right to Sanitation

Lovleen Bhullar

The realization of the right to sanitation depends on access to and use of sanitation facilities. It is also contingent upon the infrastructure for the management of human waste, that is, collection, transportation, treatment, disposal, and/or reuse of sewage, faecal sludge, and septage.[1] Thus, the realization of the right to sanitation requires environmental resources (for example, land, water, and sources of energy) and it has an impact on the environment (for example, land, water, and air). There is also a link between sanitation and the right to environment, which has been read into Article 21 of the Constitution of India by the Supreme Court of India.[2]

---

[1] United Nations Economic Commission for Europe (UNECE) and UN-Water, *The Post 2015 Water Thematic Consultation, Wastewater Management & Water Quality—Framing Paper* (UNECE, 2015). Annexure A to this chapter includes indicative definitions of the terms 'human waste', 'municipal sewage', 'faecal sludge', and 'septage'.

[2] For this purpose, the Supreme Court has re-interpreted Article 21 of the Constitution, which guarantees the fundamental right to life, and

Nevertheless it is public health concerns that have formed the primary rationale for sanitation interventions.[3] In the international context, Feris has identified a discernible silence on the environmental aspects of sanitation.[4] According to her, '[F]ew definitions link sanitation to pollution, the environment or to sustainable development as a whole, and sanitation is seldom conceptualised in environmental terms'.[5]

This chapter attempts to conceptualize the relationship between sanitation and the right to sanitation, on the one hand, and the environment and the right to environment, on the other, in the context of the domestic law and policy framework in India. The twofold objective is to contribute to the conceptual understanding of the links between the right to sanitation and the right to environment as well as to highlight the importance of including environmental considerations in the domestic framework on sanitation.

The next section examines the nature of the relationship between the lack or inadequacy of sanitation and the implementation of measures for the realization of the right to sanitation, on the one hand, and environmental pollution, degradation of environmental resources, and the right to environment, on the other. The third and fourth sections analyse the extent to which this relationship is integrated into the domestic law and policy frameworks, respectively. This is followed by some concluding remarks.

The Relationship between Sanitation and the Environment

The relationship between sanitation and the environment can be unpacked at multiple levels. The lack or inadequacy of sanitation, and in some cases, even the implementation of measures for the

---

Article 48A of the Constitution, which imposes a duty on the state to protect and improve the environment.

[3] Loretta Feris, 'The Human Right to Sanitation: A Critique on the Absence of Environmental Considerations', (2015) 24(1) *Review of European Community and International Environmental Law* 16, 17.

[4] Feris (n 3), 16.

[5] Feris (n 3), 18.

realization of the right to sanitation, may pollute the environment, degrade environmental resources, and/or infringe the right to environment.[6] This section examines the relationship in the specific context of India.

Lack of Proper Sanitation Facilities: The Practice of Open Defecation

The practice of open defecation, which is attributed to the lack of proper sanitation facilities, may violate the rights to sanitation, health, water, food, and the environment.[7] Open defecation in open areas or fields may lead to the leaching of raw human waste into underground water resources, run-off into surface water bodies, and/ or contamination of agricultural produce.[8] Faecal–oral transmission is one of the major causes of health problems, such as diarrhoea and enteropathy, among children.[9] The scale of the negative impact of the

[6] Feris (n 3), 16, 18, and 22. See also Owen McIntyre, 'Environmental Protection and the Human Right to Water: Complementarity and Tension', in Laura Westra, Colin L. Soskolne, and Donald W. Spady (eds), *Human Health and Ecological Integrity: Ethics, Law and Human Rights* (Routledge, 2012), 225.

[7] According to the 2011 Census, a section of the urban, rural, and slum population relies on public toilets and the practice of open defecation to fulfil its sanitation requirements. See Census of India 2011, 'Availability and Type of Latrine Facility: 2001–2011'; available at http://censusindia. gov.in/2011census/hlo/Data_sheet/India/Latrine.pdf; Census of India 2011, 'HH-8: Slum Households by Availability of Type of Latrine Facility'; available at www.censusindia.gov.in/2011census/hlo/Slum_table/hl-slum/ SHH2808-crc.pdf. This chapter relies on Census 2011, but there are other sources of data on toilet coverage and the availability of sewerage infrastructure, which may provide different estimates.

[8] See generally, Jay P. Graham and Matthew L. Polizzotto, 'Pit Latrines and their Impacts on Groundwater Quality: A Systematic Review', (2013) 121(5) *Environmental Health Perspectives* 521.

[9] See Joe Brown, Sandy Cairncross, and Jeroen H.J. Ensink, 'Water, Sanitation, Hygiene and Enteric Infections in Children', (2013) 98(8) *Archives of Disease in Childhood* 629.

practice of open defecation in India can be estimated from the fact that India is home to more than half of the world's open defecators (597 million people),[10] which includes 52.1 per cent of the rural population and 7.5 per cent of the urban population.[11]

Adverse Impacts of Measures for the Realization of the Right to Sanitation

Construction and use of toilets

Access to, and use of, sanitation facilities requires environmental resources as an input.[12] First, land is required for the construction of the toilet superstructure and substructure. Siting standards for construction of toilets, where prescribed, require the maintenance of a minimum distance between the toilet and the source of water supply in order to prevent water pollution.[13] However, compliance with these standards will depend, among other factors, on the availability of land. Second, water-based sanitation facilities and sewerage rely on the availability of water.[14] Water pollution, to which the discharge of untreated or partly treated human waste into water bodies is a major

[10] World Health Organization and UNICEF, *Progress on Drinking Water and Sanitation: 2014 Update* (UNICEF and WHO, 2014); available at http://apps.who.int/iris/bitstream/10665/112727/1/9789241507240_eng.pdf?ua=1.

[11] See Government of India, Ministry of Statistics and Programme Implementation, National Sample Survey Office, Swachhta Status Report 2016 (Ministry of Statistics and Programme Implementation, 2016), 47.

[12] Feris (n 3), 18.

[13] For example, The Uttar Pradesh Municipalities Act, 1916, s 227. The World Health Organization suggests minimal risk of groundwater pollution where >2 m of relatively fine soil exists between a pit and the groundwater table, assuming fill rates are <50 L/m^2/day. See R. Franceys, J. Pickford, and R. Reed, *A Guide to the Development of On-site Sanitation* (WHO, 1992).

[14] See United Nations Development Programme, *Human Development Report 2006: Beyond Scarcity: Power, Poverty and the Global Water Crisis* (Palgrave Macmillan, 2006), 35; M. Black and B. Fawcett, *The Last Taboo: Opening the Door on the Global Sanitation Crisis* (Earthscan, 2008), 8.

contributor, may also affect the availability of water for different domestic uses, including toilet flushing.[15]

The negative impact on the environment of excessive withdrawal of water to meet different requirements, including sanitation, raises concerns for the realization of the right to water and the right to environment. The failure to consider the unique features of the environment while making decisions to improve access to sanitation, such as the selection of the design of the toilet substructure, may pose another set of problems.[16] For instance, the twin-pit pour flush water seal toilet is not suitable for areas with a high water table, or rocky or coastal areas.[17] Pit latrines that penetrate the water table may transport microbes and chemicals through soil and into local groundwater sources.[18] This may occur where the pit is dug too deep, or it is unlined or improperly lined, or it collapses due to poor soil conditions and shallow groundwater table.[19]

Management of human waste

Urbanization and population growth, together with the emphasis on construction of individual household latrine (IHHL) facilities, have led to an increase in human waste as a constituent of domestic

---

[15]   The Bureau of Indian Standards has laid down the following minimum water supply requirements for the domestic and non-domestic needs of urban communities with full flushing system and (i) a population of 20,000 to 100,000 is 100–50 lphd; and (ii) a population of more than 100,000 is 150–200 lphd. See Bureau of Indian Standards, Indian Standard: 1172–1993: Code of Basic Requirements for Water Supply, Drainage and Sanitation (4th revision, 2007).

[16]   Graham and Polizzotto (n 8), 527.

[17]   Government of India, Ministry of Drinking Water and Sanitation, *Handbook on Technological Options for On-site Sanitation in Rural Areas* (Ministry of Drinking Water and Sanitation, 2016), 29. See also P.R. Pujari, C. Padmakar, P.K. Labhasetwar, P. Mahore, and A.K. Ganguly, 'Assessment of the Impact of On-site Sanitation Systems on Groundwater Pollution in Two Diverse Geological Settings: A Case Study from India', (2012) 184(1) *Environmental Monitoring Assessment* 251.

[18]   Graham and Polizzotto (n 8), 522.

[19]   Graham and Polizzotto (n 8), 522.

wastewater in India. According to the 2011 Census, the population of India had crossed 1.2 billion, 31.16 per cent of which resides in urban areas.[20] Toilet facilities within premises were present in 81.4 per cent of urban households: water closets (72.6 per cent); pit latrines (7.1 per cent); and other toilets connected to open drains, night soil removed by humans, or serviced by animals (1.7 per cent).[21] Only 30.6 per cent of rural households had toilet facilities within their premises, out of which 20.4 per cent had water closets.[22] In slums, 66 per cent of the households had toilet facilities within their premises: water closets (57.7 per cent); pit latrines (6.1 per cent); and other toilets connected to open drains, night soil removed by humans, or serviced by animals (2.2 per cent).[23] Unless properly managed, the negative impact of human waste on the environment can be significant.

A majority of the urban households with water closets, and an increasing percentage of rural households, rely on septic tanks for on-site management of human waste.[24] Human excreta disposed off in on-site sanitation systems may result in microbiological contamination (the presence of faecal coliform) and inorganic chemical contamination (especially nitrates and chloride)[25] of groundwater.

[20] See Census of India 2011, 'Provisional Population Totals: India: Census 2011'; available at http://censusindia.gov.in/2011-prov-results/indiaatglance.html; Census of India 2011, 'Rural Urban Distribution of Population (Provisional Population Totals)'; available at http://censusindia.gov.in/2011-prov-results/paper2/data_files/india/Rural_Urban_2011.pdf.

[21] See Census 2011 (n 7), 'Availability and Type of Latrine Facility: 2001–2011'.

[22] See Census 2011 (n 7), 'Availability and Type of Latrine Facility: 2001–2011'.

[23] See Census 2011 (n 7), 'HH-8: Slum Households by Availability of Type of Latrine Facility'.

[24] See Census 2011 (n 7), 'Availability and Type of Latrine Facility: 2001–2011'.

[25] The WHO-recommended guideline for nitrate in drinking water is 50 mg/L. Chloride concentrations >250 mg/L may affect the taste and acceptability of water. See World Health Organization, *Guidelines for Drinking-Water Quality* (4th edn WHO, 2011).

Environmental factors such as hydrological and soil conditions influence the occurrence and extent of groundwater pollution from the discharge of effluents from on-site sanitation facilities.[26]

Urban households with water closets, which do not rely on on-site management, require off-site management of human waste. Negative environmental impacts may follow from the absence of a sewerage network or the inadequacy (for example, poor quality) of the existing network. Leaking or overflowing drains may release their contents into storm water or other surface drains, or the contents may get retained on land to percolate, leach, or get washed off into streams or groundwater.[27] The disposal of untreated or partly treated sewage, including human waste, into public drains or on land or into water bodies, results in the pollution of surface water and groundwater.[28] The volume of dumped untreated or partly treated sewage also limits the assimilative or regenerative capacity of surface water bodies.[29] This capacity is also adversely affected by the nature of the pollutants, which may result, for example, in eutrophication due to nutrient over-enrichment of the receiving water bodies.[30]

In order to arrest this problem, sewage pumping stations and sewage treatment plants form a critical component of the sanitation interventions in the country. They may contribute towards the

[26] Graham and Polizzotto (n 8), 522 and 526. See also Pujari et al. (n 17).

[27] WaterAid, Urban Wash: An Assessment of Faecal Sludge Management Policies and Programmes at the National and Select States Level (WaterAid, 2015), 41.

[28] Untreated sewage from cities is the single biggest source of water resource pollution in India. See Government of India, Ministry of Housing and Urban Affairs, Guidelines for Swachh Bharat Mission (Urban), 2017, para 1.1; available at http://164.100.228.143:8080/sbm/content/writere-addata/SBM_Guideline.pdf.

[29] R. Kaur, S.P. Wani, A.K. Singh, and K. Lal, 'Wastewater Production, Treatment and Use in India', in UN Water, Country Report: India (UN Water, 2012), 111.

[30] Brij Gopal and K.P. Sharma, 'Ecology of Plant Populations I: Growth', in Brij Gopal (ed), Ecology and Management of Aquatic Vegetation in the Indian Sub-Continent (Kluwer Academic Publishers, 1990), 97.

realization of the right to sanitation. However, in terms of environmental inputs, land is required for their construction, and large quantities of water are required to ensure the self-cleansing velocity of underground sewerage systems (where existing) as well as the treatment of sewage. In terms of environmental impacts, insufficient capacity or inadequacies in the operation and management of the treatment facilities may result in environmental pollution.[31] The use of fossil fuel energy as well as emissions from such facilities may contribute to air pollution as well as to climate change.[32] Further, nearly 39 per cent of the existing sewage treatment plants do not conform to the general standards for discharge into streams laid down under domestic environmental laws.[33]

Off-site management is also required for the faecal sludge or septage that is left behind after on-site management of human waste. It is worse than open defecation, as the levels of pathogens and microorganisms are higher in black water.[34] As in the case of sewage, the dumping of untreated septage as well as human waste from septic tanks that are connected to an outlet, as well as waste from households with cesspools (lined tanks with no outflow) or storage tanks or unlined pit latrines, on land and into water bodies results in pollution of the soil and groundwater, once the waste percolates into the earth.[35]

In the absence of complete and reliable data to determine the total amount of human waste generated in India, it is not possible to establish the scale of the required management initiatives. The current

[31] For instance, inadequate management may result in eutrophication, which generates excessive growth of algae and microbial contamination (cyanobacteria), which removes oxygen from the water, thereby posing a threat to both marine and fresh water resources (aquatic animal and plant species and associated ecosystems). See Feris (n 3), 22.

[32] Feris (n 3), 22.

[33] Government of India, Ministry of Environment and Forests, *Inventorization of Sewage Treatment Plants*, Control of Urban Pollution Series: CUPS/ /2015 (CPCB, 2015).

[34] WaterAid (n 26), 33.

[35] Centre for Science and Environment, 'Urban Shit', 24(22) *Down to Earth* 29 (1–15 April 2016), 36.

estimates of generation of human waste in urban areas[36] do not provide the complete picture because water supply by the urban local bodies is not the only source of water supply, and these estimates do not account for sanitation facilities that are not water-based.

Sanitation, the Environment, and Laws

This section examines the extent to which the relationship between sanitation and the environment, as well as the corresponding rights, is recognized in the domestic laws relating to environment and sanitation.

Environment in Sanitation-Related Laws

As stated by Cullet in Chapter 3 in this volume, there is no specific law relating to sanitation in India. Instead, laws governing urban local bodies (municipal corporations and municipalities) and rural local bodies (panchayats), as well as public health laws, include provisions concerning sanitation. In addition, the Central Public Health and Environmental Engineering Organisation (CPHEEO)[37] and the Bureau of Indian Standards (BIS)[38] provide guidance, which,

[36] Based only on the amount of water supplied by urban local bodies, it is estimated that approximately 38,254 MLD of sewage, which includes human waste, was generated in 498 Class I cities (with population >100,000) and 410 Class II towns (with population 50,000–100,000) in 2008. See Government of India, Ministry of Environment and Forests, *Status of Water Supply, Wastewater Generation and Treatment in Class-I Cities & Class-II Towns of India*, Control of Urban Pollution Series: CUPS/70/2009-10 (CPCB, 2009), 46. The amount of sewage generated increased to 62,000 MLD in 2014. See Ministry of Environment and Forests (n 33), Foreword and 6.

[37] Government of India, Ministry of Urban Development, Central Public Health and Environmental Engineering Organisation (CPHEEO), *Manual on Sewerage and Sewage Treatment Systems*, 2013 (CPHEEO, 2013).

[38] See Bureau of Indian Standards, 'Indian Standard: 2470 (Part 1)—1985: Code of Practice for Installation of Septic Tanks: Part 1 Design Criteria and Installation', (1985); Bureau of Indian Standards (BIS), 'IS 2470 (Part 2)—1985: Code of Practice for Installation of Septic Tanks:

although non-binding, serve as the framework for the management of human waste (particularly on-site management). The implementation of these laws and guidance can contribute to the realization of the rights to sanitation and the environment. This section focuses on the provisions for on-site and off-site management of human waste.

On-site management

The CPHEEO and the BIS provide guidance on the design and installation of septic tanks, including the minimum liquid-holding capacity, the number of chambers and their size, connection of the outlet for safe dispersal of effluents, and so on.[39] In practice, many septic tanks do not conform to these recommendations. Many households have a single-chambered septic tank without any outlet, so its entire content has to be emptied.[40] In some cases, septic tanks are designed with an outlet to open ground or an open drain instead of a soak pit.[41] The BIS standards also mandate that the floor of the septic tank should be watertight.[42] Once again, in practice, due to poor quality and the absence of a watertight floor, untreated sewage may seep into the soil, and the septic tank may become a source of groundwater pollution where the groundwater level is not low.[43] Some of the local bodies are empowered to issue notice to owners of septic tanks that do not meet the standard

---

Part 2 Secondary Treatment and Disposal of Septic Tank Effluent', (1985); Bureau of Indian Standards, 'IS 9872—1981: Specification for Precast Concrete Septic Tanks', (1981). See also Bureau of Indian Standards, National Building Code of India, SP 7: 2005, 'Part 3: Development Control Rules and General Building Requirements', and 'Part 9: Plumbing Services Section 1 Water Supply, Drainage and Sanitation (Including Solid Waste Management)'.

[39] See CPHEEO (n 37); BIS (n 38), IS 2470 (Part 1).
[40] Centre for Science and Environment (n 35), 32.
[41] Centre for Science and Environment (n 35), 32.
[42] See BIS (n 38), IS 2470 (Part 1).
[43] Centre for Science and Environment (n 35), 34.

septic tank design;[44] yet, such provisions tend to remain on the statute book.

The BIS and the CPHEEO also prescribe maintenance and operational conditions that can prevent the leakage of partly treated or untreated septage into the surrounding water bodies. For instance, the maximum period for storage of sludge in a septic tank is three years.[45] This can prevent accumulation of organic sludge, reduction in effective volume, and hydraulic loading.[46] However, the ignorance of, or non-compliance with, these conditions, results in the widespread practice of desludging the tank only when it overflows.[47] At this stage, it is not possible to prevent the negative environmental impacts.

Off-Site management

Untreated human waste (where the septic tank does not have an outlet connected to a treatment system) or septage (where the septic tank has an outlet connected to a treatment system) collected from the septic tank should be treated in accordance with the provisions of domestic environmental laws (discussed in the section titled 'Sanitation in Environmental Laws') before disposal or reuse.

---

[44] For example, Government of Tamil Nadu, Municipal Administration and Water Supply (MA3) Department, *Operative Guidelines for Septage Management for Local Bodies in Tamil Nadu*, GO (Ms) No 106, MA& WS, dated 1 August 2014.

[45] The BIS standards prescribe that the septic tanks should be emptied on a half-yearly or annual basis. See BIS (n 38), IS 2470 (Part 1). According to the CPHEEO, the minimum acceptable interval between successive desludging could be one-and-a-half years, with a flexibility of provision of up to three years of storage volume in urban areas. See CPHEEO (n 37), 'Chapter 9: Onsite Sanitation'. The MoUD gives the desludging frequency as once every two to three years or when the tank becomes one-third full. See Government of India, Ministry of Urban Development, *Advisory Note on Septage Management in Urban India*, 2013 (Ministry of Urban Development, 2013), 17.

[46] Centre for Science and Environment, *Policy Paper on Septage Management in India* (Centre for Science and Environment, 2011), 13.

[47] Centre for Science and Environment (n 35), 34.

The National Building Code, 2005, specifies that 'under no circumstances shall effluent from a septic tank be allowed into an open channel drain or body of water without adequate treatment'.[48] Further, the disposal of treated septage should be at a specified, authorized, and notified location in compliance with the provisions of the Environment (Protection) Act, 1986, and the Water (Prevention and Control of Pollution) Act, 1974. But even if the untreated septage is safely transported to a treatment facility, the sewage treatment facilities are often not designed to treat the total solids, suspended solids, Biochemical Oxygen Demand, Chemical Oxygen Demand, nitrogen, and potassium found in septage.[49]

Recently, some states/cities have introduced regulations for the management of waste in septic tanks or septage.[50] These regulations incorporate environmental concerns to a varying extent. Here, the relevant provisions of two regulations are being considered for illustrative purposes. The Delhi Water Board Septic Tank Waste Management Regulations, 2015, are primarily concerned with the establishment of a licensing system for the collection, transportation, and disposal of septage to notified sewage pumping stations and sewage treatment plants. The licensee is responsible for ensuring that there is no leakage during transportation, and is fully and completely liable for any damage to the environment in case of any accident or disaster. The regulations also require that the vehicle must be fitted with equipment to take care of the threat of pollution due to any accident during movement.

The scope of the Bhubaneshwar Septage Management Regulations, 2015, is wider. The owner of premises connected to a septic tank is responsible for its operation and maintenance (O&M) to prevent a risk to human health or the environment, and for checking the sludge level so that the effluent does not reach

---

[48] National Building Code of India (n 38), para 12.15.2(c).

[49] Centre for Science and Environment (n 35), 36.

[50] See Delhi Water Board Septic Tank Waste Management Regulations, 2015; Bhubaneshwar Septage Management Regulations, 2015. See also 'Operative Guidelines on Septage Management (Collection, Transportation, Treatment and Disposal) in Greater Warangal Municipal Corporation (GWMC)', 2016.

surface waters or onto the surface of the ground. The municipal plan for inspection/supervision and monitoring of septic tanks must have regard to relevant or potential risks to human health or the environment, and in particular, risks to water, air, or soil, or to plants and animals. In terms of responsibilities, the septage transporter is required to ensure that there is no discharge or emptying of sludge and septage into locations other than approved treatment facilities, and to take immediate action to minimize the environmental impact in the event of accidental spillage. Septage must be processed and treated in approved and notified treatment facilities in accordance with the relevant laws and generally accepted methods and standards.

The legal framework also includes several provisions to facilitate the collection and transportation of untreated sewage, including human waste, to a treatment facility through the sewerage network. It is the statutory duty of urban local bodies to construct, alter, and maintain drains, drainage works, and sewerage works.[51] The owners or occupiers of premises/buildings cannot erect a new building or re-erect a building, or occupy it, without a drain.[52] They are also required to fulfil the conditions laid down in the written permission from the local body before emptying a private drain into a Corporation drain or another place lawfully set apart for this purpose.[53] Further, the local body is empowered to enforce drainage of undrained premises.[54]

In order to ensure smooth transportation of sewage from the source of its generation through drains, some laws acknowledge the need to make certain that there is no interference with the ability of drains to convey sewage. It is not uncommon to find a provision that prohibits the discharge of any substance or matter which is likely to injure a drain or to interfere with the free flow of its contents, or to prejudicially affect treatment and disposal of its contents.[55]

---

[51] For example, The Uttar Pradesh Municipal Corporations Act, 1959, ss 114(v) and (vi).

[52] Uttar Pradesh Municipal Corporations Act (n 51), s 245.

[53] Uttar Pradesh Municipal Corporations Act (n 51), s 234.

[54] Uttar Pradesh Municipal Corporations Act (n 51), ss 238 and 239.

[55] Uttar Pradesh Municipal Corporations Act (n 51), s 258.

Some other provisions can contribute to the protection of public health and the environment. For instance, the discharge of water from any drains or premises on a public street or into a source of water is prohibited or restricted.[56] Further, the local bodies are required to separate drains carrying human waste, which should be transported to sewage treatment facilities, and the storm water drains carrying rainwater, which are directly discharged into water bodies.[57]

Sanitation in Environmental Laws

Sanitation, and more specifically human waste, forms a central element of domestic environmental laws. Under certain circumstances, human waste can become an environmental pollutant under the Environment (Protection) Act.[58] Similarly, the Water (Prevention and Control of Pollution) Act applies to the prevention and control of water pollution resulting from human waste.[59] This section examines the statutory provisions that highlight the obligations of the different stakeholders in respect of human waste, the link with the assimilative capacity of water bodies, and the opportunities for recycling and reuse of treated human waste.

Obligations of different stakeholders

The Environment (Protection) Act and the Water (Prevention and Control of Pollution) Act impose obligations on urban local bodies in respect of treatment and disposal of sewage effluents. First, they are required to obtain, from the concerned state pollution control board (SPCB) or pollution control committee (PCC), a 'consent to establish' a sewage treatment plant before commencement of

---

[56] For example, Uttar Pradesh Municipalities Act (n 13), s 276.

[57] For example, Uttar Pradesh Municipal Corporations Act (n 51), s 248.

[58] See The Environment (Protection) Act, 1986, s 2(a) (definition of 'environment') and s 2(b) (definition of 'environmental pollutant').

[59] See The Water (Prevention and Control of Pollution) Act, 1974, s 2(e) (definition of 'pollution') and s 2(g) (definition of 'sewage effluent').

construction, and a 'consent to operate' the same before commencement of operations.[60] Second, sewage treatment and disposal is
subject to compliance with the prescribed standards for treatment of
sewage to be discharged into any particular stream, and the prescribed
effluent standards for the discharge of sewage.[61] Urban local bodies
are also prohibited from discharging or permitting the discharge of
pollutants in excess of the prescribed standards.[62]

In order for urban local bodies to discharge their obligations, the
SPCB/PCC is required to prescribe standards. Until recently, in the
absence of specific standards for sewage treatment plants, the prescribed mandatory general standards for discharge of pollutants into
inland surface water, public sewers, land for irrigation, and marine
coastal areas were applicable.[63] In April 2015, the Central Pollution
Control Board (CPCB) suggested specific standards for the disposal

---

[60] Water (Prevention and Control of Pollution) Act (n 59), s 25.

[61] Water (Prevention and Control of Pollution) Act (n 59), s 17(1)(k) and
s 17(1)(m), respectively. The former standards should take into account the
minimum fair weather dilution available in that stream, and the tolerance
limits of pollution permissible in the water of the stream, after the discharge
of such effluents.

[62] Environment (Protection) Act (n 58), s 7. These standards are prescribed by the Central Government through the Ministry of Environment
and Forests (now the Ministry of Environment, Forest and Climate Change)
and relate to (i) various aspects of environmental quality (Environment
(Protection) Act, s 3(2)(iii)); and (ii) emission or discharge of environmental
pollutants from various sources having regard to the quality or composition
of the emission or discharge (Environment (Protection) Act, s 3(2)(iv)). The
Central Government may also make rules for the quality of air, water, or soil
for various areas and purposes (Environment (Protection) Act, s 6(2)(a)),
as well as the maximum allowable limits of concentration of various
environmental pollutants for different areas (Environment (Protection)
Act, s 6(2)(b)).

[63] See The Environment (Protection) Rules, 1986, Schedule VI, Part
A and Annexure I, item 7 read with rule 3(3A). Additionally, the Most
Probable Number (MPN) of faecal coliform is included in the water quality standards for coastal waters marine outfalls, and primary water quality
criteria for bathing water. See Environment (Protection) Rules, Schedule I,
items 86 and 93, respectively.

of treated effluents on land or in a river or any other water body including coastal water/creek or a drain, and directed the SPCBs/PCCs to enforce consent management in accordance with these standards.[64] The SPCBs/PCCs are also required to prescribe standards for the quality of receiving waters (not being water in an interstate stream) resulting from discharge.[65] They are also responsible for the identification of economical and reliable methods of sewage treatment,[66] and efficient disposal methods on land.[67] These methods must satisfy certain conditions, which reflect a consideration of the environmental impact of sewage treatment and disposal.

The domestic environmental laws impose certain obligations on all persons in respect of prevention and control of water pollution, which can prevent the disposal or dumping of untreated or partly treated human sewage into the environment. For instance, there is a prohibition on the entry of any poisonous, noxious, or polluting matter into any stream or well or sewer or on land, as well as the entry of any matter which may tend to impede the proper flow of the water of the stream in a manner leading or likely to lead to a substantial aggravation of pollution due to other causes or the consequences of pollution.[68]

Assimilative capacity of water bodies

In addition to the concerns discussed so far, the link between sanitation and the environment can be explored in another way.

---

[64] See Ministry of Environment and Forests (n 33).

[65] Water (Prevention and Control of Pollution) Act (n 59), s 17(g).

[66] Water (Prevention and Control of Pollution) Act (n 59), s 17(h). The methods must have regard to the peculiar conditions of soils, climate, and water resources of different regions, and more particularly, the prevailing flow characteristics of water in streams and wells which render it impossible to attain even the minimum degree of dilution.

[67] Water (Prevention and Control of Pollution) Act (n 59), s 17(j). Such standards should be necessary on account of the predominant conditions of scant stream flows that do not provide the minimum degree of dilution for major part of the year.

[68] Water (Prevention and Control of Pollution) Act (n 59), s 24(1).

The problem posed by the discharge of untreated or partly treated sewage, including human waste, into water bodies is exacerbated by the overexploitation of these water bodies to meet the increasing demand for water supply for different uses, as it results in reduced availability of freshwater for dilution of the discharged sewage.[69] The domestic environmental laws recognize the need to ensure the assimilative capacity of the water bodies that receive the treated human waste for disposal. The SPCBs/PCCs are required to take into account the assimilative capacities of receiving bodies, especially water bodies, while permitting the discharge of effluent into the environment, so that the quality for intended use of the receiving body is not affected; otherwise, they should not allow the discharge.[70] In addition to ensuring water availability for different human uses, such measures can also contribute to a healthy ecosystem.

Recycling and reuse of human waste

Although generally termed as waste, treated sewage is also a resource. It can be recycled and reused for different purposes before its final disposal, such as on construction sites, for industrial cooling, for energy production, or for irrigation (with wastewater)/fertilization (with sludge). The World Health Organization (WHO) provides useful standards in this regard.[71] But until recently, this important intervening process has received relatively little attention.

The legal framework recognizes the reuse potential of treated sewage in irrigation. One of the functions of the SPCB under the Water (Prevention and Control of Pollution) Act is to evolve methods of utilization of treated sewage in agriculture.[72] Similarly, the Water Quality Assessment Authority established under the Environment (Protection) Act is vested with the power to direct government, local

---

[69] For example, Centre for Science and Environment, *Sewage Canal: How to Clean the Yamuna* (Centre for Science and Environment, 2007), 41–2.

[70] Environment (Protection) Rules (n 63), Schedule VI.

[71] World Health Organization, WHO Guidelines for the Safe Use of Wastewater, Excreta and Greywater, Volume IV; available at http://www.who.int/water_sanitation_health/wastewater/gsuweg4/en/.

[72] Water (Prevention and Control of Pollution) Act (n 59), s 17(1)(i).

bodies, and non-governmental agencies to promote recycling/reuse of treated sewage for irrigation.[73] Further, the discretionary functions of the local body in some municipal laws include arrangements within or outside municipal limits for preparation of compost manure from night soil and rubbish.[74] Some urban local bodies sell domestic sewage generated within their jurisdictional limits to farmers from surrounding villages to irrigate their crops. But in some cases, the sewage is not treated or it is partly treated. Courts have taken note of the problems associated with such use, including pollution, contamination, and foul smell.[75]

Some of the state-level or city-level bye-laws or regulations, or amendments to existing bye-laws or regulations, require cooperative group housing societies, multi-storied housing complexes, big hotels, and so on to establish and operate on-site treatment facilities for recycling and reuse of wastewater.[76] The builder is required to obtain 'consent to establish' and 'consent to operate' these facilities from the SPCB under the Water (Prevention and Control of Pollution) Act. However, there are certain practical implications/difficulties in implementing this decentralized approach, such as flaws in installation, O&M issues, and/or malfunctioning

---

[73] Government of India, Ministry of Environment and Forests, *Water Quality Assessment Authority Order*, No SO583(E), dated 29 May 2001, para 2(II)(d).

[74] Uttar Pradesh Municipalities Act (n 13), s 8.

[75] For example, *Amar Singh & Others* v *Union Territory, Chandigarh & Others* AIR 1993 P&H 100 (High Court of Punjab and Haryana, 1992). See also *Dr Subhash C. Pandey* v *Union of India & Others*, OA No 117 of 2014, National Green Tribunal (Central Zonal Bench, Bhopal).

[76] For example, Government of Kerala, Local Self Government Department, General Town Planning Scheme, Notification GO(Ms.) No 144/07/LSGD dated 31 May 2007. This was a response to the Jawaharlal Nehru National Urban Renewal Mission (JNNURM), which called upon urban local bodies to adopt the 'optional' water reuse reform and to formulate building bye-laws for reuse of wastewater for this purpose. See Government of India, Ministry of Urban Development, Jawaharlal Nehru National Urban Renewal Mission, 'Primer on O7. Bye Laws for Reuse of Wastewater: Optional Reform under JNNURM' (Ministry of Urban Development, n.d.), 2.

facilities.[77] The judiciary has also recognized the potential for use of treated sewage for non-potable purposes, and ordered the reuse of treated sewage/wastewater (instead of groundwater) for construction purposes.[78]

Further, the CPCB has prohibited the use of potable water for non-potable purposes such as industrial processes, railways and bus cleaning, flushing of toilets through dual piping, horticulture, and irrigation, and asked the SPCBs/PCCs to issue directions to all municipalities and other concerned authorities in the states/union territories responsible for treatment and disposal of sewage, to mandatorily sell secondary treated sewage for such non-potable uses.[79]

If the prescribed statutory requirements are met, recycling and reuse of human waste can help to reduce the dependence on environmental resources, particularly water and energy, as an input in other processes. At the same time, the concern remains that if untreated or partly treated human waste is reused, not only can it expose people to health risks,[80] it can also have detrimental environmental impacts.

Environmental Considerations and the Swachh Bharat Mission

The previous section has examined the link between sanitation and the environment in some of the laws relating to either or

[77] For example, M. Nazeer, 'Faulty Sewage Systems in Flats Pose Health Hazards', *The Hindu* (Kannur) (28 March 2012); available at http://www.thehindu.com/todays-paper/tp-national/tp-kerala/faulty-sewage-systems-in-flats-pose-health-hazards/article3252948.ece.

[78] For example, *Sunil Singh* v *Ministry of Environment and Forests & Others* WP (Civil) No 20032 of 2008 (High Court of Punjab and Haryana, Order dated 24 December 2010).

[79] For example, Government of India, Ministry of Environment, Forest and Climate Change, Central Pollution Control Board, Directions under Section 18(1)(b) of the Water (Prevention and Control of Pollution) Act, 1974, Regarding Treatment and Utilisation of Sewage, 21 April 2015; available at http://cpcb.nic.in/cpcbold/Uttrakhand_swg_18(1)(b)_2015.pdf.

[80] See UN-Habitat, Global Atlas of Excreta, Wastewater Sludge, and Biosolids Management: Moving Forward the Sustainable and Welcome Use of a Global Resource; available at http://esa.un.org/iys/docs/san_lib_docs/habitat2008.pdf. See also Nazeer (n 77).

both. Additionally, and overwhelmingly, the regulation of sanitation is being undertaken via policies, programmes, and schemes. In this context, it is important to discuss the extent to which the policy framework accommodates the link between sanitation and the environment. This section focuses on the Swachh Bharat Mission-Gramin (SBM-G) Guidelines[81] and the Swachh Bharat Mission-Urban (SBM-U) Guidelines, which form the basis of the ongoing Swachh Bharat Mission (SBM) of the Central Government, to make rural and urban India 'open defecation free' (ODF) by October 2019. Improved access to IHHLs, which forms a key strategy, can contribute to the prevention or control of the adverse impacts on the environment, and the realization of the right to sanitation. And yet, the unilateral focus on construction of toilets, which ignores management of human waste, fails to appreciate the overarching causes and effects of water pollution.

The text of the SBM-G Guidelines acknowledges the link between sanitation and the environment. There is an explicit reference to 'ecologically safe and sustainable' sanitation.[82] In order to 'encourage and promote ecologically sustainable long term solution for disposal of wastes', the guidelines recognize the need for further research/studies to make technology more 'environmentally safe to suit the requirements of different geo-hydrological conditions'.[83] For this purpose, they prioritize '[r]esearch/study on latrine design, sustainable methods/technologies for Solid and Liquid Waste Management in rural areas, appropriate technology to suit varying soil conditions, high water table situations, floods, water scarcity conditions, coastal areas'.[84] The guidelines also encourage ecological sanitation/on-site waste management to prevent pollution of water bodies due to discharge of untreated waste.[85]

---

[81] Government of India, Ministry of Drinking Water and Sanitation, Guidelines for Swachh Bharat Mission (Gramin), 2017; available at https://mdws.gov.in/sites/default/files/Complete%20set%20guidelines_1.pdf.

[82] SBM-G Guidelines (n 81), para 4(d).

[83] SBM-G Guidelines (n 81), para 18.2.

[84] SBM-G Guidelines (n 81), para 18.2.

[85] SBM-G Guidelines (n 81), para 18.2.

Paving the way for the incorporation of environmental considerations at the design stage, the SBM-G Guidelines also permit location-
specific technology.[86] This is unfortunately compromised by a tendency to adopt a one-size-fits-all approach in practice. Further, in
order to 'ensure the outcomes required for pollution free rivers' one
of the aims of the guidelines is 'to saturate, on priority, the States/
Districts/GPs in all major river basins of India'.[87] While the recognition of the need to prevent river pollution is welcome, this may
undermine the need to protect other water sources from pollution
linked to sanitation.

There are scant direct references to the environment in the SBM-U
Guidelines. In fact, the link between the environment and sanitation is only mentioned twice. The urban local bodies are required
to carry out periodic desludging of pits to minimize environmental
problems of the community, and behaviour change communication,
a key strategy, which is to be carried out through massive public
awareness campaigns, should establish the link between sanitation
and the environment.[88] In addition, there is one reference to the
environmental-friendly nature of biodigester toilets.[89]

Another major limitation of the policy framework is that it is
not binding. The failure to comply with the terms of the guidelines
cannot be made the subject of a judicial challenge, unlike the laws
discussed in the previous section. At the same time, it is the non-
binding policy framework that has provided the impetus to fill the
gap resulting from the absence of laws.[90] For instance, some states
and cities have prepared guidelines for septage management pursuant to SBM-U,[91] and regulations pursuant to the National Urban

---

[86] SBM-G Guidelines (n 81), para 5.2.6.

[87] SBM-G Guidelines (n 81), para 5.2.12.

[88] SBM-U Guidelines (n 28), paras 4.2.4 and 8.1–8.2, respectively.

[89] SBM-U Guidelines (n 28), 'Annexure II: Technical Options for
Toilets under SBM-U'.

[90] For further discussion on binding versus non-binding instruments,
see Cullet (Chapter 3) in this volume.

[91] See, for example, 'Guidelines for Septage Management in Maharashtra',
2016; 'Odisha Urban Septage Management Guidelines, 2016'.

Sanitation Policy (NUSP) and the Ministry of Urban Development's advisory note on septage management (see the section titled 'Off-site Management').

* * *

There is an inverse relationship between the lack or inadequacy of sanitation, on the one hand, and environmental protection and the realization of the right to environment on the other. The measures for the realization of the right to sanitation may promote environmental protection and the realization of the right to environment, just as they may hinder it. For instance, if ensuring access to a toilet is viewed as the primary indicator to measure the achievement of the target of 'improved' access to sanitation facilities, it is possible to realize this very anthropocentric formulation of the right to sanitation without paying attention to waste management and the resulting adverse environmental impacts. Further, a rights-based approach may not address purely environmental considerations that are not linked to health, which continues to form the primary focus of sanitation interventions.

Laws governing local bodies, public health laws, as well as environmental laws capture some aspects of the link between sanitation and the environment. Usually, the link is more explicit in environmental laws. In the laws governing local bodies, the link can be implied from the more obvious connection that is made between sanitation and public health, especially in terms of the impact on water supply. Compliance with these laws can promote sanitation goals and protect the environment as well as the aquatic and associated ecosystems that are utilized in waterborne sanitation or act as receptors for the sewage system. However, their non-implementation, among other reasons, has led to a situation where the generation of sewage far exceeds the amount that is being transported to treatment facilities.[92] As a result, a very large amount of untreated human waste continues to be dumped into water bodies or disposed off on land. Further,

---

[92] According to the 2011 Census, 32.7 per cent of urban households and only 2.2 per cent of rural households are connected to the sewer system. See Census 2011 (n 7), 'Availability and Type of Latrine Facility: 2001–2011'.

these laws do not address the environmental impacts of the design of sanitation facilities, the collection and transportation of human waste, or the on-site management of human waste including the prescription of standards for the treatment of septage.

Recycling and reuse of treated human waste for non-potable uses of water has a positive environmental impact—it reduces the exploitation of the available sources of water, and environmental pollution resulting from the discharge of untreated or partly treated sewage. But, in the absence of proper monitoring, the reuse of untreated or partly treated human waste may pose health and environmental hazards. The policy framework acknowledges the environmental impacts of sanitation but this is not reflected in the operative parts. The implementation of the regulatory framework is another matter of grave concern.

It is also not possible to consider the management of human waste in isolation. The mixing of sewage with industrial effluents and agricultural waste as well as with solid waste can lead to another set of environmental problems; where sewage is treated, this can undermine regulatory efforts. This is an important area for further research. Another issue that merits attention while studying the link between sanitation and the environment is the adoption of a holistic approach, which considers the different cause-and-effect relationships, as well as the unequal distribution of costs and benefits among different sections of society.

Annexure

Human waste is understood as the domestic effluent consisting of black water or excreta, urine, and faecal sludge, which forms a part of wastewater. The term 'wastewater' also includes domestic effluent consisting of grey water (kitchen and bathing wastewater); water from commercial establishments and institutions, including hospitals; industrial effluent, storm water and other urban run-off; and agricultural, horticultural, and aquaculture effluent, either dissolved or as suspended matter.[93]

---

[93] See E. Corcoran et al. (eds), Sick Water: The Central Role of Wastewater Management in Sustainable Development (UNEP and UN-Habitat, 2010), 15.

Municipal sewage is defined as '[w]aste (mostly liquid) originating from a community, may be composed of domestic wastewaters and/or industrial discharges'.[94]

'*Faecal sludge* is the solid or settled contents of pit latrines and septic tanks. It differs from sludge produced in municipal wastewater treatment plants.'[95]

Septage, in the urban context, is defined as 'the settled solid matter in semi-solid condition usually a mixture of solids and water settled at the bottom of septic tank. It has an offensive odour, appearance and is high in organics and pathogenic microorganisms'.[96] In the rural context, 'septage' is defined as 'the combination of scum, sludge, and liquid that accumulates in the septic tanks'.[97]

---

[94] See Ministry of Environment & Forests (n 36), 1.
[95] See Ministry of Urban Development (n 45), 7.
[96] Ministry of Urban Development (n 45), 7.
[97] See Ministry of Drinking Water and Sanitation (n 17), 68.

PART III

DIGNITY, SAFETY, AND VULNERABILITY

10

Safai Karmachari Andolan

An Insider's Account (Conversation with Bezwada Wilson)*

Q: How did the Safai Karmachari Andolan (SKA) start?

Bezwada Wilson (BW): The emergence of the SKA cannot be attributed to the efforts of any particular individual or group of individuals. Neither can it be attributed to any particular incident. In fact, it is very difficult to put a date to it. There are thousands of memories that made us think. In the early 1980s, when I was about 15–16 years old, I started thinking about our own lives, the life of manual scavengers. I started travelling, asking questions, talking, and discussing about our lives. The SKA emerged during a three-year period, from 1982 to 1985, when many things happened around us and when there were many like-minded individuals such as Anant Rao Samuel, Y. Moses, and P.S. Rao.

* Based on interviews with Bezwada Wilson conducted by Philippe Cullet and Sujith Koonan.

Q: What are these memories that you speak of and what are your own memories? What made you realize that the problems of your community had to be addressed?

BW: The SKA is not a registered organization or a non-governmental organization (NGO). It is a platform which emerged out of anguish. Since childhood we had heard from our parents, relatives, and other community members about the problems related to manual scavenging. However, their social and economic conditions never allowed them to raise their voice against the practice. There were many instances wherein the community members were punished for raising their voice against the practice of manual scavenging. This is embedded in our memory since childhood.

One day I was sent to be inducted into my hereditary profession, which I refused. But I can recollect thousands of narratives including the first experience of my parents and relatives about how they were convinced to join the occupation. Everybody has a story, and our mind is filled with such stories. A change in our approach and understanding began when we went out and saw the life and work of other people. This led us to realize the degrading nature of our life and work which involves carrying of human excreta. We gradually identified manual scavenging as a problem to be addressed and resolved.

Q: When did you realize the role of caste in manual scavenging?

BW: Till 1986, I used to believe that the community itself was responsible for the work they did and was not forced into doing so. At that time, it was my simple notion that we as a community were doing something wrong and that our people were useless and unable to understand because of illiteracy. I also used to think that my community members have chosen an easy job where they do not need to work hard.

From 1986 onwards, I started receiving support from the *safai karamchari* community. The period from 1986 to 1989 was crucial, since I gained a better understanding of the problems of manual scavenging. Till then, I had neither visited the villages nor experienced how the caste system works or the role it plays. By 1986, I started to realize that we are victims of the caste system. I also realized that the caste system can have an impact despite being invisible, and its influence can be considerable.

The root of the practice of manual scavenging is linked to caste. We started using caste as of the main argument to fight against manual scavenging. We started arguing that we are scavengers not because we are ugly, dirty, or lazy; but because we were born into a particular caste. Gradually we realized that the term 'scavenger' itself is a derogatory term, and we began to use the term 'safai karamchari' instead.

Karnataka is one of the pioneering states where there was a movement for the eradication of manual scavenging. Nijalingappa and Basalingappa, the chief minister and social welfare minister of Karnataka in the 1970s banned the head load system in the state. When I started talking about manual scavenging in Karnataka, I was told that the matter had already been discussed in the state assembly. I also contacted journalists who wrote on the issue. In the 1990s, I gained prominence.

Q: Since an *andolan* requires the support of the community, how did the SKA earn it? Were they able to identify the problems you were talking about or apprehensive about losing their work?

BW: First, we located the community that did the work, namely our people. Second, we asked the question why we they are doing this 'work'? Their response pointed to the issue of lack of other opportunities to earn their livelihood. For instance, their usual answer was—'if we do not do this, what else would we do, and how will we live?' This was indeed a vicious cycle. The caste system links livelihoods of people belonging to certain sections of society with their occupation. So, if they leave their occupation, they would lose their livelihood. It is never said that they can engage in only one particular occupation. But it is very clear that if they leave that occupation, they would automatically lose their livelihood. There is no doubt that this kind of internalization exists in the community.

Society also feels that this community is skilled to clean, so this is a better occupation for them. Even if the community wants to do something else, they are not allowed to enter houses of others, particularly the upper caste people. Members of the community may sweep inside the house, clean toilets, or even the garden but they are not allowed to wash clothes or cook food. Entry to the mainstream society therefore, remains restricted. How does one deal with such a situation? Thus, we linked this issue with self-respect and dignity. This happened after 1986–7, when we learnt more about Dr B.R. Ambedkar.

We felt that it is better to dispel the confusion about sanitation workers and workers who clean human excreta. Once the clarification was made, people started to understand why we described manual scavenging as inhuman and heinous, instead of calling it dirty or easy. Some people told me very clearly: How can you think that we are happy to clean somebody's shit? Why do you ask such a question and why are you expecting an answer from us? Nobody can be happy to clean somebody's shit for money.

We started learning from the members of the community. Many times, when we went to tell them something, we learnt something from them instead. This process of learning continued. The members of the community initially used to complain about the bad quality of the buckets they use, lack of availability of gloves, and the meagre amount of wages. We started creating a space where they could think and say that they did not want to be a manual scavenger. This was the actual turning point. One achievement was that we were able to make people understand. Consequently, in one or two places, people left manual scavenging themselves, and in some other places people promised us that they will leave manual scavenging. All this happened gradually, and we were satisfied with the outcome.

Q: So, you successfully mobilized the community, and by this time the SKA had started to expand its work and even confronted the government. Can you elaborate?

BW: When people left this work, they said that they felt remarkable and very happy! This made us realize that our community members are being stopped from experiencing this feeling by various social and economic factors. After this we started breaking hurdles everywhere. Gradually, we understood that manual scavenging was not just a social problem; the problem was also with the government. We also realized that it was impossible to aim for a social reform movement without the state and its intervention. The Constitution guarantees fundamental rights to its citizens, and we are political activists who can demand this. This understanding helped us to focus on the issue of non-implementation of the 1993 Act [Employment of Manual Scavengers and Construction of Dry Latrines (Prohibition) Act]. Then we moved a step ahead. Around the year 2000, we came to Delhi and started preparing the writ petition. Once we understood that we were fighting for constitutional rights, we really felt that we were not fighting against, but for what the Constitution has guaranteed to us. We became political and human rights activists in the process. Now we speak the language of 'rights' instead of 'demands'.

During the three years from 1986 to 1989, we confronted the government authorities. Out fight against the Bharat Gold Mines Limited (BGML) in Karnataka, then a public sector undertaking of the Ministry of Steel and Mines, is a good example in this regard. The BGML was located in Kolar, the town where I was born. There were dry latrines in BGML, and we took up the issue. People used to discourage me by saying that the industry had mafia gangs, but I believed that there was nothing to worry as we were not doing anything wrong.

Around 1989, we received some recognition for our work, for instance, we were invited for an interview. During the Ambedkar Centenary Celebration of 1989–90, the Andhra Pradesh *vyavasaya samiti* organized a 40-day cycle *yatra* in which I participated. The Government of India, in an effort to do something about the issue, constituted a committee which raised similar questions to the ones we were asking. Some officers from the committee contacted me, and this reflected the increasing recognition to the work of the campaign. Another important thing that happened at that point is meeting S.R. Sankaran who had just retired and did not want to take up any government assignments. Various discussions started with him, and he gave another direction to the whole movement, and made a very significant and continuous contribution up to his passing away in 2010 that was a big setback to the movement.

Around this time, we shared the copies of newspapers that had reported the issue of manual scavenging with parliamentarians.

The importance of the SKA is further reflected from the fact that, in 1992, when the draft Employment of Manual Scavengers and Construction of Dry Latrines (Prohibition) Bill was prepared, I received a copy of the Bill with a request to give my suggestions.

Q: Before 1993, there existed the Atrocities Act (Scheduled Castes and Scheduled Tribes [Prevention of Atrocities] Act) of 1989 which, according to you, was inadequate for addressing problems related to manual scavenging. What was missing, and how did the idea of a completely separate Act come about?

BW: An incident that occurred in Shimoga in the Tumkur District of Karnataka sometime during the period 1984–6 is important to address this question. The issue was some people in the village made a Dalit boy carry human excreta from one place to another. This incident became a huge issue. Many Dalit organizations started a massive movement leading to the enactment of the Atrocities Act in 1989. The incident was termed criminal. It struck me that if carrying excreta from one place to another is such a major issue, why is no one talking about a community that carries it for their entire lifetime?

Some Indian Administrative Service (IAS) officers spoke on our behalf. They suggested that the government should make a separate Act. During the Ambedkar Centenary Celebrations in the 1990s, the government appointed a task force, which recommended many laws, including the 1989 law. The Employment of Manual Scavengers and Construction of Dry Latrines (Prohibition) Act was adopted later in 1993.

Q: Also, as you have mentioned earlier, redefining the term 'sanitation' was a prerequisite because …

BW: Sanitation work has different forms like sweeping, cleaning of sewers, septic tanks, railway tracks, offices, and dry latrines. As cleaning of dry latrines is the worst form of scavenging, we suggested that this should be eradicated without any compromise. Further, we argued that cleaning of septic tanks and sewers should be mecha-nized. Sweeping is a routine activity which should not be on the basis of caste in any municipality. It should be open for everyone, and the municipalities should ensure that the sweepers do their work. This is important because there are instances where the sweepers employed by local bodies take their salaries, but do not carry out the work. Instead, they pay a small amount to the scavengers to do the work on their behalf. This creates a kind of contract labour system.

Q: You mentioned that safai karamcharis had left manual scavenging at various places. What recourse could they seek?

BW: We submitted one memorandum to Mr Salappa, a member and the vice-chairman of the National Commission for Safai Karamcharis (NCSK) constituted in 1993, when he visited Kolar gold fields. By 1995, all the dry latrines in the Kolar gold fields were demolished, and around 108 people directly involved in cleaning of dry latrines were rehabilitated to other occupations. Rehabilitation included grant of auto-rickshaws, cows, buffaloes, and fair price shops. The decision on selection of occupation was based on a discussion between the District collector and the safai karmacharis.

I attended the first rehabilitation meeting called by the collector, where he asked the safai karmacharis what they wanted for rehabilitation. Some people said two goats; others said two hens. I got angry seeing this, and told him that this should not be the way to discuss and decide rehabilitation of safai karamcharis. Someone had told the safai karamcharis that the collector had called them, and they came without preparation. I told the collector that it is inappropriate for an educated person like him to ask such questions to safai karamcharis, who are illiterate. In response, he asked me to do the work. To this, I replied that he was employed by the government with salary and other perks, and therefore, he cannot ask me to do his work.

He then held a meeting. The superintendent of police (SP) was also there. He told me that the situation had become difficult. Since local members of the legislative assembly (MLAs) and members of parliament (MPs) were side-lined, and ministers came to meet only me, he had started getting calls from the press and different ministers asking who Bezwada Wilson was. He said I had to be protected, and he would help me by giving me security. He sent a person to stay with me. When I said I cannot accommodate another person as I was staying in my brother's veranda, he told me to come and sit in his office from 8.00 am to 10.00 pm. From then onwards every day the SP would send his car to take me to his office. I was introduced to MLAs and other people who came to meet the SP. I accompanied the SP on his visits. These visits helped enhance my level of understanding of the situation. By now, many dry latrines had been demolished and rehabilitation was also over. Then many people told [me] that I should contest in the next election.

Q: How did the SKA travel to the state of Andhra Pradesh and beyond?

BW: When news about the SKA and our work appeared in newspapers, the title was 'The Shame'. We took copies of the newspaper and gave it, along with a covering letter, to all the ministers in the state assembly.

I had the experience of travelling to other parts of Karnataka and to Andhra Pradesh. Then I travelled to Chittoor, Hyderabad, Chennai, and Delhi. This gave me more space to work. I could see how the 1993 Act was working, and by 1995, we started thinking about improving it.

From 1995 to 2000, many studies were conducted and discussions held. In 1999, we decided to file a case. Government officials told us that the Act is there, but there were no rules. We found that the rules came six years after the Act, but there was nothing substantial in the rules. We asked the Andhra Pradesh government to issue a notification, and they issued eight notifications in a single day. We took the notifications to the ground level. The notifications were there, but no work had been done. We felt it was necessary to take legal action. If the Act is not getting implemented, why cannot we file a case against the collector? We realized that we cannot file a case against the collector, and that it was the collector who could file a case against the scavengers.

Q: In what way has the state progressed in terms of eradication?

BW: Only dry latrines.

Q: Should manual scavengers be rehabilitated outside the sanitation sector?

BW: Yes. In my perspective, scavengers are not needed for sanitation.

Q: What will be the solution to India's sanitation problem once manual scavenging is eradicated?

BW: Mechanization is one answer. Modernization is another answer. A third response can be the implementation of relevant laws, for instance, labour laws, to ensure safety and welfare of the people who are working in this sector. If all these things are there, people will not look at scavenging or sanitation work as a 'dirty occupation'. One is no longer a sweeper if mechanized equipment is used for the work. For example, at the airport, a person doing the cleaning work is not called a sanitation worker. When you take the broom and sweep, it has many implications. We have to come out of this very traditional way of cleaning with the broom. It has to be mechanized so that others will also enter the occupation, and people who are already there will work in a dignified way, unlike carrying human excreta. Similarly, cleaning of septic tanks must be carried out with machines, for instance, a suction machine. It needs to be ensured that there is no human entry into sewer lines at any cost. This means that the work of sewage cleaning must be mechanized. We are asking for the modernization and mechanization of sewer work. Flush toilets can replace dry latrines. So, there is a way. The only thing is that as long as the scavengers are available, the practice will continue. Further, any work or occupation including sanitation work should not be linked with caste. Right now, manual scavenging is a caste-based occupation. We need to delink the two.

Q: What do you mean when you say that there is a fundamental right to sanitation in India? What is the SKA's position on the right to sanitation?

BW: The right to sanitation should also include the rights of sanitation workers. Questions that have been raised so far are: How many people have access to public taps? How many households have water facility and toilets? Why are *bastis* and *galis* so dirty? The right to sanitation cannot be just about the rights of users. It must also include the rights of the service providers. This is my demand.

Q: What is your opinion on the 'Swachh Bharat Mission' (SBM) launched by the Government of India? Has it addressed the problems of manual scavenging?

BW: The government is promoting community toilets, which includes construction of around 2 lakh community toilets in India under the SBM. However, there is no provision for proper water facility. This could be a problem. The whole burden would again be on the manual scavengers. How will the waste from these toilets be managed? There is no model. Lack of connection with the sewer line raises the question as to how to empty them? If these toilets are used regularly by the people for whom they are built, they will require cleaning and emptying of tanks on a regular basis.

Unfortunately, 'Swachh Bharat' can make Bharat dirtier. People still go out in the open to defecate and there are no plans to collect everything in one place and no knowledge of how to deal with it. Note that 2 lakh toilets can produce at least an average of some metric tonnes of excreta, but there is no mechanism or process to decompose it. How can such a Mission be declared, and people and NGOs be sent to construct toilets? The SBM will finally lead to only construction of toilets.

Q: You say that caste is an important component, but is manual scavenging related only to the Hindu caste system or does it exist in other religions also?

BW: Dalit Christians (in south India, Punjab, and Jammu and Kashmir) and Muslims (in Jammu and Kashmir, Uttar Pradesh, Bihar, and Maharashtra) are also involved in this practice.

Q: Then why does the Hindu caste system come up in all the discussions?

BW: The origins of the caste system can be traced to Hinduism. Conversion took place from Hinduism to other religions. That is the reason why the caste system carries on. Even if I convert my religion, I cannot leave my caste. It is impossible to overcome this barrier. So, we are saying that the entire Hindu religion must be reformed. No other religion says that someone is polluted. But the Hindu religion says that the scavengers are polluted, the Dalits are polluted, and that they should not come near the caste Hindus. Therefore, it is important to talk about the Hindu caste system.

Q: You may have faced setbacks too. How did you overcome them?

BW: I have travelled to many places to tell people about the existence of the abhorrent practice of manual scavenging. However, I did not get any positive response. Everywhere, people asked me what manual scavenging was, and I was chased away from some places, not by government officers but by members of our own community. I visited the offices of municipalities, municipal corporations, and so on, and if I spoke loudly, the sanitation workers would tell me to keep quiet, and push me out. One day, I sat for almost 10 hours under a tree in front of a sanitation office, and asked myself why they had chased me away. I wondered why members of my own community were not supporting me when I was working for a genuine cause and wanted to do good for all.

Q: What are your inspirations and ultimate goal?

BW: In 2005, I was reading *Discovery of India* by Jawaharlal Nehru. He said that our people were dying year after year due to famines. He could understand that the British government was not doing anything to prevent the deaths. But, according to him, it was a crime on our part that we do not have any plans to prevent the deaths of our own people. We must have a plan to prevent these deaths. His observations struck me.

Before the 1993 Act, the government had declared that the practice will be eradicated by 1993, and once the Act is enacted, offenders will be punished. After this, they said that the practice will be eradicated by 1995, and then 1998, followed by 2000.

Our organization is not registered under any of the existing laws. The reason is that, in the case of any organization, the number of members shows its strength (if the membership is more, people will recognize it as a strong union). So, every year, the membership increases. But in the case of the SKA, we want the membership to reduce. One day it should reach zero. Our dream is that one day, we will have to close the SKA because there is no work left for us. So, for this reason we felt that there is no point in registering the organization.

Q: Finally, in your decades-long struggle, the judiciary has played an important role, and you have worked in tandem with it. Would you like to elaborate?

BW: The Supreme Court issued many directions during the pendency of the case. Many of these directions stated how the state had made blunders. We translated these directions to all vernacular languages, and took them to the administration and demanded rehabilitation. In some places, instead of sending the owner of the dry latrine to prison, the officers threatened the workers with imprisonment if they failed to scavenge or disclosed their work in the latrines to others. Our people would give them the Supreme Court's directions, and tell them that what they were saying was wrong.

We gave copies of the directions of the Supreme Court to many IAS officers. Volunteers of the SKA including women volunteers went and gave copies of the 1993 Act and the Court's directions to the District collector/magistrate in not less than 240 Districts in the country. These poor, illiterate women went to the District magistrates and asked them whether they were aware of such an Act which protects their life and dignity; whether they knew that there is a rehabilitation package. The interventions of the Supreme Court gave them the power to ask questions to government officials who were responsible to implement the law.

11

Invisible Inequalities

An Analysis of the Safai Karmachari Andolan Case

Shomona Khanna[1]

During the drafting of the Constitution of India, there was considerable discussion on the provisions relating to the abolition of untouchability and forced labour, namely Articles 17[2] and 23[3]

[1] The author would like to acknowledge the access to documentation and support provided by the Safai Karmachari Andolan (SKA), the encouragement of Bezwada Wilson, and the research and analytical inputs provided by Ms Megha Bahl, Advocate. I am also grateful to Dr Philippe Cullet for his patient encouragement and valuable editorial inputs.
[2] Constitution of India, 1950, Art. 17: Abolition of Untouchability: 'Untouchability' is abolished and its practice in any form is forbidden. The enforcement of any disability arising out of 'Untouchability' shall be an offence punishable in accordance with law.
[3] Constitution of India (n 2), Art. 23: (1) Traffic in human beings and *begar* and other similar forms of forced labour are prohibited and any contravention of this provision shall be an offence punishable in accordance with law.

of Part III of the Constitution (the fundamental rights chapter). The debates demonstrate that the members of the Constituent Assembly had no doubt in their minds that these provisions sought to address, among the myriad forms of untouchability being practised in the country at the time, in particular the practice of manual scavenging. It was understood at the time that manual scavenging is both a source and a result of abhorrently cruel social exclusion because of notions of pollution, and therefore the continued practice of this 'disability' had no place in the vision of an Independent India.

Numerous schemes[4] and commissions have come and gone in the seven decades since then, but the practice of manual scavenging, and the social exclusion it manifests and fuels, continue from one generation to the next. The enactment of statutory prohibitions[5] has, while reinforcing the constitutional embargo, failed to eradicate this practice.

The survey and identification of manual scavengers and their family members has been a central component of the Employment of Manual Scavengers and Construction of Dry Latrines (Prohibition) Act, 1993 ('1993 Act'), as well as the recently enacted Prohibition of Employment as Manual Scavengers and their Rehabilitation Act,

---

[4] The Central Government has come up with three main schemes for the eradication of manual scavenging, under which allocations are made for each state, depending upon their demand and the availability of funds. These are the National Scheme for Liberation and Rehabilitation of Scavengers and their Dependants (NSLRS); the Integrated Low Cost Sanitation Scheme (ILCS) which aims at the conversion of individual dry latrines into pour-flush latrines, thereby liberating manual scavengers (Ministry of Housing and Urban Poverty Alleviation, Revised Guidelines, 2008, for the ILCS Scheme (2008)); and the Self Employment Scheme for Rehabilitation of Manual Scavengers (SWABHIMAN).

[5] The key statutory prohibitions relating to manual scavenging are The Untouchability Offences Act, 1956, The Scheduled Castes and Scheduled Tribes (Prevention of Atrocities) Act, 1989, The Employment of Manual Scavengers and Construction of Dry Latrines (Prohibition) Act, 1993 ('1993 Act'), and The Prohibition of Employment as Manual Scavengers and their Rehabilitation Act, 2013 ('2013 Act').

2013 ('2013 Act'). However, till date there is no reliable data on the number and identity of manual scavengers in the country, an ambiguity which has been exploited to the full by the state. Even so, it is useful to examine the available data.

The Planning Commission in 1995 estimated that 6.4 lakh people were employed as manual scavengers, but activists believe that the numbers were actually more than a million. It is significant that 99 per cent of the people forced to do this work are Dalits, and 95 per cent of them are women.[6] According to the National Commission for Safai Karamcharis (NCSK), in the year 2007, the population of manual scavengers in the country was about 6.76 lakh, of whom more than 3.42 lakhs were engaged in the work, and remained to be rehabilitated.[7] The NCSK observed that: 'there is a large number of people belonging to [a] particular community who are still engaged in the demeaning practice of manual scavenging and the State Governments and Urban Local Bodies (ULBs) are not making sufficient efforts to adhere to the commitment of the Central Government to abolish this practice by December 2007'.[8]

In 2008, the Central Government acknowledged that out of 50,20,074 dry latrine units sanctioned for conversion and construction across the country, a total of 28,15,857 units had been completed, while 2,30,018 were in progress.[9] In the same document, it is noted that on the said date while 56,873 manual scavengers had been liberated, there still were 1,38,464 manual scavengers to be liberated. The most recent estimates are found in the 2011 Census, which records that of 24,66,92,667 households in the country, 7,94,390 households accessed latrines which were being 'serviced

[6] Harsh Mander, 'Barefoot: Burning Baskets of Shame', *The Hindu* (9 May 2010); available at www.thehindu.com/opinion/columns/Harsh_Mander/Barefoot-Burning-baskets-of-shame/article16123459.ece.

[7] Counter Affidavit on Behalf of Respondent No. 5 (National Commission for Safai Karamcharis), dated April 2007, in *Safai Karamchari Andolan & Others* v *Union of India & Others* Writ Petition (Civil) No. 583 of 2003, Supreme Court of India ('*SKA* v *UoI*').

[8] *SKA* v *UoI* (n 7), para 6.

[9] Revised Guidelines for ILCS (n 4), table entitled 'Cumulative Status of ILCS Schemes as on 31 March 2008'.

manually or through scavengers'.[10] Even if one makes a conservative estimate of eight latrines being 'serviced' by one manual scavenger, this would translate into 1,00,000 manual scavengers actively working in the country.

Although the official figures are incomplete and contradictory, it is also true that the numbers have greatly reduced due to the unrelenting work of organizations such as the Safai Karmachari Andolan (SKA) towards eradication and liberation, without waiting upon the fickle promises of government rehabilitation schemes.

This chapter briefly examines the constitutional and statutory framework which is meant to address the practice of manual scavenging, insofar as these relate to the writ petition filed by the SKA and other petitioners in the Supreme Court of India in 2003.[11] It then proceeds to trace the journey of this historic litigation seeking the implementation of the constitutional and statutory mandate to eradicate manual scavenging. Treated as a continuing mandamus[12] by the Court, this litigation has seen many twists and turns, which have been only partially documented. This chapter attempts, through a process of documentation, to foreground the key challenges which

---

[10]   Office of the Registrar General and Census Commissioner, Census of India 2011 (2011), Table entitled 'State/UT & Distt-wise No. of Latrines which are Serviced Manually or by Scavengers'.

[11]   *SKA* v *UoI* (n 7).

[12]   The device of 'continuing mandamus' was developed by the Supreme Court of India in the 1980s along with public interest litigation, in order to ensure compliance with its directions by the state executive. Thus, rather than following the conventional method of delivering a reasoned judgment after examining the arguments by both parties, in such cases the Court issues a set of directions in the nature of mandamus, and keeps the petitions pending. The case comes up for hearing at regular intervals to enable the Court to scrutinize whether its directions have been complied with, and whether additional directions are required. One of the largest and oldest such continuing mandamus cases is the 'Godavarman case' in the Supreme Court of India which has been pending since 1995 and comes up for hearing at regular intervals before a specially constituted 'Forest Bench'. See *TN Godavarman* v *Union of India & Others* WP (C) No. 202 of 1995 (Supreme Court of India) ('*Godavarman*').

have been faced by the petitioners in taking this writ petition forward within a legal discourse which is increasingly characterized by its neoliberal ambiguity towards enforcement of the rights of the poorest of the poor. This chapter further explores how the pendency of the writ proceedings complemented the efforts of the movement for eradication of manual scavenging, by persistently raising the visibility of what has been and continues to be an 'invisible crime'. It also explores how the Court has specifically addressed the numerous lacunae in the statutes over a period of time. This chapter explores how such interventions provided a boost to the struggle of the groups on the ground, and also breathed life into the 1993 Act, a law which has often been critiqued as being stillborn.

Since the author is a lawyer who represented the petitioners in these court proceedings from 2006 to 2012, a certain absence of objective observation is to be expected. This drawback, if it can be termed as such, may perhaps be offset by the benefit of a narrative from within the eye of the storm.[13]

What Is Manual Scavenging?

While a detailed examination of the social, historical, and economic roots of manual scavenging is beyond the scope of this chapter,[14] it would be useful to draw attention to some key aspects. Manual scavenging is the practice of manually removing night soil or human faeces by a particular sub-caste of the Dalits, known by different nomenclatures in different parts of the country. Traditionally, manual scavengers are considered to be untouchable, and so inferior in the hierarchy of caste that they are often considered untouchable even by other Dalits. The notion of pollution, which purportedly is founded upon the work they do, extends to all members of the caste whether

[13] An offshoot of the proceedings in the Supreme Court, WP (C) No. 845 of 2011 relating to manual scavenging in the Indian Railways, is pending in the High Court of Delhi. Since the matter is *sub judice*, it is not discussed in this chapter.

[14] For an examination of the socio-political roots of manual scavenging, see K. Parameshwar, 'Stink, Shame and the State' (NALSAR University of Law [unpublished, on file with the author], 2007).

they are actually engaged in manual scavenging or not. For this reason, there is active, often violent, resistance to their engagement in other employment. Thus, an integral aspect of manual scavenging is systemic oppression, where the polluting nature of the work precludes transition to other 'less' polluting work in a never-ending circularity which extends from generation to generation.[15]

The engagement or employment of any person for manually carrying human excreta, as well as the construction and maintenance of dry latrines, is prohibited under Section 3(1) of the 1993 Act, and the contravention of this provision is a punishable criminal offence inviting a maximum punishment of up to one year of imprisonment.[16]

According to the 1993 Act, 'manual scavenger' means 'a person engaged in or employed for manually carrying human excreta'.[17] The term 'dry latrine' is defined as 'a latrine other than a water-seal latrine'.[18] The Act goes further to define a 'water-seal latrine' to mean 'a pour-flush latrine, water flush latrine or a sanitary latrine with a minimum water-seal of 20 millimetres diameter in which human excreta is pushed in or flushed by water'.[19]

In practice, these definitions are skeletal at best, and it is important, therefore, to turn to other social and historical materials to understand what manual scavenging really means. The Asian Human Rights Commission, for instance, describes manual scavenging in the following terms:

> Manual scavenging in India is officially defined as 'lifting and removal of human excreta manually', at private homes and toilets maintained by municipal authorities. The practice consists of gathering human excreta from individual or community dry latrines with bare hands, brooms or metal scrapers into woven baskets or buckets. This the scavengers then carry on their heads, shoulders or against their hips, (and in wheelbarrows if they can afford it) into dumping sites or water bodies. Apart from this, many scavengers are similarly employed to

---

[15] Parameshwar (n 14).
[16] 1993 Act (n 5), s 14.
[17] 1993 Act (n 5), s 2(j).
[18] 1993 Act (n 5), s 2(c).
[19] 1993 Act (n 5), s 2(n).

collect, carry and dispose excreta from sewers, septic tanks, drains and railway tracks.[20]

Another report explains:

There are two ways in which this is done:

- By scavenging manually from the dry toilets with the help of broom, tin plate, stone, bamboo or tin basket, plastic bucket, tin boxes and disposing it off in a safe place designated for this purpose.
- The other way is to clean the sewage pits of the toilets manually. Mostly men do the work of cleaning sewage pits in the night or early morning. Women clean the dry toilets individually in homes and public places.[21]

It is important to keep in mind that in the vernacular, manual scavengers are described as 'those who carry night soil on the head',[22] a description which emerges from the traditional practice of carrying headloads of night soil in wicker baskets in the early hours of the morning. Many of the practices of social exclusion, and the struggles challenging these practices, resonate with these words. Therefore, in rebuttal of the assertion by the NCSK that manual scavenging is rampant in Delhi,[23] the government of Delhi submitted an affidavit before the Supreme Court stating that there were no manual scavengers because 'the practice of manual scavenging in its strict sense

[20] Avinash Pandey, *Caste Based Discrimination: The Continuing Curse of Manual Scavenging* (Asian Human Rights Commission, AHRC-SPR-003-2009, 2009), 24.

[21] WaterAid India, *Burden of Inheritance: Can We Stop Manual Scavenging? Yes But First We Need to Accept It Exists* (WaterAid India, 2009), 5.

[22] The Hindi phrase is 'sarpe maila dhoney waaley'.

[23] According to state-wise data submitted before the court by the NCSK on 8 June 2007, there were 14,479 manual scavengers in Delhi. In a response dated 26 May 2008 to an application by the petitioners under The Right to Information (RTI) Act, 2005, the Delhi SC/ST/OBC/Minorities and the Handicapped Financial and Development Corporation Ltd. stated that a survey conducted by the University of Delhi, Department of Social Work found 1085 scavengers in Delhi. The Delhi Government, however, continued to maintain that there were no manual scavengers in Delhi.

i.e. carrying night soil on head does not exist as per MCD'.[24] The state government asserted that those who carry excreta on the side, or in wheeled barrows or buckets, or manually remove it from drains, are not manual scavengers, and therefore not entitled to the protection of the law.[25]

When the SKA decided to shift gears and transform itself into a movement not only for the eradication of manual scavenging, but also for the liberation of manual scavengers, it tellingly called its campaign 'burning the basket'.[26] Hundreds of manual scavengers have participated in demonstrations and rallies across India where they have symbolically burnt the baskets, which represent their enslavement, and asserted their commitment to a life liberated from the indignity of manual scavenging itself. One such demonstration where baskets were symbolically burnt took place in March 2012 outside the Office of the High Commissioner for Human Rights in Geneva.[27]

An effort has been made to address some of these definitional conundrums in the recently enacted 2013 Act. This statute, unlike the 1993 Act, gives a detailed definition of 'manual scavenger' as follows:

> a person engaged or employed, at the commencement of this Act or at any time thereafter, by an individual or local authority or an agency or a contractor, for manually cleaning, carrying, disposing of, or otherwise handling in any manner, human excreta in an insanitary latrine or in an open drain or pit into which the human excreta from the insanitary latrines is disposed of, or on a railway track or in such other spaces or premises, as the Central Government or a State Government

---

[24] Affidavit filed by Respondent No. 33 (Government of NCT of Delhi) dated 10 March 2008, 3, para 6 in *SKA* v *UoI* (n 7).

[25] The petitioners placed a multiplicity of evidence before the Court in this regard, but the state government refused to adopt the 1993 Act till 2010, after repeated directions from the Court.

[26] Bezwada Wilson, 'Why is it so Difficult to Free India of Manual Scavenging?', *Kafila* (22 December 2010); available at https://kafila.online/2010/12/22/why-is-it-so-difficult-to-free-india-of-manual-scavenging.

[27] Mander (n 6).

may notify, before the excreta fully decomposes in such manner as may be prescribed ...[28]

Unfortunately, the same provision retreats from the promise of a realistic definition, and goes on to exclude 'persons engaged or employed to clean excreta with the help of such devices and using *such protective gear* as the Central Government may notify in this behalf' (emphasis added). This would mean that engaging sanitation workers to clean human excreta from an insanitary latrine or open drain or pit or railway track, while wearing 'notified' protective gear such as gumboots and plastic overalls, would not be proscribed by the law; the fundamental relationship of the caste component to the task would be irrelevant under such law.[29]

The SKA has all along maintained that the practice of manual scavenging relates to notions of pollution and untouchability, and therefore no amount of protective gear can obviate the pernicious consequences of this work. Manual scavenging needs to be eradicated, and the manual scavengers liberated, with no exceptions. The 2013 Act appears to have missed this point completely, so that the definition of manual scavenging remains open to interpretation and ambiguity.

The Constitutional and Statutory Framework

The practice of untouchability in general and of manual scavenging in particular was deprecated in no uncertain terms by the Constituent Assembly at the time of the drafting of the Constitution of India. During the debate around the present Articles 17 and 23 of the Constitution, some members expressed their anguish in the following words:

---

[28] 2013 Act (n 5), s 2(1)(g).

[29] Predictably, the Ministry of Railways, through a series of notifications in 2014, notified the nature of the protective gear and devices, the use of which would immunize such employment from the proscription of the law. Notification No. G.S.R. 376(E), dated 4 June 2014 and Notification No. G.S.R. 726(E), dated 15 October 2014 as published in the Gazette of India, Extraordinary, Part II.

The very clause about untouchability and its abolition goes a long way to show to the world that the unfortunate communities that are called 'untouchables' will find solace when this constitution comes into effect. It is not a certain section of the Indian Community that will be benefitted by this enactment, but a sixth of the population of the whole of India will welcome the introduction and the adoption of a section to root out the very practice of untouchability in this country.[30]

... The working of the Constitution will depend upon how the people will conduct themselves in the future, not on the actual execution of the law. So, I hope that in course of time there will not be such a community known as untouchables and that our delegates abroad will not have to hang their heads in shame if somebody raises such a question in an organisation of international nature.[31]

While discussing the freedom to practice a profession of one's choice, another member of the Constituent Assembly pointed out how meaningless such a right is for the untouchables in the following words:

The most unfortunate people in this country, in my opinion, are the sweepers. Whatever we may talk about the grant of rights to these unfortunate sweepers the fact remains that these unfortunate people have never been given any rights by any person in India nor have they ever enjoyed any right said to have been granted to them. To talk of their 'freedom to practise any profession or trade' is a mockery to them. I do not know of the conditions prevailing in other provinces but I know what happens in my province. If a sweeper working under a Municipal Committee desires to give up his work, in my province, he would have to give a notice in writing addressed to the District

---

[30] Views expressed by Shri V.I. Muniswamy Pillai during the discussion on 29 November 1948 on Article 11 (present Article 17) in the Constituent Assembly, Constituent Assembly Debates, Volume VII, 665–8.

[31] Views expressed by Smt. Dakshayani Velayudhan during the discussion on 29 November 1948 on Article 11 (present Article 17) in the Constituent Assembly, Constituent Assembly Debates, Volume VII, 665–8.

Magistrate of his intention to do so and can leave his service only if that officer agrees to release him.[32]

Dr B.R. Ambedkar, who presided over the Constituent Assembly and is widely recognized as the founder the Constitution of India, made his views very clear both within the Constituent Assembly and outside. In his widely celebrated work *Annihilation of Caste*, he described the abominable permutations of the practice of untouchability across the country, and rubbished the defence of the caste system as being a method of efficiency. He stated:

> Now the first thing to be urged against this view is that the Caste System is not merely division of labour. *It is also a division of labourers.*... Social and individual efficiency requires us to develop the capacity of an individual to the point of competency to choose and to make his own career. This principle is violated in the Caste System in so far as it involves an attempt to appoint tasks to individuals in advance, selected not on the basis of trained original capacities, but on that of the social status of the parents.[33] (emphasis in the original).

Clearly, Ambedkar was fully aware of the pernicious exclusion and subordination of people—now citizens of Independent India—which result from the so-called 'efficiency' rationale of the caste system. These debates resulted in the inclusion of Article 17 in Part III of the Constitution, entitled 'Fundamental Rights', which abolished untouchability in Independent India.

[32] Views expressed by Shri H.J. Khandekar during the discussion on 2 December 1948 on Article 19, Constituent Assembly Debates, Volume VII. Although this speaker used the genteel 'sweeper' throughout his submission, it is clear from the content that he is referring to manual scavengers. This is further made clear in the response to his submission by another member, where the term '*bhangi*' is used, which denotes the specific sub-caste group. Use of the word '*bhangi*' to describe a person belonging to a lower caste is now a criminal offence under Section 3(1)(r) and (s) of The Scheduled Castes and Scheduled Tribes (Prevention of Atrocities) Act, 1986.

[33] B.R. Ambedkar, *Annihilation of Caste* (3rd Edn, Gautam Book Centre, 1945).

Article 17 of the Constitution was initially implemented through the enactment of the Protection of Civil Rights Act, 1955, (formerly known as the Untouchability (Offences) Act, 1955) ('1955 Act'). Section 7A of the 1955 Act provides that whoever compels any person on the ground of untouchability to do any scavenging, shall be deemed to have enforced a disability arising of untouchability, and thus is punishable with imprisonment.

Section 3(1)(j) of the Scheduled Castes and Scheduled Tribes (Prevention of Atrocities) Act, 1989, recognizes that it is an offence for a person, not being a member of a scheduled tribe (ST) or scheduled caste (SC), to make a member of such caste or tribe to do manual scavenging or to employ or permit employment for such purpose. The offence is punishable with a minimum of six months imprisonment, which may extend to five years. The statute also provides for the imposition of collective fines as provided in the 1955 Act. No documented case has been registered under this law, however, to prosecute persons for employment of manual scavengers.

While these constitutional and statutory provisions were path-breaking in themselves, they were found to be inadequate to address the continuation of the obnoxious practice of manual scavenging across the country. Therefore, on 5 June 1993, Parliament enacted the 1993 Act,[34] which is described in its long title as: 'An Act to provide for the prohibition of employment of manual scavengers as well as construction or continuance of dry latrines and for the regulation of construction and maintenance of water-seal latrines and for matters connected therewith or incidental thereto.' As stated earlier, Section 3 of the 1993 Act prohibits the engagement or employment of persons for manually carrying human excreta, and further prohibits the construction or maintenance of dry latrines.

It is important to note that the 1993 Act places the executive authorities in a pivotal position insofar as implementation of the constitutional and statutory mandate is concerned. Section 5 provides that the District magistrate or sub-divisional magistrate shall be the executive authority under the Act empowered to rehabilitate

---

[34] The 1993 Act was not brought into force immediately. It was brought into force by way of a notification on 26 January 1997.

and promote the welfare of persons engaged as manual scavengers, and for implementation of schemes for conversion of dry latrines into water-seal latrines.

Penalties for violation can extend to imprisonment up to one year or fine up to Rs 2,000 or both.[35] The offences are cognizable, and triable by a court of a metropolitan magistrate or judicial magistrate first class.[36] However, the court can take cognizance of a complaint only if the same is duly authorized by the executive authority, and prosecutions under the Act require the previous sanction of the executive authority.

The enactment of the 2013 Act marks another milestone in the law relating to manual scavenging in India.[37] In its preamble, the statute draws attention to notions of dignity enshrined in the preamble to the Constitution as well as in the fundamental rights chapter. It notes that: 'the dehumanising practice of manual scavenging arising from the continuing existence of insanitary latrines and a highly iniquitous caste system, still persists in various parts of the country, and the existing laws have not proved adequate in eliminating the twin evils of insanitary latrines and manual scavenging.' It goes on to say that it is necessary to correct the historical injustice and indignity suffered by the manual scavengers, and rehabilitate them to a life of dignity.

The definition of 'manual scavenger' in the 2013 Act excludes all those who stopped working as manual scavengers before the statute came into force, either through necessity or through their own efforts to liberate themselves. By incorporating this fictional boundary in the definition itself, the statute belies its purported objective of addressing 'historical injustice', losing sight of the pernicious notions of pollution and untouchability which continue to oppress people from the community long after they have 'stopped'

---

[35] 1993 Act (n 5), s 14.

[36] 1993 Act (n 5), ss 16 and 17.

[37] Although the statute was published in the Gazette of India on 19 September 2013, it remained inoperative for more than a year. It was brought into force finally on 12 December 2013, along with the notification of the Prohibition of Employment of Manual Scavengers and their Rehabilitation Rules, 2013.

the work, and which leave them socially and economically vulnerable to being coerced by dominant groups into returning to the work when required.[38]

While prohibiting the construction of dry latrines and the employment of manual scavengers, the 2013 Act provides a statutory period of six months for demolition of all dry latrines,[39] placing the burden for this exercise upon the 'occupier'. These must be replaced with sanitary latrines within nine months, which period is extended to three years for municipalities, cantonment boards, and railway authorities.[40] Contravention of these provisions is a criminal offence punishable with imprisonment, which could extend to one year and also a fine.[41] Repeat offences invite more stringent punishments. However, cognizance can be taken of such an offence only within three months,[42] a limitation period which is significantly restrictive in comparison with ordinary criminal law.

A primary area of focus of the statute is the identification of manual scavengers through a nation-wide survey, and their subsequent rehabilitation. A fairly complex mechanism for the conduct of such surveys is provided, with detailed timelines. Various committees are established at the District and state level for implementation and monitoring. However, the failure of state functionaries to adhere to such timelines, or of the committees to perform their statutory functions, invites no disciplinary or criminal consequences.

---

[38] A key reason why the movement for liberation spearheaded by the SKA has insisted upon actual demolition of dry latrines is the reality that members of the manual scavenger community are coerced to return to this work at the first hint of failure of pour-flush latrines. The movement has always remained conscious of the danger of regression due to social and economic pressure, which the communities, subjected to generations of oppression, are unable to withstand. Years of work towards rehabilitation can be obliterated by one incident of backsliding.

[39] 2013 Act (n 5), s 5(2) read with s 4(1)(b).

[40] 2013 Act (n 5), ss 4(1)(c) and 4(2).

[41] 2013 Act (n 5), s 8.

[42] 2013 Act (n 5), s 10. Under Section 468 of the Criminal Procedure Code, 1973, the normal period of limitation for criminal offences inviting similar punishments is one year, and for a repeat offence, it is three years.

The statute includes within its purview 'hazardous cleaning' of sewers and septic tanks, which has been the subject matter of considerable litigation itself. The enactment of the 2013 Act has pushed the 1993 Act into a statutory grey area. While the 2013 Act makes no provision for repeal of the earlier statute, it categorically states that its provisions shall have overriding effect over the 1993 Act, and all other law or legal instruments.[43] What this means in its entirety remains to be seen. What is, however, apparent is that the unambiguous illegality of the practice of manual scavenging has now been watered down with exemptions, exceptions, and provisos.

Failure of Implementation

The NCSK, a statutory body set up under the National Commission for Safai Karamcharis Act, 1993,[44] in its third and fourth reports submitted to Parliament in November 2001, noted that the 1993 Act was not being implemented effectively and further noted that the estimated number of dry latrines in the country is 96 lakhs and the estimated number of manual scavengers identified is 5,77,228.[45] In the third report, it observed that manual scavengers were being employed in the military engineering services, the army, public sector undertakings, and for the purpose of cleaning of railways tracks by the Indian Railways.[46]

[43] 2013 Act (n 5), s 3.

[44] The National Commission for Safai Karamcharis Act, 1993, is no longer in force, and the NCSK functions under the aegis of the Ministry of Social Justice and Empowerment on the basis of a government resolution. The first four reports of the NCSK were made public after being placed before Parliament, the last of these being in 2001. Since then, none of its reports have been publicly released.

[45] Government of India, *Report of the National Commission for Safai Karamcharis: Third Report 1996–97 & 1997–98* (Government of India, 2000) ('NCSK Third Report'); Government of India, *Report of the National Commission for Safai Karamcharis: Fourth Report 1999–2000* (Government of India, 2000) ('NCSK Fourth Report').

[46] NCSK Third Report (n 45), para 3.13.

In 2003, a report was submitted by the Comptroller and Auditor General (CAG) that evaluated the National Scheme for Liberation and Rehabilitation of Scavengers and their Dependents.[47] Noting that 'the Scheme began, and continues to remain until now, a prisoner of its own statistics',[48] the CAG report is critical of the absence of a credible baseline census of the targeted beneficiaries. At the time of its institution in March 1991, the Scheme visualized the rehabilitation of all the 4 lakh scavengers and their dependents by the end of the Eighth Plan period (1992–7). However, far from a reduction in numbers, subsequent surveys conducted between 1994–5 and 2001–2 estimated the number as 7.87 lakh.[49]

The CAG found that the scheme lost its focus as a result of the failure to link 'liberation' and 'rehabilitation'. Liberation, interpreted to mean removal of the very cause and basis of manual scavenging, thereby allowing the beneficiary to be released from the stigmatized occupation, should have been the cornerstone of the scheme. The CAG found that:

> The most serious lapse in the conceptualization and operationalisation of the scheme was its failure to employ the law that prohibited the occupation. The law could have been invoked to ensure that the condition and circumstance of occupational entrapment were not created. As a matter of fact, the law itself expected that the schemes implemented by the both the State and Central Governments would draw their strength from it. The law was rarely used.[50]

[47] See Report of the Comptroller and Auditor General of India for the year ended March 2002: Union Government Performance Appraisal No. 3 of 2003: Ministry of Social Justice and Empowerment: National Scheme of Liberation and Rehabilitation of Scavengers and their Dependents ('CAG Report'), as placed on record before the Supreme Court of India in *SKA* v *UoI* by the Government of India. It may be pointed out that this report was not available in the public domain at the time of filing of the writ petition, and was made available by the Central Government as part of its counter affidavit in September 2004. The report has since been removed from government websites.

[48] CAG Report (n 47), 32.

[49] CAG Report (n 47), 32.

[50] CAG Report (n 47), 33.

The report concluded that this scheme 'has failed to achieve its objectives even after ten years of implementation involving investments of more than Rs. 600 crores'.[51]

The continuing practice of manual scavenging in India has also invited censure from various United Nations (UN) bodies. In 2004, the Committee on the Rights of the Child recorded its concern at the persistent social discrimination against children belonging to the SCs.[52] The UN Committee on the Elimination of Discrimination against Women in 2007 expressed concern that 'despite a law banning manual scavenging, this degrading practice continues with grave implications for the dignity and health of the Dalit women who are engaged in this activity'.[53] Also in 2007, the UN Committee on the Elimination of Racial Discrimination recognized the inclusion of 'untouchability' as a practice emerging from caste discrimination as part of the mandate of the Committee.[54]

---

[51] CAG Report (n 47), 1.

[52] The Committee on the Rights of the Child recommended that India 'in accordance with Article 17 of its Constitution and Article 2 of the Convention, take all necessary steps to abolish the discriminatory practice of "untouchability" and further recommended "the full implementation of the ... Employment of Manual Scavengers and Construction of Dry Latrines (Prohibition) Act, 1993'. See Concluding Comments of the Committee on the Rights of the Child: India, 35th Session, 26 February 2004, UN Doc. CRC/C/15/Add.228, paras 28 and 73.

[53] Concluding Comments of the Committee on the Elimination of Discrimination against Women: India, 37th Session, 2 February 2007, UN Doc. CEDAW/C/IND/CO/3, para 28. In the next paragraph (para 29), the Committee urged 'the State party to study the health implications of manual scavenging on Dalits engaged in this profession and on the community as a whole, and to address all the impediments to eradicating this practice, including by putting in place modern sanitation facilities and providing the Dalit women engaged in this practice with vocational training and alternative means of livelihood'.

[54] The Committee on the Elimination of Racial Discrimination (CERD) noted 'with concern that very large numbers of Dalits are forced to work as manual scavengers and child workers, and are subject to extremely unhealthy working conditions and exploitative labour arrangements, including debt bondage'. Concluding observations of the Committee on

The UN Committee on Economic, Social and Cultural Rights reiterated these concerns in 2008.[55] The scrutiny by international treaty bodies has gone a long way in raising the visibility of the practice of manual scavenging.

As part of its planning process for the Eleventh Five-year Plan (FYP), the Planning Commission of India constituted a seven-member 'Sub-Group on Safai Karamcharis',[56] which submitted a detailed report in 2006, observing:

> It is painful to note that in a country with a billion people, with social welfare measures, planned development programmes, a small group of people involved in an obnoxious task, despite legal provisions and planned programmes are yet to be released and rehabilitated. The continuing stranglehold of the social structure, viz caste system and internalization of social exclusion, untouchability and discrimination is evident in this manifestation. What is needed is special focus to liberate our society from the norms of social exclusion and discrimination along with an action plan with 'Implementation' as the 'Buzz' word in the XIth Plan, with full ownership and participation of the persons involved in these occupations. It should be recognised that the basic issue is that of reclaiming human dignity of people engaged

---

the Elimination of Racial Discrimination: India, 70th Session, 5 May 2007, UN Doc. CERD/C/IND/CO/19, para 23.

[55] The Committee on Economic, Social and Cultural Rights recommended that: 'the State party should take effective measures to ensure that violations concerning prohibited labour practices, such as … manual scavenging … are stringently prosecuted and employers duly sanctioned. The Committee recommends that the State party launch a national campaign to abolish manual scavenging and other degrading forms of work and provide information on the results achieved in its next periodic report.' Concluding Observations of the Committee on Economic, Social and Cultural Rights: India, 40th Session, 8 August 2008, UN Doc. E/C.12/IND/CO/5, para 59.

[56] This sub-group was set up by the Working Group on the Empowerment of Scheduled Castes under the chairmanship of Prof. S.K. Thorat vide notification dated 23 May 2006 bearing F. No. M-12052/4/2005-BC, issued by the Backward Classes Division of the Planning Commission of India; available at http://planningcommission.gov.in/aboutus/committee/wrkgrp11/wg11_bc2.pdf (last accessed on 10.10.2018).

in manual scavenging; a dignity assured in the very Preamble to the Indian Constitution.[57]

The report proceeded to make detailed recommendations for the purpose of achieving this goal in the Eleventh FYP, including a national-level survey to enumerate manual scavengers in the country, creation of a nodal agency to ensure total eradication, review of the 1993 Act including the problems being experienced on the subject of definition, review of rehabilitation already provided, strengthening of the NCSK, and so on.

It supplemented these recommendations with projections for required budgetary allocations. With regard to the allocation of funds for the various schemes in the past, the report observed:

> There is a disjunction between intent and actual performance. For e.g. Rs. 460/ crores were allocated by the Planning Commission for the 10th Plan period, but only Rs. 146.04 crores were released during the Plan period. Additionally, no funds have been allocated in the Annual Plan for 2005–2006. Since the inception of National Scheme of [sic] liberation and rehabilitation of Scavengers and their dependants (NSLRS) in 1991–92 only Rs. 747.11 crores have been released up to 2004–05 and 1,72,681 scavengers have been assisted for training and 4,43,925 for rehabilitation. There are nearly 12 lakhs of manual scavengers still awaiting liberation and rehabilitation.[58]

These findings were significant for the SKA in that they acknowledged the existence of the problem, moving away from the malaise of invisibility and denial, which had dogged the progress of government initiatives with failure in the past. Clearly, the government's own reports as well as reports of official commissions and international bodies acknowledged what civil society had been saying for a while—that the invisibilization of manual scavenging was hindering the efforts towards its eradication.

---

[57] Planning Commission of India, *Report of Sub-group on Safai Karmacharis*, Working Group on the 'Empowerment of Scheduled Castes (SCs)', for the Eleventh Five-year Plan (2007–12) 8.

[58] Planning Commission of India (n 57), 11.

Writ Petition in the Supreme Court

By 2003, it had become apparent that the government initiatives and schemes for eradication of manual scavenging were ineffective, a fact which was acknowledged by the NCSK itself.[59] It was also obvious that the 1993 Act, which ought to have realized the constitutional protections, such as Article 17 of the Constitution, had failed to have any impact. The political and social will to implement the law was simply absent.

For the SKA, an emerging federation of non-governmental organizations (NGOs) across the country working with manual scavengers, it became imperative to alert the constitutional court. In December 2003, the SKA, along with six other civil society organizations,[60] as well as seven individuals belonging to the community of manual scavengers, filed a writ petition in the Supreme Court under Article 32 of the Constitution of India.[61]

This writ petition, which evolved over a year of discussions, meetings, and debates held in different parts of the country, placed before the Court a plethora of material regarding the continuing practice of manual scavenging in the teeth of a prohibitory law, many of which were reports by government bodies themselves. Among these were the reports submitted to Parliament by the NCSK referred to earlier, which had expressed its anguish in no uncertain terms, and a reference to the scathing report of the CAG.

The writ petition argued that the continuation of the practice of manual scavenging as well as the existence of dry latrines is illegal and unconstitutional, since it violates the fundamental rights guaranteed under Articles 14, 17, 21, and 23 of the Constitution of India, and

---

[59] See NCSK Third Report (n 45); NCSK Fourth Report (n 45).

[60] The other civil society organizations who joined the writ petition as petitioners were Jan Sahas, Madhya Pradesh (Petitioner No. 2); Adharshila, Uttar Pradesh (Petitioner No. 3); the Young Women's Christian Association, Chennai (Petitioner No. 4); the Safai Kamgar Parivartan Sangh, Maharashtra (Petitioner No. 5); the Dalit Research Institute, Uttar Pradesh (Petitioner No. 6); and the National Campaign for Dalit Human Rights, Hyderabad (Petitioner No. 7).

[61] *SKA* v *UoI* (n 7).

the 1993 Act. The petitioners sought, among other things, the implementation of the 1993 Act in its fullness. Towards this end, they sought issue of writs of mandamus to the various state governments as well as to the Central Government to take effective steps to ensure complete eradication of this practice. Finally, they sought directions from the Court to bind the respondents to a rigid time schedule in order to achieve the said objective.

From 2003 till its disposal through a reasoned judgment in March 2014, the writ petition was treated as a continuing mandamus, coming up at regular intervals for hearing in the Supreme Court, which passed numerous far-reaching orders and directions taking the matter forward. The state governments, the Central Government, as well as the petitioners filed affidavits from time to time as per the directions of the court, and to ascertain their compliance of these orders.

The Supreme Court of India Issues 'Notice'

When the writ petition came up for hearing for the first time, the bench hearing it was so taken aback by the revelations contained in it that they heard the submissions of the petitioners' counsel for close to an hour, putting on hold a large number of other cases. Bezwada Wilson, convenor of the SKA and himself a member of the community, had come to the Supreme Court for the first time in his life. Although he has made numerous visits since then, he recalls the overwhelming sense of confusion quite clearly. As a result, he recollects how the significance of the words 'issue notice' spoken by the judges in their characteristically stern manner quite escaped him at the time.[62]

It was only a few months later that the SKA realized that in a quiet but significant manner, the ground had shifted. Wilson describes how previously, efforts to meet with District administration officials would usually end in disappointment. Officers of the government often treated representatives of the SKA with derision and contempt, unmistakable resonances of their own fear of 'pollution' from such interactions, rare as they were. But as the 'notices' issued by the

[62] Discussion with legal team on 7 April 2014, organized by the SKA at India International Centre, New Delhi.

Supreme Court quietly made their way down the bureaucratic chain of command through various ministries of the Central Government,[63] and departments of state and union territory governments,[64] the SKA found they were being treated with new respect, and sometimes, with a degree of apprehension. The movement found itself galvanized into new areas of intervention and mobilization, which included campaigns and demonstrations demanding, and often carrying out, the demolition of dry latrines in different parts of the country.[65]

Early Stages of the Litigation

It is an unfortunate reality of litigation in the constitutional courts that writ petitions raising issues of violations of fundamental and human rights are given short shrift by the state and its lawyers. In the initial year, therefore, a number of the respondent state governments, as well as some ministries of the Central Government, treated the issue in a cavalier manner. Filing short affidavits sometimes running into two or three paragraphs, the central and state governments simply denied the existence of manual scavenging in their jurisdiction. Some of the state governments even took the trouble to explain to the Court that they have declared themselves 'manual scavenger free', and therefore, they have nothing further to contribute to the proceedings before the Court, and that the writ petition should be 'dismissed'.[66] Many simply failed to file any affidavits at all until the Court passed

[63] A total of four Central Government ministries were arrayed as respondent parties in the writ petition, namely the Ministry of Social Justice and Empowerment (Respondent No. 1), the Ministry of Railways (Respondent No. 2), the Ministry of Industries (Respondent No. 3), and the Ministry of Defence (Respondent No. 4).

[64] All the states and union territories in existence at the time, a total of 35, were arrayed as separate respondent parties.

[65] See, for instance, Additional Affidavit on behalf of Petitioners dated 27 April 2009, paras 43–5 in *SKA* v *UoI* (n 7).

[66] This included several states from Northeast India, which argued that no manual scavenging takes place in their jurisdictions because of the primarily rural and mountainous nature of these areas, and also the socio-cultural difference from the rest of India.

orders threatening action against senior bureaucrats, and requiring their personal presence in Court.[67]

Confronted with a wall of denial, the petitioners were compelled to place before the Court several hundred pages of photographic evidence painstakingly collected from different parts of the country.[68] The petitioners also drew the attention of the Court to the budget allocations being made by the Central Government to different states for purported implementation of schemes for eradication of manual scavenging and construction of water-flush latrines. Placing this material before the Court, the petitioners challenged the numerous affidavits filed by the state governments as misleading and even false. Addressing the matter with the seriousness it deserved, the Supreme Court issued these directions in April 2005:[69]

- The Central and each state government shall place before the Court sworn affidavits giving details of whether or not manual scavenging is being resorted to in any department or corporation in its jurisdiction. If so, details of the scheme for eradicating this practice, and rehabilitating the concerned persons, as well as the time frame, should also be provided.
- The Central government was directed to give details of the budget allocations made for various schemes, the utilization of these funds, and the number of people actually rehabilitated each year since 1993.
- The Court specifically directed that these affidavits be filed by the person who is responsible for taking a decision in the matter, and 'on personal information as we propose to hold the person responsible if it is found that the affidavit does not contain the truth'.[70]

The message to state functionaries was unambiguous—the Court was treating the matter seriously, and would not react kindly to irresponsible statements.

---

[67] Order dated 13 September 2004 (unreported) in *SKA* v *UoI* (n 7).

[68] Rejoinder Affidavit on behalf of the Petitioners dated 1 February 2005 in *SKA* v *UoI* (n 7).

[69] Order dated 29 April 2005 (unreported) in *SKA* v *UoI* (n 7).

[70] This direction was clearly in response to the perfunctory affidavits, which had been filed by the respondent governments till then.

Over the next six months, the state governments filed fresh affidavits with better details but there continued to be discrepancies and gaps. Accordingly, the Court issued further directions in November 2005 as follows, this time addressed to the Central Government and its concerned ministries:

- The Ministry of Social Justice and Empowerment, Government of India, which is the nodal agency of the Centre for the implementation of the NLSRS, 'shall file the detailed affidavit by a responsible person not below the rank of Secretary of Department who is responsible for taking decision in the matter'.
- The Ministry of Railways, Government of India, through the Secretary, Railway Board, 'shall file a detailed affidavit showing the scheme/proposed scheme prepared by the Railway Board and implementation of the scheme in time-bound programme for total elimination of Manual Scavenging'.[71]

Again, a specific direction from the Court that the senior-most officer of the concerned department file affidavits sent a ripple of anxiety down the chain of command in the state executive. During the next year or so, state governments, municipal corporations, public sector corporations, and even government banks filed affidavits, stating on oath that there were no manual scavengers or dry latrines in their jurisdiction. The SKA and its associate organizations, meanwhile, kept up the pressure on the ground. This was done through ground-truthing exercises, where they tested the reality against these affirmations, and where an anomaly was found, these were quickly corrected by ensuring the state agency destroyed the dry latrine.

In several states, volunteers of the petitioner organizations, armed with affidavits of the state government denying the existence of manual scavenging and dry latrines, went and demolished these 'non-existent' dry latrines themselves, much to the consternation of local officials. One such initiative related to two dry latrines in the compound of the junior civil judge, Yellareddy in the pre-bifurcation state of Andhra Pradesh, and the 'part time scavenger' employed by the said court (see Box 11.1).

---

[71] Order dated 14 November 2005 in *SKA* v *UoI* (n 7).

Box 11.1 Part-Time Scavenger Employed by Civil Judge

While conducting their campaign for the demolition of dry latrines in the pre-bifurcation state of Andhra Pradesh, the petitioners came across a manual scavenger working in two dry latrines within the court premises of a junior civil judge, Yellareddy. When the volunteers of the organization went to the site to demolish the dry latrines, they were stopped by the civil judge, who also issued an order directing that 'in order to protect the property of the court they [Safai Karamchari volunteers] are prevented from demolishing the same till the necessary permission is obtained from the Hon'ble District Judge, Nizamabad'.[72]

A few days later, a show cause notice was issued to

> Sri Vinod Part Time Scavenger' stating that he has committed misconduct by showing the volunteers the dry latrines, and participating in their efforts to demolish them. It appears, he also spoke to some television reporters, showed them the toilets, and also told them that he earns a monthly salary of Rs 750/-. The notice stated that '(t)herefore, your conduct on both the occasions is highly objectionable and amounts of [*sic*] misconduct, attracting severe action against you.[73]

The petitioners immediately placed all this material before the Supreme Court of India in the pending writ petition, seeking urgent directions in light of the fact that the judicial officers themselves were clearly perpetuating manual scavenging in violation of the law.[74] Shockingly, a reply affidavit was filed by the District and Sessions Judge, Nizamabad supporting the action of his subordinate judge. He asserted that the two dry latrines had fallen into disuse for 20 years, and were surrounded by thorny bushes, submitting that these have now been demolished by the Public Works Department. Repeatedly referring to him as 'Vinod Part Time Scavenger', the judge dismissed the incident as an attempt by the employee to get his job converted into a permanent one.[75]

---

[72] Order dated 16 August 2004 passed by Junior Civil Judge, Yellareddy, cited in IA No. 3, 6 in *SKA* v *UoI* (n 7).

[73] Memo dated 31 August 2004 passed by the District and Sessions Court, Nizamabad in Dis. No. 6788, cited in IA No. 3, 7–8 and 24–5 in *SKA* v *UoI* (n 7).

[74] IA No. 4 of 2004 in *SKA* v *UoI* (n 7).

[75] Affidavit dated 22 February 2005 submitted by Shri V. Suri Appa Rao, District and Sessions Judge, Nizamabad, in reply to IA No. 3 in *SKA* v *UoI* (n 7).

Unlocking the 1993 Act

Even as the movement grew from strength to strength on the ground, it was becoming increasingly clear that the state govern-ments were continuing to either deny or underplay the practice of manual scavenging before the Court. Other states, while maintain-ing that there was no manual scavenging or dry latrines in their jurisdictions, placed contradictory reports on record. The state of Gujarat, for instance, filed numerous affidavits denying the exis-tence of manual scavenging in the state. In an early affidavit, the state government asserted that 'there is no such practice of carrying night soil or dry and *dabba* latrines on head and there is no manual scavenging'.[76] However, 'supporting' documentation and reports from their District functionaries filed along with these affidavits contradicted these assertions.[77]

Thus in July 2007, the petitioners sought specific directions to the NCSK[78] to present the correct picture before the Court.[79] In doing so, the petitioners were hopeful not only of surmounting the infor-mation conundrum, but also of energizing the NCSK to play a more active role in the proceedings before the Court, and fulfil its avowed

[76] Affidavit-in-reply on behalf of the State of Gujarat dated 13 September 2004, para 7.3 in *SKA* v *UoI* (n 7).

[77] For instance, in an affidavit dated 11 November 2005 filed by the Social Justice and Empowerment Department, State of Gujarat, several reports were annexed which admitted that the practice of manual scav-enging was continuing. This was sought to be underplayed. One report, submitted by the Paliyad Gram Panchayat Office, Batod (Bhavnagar) and signed by all five *pancha*s, acknowledged that there are four open toilets in operation, but asserted that: 'At present these open toilets are being used as ladies' toilet. The excreata [*sic*] is cleaned naturally as it is being eaten by animals. The question of scavenging does not arise at all. There is no need to use machinery to dispose of the excreata [*sic*]. The petition before this court is that there is act of scavenging going on in this village, which is absolutely false and totally denied'.

[78] The NCSK had been arrayed as Respondent No. 5 in the writ peti-tion, but had not filed any report or affidavit before the Court separate from the Union Government.

[79] Order dated 8 December 2006 (unreported) in *SKA* v *UoI* (n 7).

statutory objectives.[80] While the NCSK had consistently refused to take on any leadership or advisory role in these proceedings, it did play an important part in placing before the Court the state-wise data on the number of manual scavengers and dry latrines in existence at the time.[81] This data acknowledged that in the year 2007, the population of manual scavengers in the country was 6,76,009, of whom 3,42,468 were engaged in the practice of manual scavenging, and were still to be rehabilitated.

Evidence regarding the continuing practice of manual scavenging was irrefutable, being acknowledged by government as well as civil society reports. Inside the courtroom, however, the problem of denial continued to persist. While at the time of filing of the writ petition, there was fragmented information on the prevalence of manual scavenging in the country, with the numerous affidavits and reports now on record, accompanied by the detailed affidavit of the NCSK, a wealth of information was available. However, as the state governments did not acknowledge the problem of manual scavenging, they felt no need to pass the necessary legislative resolutions to adopt the 1993 Act, and start implementing it.[82] The Planning Commission of

[80] The Statement of Objects and Reasons of the National Commission for Safai Karamcharis Act, 1993, acknowledges that in spite of a 'number of steps for the social, economic and educational upliftment of Safai Karamcharis ... the obnoxious practice of manual scavenging still continues in many parts of the country. Since this practice is a continuing stigma on our social fabric, Government is determined to eradicate the practice within a fixed time-frame'. Towards this end, the NCSK was set up as 'a separate statutory National commission ... for monitoring the schemes for the liberation and rehabilitation of Safai Karamcharis'. However, the statute has since lapsed, and the NCSK now functions as a subordinate of the Ministry of Social Justice and Empowerment, Government of India, which perhaps explains its lack of enthusiasm for taking a leadership role in the writ proceedings.

[81] Counter Affidavit on behalf of Respondent No. 5 (National Commission for Safai Karamcharis) dated April 2007 in *SKA* v *UoI* (n 7).

[82] The 1993 Act was enacted by Parliament under Article 252(1) of the Constitution of India, since a state subject was directly in issue. Accordingly, for the statute to come into force in each state, a resolution was required to be passed by the concerned state legislature adopting it.

India itself acknowledged that: 'Despite commitments made to the eradication of the obnoxious and dehumanizing practice of handling night soil manually, it still continues. Only 19 States and all UTs have adopted the Employment of Manual Scavengers and Construction of Dry Latrines (Prohibition Act, 1993) [sic]. Nine States are yet to adopt the Act.'[83]

In the few states where the legislatures had adopted the law, the executive machinery had not been put in place. As stated earlier, the 1993 Act is not a self-starting law; the necessary executive machinery at the state, District, and Block level has to be appointed and notified, so that its provisions can be activated. This had not been done. In a handful of states where the implementation machinery was, in fact, in place, it was found that no prosecutions were launched under the 1993 Act or otherwise. According to the government's own records, not a single prosecution was registered under the law. Convictions were unheard of.

In October 2007, the petitioners placed a detailed chart before the Supreme Court giving the state-wise status of prevalence of manual scavenging, and juxtaposing this information with the status of adoption/implementation of the 1993 Act. They also drew the attention of the Court to current data as placed on record by the NCSK. Confronted with this irrefutable evidence that state governments were grossly underplaying the problem and falsifying data, a clearly agitated bench passed the following set of directions:

> We direct that any State who [sic] has not issued notification in terms of Section 5(1) of the Act to do so within a period of two months. Such agencies shall carry out investigation as empowered under Section 5(1) of the Act and also impose the penalties to the defaulters in terms of Section 14 of the Act, in the meantime.[84]

According to this direction, the state governments were expected to immediately put in place the implementing authorities under the

---

[83] Planning Commission of India, Eleventh Five Year Plan, 'Chapter 6: Social Justice: Scheduled Castes, Scheduled Tribes, Other Backward Classes, Minorities, and Other Vulnerable Groups', 2018, 109, para 6.47.

[84] Order dated 5 October 2007 in *SKA* v *UoI* (n 7).

1993 Act, namely a District magistrate or sub-divisional magistrate, through a notification published in the official gazette.

A few months later, the Court followed up with a further set of directions in continuation of its previous order as follows:[85]

- Affidavits explaining the reasons for non-adoption of the 1993 Act in their respective states: to be filed by the states of Jammu and Kashmir, Nagaland, Himachal Pradesh, Manipur, Meghalaya, Sikkim, Mizoram, Arunachal Pradesh, Delhi, and the union territory of Chandigarh.
- Affidavits explaining the reasons why, having adopted the 1993 Act, no executive authorities have been appointed: to be filed by the states of Assam, West Bengal, Haryana, Tripura, Goa, Uttaranchal, Jharkhand, Madhya Pradesh, Tamil Nadu, Maharashtra, Punjab, and the union territories of Andaman and Nicobar, Lakshadweep, Dadra and Nagar Haveli, and Pondicherry.
- Affidavits explaining why, having appointed executive authorities, no investigation or prosecution of violations of the 1993 Act has been initiated: to be filed by the states of Andhra Pradesh, Chhattisgarh, Gujarat, Kerala, Karnataka, Odisha, Rajasthan, and the union territory of Daman and Diu.

Although the Court gave three months' time for the errant state governments to rectify these gaps, the mood of the Court was anything but patient, a message which soon trickled down to the concerned executive functionaries. During this period, the petitioners found that there was also an increased interest in the media and civil society about the abhorrent practice of manual scavenging and its continuance. The movement for eradication, therefore, gained in strength even as pressure mounted on state governments to adopt the 1993 Act, and set up the implementation machinery required for ensuring that the law does not remain a dead letter.

This process took more than a year, with the writ proceedings coming up for hearing before the Supreme Court at regular intervals, putting the spotlight on the recalcitrant states. That the Court was taking the issue up in utmost seriousness was apparent to the

[85] Order dated 11 December 2007 (unreported) in *SKA* v *UoI* (n 7).

petitioners in a multiplicity of gestures of inclusion made by the bench. During one memorable hearing, one of the judges observed that the Court would not rest until the last manual scavenger in the country had been liberated and rehabilitated.

The Tide Turns

Looking back, it seems inevitable that after so many years of remarkable progress in the writ proceedings, the fortunes of the petitioners were bound to take a downturn. As it is, the day caught the petitioners by surprise. In August 2008, what was expected to be a routine hearing to take stock of the compliance by different states of the Court's previous orders, went very wrong. The writ petition was listed before a different bench, which raised a barrage of questions challenging the very foundation of the proceedings. Indeed, the Court expressed its disbelief that the practice of manual scavenging continues, insisting that it has been eradicated decades ago.

Unfortunately, the law officers representing the government in Court that day seized the opportunity to press the argument they had made repeatedly over many years—that the writ petition relies upon outdated information, and that manual scavenging is a thing of the past. On the verge of dismissing the writ proceedings as frivolous, the Court relented at the last moment, but only to the extent that the petitioner had to discharge the burden of demonstrating the existence of manual scavenging all over again. The following order was passed: 'The petitioner will furnish the details by way of an affidavit as to whether the manual scavenging is still continued and if so, in which parts of the country, within eight weeks.'[86]

Immediately after this hearing, this author, who had been at the receiving end of the Court's antagonism, was overcome with a sense of desolation. After seven years of crawling forward one painful inch at a time, the petitioners were back at square one. Indeed, it was a setback of mammoth proportions. In a telling reversal of roles, it was Bezwada Wilson of the SKA who reassured this author that this was

---

[86] Order dated 5 August 2008 (unreported) in *SKA* v *UoI* (n 7).

not the end of the road, and that they would find a way to surmount this hurdle too.[87]

The SKA turned what was the lowest point of the litigation into an opportunity for growth. Pulling out all the stops, it launched a mobilization on the ground, which saw hundreds of volunteers, themselves drawn from the community, fan out across the country to conduct surveys of people engaged in manual scavenging. Six months later, the petitioners placed before the Court detailed survey reports of five sample states,[88] giving not only the numbers of manual scavengers actually engaged in the practice every day, but details of their socio-economic status, their locations, their dependents, the names and addresses of the owners of the dry latrines where they worked, and a glimpse into their aspirations for advancement.[89] Hundreds of pages of carefully collated data submitted on sworn affidavits, were supplemented by photographic evidence chronicling the lives of some of the manual scavengers who had consented to have their private horror stories narrated before the Court.[90]

The petitioners sought to draw attention to the central problem in these writ proceedings—the tendency of the state governments in general, and the local implementing authorities in particular, to deny the existence of the practice of manual scavenging entirely, or to underplay its existence through definitional gymnastics which have

[87] In subsequent discussions, Bezwada Wilson has acknowledged the prominent role played by late S.R. Sankaran, a founding member of the SKA, and its advisor and mentor, until his sudden demise in 2010. Sankarangaru, as he is fondly referred to even today, galvanized the SKA in his inimitably gentle style, to meet this setback as a new challenge.

[88] The five states included in this sample survey were Punjab, Haryana, Rajasthan, Delhi, and Uttarakhand.

[89] One of the questions in the survey form was 'what would you like to do instead of manual scavenging'? Many of the survey forms contain heart-rending responses. While some wanted to work as a tailor, or start a small paan-shop, others expressed a desire to own and rear a cow or a pig. A sociological analysis is waiting to be done into these responses of how untouchability practices have truncated the ability of oppressed peoples to aspire for a better life.

[90] See Additional Affidavit on Behalf of the Petitioners dated 27 April 2009 in *SKA* v *UoI* (n 7).

no basis in law or in fact. It was pointed out to the Court that it is a matter of grave concern that the state governments are attempting to defeat the purpose of the constitutional provisions as well as the 1993 Act through these acts of denial.

After examining the detailed survey reports placed on record by the petitioners regarding the continuation of the practice of manual scavenging, the same bench, which had a few short months earlier directed its ire at the petitioners, now turned upon the state governments. Going beyond the framework of the 'prayers' sought by the petitioners in their writ petition, the Court issued 'show cause' notices to the District collectors of all the areas where the petitioners had demonstrated that manual scavenging is continuing, as follows:

> The petitioner has submitted a detailed report to the effect that in the State of Rajasthan, manual scavenger work is widely prevalent in various districts. The details i.e. names and addresses etc. of the workers and also the persons who employed these workers are also being given. It is noticed that this is prevalent in the districts of Jhunjhunu, Ajmer, Nagaur, Bikaner, Bharatpur, Churu, Karoli, Seekar and Alwar. Registry to send a copy of these details i.e. names and addresses of the Dry Latrine owners and employers along with a copy of the report submitted by the petitioner to each of the District Collectors mentioned above. Each District Collector has to explain as to why steps are not being taken against the employers who employed the manual scavengers under the Employment of Manual Scavengers and Construction of Dry Latrines (Prohibition) Act, 1993 (hereinafter referred to as 'the 1993 Act').[91]

Similar directions were issued to District collectors in the other states regarding which the petitioners had submitted data.[92] The Court was particularly shocked by the fact that in the national capital of Delhi, a few kilometres from the Court premises, there were dry latrines in use where manual scavengers were currently working. In this regard, the Court also issued notice to the State of Delhi (Respondent

---

[91] Orders dated 30 April 2009 and 8 May 2009 in *SKA* v *UoI* (n 7).
[92] Other than the state of Rajasthan, similar orders were passed in relation to the states of Punjab, Haryana, Uttarakhand, and Delhi.

No. 34) to submit a detailed affidavit explaining why it has not even adopted the 1993 Act till date.[93]

Impact of the Supreme Court's Directions

The directions, issued by a bench headed by the then Chief Justice of India, were widely reported in the press and caused an unprecedented wave of action. The registry of the Supreme Court addressed show cause notices to each concerned District collector by name, along with the names and addresses provided by the petitioners through their survey. In almost all these areas, the District administration swung into action, and armed with these lists, conducted rapid operations to demolish the dry latrines and provide alternative employment to manual scavengers. In the state of Haryana, the first criminal prosecutions in the history of the 1993 Act were launched against 22 dry-latrine owners, who were also arrested and imprisoned, albeit only for a few days. The same volunteers who had assisted in conducting these surveys were now mobilized to play an active role in advancing the movement itself.

The impact resonated not only in the five concerned states, but also in adjoining areas. On the basis of these orders, activists of the SKA were able to convince the District administration in other parts of the country to take pre-emptive steps, and remove dry latrines from their areas. In several areas, manual scavengers who had been working in these dry latrines were provided rehabilitation under previously languishing government schemes, and some were even provided employment.

In addition, the petitioners and many other civil society organizations made innumerable personal visits to the local authorities and state government officials such as District magistrates, National Scheduled Caste Finance and Development Corporation (NSFDC) executive officers, municipal authorities and their chairpersons, and personally handed over the Supreme Court's orders along with copies of the 1993 Act. Several officials took up the matter and initiated the necessary steps towards eradication of manual scavenging, demolition of dry latrines, and liberation of manual scavengers. To cite one example, in the state of Tamil Nadu, where the practice of manual

[93] Order dated 8 May 2009 in *SKA* v *UoI* (n 7).

scavenging was rampant at the time of filing the writ petition in 2003,[94] the state government has been motivated by the Supreme Court's orders to demolish virtually all dry latrines in the state, and the practice of manual scavenging has been all but eliminated, even though rehabilitation is far from complete.[95]

The movement also drew the attention of the National Advisory Council (NAC). The NAC took serious note of the continued existence of manual scavenging, passing the following resolution:

> The NAC urges the Central Government to coordinate with all state, local governments and also Central Government departments including the Railways, to ensure that this practice is fully abolished latest by the end of the 11th Plan period. This would require a) new survey in every state and UT, with wide public involvement, of remaining dry latrines and manual scavengers b) demolition of all dry latrines c) psycho-social and livelihood rehabilitation in modern marketable skills of all manual scavengers and their families; and d) special programme for education, including higher education and computer education of all children of manual scavengers. The Ministry of Social Justice should formulate 100% centrally sponsored scheme to support the rehabilitation initiatives. The law also needs to be amended to ensure sharper definitions of manual scavenging, and accountability of public officials who employ, or fail to prevent, manual scavenging.[96]

[94] According to the chart prepared by the Ministry of Social Justice and Empowerment, during the year 2002–3, there were 35,561 manual scavengers and their dependents in the state of Tamil Nadu alone. See *SKA v UoI* (n 7), Annexure P/12, 91.

[95] According to information available with the SKA, the practice of manual scavenging with regard to cleaning of dry latrines has practically been eradicated in Tamil Nadu. However, it must be clarified that manual cleaning of sewers and septic tanks, a practice which is proscribed under the 2013 Act, continues.

[96] Resolution adopted on Manual Scavenging at the meeting of the National Advisory Council on 23 October 2010 with recommendations to the Government, as forwarded to the Prime Minister of India vide letter dated 9 November 2010 (No. N.11017/1/2010-NAC-775), para 4. See also National Advisory Council, Recommendations for Follow up Measures to Eradicate Manual Scavenging, 25 May 2011.

While government spending for rehabilitation did not form the subject matter of the Court orders, the increased attention to the issue enabled the movement to advocate for increased budget allocations as well. The allocation for rehabilitation of manual scavengers went from a paltry Rs 1.2 crores for the year 2010–11, to Rs 98 crores in 2011–12, and a similar amount for 2012–13.[97]

The Tide Turns—Again

Even as the petitioners' campaign for eradication of manual scavenging went from strength to strength on the ground, in the hallowed portals of the highest Court of the land, things were changing rapidly. For several years, even decades, numerous public interest litigations (PILs) on various issues of fundamental rights and welfare functions of the state, had been given the status of continuing mandamus, thus receiving the close attention of the Court.[98] However, many of these were rapidly being wound up.[99]

At a critical juncture in the writ proceedings relating to manual scavenging, with show cause notices issued to District officials across the country still awaiting responses, the petitioners found themselves caught inside this wave. In a startling development towards the end of 2011, the Supreme Court directed the senior counsel for the petitioners to address arguments on the preliminary issue of

[97] It is a different matter that during the year 2012–13, the entire amount allocated in the budget for rehabilitation of manual scavengers remained unspent.

[98] For example, *Godavarman* (n 12). See also Shomona Khanna, 'Boundaries of Forest Land: The Godavarman Case and Beyond', in Sharadchandra Lele and Ajit Menon (eds), *Democratizing Forest Governance in India* (Oxford University Press, 2014).

[99] Indeed, a cognate bench of the same Supreme Court, through a detailed judgment in *Delhi Jal Board* v *National Campaign for Dignity & Rights of Sewerage and Allied Workers* (2011) 8 SCC 568, deprecated the urgency with which the Supreme Court appeared to be clearing its board of public interest writ petitions (paras 31–3).

maintainability.[100] It further directed the Attorney General of India, the late Mr Goolam N. Vahanvati, a leading constitutional expert in his own right, to address arguments on this fundamental question.[101]

When this issue was argued in January 2012 for almost three hours, the senior counsel appearing for the petitioners struggled to convince the Court that the continued practice of manual scavenging, regarding which a wealth of information based on government studies as well as the petitioners' own surveys has already been placed on record, itself demonstrates that the 1993 Act has proved to be a dead letter in protecting the fundamental rights of hundreds of thousands of citizens. Without the continuing intervention, direction, and supervision of the Supreme Court, and the numerous directions it has issued which are in the nature of mandamus, the petitioners and the manual scavengers they represent would be bereft of hope.

The Court directed that the writ petition be transferred to all the high courts in the country for further monitoring, and for implementation of the 1993 Act and the various orders passed by it, as follows:

> We have examined the writ petition. We find that the prayers made in the writ petition are very wide. Be that as it may, in the present case, this Court has been monitoring the issue concerning prohibition and employment of manual scavengers as well as construction or continuance of dry latrines for the last decade. Detailed directions have been given from time to time by this Court ... For implementation of those directions, we direct the Registry of this Court to forward a copy of the writ petition along with (relevant) Orders ... to respective High Court and we request those High Courts to enforce the directions given by this Court from time to time. We make it clear that the High Courts will see to it that the provisions of 1993 Act are implemented by the Authorities within their respective jurisdiction.[102]

---

[100] More specifically, the Court framed the question thus: 'Can the Supreme Court, in a writ proceeding under Article 32 of the Constitution, issue a writ of mandamus to the state machinery for protection of a fundamental right, when a statute in this regard already exists?'

[101] Order dated 8 November 2011 (unreported) in *SKA* v *UoI* (n 7).

[102] Order dated 12 January 2011 in *SKA* v *UoI* (n 7).

As the Court passed an order directing that the writ petition no longer requires the attention of the country's highest constitutional court, the petitioners with some difficulty convinced it to keep the matter pending for the limited extent of compliance. This was possible only in the context of the writ proceedings having been treated as a continuing mandamus for almost nine years; in other circumstances the case would have been closed with these minimalistic observations.

The direction that a writ petition under Article 32 of the Constitution be converted into multiple writ petitions before the 21 high courts of the country, unprecedented in Indian jurisprudence, proved impossible to implement. Despite strenuous efforts by the petitioners to activate the various high courts, the fact that there is no procedural provision for such conversion[103] remained an insurmountable barrier, and therefore nothing came of this direction except in the Delhi High Court.[104]

Faced with this impasse in the writ proceedings, the petitioners once again turned their attention to advancing mobilization around the eradication campaign, and implementation of the previous directions passed by the Supreme Court to the District collectors in different parts of the country. The lull in the court proceedings became an opportunity to explore new strategies and campaigns for bringing public attention to the issue, such as demonstrations, public meetings, country-wide arts, awareness raising among school

---

[103] A provision for the reverse process, namely, transfer of two or more writ petitions from different high courts to the Supreme Court, exists both in the Constitution of India (Article 139-A) as well as the Supreme Court Rules, 1966 (Order XL).

[104] As it turned out, a key factor was the specific direction relating to the High Court of Delhi in the order dated 12 January 2012 as follows: 'In cases where the Railways is the employer, we request the Delhi High Court to enforce the provisions of 1993 Act as also the directions issued by this Court from time to time'. Pursuant to this direction by the Supreme Court, the Delhi High Court converted the writ petition into WP (C) No. 845 of 2011, where it has been dealing with the issue of manual scavenging in the Indian Railways. Several orders and directions relating to the Indian Railways have been passed from time to time.

children,[105] and mobilization of legislators. A remarkable effort, which provided a tremendous boost for the movement, was the 10,000 km march across 18 states and 200 Districts in 2010.

Reflecting upon this time, Bezwada Wilson opines that despite the setback in the Court, the petitioners had to a great extent achieved the larger objective of bringing to the forefront of public discourse a practice that had for centuries remained an invisible crime.[106]

Final Judgment

A decade of pursuing this litigation in the highest constitutional court naturally led to some introspection by the petitioners about the journey. In the above narrative, the key turning points in the ebb and flow have been described, but behind this brief narrative lie a hundred stories of lived experience, ranging from elation to dismay.[107] It became clear to the petitioners that with every new officer at the helm of a District, with every new judge at the head of a bench, indeed with every new political dispensation, they were compelled to repeat the same arguments again and again. At every

[105] Working with educators in the National Council of Educational Research and Training (NCERT), the movement was able to advance awareness among school students and educationists regarding the abhorrent practice of manual scavenging in India. As part of this initiative, a section entitled 'The Scourge of Manual Scavenging' giving, inter alia, a summary of the Supreme Court directions was included in the Social Studies Textbook for Class VIII in a chapter titled 'Confronting Marginalisation'.

[106] Shortly after the final judgment was delivered, the SKA held a meeting to acknowledge all the lawyers who had been part of the process over this 10 year journey. Of the 22 lawyers who are on this list, more than 15 came together to share their recollections, and the ways in which the SKA touched their lives. It also provided an opportunity to process some of the key lessons learned during this journey. 'The Way Forward' meeting was held in India International Centre, Delhi on 7 April 2015.

[107] For a deeper understanding of the human impact of the SKA's campaign for eradication of manual scavenging, including the litigation, see Bhasha Singh, *Unseen: The Truth about India's Manual Scavengers* (Penguin Books, 2012).

stage in the litigation, the petitioners were compelled to reiterate the constitutional and jurisprudential principles on which their movement is premised.

It was also inescapable that the crucial link between the notion of pollution and untouchability and the practice of manual scavenging would never be immediately apparent to those who have not experienced it. The urgency with which the movement viewed the need to eradicate manual scavenging and the loathsome dry latrines, their commitment to the principles of human dignity as overriding the pragmatism of daily existence, and their anguish in the face of officers who either refused to acknowledge the problem or suggested the provision of 'safety gear' and other such self-serving solutions, was clearly becoming a vicious cycle. The petitioners found that although a wealth of orders and directions had been passed by the Supreme Court over the years in these proceedings, there existed no exposition of the jurisprudence connecting the practice of manual scavenging with the right to equality (Article 14), the right against discrimination (Article 15), the right to life with dignity (Article 21), the prohibition of untouchability (Article 17), and the prohibition of forced labour (Article 23), among other important constitutional protections. Thus, in February 2013, when the incumbent Chief Justice of India suggested to the petitioners that it was time to finally hear the matter and bring the continuing mandamus to a close, the petitioners welcomed the opportunity to place before the Court their arguments regarding the constitutional framework within which a solution must be envisaged.

In March 2014, the Supreme Court pronounced a detailed judgment bringing the decade long writ proceedings to a close.[108] The judgment, which was widely reported, traced the historical connection between the constitutional prohibition of untouchability under Article 17, and the practice of manual scavenging. The judgment asserted that the practice of manual scavenging is continuing in violation of the constitutional mandate; whether or not the statute is violated is a secondary issue.

---

[108] *Safai Karamchari Andolan & Others* v *Union of India & Others* (2014) 11 SCC 224 (Supreme Court of India) ('*SKA v UoI* judgment').

The Court endorsed the provisions of the 1993 Act, and also the various orders passed in the writ proceedings, which ensured that the executive machinery was put in place.[109] It also, quite unambiguously, endorsed the provisions of the 2013 Act, which relate to the prohibition of manual scavenging, unsanitary latrines, hazardous cleaning of sewers and septic tanks, and cleaning of railway tracks. Equally unambiguously, the judgment endorsed the statutory provisions regarding rehabilitation of manual scavengers. The Court further drew upon the provisions of a variety of international conventions and covenants,[110] to which India is a party, and which proscribe the inhuman practice of manual scavenging, observing that since these have been ratified by India, these 'are binding to the extent that they are not inconsistent with the provisions of the domestic law'.[111]

Significantly, the judgment issued numerous directions in the nature of mandamus to the Central Government and the state governments, with a further direction that appropriate action be taken in case of non-implementation or violation of such directions. Some of these are:

- *Survey and Rehabilitation*: Asserting that the approach of the state must be based on principles of justice and transformation, the Court directed identification of manual scavengers through a country-wide survey. It further directed that they must be provided with proper rehabilitation through cash assistance, provision of housing, education scholarships to children, monthly stipend during skill development training, and subsidy/concessional loan for taking up alternative occupation.

[109] The 1993 Act is discussed in the section 'Unlocking the 1993 Act' of this chapter.

[110] Some of the key international instruments, which the judgment of the Supreme Court relies upon, are: The Universal Declaration of Human Rights, New York, 10 December 1948 (Arts 1, 2.1, 23.3); the Convention on the Elimination of All Forms of Discrimination against Women, New York, 18 December 1979 (art 5.a); and the Convention on the Elimination of All Forms of Racial Discrimination, New York, 7 March 1966 (art 2.1).

[111] *SKA* v *UoI* judgment (n 108), para 7.

- *Sewer Workers*: The Court opined that in order to ensure that the practice of manual scavenging is brought to a close, and to prevent future generations from being drawn into it again, rehabilitation measures must also include sewer workers, further directing that being made to enter 'sewer lines without safety gear should be a crime even in emergency situations'.[112] The Court directed that families of all persons who have died in sewerage work, including manholes, septic tanks, and so on since 1993 must be identified and awarded compensation of Rs 10 lakhs each.
- *Workers on Indian Railways*: Having noted that the 2013 Act expressly acknowledges that Article 17 and Article 21 of the Constitution protect the rights of persons engaged in cleaning human excreta on railway tracks, the Court directed that the '(r)ailways should take time-bound strategy to end manual scavenging on the tracks'.[113]
- *Women Workers* should be provided support for dignified livelihood, and choice of livelihood schemes.

In closing, the Court directed as follows:

> In the light of various provisions of the Act referred to above and the Rules in addition to various directions issued by this Court, we hereby direct all the State Governments and the Union Territories to fully implement the same and take appropriate action for non-implementation as well as violation of the provisions contained in the 2013 Act. Inasmuch as the Act 2013 occupies the entire field, we are of the view that no further monitoring is required by this Court. However, we once again reiterate that the duty is cast on all the States and the Union Territories to fully implement and to take action against the violators. Henceforth, persons aggrieved are permitted to approach the authorities concerned at the first instance and thereafter the High Court having jurisdiction.[114]

With these directions and exhortations to the state machinery, coupled with the liberty to the petitioners and 'persons aggrieved' to approach the concerned authorities or the high courts if these directions are not complied with, the decade-long litigation drew to a close.

---

[112] *SKA* v *UoI* judgment (n 108), para 14(2)(a).

[113] *SKA* v *UoI* judgment (n 108), paras 12 and 14(ii)(b).

[114] *SKA* v *UoI* judgment (n 108), para 15.

Of Lessons, Endings, and Beginnings

Treating the writ proceeding as a continuing mandamus for close to ten years had its advantages, generating visibility for the issue as well as for the petitioners and other civil society organizations working on the frontlines. As information regarding the Court's orders travelled down the chain of command, no doubt accompanied by stern exhortations from government counsel when the Court expressed its displeasure, officers within the executive branch were more amenable to meeting and collaborating with the petitioners. This was no small achievement for those who have been severed from their status as equal citizens, and from the promise and aspirations of the Constitution. Even the most recalcitrant of state governments were compelled eventually to collaborate with the petitioners towards the goal of eradication, and surrender their hardened positions of denial (see Box 11.2). Numerous state governments, which

---

Box 11.2   A 'Holy' City in Uttarakhand

One state which remained unmoved by the specific Court orders directed at it was the state of Uttarakhand. The petitioners had placed before the Court a detailed survey report and evidence to demonstrate that the practice of manual scavenging was rampant in the 'holy' city of Haridwar, which is an important pilgrimage site for Hindus. Not only were the directions of the Supreme Court not complied with, the District collector, to whom a 'show cause' notice had been issued by the Supreme Court, did not deem it necessary to even file an affidavit in response. Almost two years later, sample surveys conducted by the petitioners in four Districts of the state found that there was an alarming increase in the numbers of manual scavengers and dry latrines.[115]

For the first time in the history of the litigation, confronted by the intractable refusal of the state government to implement the Supreme Court's specific directions, the petitioners were compelled to initiate contempt of court proceedings.[116] When the petitions came up for

---

[115] According to the sample surveys conducted by the petitioners from December 2011 through January 2012 in four Districts of Haridwar, Udhamsingh Nagar, Dehradun, and Pauri Garhwal, there were 288 manual scavengers working in 1,963 dry latrines at the time.

[116] *Safai Karmachari Andolan* v *Shri Subhash Kumar & Others* Contempt Petition (Civil) No. 132 of 2012, (Supreme Court of India).

hearing, the petitioners also placed before the Court the recently released findings of the Census of India report of 2011, which revealed a shocking state of affairs that out of a total number of 24.6 crore households in the country, approximately 8 lakhs were being 'serviced manually'.[117] State-wise and District-wise break-up of this outrage was also placed before the Court.[118]

This time the Court was neither tardy nor grudging in its response, and issued directions to several of the state governments that it would initiate contempt of court proceedings against all of them if immediate remedial steps were not taken.[119] While some of the states continued to take a position that manual scavenging has ceased to exist,[120] this order and those passed subsequently, provided an additional opportunity to the petitioners to take up important initiatives with the local bureaucracy, such as demolition of dry latrines and provision of rehabilitation. Indeed, the contempt petition relating to the state of Uttarakhand, which initially saw dogged opposition from the state government,[121] eventually culminated in a joint inspection being conducted by the representatives of the SKA and the District collector himself.

[117] Office of the Registrar General and Census Commissioner (n 10).

[118] See Short Affidavit on Behalf of Petitioners dated 20 September 2012 in *SKA* v *UoI* (n 7).

[119] Order dated 3 September 2012 (unreported) in *SKA* v *UoI* (n 7).

[120] The state of Madhya Pradesh, for instance, in a detailed affidavit placed before the Court pursuant to this order, challenged the Census of India 2011 findings that out of 1,49,67,597 households in the state, 5,664 were being 'serviced manually'. It argued that 'the persons engaged in Census work for survey and information collection had to note the information given by house owners using due diligence, wherein they had drawn wrong inferences, for e.g. families practicing open defecation were clubbed with latrine in open drain, similarly "katcha sauchalay" means temporary super structure of sheet roofing, which has been inferred as dry latrines. Thus the information for Census-2011 is not fully accurate'. See Affidavit filed by the State of Madhya Pradesh dated nil 2012, para 29 in *SKA* v *UoI* (n 7).

[121] The state of Uttarakhand and the District collector of Haridwar filed numerous affidavits before the Court challenging the survey findings of the petitioners, compelling the SKA to re-conduct the survey and present even more detailed information before the Court. At one point, the impasse appeared to be insurmountable.

had hitherto failed to bring the 1993 Act into force, have taken positive steps to notify the statute and bring the same into force, as well as set up the implementing machinery under the statute. Executive authorities, which are empowered to take note of violations, initiate proceedings against violators, as well as implement schemes for liberation and rehabilitation, have now been notified in almost all states, while some states enacted state-level legislation on the subject.[122]

The SKA was also compelled to draw upon a wealth of legal talent during this 10 year journey. Rather than let these interactions remain fleeting, it invested time, effort, and patience into developing relationships which have weathered many storms.[123] Even the setbacks were converted into opportunities for new and creative initiatives, and hindsight reveals how the movement for eradication gained strength, visibility, and penetration as a result. To a large extent, the intrinsic flaws in the 1993 Act, key among these being its complete dependence upon the state executive for implementation, were addressed by the directions of, and persistent monitoring by, the Supreme Court.

However, there were also some disadvantages of the continuing mandamus approach. It is in the nature of litigation that judicial officers change at regular intervals, either when they retire or because benches are re-constituted. Since there is no mechanism for preserving institutional memory,[124] it is difficult for one judge

---

[122] The State of Jammu and Kashmir, for instance, does not come within the purview of the 1993 Act, since it has a special constitutional status. During the initial years of the litigation, the state government had maintained that it does not require any such law. However, confronted with evidence highlighted by the petitioners that a significant number of manual scavengers are continuing to work in the state, it eventually enacted The Jammu and Kashmir Employment of Manual Scavengers and Construction of Dry Latrines (Prohibition) Act, 2010.

[123] See SKA Meeting (n 106).

[124] The lack of institutional memory is a vacuum, which afflicts many public interest and continuing mandamus litigations in the constitutional courts. The key reason is that the views of the Court are recorded only in perfunctory 'orders', and there is no method of recording the discussions, developments, and thought processes, which resulted in such orders being passed. While clues are no doubt available in the pleadings, these are usually voluminous, and not easy to navigate.

to understand why his or her predecessor may have been pursuing a particular line of approach, or chose not to pursue another. Further, different judicial officers have their own perceptions about how issues relating to fundamental rights violations should be addressed, and may not agree with their predecessor's approach. While proceedings in a public interest writ petition are meant to be non-adversarial, it is difficult for the Court and the law officers to completely switch off their natural wariness of the petitioners' counsel, the only officer who actually has a recollection of the proceedings from start to finish in the absence of an amicus curiae.[125] The lack of any mechanism for recording institutional memory has proved to be problematic for many continuing mandamus cases which have carried on for a long period of time.[126]

It is also true that writ proceedings by definition involve issues with social, political, economic, and technical complexities, often outside the comfort zone of most lawyers and judges. This means that intense efforts are required towards research, collection and collation of information, and its presentation to the court in a form which is accessible, in order to advance the proceedings in a meaningful way. Intense human and financial resources are required, sometimes within impossible time frames. The SKA found itself pushed to its limits just to be able to meet the demands the Court often made in a brief one-line order. Eventually, the challenge is located in the ability of the organization to translate the orders of the Court into reality on the ground.

At a meeting of the lawyers' team in April 2014, even as they exchanged experiences they never had time to share before, listened and talked and laughed in a rare moment of solidarity, it was clear that the respite was going to be short-lived as the SKA chalked out its plan for ensuring that the Court's directions do not become a mere paper victory.

One year later, the SKA addressed a letter to the President of India expressing its anguish at the failure of the state machinery to identify

---

[125] In the *Godavarman case*, for instance, the Court appointed an amicus curiae as far back as 1995 who has continued to assist the Court through the last 23 years, even as more officers have been appointed to assist him! This kind of continuity is, however, very unusual. See *Godavarman* (n 12).

[126] See, for example, Khanna (n 98).

the manual scavengers entitled to rehabilitation under the Court's directions, and the niggardly fashion in which the families of workers who died in sewers were being identified, with only 16 deaths having been compensated as on March 2015.[127] Four years down the line, the enumeration of manual scavengers working on railway tracks under the Indian Railways across the country has not even been conceptualized, while survey of the manual scavengers in the country, identified as a key gap by the CAG in 2003 and one of the main directions in the Supreme Court judgment of 2014, remains mired in a bureaucratic morass.

The Swachh Bharat Mission (SBM) launched by the current government is being implemented in mission mode across the country, in anticipation of the increased traffic of foreign capital, as India prepares to breach the walls that separate it from the developed world. But the existing practice of manual scavenging finds only passing mention in this campaign in the context of conversion of 'insanitary latrines' into 'sanitary latrines',[128] bringing an unmistakable sense of déjà vu.[129]

---

[127] See letter dated 27 March 2015 addressed by the SKA to the President of India (on file with the author). The letter records that the SKA has collected and verified details of 436 deaths from across the country, but only 16 families have been awarded compensation as per the Court's directions.

[128] The Guidelines for Swachh Bharat Mission (Urban) (SBM-U), 2017, mention 'eradication of manual scavenging' as one of its objectives (2.1.2 and 10.3.3), and further identify them as a 'special focus group' for which state governments are required to ensure that '[a]ll manual scavengers in urban areas are identified, insanitary toilets linked to their employment are upgraded to sanitary toilets, and that the manual scavengers are adequately rehabilitated' (para 2.5.5). Whether the actual performance of the Scheme meets the standards of the Constitution, the 1993 Act, and the 2013 Act, remains to be seen. The Guidelines for Swachh Bharat Mission (Gramin) (SBM-G) refer to the provisions of the 2013 Act which prohibit construction of insanitary latrines, and observe that 'existing "insanitary latrines" if any, should be converted to sanitary latrines and the sharing pattern for incentive for the targeted beneficiaries shall be identical to that of construction of individual house hold latrines' (para 5.4.6). Clearly, the beneficiaries being referred to here are not the manual scavengers who work in such latrines, if any.

[129] Bolla Alekhya, 'Swachh Bharat Campaign Finds Place in 66th Republic Day Tableau; Manual Scavenging Still Continues in India' (29 January 2015);

In an order passed close upon the heels of the Supreme Court's declaratory judgment in the SKA case, the Bombay High Court took serious note of manual scavenging in the pilgrim town of Pandharpur, directing the state government to release Rs 5 crores immediately to the municipal council to help deploy mobile toilets on a war-footing. The Court expressed its shock that human beings are being employed to clean human waste in this day and age, in violation of basic human rights, and recorded that the directions issued in the aforesaid judgment of the Supreme Court are mandatory, and have to be complied with.[130] Within a year, the focus of the High Court had shifted towards overseeing administrative arrangements for ensuring sanitary toilets for the pilgrims, and away from the failure of the state government to ensure that manual scavenging in the temple town is discontinued.[131] It may well be that the judiciary holds the key to unlock the door behind which this crime is rendered invisible.

The greatest challenge remains to advance the aspiration, visualized over six decades ago by the makers of the Constitution of India, for a country free from the pernicious practice of untouchability and the caste system, and which has now been recognized by the judgment of the Supreme Court. Without a commitment to this fundamental goal, the Indian state will continue to treat each deadline for eradication of manual scavenging with nonchalance, and each target as a shifting goalpost in perpetuity.

---

available at www.merinews.com/article/swachh-bharat-campaign-finds-place-in-66th-republic-day-tableau-manual-scavenging-still-continues-in-india/15903785.shtml.

[130] Vinaya Deshpande, 'End Manual Scavenging in Pandharpur', *The Hindu* (17 April 2014); available at www.thehindu.com/news/national/other-states/end-manual-scavenging-in-pandharpur/article5921391.ece.

[131] See *Campaign Against Manual Scavenging* v *State of Maharashtra & Others* PIL No. 8 of 2012, Order dated 5 March 2015 (Bombay High Court).

12

Rights of Sanitation Workers in India

P. Sakthivel, M. Nirmalkumar, and *Akshayaa Benjamin*

Since time immemorial, sanitation workers have been subjected to a hazardous work environment in India, and this position has not changed in spite of the early recognition of labour rights in the country.[1] The rights of sanitation workers are a matter of serious concern mainly due to issues such as deaths and diseases due to unsafe working conditions despite the existence of several laws on the subject. Regrettably, the safety of sanitation workers has not been asserted as a component of the right to sanitation in the regulatory instruments relating to sanitation.

Sanitation work in India is deeply connected to the caste system. The caste system has played an important role in the history of

[1] India has more than 80 years of legislative history on protecting labour rights. The Workmen's Compensation Act, 1923, The Trade Unions Act, 1926, and The Trade Disputes Act, 1929, were followed by legislation on labour subjects such as payment of wages, factories, minimum wages, abolition of child labour, maternity benefits, provident fund, bonus, and abolition of contract labour. Thus, a general legal framework was available for labour protection by the end of the 1960s.

occupations in India, and it remains relevant for sanitation workers of every category.[2] The 'unclean' occupations were forced on the scheduled castes (SCs),[3] and in modern times, sanitation work is indirectly forced on these communities.[4] This has been economically advantageous for the managers of sanitation work as there is a lower demand for health and monetary satisfaction from these communities due to poverty and denial of other employment opportunities owing to their caste. In the Indian context, therefore, a 'sanitation worker' must be defined based on the nature of work performed by him/her, and any discussion about sanitation workers will be incomplete if it does not delve into issues relating to caste. The caste-based division of occupations in India, and the denial of dignity to this occupation as well as to those who are engaged in it, has turned into a vicious cycle.

The term 'sanitation work' has necessarily evolved with advancements in science, technology, and urban management. Generally, sanitation work involves collection, transport, treatment, and disposal of human excreta, domestic wastewater, and solid waste, and associated hygiene promotion.[5] All those who are directly employed in the aforesaid work in India must be considered sanitation workers, as they are involved in a common employment dealing with human

[2] There is a clear link between historical discrimination and the present status of sanitation work, as caste sustains modernization and it is capable of reproduction. See Surinder S. Jodhka, *Caste in Contemporary India* (Routledge, 2015), 229.

[3] The historically disadvantaged castes have been known by different names, including Dalits, Harijans, untouchables, and lower castes. This chapter adopts the term 'scheduled castes' from the illustrative definition provided under Article 341 read with Article 366(24) of the Constitution of India.

[4] Social and economic compulsions, specifically, lack of other opportunities, uneducated families, and easy access to sanitation work through references, are the factors that indirectly force SCs in India to take up sanitation work. As a corollary, SCs are the least preferred in other employments.

[5] The term 'sanitation work' is based on the United Nations' understanding of 'sanitation' and 'sanitation work'. See Centre on Housing Rights and Evictions (COHRE), WaterAid, SDC and UN-Habitat, *Sanitation: A Human Rights Imperative* (COHRE, 2008), 2.

excreta and other municipal waste. Thus, the term 'sanitation workers' includes sweepers,[6] scavengers,[7] those who are involved in the cleaning of toilets, those involved in clearing of garbage, those assisting in the transportation of municipal solid waste, workers at landfills and disposal units, sewerage workers, assistants in sewage pumping stations, workers at sewage treatment plants, septic tank cleaners, cremators, post-mortem assistants, and any other person doing similar work.[8]

This chapter analyses to what extent the existing legal framework protects the rights of sanitation workers, most importantly, their safety, dignity, and health. The authors have adopted two methods to understand the working of laws and policies relating to sanitation workers. The first method is the responses to applications filed under the Right to Information (RTI) Act, 2005, which were addressed to various local authorities in the state of Tamil Nadu. The Annexure lists selected RTI responses, which are referred to in the chapter. Second, the authors interviewed around 100 sanitation workers employed in different categories of

[6] Takashi Shinoda classifies sweepers into dry and wet sweepers based on their primary duties in relation to disposal of wastes such as solid waste or sewage. But this chapter assumes that such distinctions are not necessary. See Takashi Shinoda, 'The Structure of Stagnancy: Sweepers in Ahmadabad District', in Ghanshyam Shah (ed), *Dalits and the State* (Centre for Rural Studies, 2002), 250.

[7] Though the term 'scavengers' is not used officially, those who are involved in cleaning toilets are still called 'scavengers' in most unofficial communications such as telephonic conversations.

[8] People are employed to clear dead bodies from railway tracks by the police and the railways, and there are persons who clean human waste of severely sick and hospitalized people. These persons also fit into the category of sanitation workers, as they are also employed in handling human waste. This definition also includes rag pickers as far as their services are not illegal. Rag pickers and other informal waste collectors are defined as 'waste picker' under rule 3(1) (58) of the Solid Waste Management Rules, 2016. See also Ministry of Environment, Forest and Climate Change, *Report of the High Level Committee to Review Various Acts administrated*, (Government of India, 2014) 90. It is to be noted that a Select Committee of Parliament has rejected the report.

sanitation work in different institutions. Applications under the RTI Act were filed and interviews were conducted to find out the nature of safety gadgets provided to the workers, the applicability of communal reservation policies, employment conditions, and health aspects including issues related to the consumption of alcohol and family status. The authors also relied on a host of secondary literature including empirical studies. This chapter adopts a national approach in analysing the rights of sanitation workers while drawing conclusions as to their implementation in the state of Tamil Nadu.[9]

Rights of Sanitation Workers

There is no single law in India that addresses the rights of sanitation workers. Instead, there are a number of laws that deal with different aspects of their rights. This section consolidates and discusses the rights of sanitation workers in the light of various relevant laws, for instance, laws relating to health, working conditions, safety, caste, and dignity. The enforcement of these laws is analysed mainly in the light of the fieldwork conducted by the authors in the state of Tamil Nadu.

Health and Safety

Sanitation work is perilous in nature, and results in several occupational hazards. Several technological measures have been introduced to overcome the repercussions of occupational hazards in the advanced sewerage and waste management systems of developed countries, whereas the legal instruments relating to solid waste and sewage in India seldom consider the health aspects of sanitation workers.[10] In general, the law relating to waste management in India has been a

---

[9] The state of Tamil Nadu is highly urbanized with 50 per cent of its population living in urban areas. SC constitute around 20 per cent of the total population in the state.

[10] For example, Solid Waste Management Rules, 2016.

failure mainly due to the lack of effective implementation.[11] In particular, in the context of the rights of sanitation workers, the minimal safety concerns expressed in these manuals have been largely ignored. This is evident, for instance, from field visits, newspaper reports, and documents obtained from various authorities in the state of Tamil Nadu.

For instance, as many as 30 sanitation workers died in sewerage systems between February 2012 and September 2013 in Tamil Nadu alone.[12] This is despite an order of the High Court of Madras regulating the entry of sewerage workers into manholes. These deaths were due to improper usage of machines, inadequate and unsuitable clothing, unsuitable boots and equipment, narrow streets and openings not suited to the available safety gadgets, and sewerage systems which are not modernized to use the equipment. Further, the higher officials refuse to insist on safety gadgets and devices partly due to their indifferent attitude, and partly due to the work pressure. For instance, an engineer narrated an incident where he was pressurized to clear a minor sewage leakage on a road used by the Chief Minister's convoy.[13] This forced the engineer not to insist on the safety gadgets for the sake of urgency. This explains how the

[11] Satwik Mudgal, 'A Clean Country in the Offing with New Solid Waste Management Rules', *Down to Earth* (30 November 2015); available at www.downtoearth.org.in/blog/a-clean-country-in-the-offing-with-new-solid-waste-rules-49484.

[12] A group of non-governmental organizations (NGOs) submitted a memorandum to the Government of Tamil Nadu to provide compensation to the families of deceased sewerage and septic tank workers. The group submitted a list of around 154 such workers. The list was primarily drawn from newspaper reports and workers' unions. It was very difficult to trace other victims as the police register these deaths under Section 174 of the Code of Criminal Procedure, 1973, which records deaths under all suspicious circumstances. A copy of the memorandum is available on file with the authors. See also B. Kolappan, 'New Law No Relief for Manual Scavengers', *The Hindu* (12 September 2013); available at www.thehindu. com/news/national/tamil-nadu/New-law-no-relief-to-manual-scavengers/article11864581.ece.

[13] Interview conducted by Sakthivel with Metro Water engineer, May 2012.

administration gets its routine work done, often by exposing workers to an unsafe working environment.

Sanitation workers are prone to a number of diseases. For instance, a report estimates that sanitation workers are vulnerable to at least 680 ailments.[14] The field study conducted by the authors also reveals that sanitation workers are prone to serious injuries due to solid objects such as blades, projecting glass, and other sharp-edged or pointed objects, and contaminated water which could lead to skin diseases, besides damage to their eyes due to gases like hydrogen sulphide.[15] It is evident from the authors' visits to hospitals that sanitation workers carry out their work without any protection, and thus are exposed to various medical and other wastes. All sanitation workers are not exposed to a uniform set of health hazards; however, the nature of ailments is equally serious.[16] Most of the workers do not understand the side effects of working in such environments, and they are unaware of the minimal legal protection available to them through enactments and judgments. They continue their work with severe implications for their health and safety, because alternative employments are not open to them due to lack of social recognition or unemployability.

The situation of sanitation workers employed by local bodies to maintain drainage systems, latrines, and urinals, or to remove filth

---

[14] The cited report was prepared by the NGO Kamdar Swasthya Suraksha Mandal, and referred to by the High Court of Gujarat in *Praveen Rashtrapal, IRS & Others* v *Chief Officer, Kadi Municipality* (2006) 3 GLR 1809 (High Court of Gujarat, 2006) ('*Praveen Rashtrapal*').

[15] See also A. Selvaraj, 'Worker Dies While Cleaning Sewage Tank', *The Times of India* (11 February 2012); available at http://articles.timesofindia.indiatimes.com/2012-02-11/chennai/31049799_1_sewage-scb-officials-sanitary-worker.

[16] The authors witnessed the different types of health hazards faced by sanitation workers during field visits in Tamil Nadu. A report also suggests that around 66 per cent of sanitation workers in Delhi are affected by occupational diseases. See Praxis Institute for Participatory Practices, *Down the Drain: A Study on Occupational and Health Hazards and the Perils of Contracting Faced by Sewerage Workers in Delhi* (Praxis Institute for Participatory Practices, 2014), 34.

and rubbish within their local jurisdiction is also no different from the general scenario.[17] The working conditions of sanitation workers of all local bodies are repulsive and relatively similar, as their common workplaces such as streets and public places do not have proper waste disposal mechanisms. Various officers are employed as sanitary inspectors and under other titles in the state establishments. These officers are supposed to maintain a hygienic environment for the locality. While the local bodies are entrusted with the duty to maintain a clean and hygienic environment in a locality, they are not under any legal obligation to maintain safe and dignified working conditions for sanitation workers. There is no legal mechanism to ensure the safety and health of sanitation workers. The local bodies have never assumed a protective role for sanitation workers in spirit, practice, or law.

The obligation of the state to provide medical and insurance facilities to sanitation workers was discussed in a high court judgment.[18] However, no such insurance or health programme is available specifically for sanitation workers. Very few municipalities conduct regular medical check-ups for their employees. Health insurance schemes are available only to permanent employees of these local bodies.[19] This being the case, workers who are employed temporarily and on contract basis, cannot avail these schemes. Due to their vulnerabilities, non-permanent workers of local bodies are the victims of a majority of the accidents.

Some of the labour laws are not applicable to sanitation workers. However, they occasionally deal with situations and hazards similar to the ones faced by them. For instance, the Factories Act, 1948,

---

[17] Chapter VII of The Chennai City Municipal Corporation Act, 1919, deals with 'Water Supply, Lighting and Drainage'. Similarly, The Gujarat Municipalities Act, 1964, includes provisions relating to public health and sanitation (For example, s 87).

[18] *Praveen Rashtrapal* (n 14).

[19] These health insurance schemes and annual medical check-ups are meant for all public sector employees without discrimination. The insurance coverage under these insurance schemes is limited to scheduled diseases, which are common for everyone; it is not occupation specific. Moreover, the non-applicability of these schemes to other sanitation workers makes them less meaningful.

provides a series of procedures and medical check-ups for people employed in factories. It provides safeguards against the entry of a person into confined spaces by stipulating a manhole of adequate size or other effective means of egress, breathing apparatus, and other measures. This provision addresses situations similar to those faced by sewerage workers. Despite the inapplicability of the law to sanitation workers, it illustrates the legal protection available to workers facing similar hazards.[20]

The Contract Labour (Regulation and Abolition) Act, 1970, imposes certain liabilities on the principal employer and contractor for the welfare of the contract labourers in the workplace. Section 19 of the Act, which is entitled 'First-aid Facilities', states that when a contract worker is employed for doing sanitation work, the contractor shall provide and maintain a first aid box readily accessible during all working hours with the prescribed contents at the place of work. According to the Child Labour (Prohibition and Regulation) Act, 1986, a child is prohibited from engaging in an occupation connected with cinder picking, clearing of ash pits, or building operations in railways; work in abattoirs/slaughterhouses; or as domestic workers or servants.[21] It further forbids children to work in processes connected with rag picking and scavenging.[22]

Some labour legislation provides social security for workers who are injured in the course of employment. For instance, the Employees State Insurance Act, 1948, provides for better health conditions and insurance benefits to industrial workers. The Act further speaks of sickness, maternity, and disablement benefits. The benefits under this law are also available to contract workers and casual workers as

---

[20] The Factories Act, 1948, s 36. These procedures are not available to sanitation workers since the scope of The Factories Act, 1948, is narrow, and applicable only to establishments which could be defined as a factory.

[21] The Child Labour (Prohibition and Regulation) Act, 1986, s 3, Part A of the Schedule, entries 2, 7, and 14, respectively. Section 3, which is titled 'Prohibition of Employment of Children in Certain Occupations and Processes', prohibits the employment of children in any occupations set forth in Part A of the Schedule.

[22] The Child Labour (Prohibition and Regulation) Act (n 21), s 3, Part B of the Schedule, entry 57.

held by the Supreme Court.[23] The occupational diseases listed in this Act include skin diseases, diseases due to contact with certain chemicals including nitrous fumes, halogen derivatives of hydrocarbons, chromium, and so on, which are not uncommon in the field of sanitation work.[24] Similarly, the Employee's Compensation Act, 1923, makes provision for the payment of compensation by certain classes of employers to their workmen for injury by accident. Only a few states like Tamil Nadu and Kerala have extended the benefits of this law to sanitation workers.[25]

Waste management is regulated by the rules made by the Central Government under the Environment (Protection) Act, 1986. The Solid Waste Management Rules, 2016, provide that the local authorities are responsible for the proper disposal of wastes, and they also prescribe standards concerning working conditions.[26] The

---

[23] The Employees State Insurance Act, 1948, ss 49, 50, and 51 deals with sickness benefit, maternity benefits, and disablement benefit, respectively. In *ESI Corporation* v *South India Flour Mills (Pvt.) Ltd.* AIR 1986 SC 1686 (Supreme Court of India, 1986), the Court clearly held that this Act is also applicable for the welfare of casual workers. In *ESI Corporation* v *Vijayamohini Mills* 76 FJR 246 (Kerala) (High Court of Kerala, 1990), the court applied this Act to workers engaged by contractors.

[24] The Employees State Insurance Act (n 23), Schedule III, List of Occupational Diseases.

[25] The Government of Kerala has included persons 'employed in any sewage farming, planting, irrigating or harvesting of fodder grass or in diverting of sewage water or in cleaning of main channel or sub-carriers' (Kerala Gazette, 9 November 1982) and those 'employed in cleaning of sewers or septic tanks by any local authority' (Kerala Gazette, 27 January 1990). Similarly, the Government of Tamil Nadu has included persons 'employed as a sweeper or scavenger under a local authority' (Tamil Nadu Gazette, 14 November 1973) and persons 'employed in cleaning of sewers or septic tanks within the local limits of a local authority' (Tamil Nadu Gazette, 5 August 1987).

[26] The Solid Waste Management Rules, 2016, replaced the Municipal Solid Wastes (Management and Handling) Rules, 2000. The new rules have similar provisions regarding safety gadgets and training for workers. The conclusions arrived at, by the authors, are based on the working of the previous rules.

rules expressly prohibit the manual handling of waste. However, there is lack of awareness and coordination, and non-availability of suitable safety gadgets for handling municipal solid waste. The same explanation could be given for the failure to comply with the safety procedures for sewerage management. The rules and judgments mandating safety gadgets do not have adequate enforcement mechanisms. Moreover, the workers are not in a position to demand their rights due to the temporary nature of their employment and/or the attitude of the authorities and public alike towards them.

Other waste management rules such as the Hazardous and Other Wastes (Management and Transboundary Movement) Rules, 2016, require the occupiers to take adequate steps to ensure safety while handling hazardous wastes to contain contaminants, prevent accidents, and limit their consequences for human beings and the environment. The occupiers' responsibility extends to providing persons working on the site with training, equipment, and information necessary to ensure their safety.[27] Similar provisions are enumerated in the E-Waste (Management and Handling) Rules, 2010, the waste management rules relating to plastic wastes, and bio medical wastes.[28] The waste management rules are complicated in terms of creating a protective mechanism for sanitation workers due to the multiplicity of agencies involved in the implementation process. For instance, the Solid Waste Management Rules, 2016, create obligations for six central ministries, state governments, the Central Pollution Control Board (CPCB) and state pollution control boards (SPCBs), local bodies, and District magistrates. Further,

---

[27] Rule 4 is entitled 'Responsibility of Occupier for the Handling of Hazardous Wastes'. Hazardous wastes include wastes such as cyanide wastes, metal-finishing wastes, and other chemical compounds as per the Schedule to the Rules. These rules replace the Hazardous Waste (Management, Handling and Transboundary Movement) Rules, 2008, without any significance for sanitation workers.

[28] The Plastics (Manufacture, Usage and Waste Management) Rules, 2009, and the Bio Medical Wastes (Management and Handling) Rules, 1998, were replaced by the Plastic Waste Management Rules, 2016, and the Bio-medical Waste Management Rules, 2016, respectively.

they establish state-level advisory bodies to monitor the implementation of the rules.[29]

The courts in India have shown some concern for the health and welfare of workers in hazardous employments when claims of serious human rights violations are addressed to it. One such case is *Delhi Jal Board* v *National Campaign for Dignity and Rights of Sewerage and Allied Workers & Others*,[30] where the Supreme Court observed that there is no legal protection for workers in the unorganized sector despite their services being used for the benefit of the public at large and involving huge risks that frequently cost them their lives. The case also brought to light the fact that the contractors did not provide first aid kits, respiratory masks, or portable ladders to the workers as required by the guidelines issued by the National Human Rights Commission (NHRC).[31] The Madras High Court formulated a set of guidelines to be followed while employing sewerage workers.[32] The court issued directions prohibiting the entry of workers into manholes except under certain circumstances, which are elucidated in the order. Even in those extraordinary circumstances, the worker must be given adequate safety gadgets and equipment.[33] The judgments of higher courts have been influential in creating awareness amongst workers and authorities, although the rights declared in these judgments have hardly been realized.[34]

---

[29] The Solid Waste Management Rules, 2016, rule 23.

[30] 2011 STPL (Web) 593 SC (Supreme Court of India, 2011).

[31] The NHRC has been intervening in the issue of manual scavenging since the 1990s. Its recommendations and proceedings have influenced policymakers and the judiciary. But its recommendations have lost their relevance due to the passage of The Prohibition of Employment as Manual Scavengers and their Rehabilitation Act, 2013. See National Human Rights Commission, *Human Rights and Manual Scavenging* (NHRC, 2011).

[32] *A. Narayanan* v *The Chief Secretary, Government of Tamil Nadu & Others* WP No. 24403 of 2008 (High Court of Madras, Judgment dated 20 November 2008) ('*Narayanan*').

[33] *Narayanan* (n 32).

[34] Judgments insist on the safety of workers, but on a larger scale, these orders do not influence the field engineers who are supposed to monitor the sanitation workers. Even if they know the importance given to sanitation workers in the enactments and judgments, they do not care about the

The unsafe working conditions have also led to other issues affecting the social and personal life, and health of sanitation workers. Based on the interviews conducted by the authors with sanitation workers in Tamil Nadu, it is evident that a large number of workers are alcoholics, and fall into the trap of other such habits that are injurious to their health. As a matter of fact, the general public and local body officers offer alcohol to the workers involved in sanitation work in exchange for their services.[35] The workers usually consume alcohol, as the stink may not permit them to work under normal circumstances. During the interviews, 43 out of 100 workers admitted that they consume alcohol because of their workload, and the stink that emanates during their work. 20 of them said that they drink during work. Alcohol is consumed generally by men as women workers are not usually engaged in severely foul-smelling operations such as sewage cleaning in manholes.[36] The alcohol consumption is proportionately higher with increased level of stench and hazard. Alternatively, or in addition to alcohol, smoking and tobacco chewing are common among sanitation workers. Apart from health hazards, these practices affect their matrimonial life, children, and social status.[37]

---

consequences, as their superiors will not take any strict action against them since they belong to the same cadre. According to one engineer: 'if we strictly implement the court orders, we can't maintain sewerage system'. See Pon Vasanth Arunachalam, 'Engineers Not Booked Under Scavenging Act', *The New Indian Express* (16 October 2015), 9.

[35] This seems to be an age-old practice. See S. Ramakrishnan, *Maraikkappatta India (Tamil)* (4th edn, Vikatan Publications, 2015), 278, indicating that the 'British Government supplied free food and alcohol for who came forward to clean human corpse [*sic*] during Bengal riots in August 1946'. The authors are personally aware of the practice of giving money to purchase alcohol for those who are engaged in cremation work. Because of this practice, at times, the workers also refuse to dig burial pits or make arrangements for cremation if they are not provided with alcohol.

[36] The authors limit themselves to this observation about women workers in the workplace. There may also be cultural limitations restricting women from consuming alcohol.

[37] A large percentage of workers obtained loans for health and family expenses from the unorganized sector at a higher interest rate, leading to unproductive family expenditure. This research work has not particularly

Right against Caste-Based Exploitation and Discrimination

There is empirical evidence and theoretical understanding of the continuing link between caste and sanitation work. An overwhelming majority of sanitation workers belong to the lowest strata of the caste hierarchy.[38] Invariably, they are members of the untouchable caste. A study on the caste system demonstrates its continuing presence in modern India; not of caste's traditional face but its 'modern' face.[39] It is argued that against the assumptions of modernization, caste continues to be 'performed with ever more vigour and resilience in post-independence India'.[40] Dr B.R. Ambedkar believed that the SCs must collectively and permanently withdraw from menial occupations.[41] Unfortunately, such a call was difficult to be complied with by the community due to several factors.

The Constitution of India guarantees the right to equality as a fundamental right. Article 15 of the Constitution declares that the state shall not discriminate against any person on the basis of caste. Moreover, Article 17 categorically abolishes untouchability and declares it an offence. The constitutionally guaranteed reservation for members of the SCs and STs is aimed at equilibrium in public employment. There are various pieces of legislation, for example, the Protection of Civil Rights Act, 1955, which punish infliction of social disabilities on the basis of caste. Nevertheless, caste continues to be the basis of many forms of discrimination against people belonging to the lower castes, particularly, the SCs and

---

investigated the debt conditions of sanitation workers, but this fact was revealed during interviews. This observation is supported by an empirical study on the debt conditions of sanitation workers elsewhere. See Takashi Shinoda, *Marginalization in the Midst of Modernization: A Study of Sweepers in Western India* (Manohar, 2005), 246.

[38] Jodhka (n 2), 31.

[39] Subrata Misra, 'Caste, Democracy and Politics of Community Formation in India', in Margaret Searle-Chatterjee and Ursula Sharma (eds), *Contextualizing Caste* (Blackwell, 1994) 49.

[40] Misra (n 39).

[41] Vijay Prashad, *Untouchable Freedom: A Social History of a Dalit Community* (Oxford University Press, 2000), 168.

STs.[42] Thus, the High Court of Punjab and Haryana has declared, in a case concerning the rights of sewerage workers, that employment of a person in cleaning sewage is nothing but a modern extension of abhorrent practices like untouchability and manual scavenging.[43] For instance, in Gobichettipalayam municipality in Tamil Nadu, where manual scavenging was abolished long ago,[44] the authors witnessed the continuation of insanitary work practices, with 100 per cent of the workforce belonging to the SCs.

People from other castes seldom take up sanitation work as it is considered undignified. The caste dimension of sanitation work is clear from the responses received under the RTI Act. Local bodies such as municipalities in Tamil Nadu do not have a recruitment policy for the employment of sanitation workers. Information received under the RTI Act reveals that certain municipalities have employed only members of SCs for sanitation work (for instance, Kancheepuram and Sathyamangalam). In all the municipalities analysed, SCs and STs constituted 90–00 per cent of sanitation workers.[45] The remaining 10 per cent of sanitation workers belonged to other disadvantaged communities.[46] Some municipalities responded that they neither

[42] The Scheduled Castes and Scheduled Tribes (Prevention of Atrocities) Act, 1989, lists and prohibits atrocities and discriminatory practices against the SCs and STs. A report suggests that none of the rules under this Act have been fully complied with by state governments. See Aloysius Irudayam S.J. and Jayashree Mangubhai, *20 Years of Scheduled Castes and Scheduled Tribes (Prevention of Atrocities) Act, 1988: A Report Card* (National Coalition for Strengthening SC and ST (PoA) Act, 2010), 33; available at https://idsn. org/wp-content/uploads/user_folder/pdf/New_files/India/SCST_PoA_ Act_20_years_report_card_-_NCDHR.pdf.

[43] *Sewerage Employees Union (Registered), MC Chandigarh & Another* v *Union of India & Another* CWP No. 1983 of 2008 (High Court of Punjab and Haryana, Judgment dated 10 December 2008) ('Sewerage Employees Union').

[44] 'Crusader against Caste Oppression and Untouchability', *The Hindu* (6 February 2007); available at www.thehindu.com/todays-paper/tp-national/ tp-tamilnadu/crusader-against-caste-oppression-and-untouchability/ article1792408.ece.

[45] See the Annexure to this chapter.

[46] The backward communities in Tamil Nadu are further divided into two categories: Backward and Most Backward. There are as many as 41

follow state employment reservation policies and laws, nor do they maintain community-wise details of sanitation workers. This could be to suppress the fact that sanitation workers are predominantly members of the SCs. In most of the municipalities, workers are initially recruited on contract basis. After suffering as contract workers on a meagre salary in an unsecure environment, their work is regularized on the ground of charity, and not as a matter of right. This malicious process ensures their continuous and unconditional subordination to superiors. Thus, sanitation workers are often reminded of their route of entry into the employment if they claim any of their rights. Statutory salary is the only advantage realized by sanitation workers who are permanent employees of local bodies.

The commissions established to protect the rights of SCs and STs such as the National Commission for Scheduled Castes and Scheduled Tribes and the National Commission for Safai Karamcharis (NCSK), have expressed dismay that their recommendations are not taken seriously. It is clear that the legislative mechanisms have not safeguarded the rights of sanitation workers against caste discrimination and untouchability.[47]

Working Conditions and Dignity

It is constitutionally recognized that the right to life means the right to live with dignity as against mere animal existence. The Supreme Court, while elaborating this view, has held that the right to life means something more than just physical survival.[48] Moreover, it is the obligation of the state to promote the welfare of the people by securing and protecting a social order in which justice—social, economic, and political—shall inform all the institutions of national

---

communities notified as Most Backward Communities (MBCs), and 68 communities recognized as Denotified Communities by the Government of Tamil Nadu.

[47] Report of the Subgroup on Safai Karamcharies, submitted to the Working Group on the 'Empowerment of Scheduled Castes' for the Eleventh Five Year Plan (2007–12).

[48] *Kharak Singh* v *State of Uttar Pradesh* AIR 1963 SC 1295 (Supreme Court of India, 1962).

life.[49] This directive principle incorporates part of the preamble in the Constitution concerning social, economic, and political justice.[50] In *Air India Statutory Corporation*,[51] a full bench of the Supreme Court declared that the concept of social justice in Article 38 of the Constitution is a dynamic device to mitigate the sufferings of the poor, the weak, Dalits, the tribes, and the deprived sections of the society, and to elevate them to live a life with dignity. It is a constitutional mandate under Article 42 that the state must secure just and humane conditions of work.

A perusal of legislation regarding the abolition of manual scavenging and its various forms in India is required to understand the link between manual scavenging and sanitation work. The Employment of Manual Scavengers and Construction of Dry Latrines (Prohibition) Act, 1993 ('1993 Act'), prohibited manual scavenging and its various forms as carried out by sanitation workers. The 1993 Act was often criticized for its very narrow application as far as 'manual scavenging' is concerned.[52] This is because most of the sanitation workers are in effect manual scavengers. In this context, it is worthwhile to note that the Prohibition of Employment as Manual Scavengers and their Rehabilitation Act, 2013 ('2013 Act'), prohibits all persons, local authorities, or any agency from engaging or employing, either directly or indirectly, any person for hazardous cleaning of a sewer or a septic tank.[53] Hazardous cleaning for this purpose means manual cleaning of a sewer or a septic tank without the employer fulfilling his obligations to provide protective

[49] Constitution of India, Art. 38 (1).

[50] Constitution of India, preamble, Art. 38(1). See generally V.N. Shukla, *Constitution of India* (10th edn, Eastern Book Company, reprint, 2006), 302.

[51] *Air India Statutory Corporation* v *United Labour Union* AIR 1997 SC 645 (Supreme Court of India, 1996).

[52] Samuel Sathyaseelan, 'Neglect of Sewerage Workers: Concerns about the New Act', (2013) XLVII(49) *Economic & Political Weekly* 33.

[53] The Prohibition of Employment as Manual Scavengers and their Rehabilitation Act, 2013 ('2013 Act'), s 7 deals with 'Prohibition of Persons from Engagement or Employment for Hazardous Cleaning of Sewers and Septic Tanks'.

gear and other cleaning devices, and ensuring observance of safety precautions.[54] Therefore, the 2013 Act prohibits certain manifestations of manual scavenging work undertaken by sanitation workers. However, an extended definition of manual scavenging or benefits will provide limited help to sanitation workers, as experiences with these enactments are not optimistic.

State governments have shown reluctance to implement the provisions of the 2013 Act. The rule-making power under the Act is vested with governments;[55] officers are to be appointed[56] for the monitoring and implementation of the Act, and committees[57] are to be established. Tamil Nadu has notified this legislation.[58] The identification of manual scavengers,[59] for the purpose of ensuring that the benefits reach them, faces many constraints at the administrative level. For instance, workers with a job description 'sweepers' or 'menials' are not accepted as manual scavengers in the identification process though many of them directly carry human waste. Consequently, even a state agency has opined that the identification of manual scavengers is incomplete.[60] This is one reason for adopting a different

[54] 2013 Act (n 53), s 2(d) defines the expression 'hazardous cleaning'.

[55] 2013 Act (n 53), s 36(1).

[56] 2013 Act (n 53), s 20(1).

[57] 2013 Act (n 53), ss 24(1), 26(1), and 29(1).

[58] GOM No. 40, Municipal Administration and Water Supply, Government of Tamil Nadu, 5 March 2015.

[59] Discussions with various organizations revealed that a large number of sanitation workers employed in various forms of manual scavenging are not permitted to enrol in the list of manual scavengers to receive benefits under various schemes.

[60] Press Information Bureau, Ministry of Social Justice and Empowerment, Government of India, 'National Commission for Safai Karamcharis Reviews Implementation of the Prohibition of Employment as Manual Scavengers and their Rehabilitation Act 2013' (29 September 2014). The Chairman of the Commission opined: 'The progress of the implementation of the Act is extremely poor. The surveys reportedly conducted by the States to identify the manual scavengers and the insanitary latrines are not done in a proper manner and the questions are being raised about their credibility and accuracy of figures.' Ministry of Social Justice and Empowerment, 'National Commission for Safai Karamcharis Reviews Implementation'.

approach towards abolishing manual scavenging in this chapter; an approach to protect all sanitation workers during their regular course of employment, irrespective of arbitrary nomenclatures used by the administration or employers.[61]

The dignity of a worker involved in waste management is directly related to the safety of the working environment. According to the Solid Waste Management Rules, 2016, the facilities that are to be provided at the site[62] include drinking water, bathing facilities, and lighting arrangements for easy landfill operations, and safety provisions including periodic health inspection of workers at the landfill site.[63]

Labour legislation provides certain safeguards with the general object of protecting all workers. For instance, the Minimum Wages Act, 1948, secures a minimum limit of wages for certain employments, which are enumerated in the Schedule of the Act, and in certain cases may, at the discretion of the appropriate government, be extended to any other employment. In the case of contract employment, it is the duty of the principal employer to ensure that the contract workers are paid minimum wages.[64] Similarly, the Employees Provident Funds

[61] 'Sanitation workers' have many job titles such as scavengers, sweepers, sewerage workers, sanitary workers, sanitation workers, cleanliness workers, and other names used in their respective establishments. But the authors argue that sanitation practices in India and working conditions obviously compel every worker involved in 'sanitation work' to be a 'manual scavenger'.

[62] Schedule I of the Solid Waste Management Rules, 2016, provides 'Specifications for Sanitary Landfill'. The term 'landfilling' is not defined in the 2016 rules. According to rule 3(xi) of the 2000 rules, 'landfilling' means 'disposal of residual solid wastes on land in a facility designed with protective measures against pollution of ground water, surface water and air fugitive dust, wind-blown litter, bad odour, fire hazard, bird menace, pest rodents, greenhouse gas emissions, slope instability and erosion'. Instead, the 2016 rules define 'dump site', which means land utilized by a local body for disposal of solid waste without following the principles of sanitary land filling.

[63] Solid Waste Management Rules, 2016, Schedule I, part B.

[64] *General Manager, Aligarh Dugdh Utpadak Sahakari Sangh Ltd. (Parag Dairy) Sasni, Hathras* v *Prescribed Authority, Minimum Wages & Dy. Labour Commissioner, Aligarh* 2009 LLR 316 (Allahabad High Court, 2009).

and Miscellaneous Provisions Act, 1952, also applies to sanitation workers engaged through contractors. The responsibility of the contractors cannot be cavilled anymore in the opinion of the courts.[65] The Employers Liability Act, 1938, was framed with a view that the employer shall not be allowed to take the defence of common employment in case an injury is caused to the workman by his direct negligence or the negligence of any other person under his delegation or supervision.[66] It also makes void any contract that limits or excludes the liability of the employer if an employee suffers personal injuries due to the negligence of persons in common employment with him.[67] The Contract Labour (Regulation and Abolition) Act, 1970, directs the appropriate government to make rules relating to the provision of canteens, restrooms, and other facilities including wholesome drinking water, urinals, latrines, and washing facilities.[68] This enabling provision is not used by governments for the benefit of sanitation workers despite the increasing number of contractual workers in sanitation work.

The failure of these laws is exposed by cases filed by workers' associations, non-governmental organizations (NGOs), and public-spirited individuals, highlighting the undignified treatment meted out to sanitation workers. For example, in *Sewerage Employees Union*,[69] the Supreme Court took cognizance of the fact that sewer lines contain human excreta in solid and semi-solid forms, and hence, the cleaning of a sewer line is nothing but the practice of manual scavenging. The Court observed that this constituted a derogation of the dignity, health, and safety of the workers. Similarly, in *Praveen Rashtrapal*,[70] the High Court of Gujarat prohibited the employment of human

---

[65] See *M/s S.K. Nasiruddin Beedi Merchant Ltd* v *Central Provident Fund Commissioner* AIR 2001 SC 850 (Supreme Court of India, 2001).

[66] The Employers Liability Act, 1938, s 3 bars the defence of common employment in certain cases.

[67] The Employers Liability Act (n 66), s 3A on 'Contracting Out'.

[68] Sections 16, 17, and 18 of The Contract Labour (Regulation and Abolition) Act, 1970, direct the appropriate government to make rules in this regard.

[69] *Sewerage Employees Union* (n 43).

[70] *Praveen Rashtrapal* (n 14).

agency in sewerage lines unless it was absolutely necessary. The court provided a schedule of equipment, which is to be purchased by local bodies for cleaning sewer lines. Even in extraordinary cases where human beings have to be employed in manholes, the court prescribed a number of steps for the protection of the workers. It directed the officials to impart training to the workers, equip them with safety gadgets when they dive into a manhole, conduct periodic medical check-ups, and implement a comprehensive insurance policy. In *Narayanan*,[71] the Madras High Court gave a similar ruling.

The dignity of sanitation workers has always been at stake, and discrimination continues even today in the working of the legal framework. Sanitation workers are not provided with adequate safety gadgets or with just and humane working conditions. Based on interviews with sanitation workers and information obtained on the basis of RTI applications, it appears that the protection or safety aspects dealt with in the Solid Waste Management Rules are seldom respected. It is to be noted that 29 out of 100 respondents stated that they clean human excreta manually or with a broom as a matter of routine work. Similarly, RTI responses show that many municipalities do not provide holidays to sanitation workers. It is mandatory for them to work half day on any public holiday and Sundays. They are not even paid extra wages for the work done on holidays. There is no approved break time for breakfast or refreshments. In one instance, a worker was not permitted to sign the attendance register for drinking a cup of tea during her working hours. Assuming that her deviation is not proper, the denial of attendance, which may have implications for her remuneration, is disproportionate and illegal. The workers are not provided with common rooms for leisure, and facilities to even sit in the office or workplace. It is not uncommon to see sanitation workers sitting in the veranda of the office waiting for instructions from their employers or supervisors. If anything goes missing in the office, the first call goes to them, coupled with a suspicion. Ensuring safety of sanitation workers and creating a safe working environment are merely starting points towards recognizing their 'dignity'. It is equally important to address the issue of indifference of society in general.

[71] *Narayanan* (n 32).

Political Movements and Legal Reforms

The politicization of the plight of sanitation workers and their struggles to get recognition for their rights has been shaped since the British Raj in India.[72] It was on the political agenda of almost all the political parties to abolish manual scavenging and modernize sanitation services to improve the working conditions of sanitation workers. Abolition of manual scavenging involves caste politics and mobilizing the sanitation workforce, besides legislative measures. The political efforts have culminated in various debates both inside and outside Parliament. There have been consistent efforts by various organizations to improve the working conditions of sanitation workers by organized bargaining and litigation.[73] Many committees and recommendations have preceded the present political and legal position in respect of the issue.

Sanitation Workers and Politics

There were at least three committees on the working conditions of scavengers and sweepers within 20 years of independence. The first committee concerned the state of Bombay, and its report, published in 1958, dealt with abolition of the customary rights of sanitation workers,[74] elimination of the hand removal method, minimum wages, and other service conditions. Thereafter a number of committees were appointed by the Central Government. Some

[72] See Susan E. Chaplin, *The Politics of Sanitation in India: Cities, Services and the State* (Orient BlackSwan, 2011), 160. The author discusses political and legal developments since the British era in detail.

[73] See generally Vijay Prashad, 'Between Economism and Emancipation: Untouchables and Indian Nationalism, 1920–1950', (1995) 3(1) *Left History* 5.

[74] 'Customary rights' are the claims of certain North-Indian communities over taking up cleansing work in certain areas, or/and collecting night soil to be sold as manure. Though 'customary rights' are abolished, the process of abolition was the subject of some protest. See Susan E. Chaplin, 'Scavengers: Still Marginalized', in Ghanshyam Shah (ed), *Dalits and the State* (Centre for Rural Studies, 2002), 220.

of their recommendations were converted into binding rules, while many recommendations were ignored. Though these committees were empathetic towards sanitation workers, they assumed that particular castes would remain in sanitation work.[75] The recommendations of these committees were never considered seriously. For instance, in the 1950s, the Barve Committee recommended the abolition and criminalization of manual scavenging, which is yet to be fully accomplished.

It is appropriate to look into the political, policy, and legal developments relating to sanitation workers in the subsequent years. A few organizations successfully espoused and politicized the cause of sanitation workers, and their first challenge was the abolition of manual scavenging in law and practice. Among others, the Safai Karmachari Andolan (SKA) has contributed significantly by reaching the masses and public institutions. The Nagpur Declaration adopted by the People's Alliance against Untouchability, inter alia, demanded an expansion of the definition of the term 'manual scavenger'.[76] In a march towards the South Asian Association for Regional Cooperation (SAARC) Secretariat in Kathmandu, the South Asia Regional Campaign consisting of members of parliament (MPs), civil society organizations, and campaigners from countries including India, demanded a 'Right to Sanitation for All'. The entourage submitted a Citizens Charter, which demanded that the governments of South Asia eliminate all forms of manual scavenging and ensure dignity and equality for

[75] 'The Barve, Malkani and Pandya reports have been emphatic on the need for providing employment to holders of customary rights in the sewage and cleaning departments of the municipalities, and on the improvement of the employment and working conditions of these employees. This view is based on the premise that the sweeper caste would remain in their monopolised labour market, and that the government and local bodies would continue to absorb them in sufficient numbers. The proposals in these reports aim at normalising the unstable and severe employment and working conditions of the most backward community among the SCs.' See Shinoda (n 37).

[76] The Nagpur Declaration (29 August 2010); available at http:/ dalitkerala.files.wordpress.com/2010/09/nagpur-declaration.doc. Some of the demands have been accepted through the 2013 Act.

the sanitation workforce.[77] It further insisted that the disposal and management of human waste should be carried out in strict conformity with the principles of protection of human rights, health, and environmental sustainability.[78]

The Aadi Tamilar Pervai (ATP), the social movement of the Arunthathiar community,[79] has organized political agitations in the state of Tamil Nadu to demonstrate the plight of sanitation workers. The organization has conducted conferences, and demanded that the state improve the working conditions and wages, and provide retirement benefits, as well as dignified treatment for sanitation workers.[80] The efforts of such organizations have led to a 3 per cent inner reservation for the Arunthathiar community in Tamil Nadu.[81] This has been hailed in other parts of India, and similar reservations have been demanded in some other states.[82]

The health of sanitation workers has also been the subject matter of parliamentary debates. Shri Arjun Ram Meghwal, an MP,

[77] End Water Poverty, 'South Asia Regional Campaign on Right to Sanitation Launches Today' (19 March 2013); available at www.endwaterpoverty.org/blog/south-asia-regional-campaign-right-sanitation-launches-today.

[78] End Water Poverty (n 77). Articles 10 and 11 of the Charter speak of elimination of all forms of manual scavenging, and state that disposal of human waste be done in strict compliance with principles of human rights.

[79] This community is one of the most vulnerable SCs in terms of poverty, relatively less access to state institutions, and public employment. Unclean occupations, such as manual scavenging, are usually associated with this caste. They stand as the lowest of the SCs in the hierarchy.

[80] Resolution passed in the conference held in Coimbatore on 26 December 2004, cited in 'Another Battle to Fight against Indignity' (In Tamil, *Ilivai Olikka Innumor Por*) (Coimbatore, Aadi Tamilar Peravai, 2008), 64.

[81] The Tamil Nadu *Arunthathiyars* (Special Reservation of Seats in Educational Institutions Including Private Educational Institutions and of Appointments or Posts in the Services under the State within the Reservation for the Scheduled Castes) Act, 2009.

[82] The Nagpur Declaration (n 76) seeks 5 per cent reservation for children of manual scavengers in educational institutions on par with the inner reservation followed in Tamil Nadu.

urged the Union Government to extend appropriate insurance schemes to sewerage workers. The debate widely discussed all aspects of the safety of sewerage workers in India.[83] Earlier Mr Kharventhan, another MP, urged the government to allot necessary funds under the Jawaharlal Nehru National Urban Renewal Mission (JNNURM) to humanize sewerage and garbage work.[84] Unfortunately, these debates did not lead to any fruitful policy suggestions or schemes.

The National Urban Sanitation Policy (NUSP) does not speak specifically about the welfare of sanitation workers, except for the obligations of implementing agencies to suggest specific rules, though such efforts are not traceable.[85] In 2010, the Government of Tamil Nadu drafted a policy, which declares that access to sanitation is a fundamental human right, and ensures the dignity of individuals. The draft recognizes the occupational hazard faced by sanitary workers and states, '... the government has taken steps to fully mechanise the sewer clearing operation in the underground sewerage system in the urban local bodies of the state. The Government is keen in taking care of the interest of the workers in sanitation area and in ensuring occupational safety of urban operation'. The draft policy was presented to the general public.[86] Unfortunately, a 2012 draft of the policy omits the concerns of the sanitation

[83] Lok Sabha debate, Shri Arjun Ram Meghwal called the attention of the Minister of Social Justice and Empowerment to the need to take adequate safety measures to protect the lives of safai karamcharis (sewer cleaners), and provide health insurance cover to them (20 December 2011); available at http://indiankanoon.org/doc/58005662/.

[84] Lok Sabha debate, Need to Provide Protection to the Sewage Workers Working in Man-made Holes in the Country (4 December 2007); available at https://indiankanoon.org/doc/394843/.

[85] Annexure II to the NUSP, 'Specifying Legal and Regulatory Institutional Responsibilities' states that an 'implementing agency will examine the law and rules in this regard and make recommendations for the task force to make rules explicit regarding ... designs and systems for safe collection'.

[86] The Director of Municipal Administration presented the draft policy to the public on 20 June 2010.

workers.[87] The status of rural sanitation workers is also mostly neglected in schemes and policy documents.[88] For example, a draft of the Rajasthan Rural Sanitation Policy does not refer to anything related to sanitation workers.[89]

In the context of reservation, the state of Tamil Nadu mandates that a minimum of 50 per cent of seats are to be reserved in public employment and educational institutions for other backward classes (OBCs), 18 per cent for SCs including 3 per cent inner reservation for the Arunthathiar community, one per cent for STs, and the remaining to be filled by open competition.[90] This law does not seem to have been followed in the context of sanitation work; otherwise nearly 100 per cent of the sanitation workers would not belong to the SCs. During the fieldwork, a few authorities expressly accepted that reservation is not followed in their institutions.[91]

Sub-reservation in Tamil Nadu may have benefitted the down-trodden Arunthathiar community by improving access to public employment and securing seats in educational institutions.[92] But it will take a long time to improve the situation of families (including other castes, especially SCs) involved in sanitation work through communal reservation in state employment. To put it plainly, nearly all sanitation workers belong to the SCs (or a specific SC group), but not all the SCs are involved in sanitation work. The RTI responses

[87] The draft is available at www.ielrc.org/content/e1218.pdf.

[88] For instance, the Total Sanitation Campaign (TSC) guidelines did not mention sanitation workers.

[89] Government of Rajasthan, Rural Sanitation and Hygiene Policy 2011.

[90] Section 5 of The Tamil Nadu Backward Classes, Scheduled Castes and Scheduled Tribes (Reservation of Seats in Educational Institutions and of Appointments or Posts in the Services under the State) Act, 1993, stipulates the percentage of reservation to be followed in the state by all authorities including local bodies, and Section 6 permits the reserved classes to compete for open seats.

[91] The Annexure to this chapter includes information received from local bodies and state agencies.

[92] See generally M.S.S. Pandian, 'Caste in Tamil Nadu—III: Denying Difference', (2013) XLVII(8) *Economic & Political Weekly* 19.

suggest that a significant percentage of sanitation workers in Tamil Nadu are from other SCs (apart from the Arunthathiar community). This phenomenon could be related to the availability/lack of Arunthathiar people living in those towns. Therefore, the political movements to achieve communal reservation for castes such as Arunthathiars, who are generally involved in sanitation work, do not benefit all sanitation workers. Instead, reservation or other benefits must be directly accorded to sanitation workers, which may encourage any person regardless of caste to take up sanitation work.

The schemes to improve the lives of manual scavengers have miserably failed to achieve their objectives for reasons such as lack of education, corruption, poverty, and caste.[93] A Union-Government-sponsored scheme to provide assistance to school-going children of sanitation workers has resulted in allegations of corruption in the primary education department of Tamil Nadu.[94] A syndicate of teachers and government officials had reportedly accepted bribes to provide assistance to children. The scheme has also not uniformly helped all sanitation workers in other states as noted by the Comptroller and Auditor General (CAG).[95] One fundamental issue is that all sanitation workers are not properly surveyed in the states, and unless a general list of all sanitation workers is made available to the public authorities, the welfare schemes may not achieve their purpose. This is further complicated by the fact that sanitation workers are not aware of these schemes.[96] Further, some of these schemes

[93] Bhumasha Janamitra, 'Traditional Profession and Livelihood: A Study on Scavengers' (PhD Thesis, Gulbarga University, 2015), 88–90.

[94] R. Sivakumar, 'Scholarship Scam: Top ADW Officials under Scanner', *The New Indian Express* (7 August 2012); available at http://www.newindianexpress.com/states/tamil-nadu/2012/aug/07/scholarship-scam-top-adw-officials-under-scanner-394616.html.

[95] Cited in *Safai Karamchari Andolan & Others* v *Union of India & Others*, Contempt Petition (C) No 132 of 2012 in Writ Petition (Civil) No. 583 of 2003 (Supreme Court of India, Judgment dated 27 March 2014), para 2 (ix).

[96] Most of the sanitation workers interviewed by the authors were illiterate or not very educated and unaware of the schemes. A member of the NCSK has also acknowledged this issue. See 'Sanitation Workers Unaware of

are not applicable to all sanitation workers. For instance, while the Scavengers Welfare Board is established under the government-run Tamil Nadu Adi Dravidar Housing and Development Corporation Limited (TAHDCO), the schemes available are limited to the members of TAHDCO, and this does not contribute significantly to the overall welfare of sanitation workers.

Legislative Reforms and Agenda

The long struggle to bring changes to the 1993 Act is partly fulfilled. The new law has expanded the scope for certain sanitation workers to come under the purview of manual scavenging. But the implementation of the various provisions of the law is subject to issuance of notifications and identification of manual scavengers. Further, the objectives of the law are limited to secure the dignity and safety of sanitation workers who suffer the most. The 1993 Act and the 2013 Act secure only a part of the rights of sanitation workers. It is imperative to enact a law to secure the rights of sanitation workers relating to health, safety, and dignity. This gains importance in the absence of state and local laws relating to sanitation workers, and failures to implement the recommendations of various committees by states, the Union Government, and local governments. The neglected sanitation workers employed by private entities, and the contract system and other modes of temporary employment should be regulated. The safety of all the workers should be brought under an umbrella legislation. In this context, it is pertinent to elucidate an ambitious bill prepared by a working group[97] of the Ministry of Labour, that is, the Manual Scavengers and Other Sanitation Labourers (Total

---

Welfare Schemes for Them', *Hindustan Times* (28 December 2012); available at http://www.hindustantimes.com/punjab/sanitation-workers-unaware-of-welfare-schemes-for-them/story-sT0MF0CbJBx6s4b3j6d93N.html.

[97] It is understood that the Ministry of Labour constituted this working group for the welfare of sanitation and leather workers, and this draft is a product of the committee. However, the ministry does not appear to have published the draft. The authors hold a copy of the draft on file. It is further understood that there are similar drafts with a common object to regulate sanitation work.

Liberation, Comprehensive Rehabilitation and Humanization of Working Conditions) Bill, 2010.

The draft attempts to enact legislation through a Union law.[98] The Ministry of Labour proposed the draft. In contrast, the Ministry of Social Justice and Empowerment was involved in the enactment of the 2013 Act, and the 1993 Act was enacted with the consent of states under Article 252 of the Indian Constitution, which requires a dual process for the acceptance of enactments by states. The draft elaborates the equipment required by sanitation workers such as gloves, gumboots, safety goggles, gas monitors, and breathing apparatus. It specifies that workplace exposure assessment, and safety and health audit shall be conducted on a regular basis.

Further, the draft distinguishes sanitation workers of two categories: sweepers and sewage workers. A separate set of safety measures and service conditions are suggested for each category. This significantly differs from the understanding of this chapter, which argues that sanitation workers together face a lot of common problems and it would not be possible to distinguish a sweeper from a sewerage worker in their regular course of employment. It is not merely the caste and dignity questions that are common to all sanitation workers, but the hazards faced by all categories of sanitation workers are generally comparable. Instead of adopting nomenclatures such as sweeper or sewage workers, safety and health measures should have been based on a comprehensive assessment of hazards faced by sanitation workers at their workplace such as streets, streets with human waste, public toilets, sewerage, railway stations or lines, hospitals, and waste-disposal units. Indeed, these categories must be elaborated after conducting a comprehensive assessment of hazards in a particular workplace; the hazards faced by workers in hospitals, in a mortuary, and in medical waste disposal are not similar.

The draft suggests that all types of temporary employment in sanitation work should be abolished. Though this sounds impractical, the reasons for such a suggestion are well understood, as the worst sufferers are non-permanent employees of local bodies, with higher

[98] Constitution of India, Seventh Schedule, List III, entry 24 gives concurrent powers to the Union and state legislatures to legislate on labour matters.

rates of death, and ailments.[99] The abolition of contract employment will also ensure the discontinuance of child labour in sanitation work; the authors have witnessed children working with the contractors of municipalities. However, no such data was accessible through the RTI Act, except the number of non-permanent workers in any municipality.

It is also important to take note of the employment of self-help groups (SHGs) in sanitation work by several municipalities in Tamil Nadu (see Annexure). These SHGs have been created with an entirely different objective, that is, the promotion of women and the rural poor.[100] Unfortunately, the municipalities compel the workers to form SHGs to obtain temporary work. The nature of work assigned to SHGs is the same as the work of any non-permanent employee under contract employment or regular work. The employment of SHGs is merely to evade the minimal protection available to workers under contract employment laws. Regrettably, the Waste Management Rules, 2016, encourage the employment of SHGs and other informal workers, without explaining the reasons for their engagement and providing any guidelines for their work.[101]

There is a need to reform and regulate the working conditions of sanitation workers in the private sector, from large industries to

[99] For instance, the state government argued that a contract worker's family is not eligible for compensation, irrespective of the fact that he died while doing sanitation work. Though the court did not accept this argument, it is evident that contract workers are unnoticed sufferers in sanitation work. See *P. Ayyaswami* v *The Chief Secretary* WP No. 25717 of 2012 (High Court of Madras, Judgment dated 6 March 2015).

[100] An SHG is a small voluntary association of poor people, preferably from the same socio-economic background. They come together for the purpose of solving their common problems through self-help and mutual help. The SHGs promote small savings among their members. The savings are kept in a bank. This common fund is in the name of the SHG. The SHG is a group formed by the community, which has a specific number of members like 15 or 20. Usually the number of members in one SHG does not exceed 20. In such a group, the poorest come together during emergencies or disasters, to provide economic support to each other and have ease of conversation, and for social and economic interaction.

[101] Solid Waste Management Rules, 2016, rules 11 and 15.

schools and hospitals, as they form a large workforce vulnerable to all the health- and safety-related, and social disadvantages attached to their work. There are many questions and suggestions, which are left open, as this chapter deals with fundamental issues relating to the rights of sanitation workers. For instance, why cannot India have a certification for sanitation workers? What makes sanitation work in other countries attractive?[102]

* * *

The rights of sanitation workers may be secured through the following measures: mechanized sewerage system, proper safety equipment, licensed and safe manhole entry, life and medical insurance, wages commensurate with the risk undertaken by employees, dignified workplace and treatment, and protection from caste-based discrimination. When the state allows them to engage in this employment without adequate protection, it impliedly permits slavery and caste-based discrimination.

At this juncture, the importance of sanitation infrastructure, and the role of sanitation workers for the realization of the right to sanitation assume importance. Proper sanitation facilities are necessary at every public place such as railway stations, bus stands, hotels, and parks to protect sanitation workers from manually cleaning human excreta and other waste. Indeed, any project to improve sanitation infrastructure must take note of the need for safe working conditions for sanitation workers. Most of the sanitation infrastructure in India is not equipped with safety mechanisms, and is hostile to sanitation workers; this presumably hinders the realization of their right to sanitation.

State negligence of sanitation workers is increasingly observed and documented by the media, courts, and politicians in recent times.

---

[102] A news item refers to the number of applications filed for New York City's sanitation work force. There were more than 94,000 applications from different ethnic groups for around 500 positions. See Lisa Colangelo, 'New York City Sanitation Worker Civil Service Exam Set for February Draws More than 94,000 Applications', *Daily News* (8 December 2014); available on http://www.nydailynews.com/new-york/queens/94-000-people-sign-city-sanitation-worker-exam-article-1.2000751.

Despite the existence of a number of associations linked to sanitation workers and their castes, their concerns have not been adequately addressed in policies and enactments relating to various aspects of sanitation work. India, as a modern state, has failed to protect the basic human and labour rights of sanitation workers.

Compared to other working classes in India, sanitation workers tend to succumb to various psychological, economic, and social pressures. It is a shame for a country to suppress the ignorant. Social justice and dignity for sanitation workers can be attained only if all sections of society and the different agencies of the government come forward to help realize the rights of sanitation workers. Only cooperation and coordination amongst various organs of the state can result in an environment conducive to sanitation work. The first step towards a 'clean India' must be to humanize sanitation work, and secure the rights of sanitation workers.

Annexure 12A

Table 12A.1 lists selected RTI responses from municipalities and corporations located in different regions of Tamil Nadu. All the local bodies are governed by a similar set of laws. A number of local bodies provided only partial information. Caste-wise details are available only for permanent workers. All the responses were received during the period 2012–13.

Table 12A.1 Selected Right to Information Responses

No.	Municipality	Caste (only permanent workers)	Contract/Casual Workers/SHG	Leave Conditions	Training Given to Workers	Supply of Safety Gadgets
1	Thindivanam	SC-62 BC-2 MBC-6	CW-0 SHG-3	Half-day work on government holidays.	No training is provided.	Raincoat, gloves, boots, mask and other safety equipment.
2	Sathyamangalam	SC-42	CW-0 SHG-0	All government holidays.	Information not available.	Footwear, safety caps, raincoat, gloves.
3	Vilupuram	SC-151 SC(A)-10 MBC-1 BC-5	CW-0 SHG-72	All Sundays, and half-day work on government holidays.	No training is provided.	Safety equipment provided. Gloves, footwear, mask, boots, and a raincoat.
4	Kodaikanal	SC-79 MBC-0 BC-1	CW-10 SHG-0	10 days per year for workers employed for less than 15 years.	Information not available.	Gloves, footwear, mask, boots, and a raincoat.
5	Kudiyaatham	SC-120 MBC-0 BC-0	CW-0 SHG-0	Half-day work on government holidays. 12 days casual leave.	Information not available.	Safety equipment given once in three years.

(Cont'd)

Table 12.A1 (Cont'd)

No.	Municipality	Caste (only permanent workers)	Contract/Casual Workers/SHG	Leave Conditions	Training Given to Workers	Supply of Safety Gadgets
6	Koodalur	SC-48	CW-24 SHG-0	All government-declared holidays	Information not available.	Gloves, footwear, mask, cap, reflecting jacket, and other necessary equipment
7	Karaikudi	Caste-wise details not available with the municipality.	CW-0 SHG-0	All government-declared holidays.	Information not available.	Raincoat, gloves, boots, and mask.
8	Kancheepuram	SC-237	CW-20 SHG-0	All government-declared holidays.	Civic sense awareness training given	Basket, broomstick, and other related equipment.
9	Tirupur	Total 838, caste-wise information not provided.	CW-0 SHG-60	All government-declared holidays.	Mentions that relevant training is given.	Mentions that all safety gadgets are provided.
10	Gobichettypalayam	SC-144	CW-0 SHG-0	Sundays, and all government-declared holidays.	No training is provided	Gloves, shoes, and mask.
11	Sirkazhi	SC-30 ST-25 MBC-2 BC-0	CW-20 SHG-0	All government-declared holidays.	No training is provided.	Garden fork, gloves, raincoat, boots, and so on.

No.	Municipality	Caste (only permanent workers)	Contract/Casual Workers/SHG	Leave Conditions	Training Given to Workers	Supply of Safety Gadgets
12	Sivagangai	Total-76, caste-wise information not available with the municipality.	CW-0 SHG-0	All government-declared holidays.	Training depends upon the educational qualification.	Only work equipment mentioned.
13	Thiruvallur	SC-49 BC-7 ST-13 MBC-4	CW-55 SHG-0	Half-day holiday on all government-declared holidays.	Solid waste management. Dog, pig, rat, and monkey catching, awareness on the ban on manual cleaning of man holes.	Raincoat, gloves, cap.

Notes: ST: Scheduled Tribe; SC: Scheduled Caste; SC(A): Scheduled Caste (Arunthathiar); BC: Backward Caste; MBC: Most Backward Caste;; CW: Casual/contract/daily wage; SHG: Member of a Self-Help Group (they may not get any protection available for permanent/ contract/casual or temporary workers).

13

Sanitation, Gender Inequality, and Implications for Rights

Sujith Koonan and *Lovleen Bhullar*

Sanitation needs and concerns are gendered. Social and cultural norms coupled with the lack of basic sanitation facilities such as toilets render the performance of daily sanitation functions by women burdensome and a source of embarrassment. Women are required to manage their sanitation needs in private, whereas similar restrictions are not imposed on men. Women should not be seen while defecating or urinating, but it is 'acceptable' for men to urinate in public. These norms further pose risks to the safety and health of women. The impact of socio-cultural factors on the sanitation behaviour of women is further clear from the fact that certain spatial and temporal restrictions are imposed on women, which may result in their going for defecation or urination under the cover of darkness and/or travelling farther from their home to find a secluded place for this private activity. There is an increased risk of violence including sexual violence while accessing a community toilet or engaging in open defecation.[1]

[1] Marni Sommer, Suzanne Ferron, Sue Cavill, and Sarah House, 'Violence, Gender and WASH: Spurring Action on a Complex, Under-documented

Women tend to cope with the lack of adequate facilities for sanitation by restricting their food and water intake in order to control the urge to defecate or urinate during the day.[2] This may lead to health problems such as urinary tract infections, chronic constipation, and other gastric disorders.[3] Further, women's bodies are biologically different, and therefore they have specific sanitation needs, such as during menstruation, pregnancy, and the post-natal period.[4] A related issue is the lack or inadequacy of sanitation facilities in schools, which affects the realization of the right to sanitation as well as the right to education of girl students disproportionately. It has been reported that girl students miss school days during their periods or drop out of school due to lack of adequate sanitation facilities.[5]

The gender dimensions of the right to sanitation require the law and policy framework to adopt a gender-sensitive approach to address specific sanitation-related needs and concerns of women. They also require interventions not only at the substantive level, but also at the

and Sensitive Topic', (2014) 27(1) *Environment & Urbanization* 105; Tina Khanna and Madhumita Das, 'Why Gender Matters in the Solution towards Safe Sanitation? Reflections from Rural India', (2016) 11(10) *Global Public Health* 1185.

[2] Meera Bapat and Indu Agarwal, 'Our Needs, Our Priorities; Women and Men from the Slums in Mumbai and Pune Talk About Their Needs for Water and Sanitation', (2003) 15(2) *Environment & Urbanization* 71. At the same time, this cannot be generalized beyond a point. During fieldwork, at least a few women in rural Rajasthan have mentioned that they generally do not follow the 'before sunrise, after sunset' approach to the fulfilment of their sanitation needs. This may be because finding a secluded place for open defecation is not a major challenge for them, due to abundant availability of land.

[3] Sundar Burra, Sheela Patel, and Thomas Kerr, 'Community-Designed, Built and Managed Toilet Blocks in Indian Cities', (2003) 15(2) *Environment & Urbanization* 11; Geeta Pardeshi, 'Women in Total Sanitation Campaign: A Case Study from Yavatmal District, Maharashtra, India', (2009) 25(2) *Journal of Human Ecology* 79, 80.

[4] Khanna and Das (n 1).

[5] Water Supply & Sanitation Collaborative Council, *For Her It's the Big Issue: Putting Women at the Centre for Water Supply, Sanitation and Hygiene* (Water Supply & Sanitation Collaborative Council, 2006), 15.

procedural level. The latter will involve ensuring the participation of women in the framing and implementation of the sanitation framework. The non-realization of the right to sanitation for women may also have implications for their other rights, for instance, the rights to gender equality and education.

This chapter unpacks specific gender dimensions of the law and policy framework for rural sanitation in India and its implementation in order to assess its contribution to the realization of the right to sanitation of women. The core question that informs the discussion is whether the framework represents a shift towards or away from gender equality. This chapter focuses on three aspects in particular. The first section examines the extent to which the issues of privacy and dignity of women as well as certain women-specific sanitation needs are accommodated. This is followed by the second section that contextualizes the position of women in terms of participation and agency. The third section analyses the issue of safety, particularly gender-based violence, in the context of open defecation or access to public toilets. In addition to the primary sources and secondary literature, the chapter draws upon fieldwork conducted in rural areas in the states of Rajasthan and Uttar Pradesh (UP) during the period 2014–16.[6]

Sanitation Needs of Women: Evolving Law and Policy Norms

Basic sanitation-related functions such as defecation and urination are per se gender neutral in nature. However, social and cultural factors add a significant gender dimension to these bodily functions. The differential application of the norms of privacy and dignity to women and men makes the performance of these biological functions challenging and burdensome for women. Women are expected

---

[6] Fieldwork was conducted in selected Districts in two states—Rajasthan and Uttar Pradesh—during the period 2014–16. Following are the Districts where fieldwork was conducted: Rajasthan: Bikaner, Churu, Jaipur, and Tonk; and Uttar Pradesh: Chitrakoot, Kushinagar, Lucknow, and Pratapgarh.

to defecate and urinate in private whereas such stipulations do not apply to men. This is evident more than anything else in the common occurrence of men urinating in public places whereas this 'option' is considered to be 'undignified' for women. This social construction of permissible and impermissible sanitation-related behaviour extends to boys and girls in schools. Thus, even biologically similar sanitation-related bodily functions are given a gender orientation through cultural norms rooted in patriarchy. The impact of social and cultural factors, and the consequent sanitation challenges or sanitation-related burden for women is even more serious in the case of women-specific sanitation needs and concerns, for instance, in the case of menstrual hygiene management (MHM).

This issue of differential application of the norms of privacy and dignity must be addressed in order to ensure gender equality. At a fundamental level, this requires reorientation of the social imagination, which is a daunting but essential task. In the contemporary social context, the lack of adequate sanitation facilities, such as toilets and facilities for MHM, which can contribute to addressing this process, poses a significant challenge to the realization of women's right to sanitation. In this context, this section first considers the scope and limits of the existing law and policy framework in addressing these issues, and then examines the state of its implementation—first, through the lens of privacy and dignity of women in the context of toilet construction, and then by considering one of the women-specific sanitation needs, that is, menstruation.

Law and Policy Framework

The Constitution of India guarantees privacy and dignity to everyone. Dignity is an essential component of the fundamental right to life,[7] from which the right to sanitation is also derived (see Cullet, Chapter 3, in this volume). Further, the existence of gender-based inequality in society has been recognized as an issue under the Constitution of India. The principle of gender equality, as enshrined

---

[7] *Francis Coralie Mullin* v *The Administrator, Union Territory of Delhi & Others* (1981) 1 SCC 608 (Supreme Court of India, 1981).

in the Constitution, demands affirmative action from the state.[8] Given the fact that the right to sanitation is also a fundamental right, the principle of gender equality must be a basic organizing principle for its implementation.

The statutory framework relating to the realization of the right to sanitation, to some extent, recognizes the need to ensure the dignity and privacy of women. Several statutes address sanitation needs in workplaces, and provide for separate toilets for women.[9] The Right of Children to Free and Compulsory Education Act, 2009, specifies norms for schools to provide toilet facilities, and the separate provision of toilets for girls. In a case concerning the right to education, the Supreme Court of India has held that the lack of toilet facilities in schools violates the fundamental right guaranteed under Article 21A of the Constitution.[10] The Supreme Court went on to direct all schools, whether state owned or privately owned, aided or unaided, minority or non-minority, to provide toilet facilities for boys and girls. Proper implementation of these constitutional and statutory provisions could contribute significantly to the realization of the right to sanitation of women and girls.

The rural sanitation policy framework also acknowledges the importance of privacy and dignity for women in the context of sanitation. One of the main objectives of the first flagship programme on rural sanitation—the Central Rural Sanitation Programme (CRSP), which was adopted by the Central Government in 1986, was to provide privacy to women and protect their dignity.[11] In 1999, the Total Sanitation Campaign (TSC) was adopted to replace the CRSP. The

---

[8] Article 14 of the Constitution guarantees equality before law to all persons, and Article 15 prohibits discrimination against any citizen, inter alia, on grounds of sex.

[9] For example, The Contract Labour (Regulation and Abolition) Act, 1970, s 18(b); The Building and Other Construction Workers (Regulation of Employment and Conditions of Service) Act, 1996, s 33.

[10] *Environmental & Consumer Protection Foundation* v *Delhi Administration & Others* 2012 (9) SCALE 692 (Supreme Court of India, 2012), para 4.

[11] Government of India, Ministry of Drinking Water and Sanitation, Nirmal Bharat Abhiyan Guidelines, 2012 (Ministry of Drinking Water and Sanitation, 2012), 5.

TSC Guidelines, 2011, also included explicit provisions addressing the concerns of women. For instance, a key factor for determining the location of community sanitary complexes was their acceptability to and accessibility for women.[12]

In 2012, the Nirmal Bharat Abhiyan (NBA) replaced the TSC. The NBA represented a step backwards because while it re-asserted the objectives of the CRSP, it stated that the location of community sanitary complexes should be acceptable and accessible to 'all'—thus, removing the previous reference to specific vulnerable groups, including women.[13] Similarly, while the Rural Sanitation and Hygiene Strategy emphasizes the importance of 'addressing inequalities in access with special attention to vulnerable groups such as women',[14] the engagement is peripheral in nature, and it fails to provide guidance as to the necessary mechanisms for this purpose. The ongoing SBM that replaced the NBA in 2014, seems to be no different from its predecessors in failing to address the issues relating to the realization of the right to sanitation for women.

Implementation of the Framework: Privacy and Dignity of Women

The rural sanitation policy framework has relied on the dignity and privacy of women as a rationale for various sanitation interventions. However, references to dignity and privacy of women mostly remain on paper, and the concern is hardly reflected in the implementation of the framework. The need to ensure the dignity and privacy of women does not seem to have motivated the state governments to undertake sanitation interventions.

The insensitivity of the government to the issues of privacy and dignity of women is clear from the manner in which access to toilets

---

[12] Government of India, Ministry of Rural Development, Total Sanitation Campaign Guidelines, 2010 (Ministry of Rural Development, 2010), 8.

[13] Nirmal Bharat Abhiyan Guidelines (n 11), para 5.7.1.

[14] Government of India, Ministry of Rural Development, Department of Drinking Water and Sanitation, Rural Sanitation and Hygiene Strategy 2012–22 (Ministry of Rural Development, 2011), 6.

is promoted in rural areas. For instance, implementing agencies at the local level seem to believe that the availability of a toilet would by itself lead to its use by everyone. This approach is myopic, and fails to take into account the social and cultural norms that constrain the ways in which women take care of their sanitation needs. For instance, some household toilets in rural Rajasthan were located at the front side of the house, which makes it difficult for women to use them because men and guests usually occupy this space.[15] Further, a large number of toilets constructed as part of rural sanitation programmes are non-functional or unusable, and therefore, contribute little to the realization of the right to sanitation in general, and particularly, for women.

Similarly, in the case of public/community toilets in urban and peri-urban areas, it is assumed that the provision of separate toilets for women is sufficient for ensuring the dignity and privacy of women. Factors such as their inadequacy,[16] safety concerns,[17] lack of hygiene,[18] or inaccessibility[19] are generally overlooked. The

---

[15] See also Kathleen O'Reilly, 'Combining Sanitation and Women's Participation in Water Supply: An Example from Rajasthan', (2010) 20(1) *Development in Practice* 45.

[16] One reason is high density of population. See Shahana Sheikh, *Public Toilets in Delhi: An Emphasis on the Facilities for Women in Slum/Resettlement Areas*, CCS Working Paper No. 92 (Centre for Civil Society, New Delhi, 2008), 23. Another reason is lack of sewerage, water, and/or electricity connections. See Colin McFarlane, 'Sanitation in Mumbai's Informal Settlements: Governance, Infrastructure, and Cost Recovery', in Klaus J. Bade, Bernhard Lorentz, and Ludger Pries (eds), *Migration and Integration: Reflections on Our Common Future* (Europaische Verlagsanstalt, 2011).

[17] Examples include inconvenient opening and closing hours, broken doors/roofs, and absence of latches on doors, and so on.

[18] Examples include mismanagement/poor maintenance, and lack of facilities such as dustbins for disposal of menstrual waste. See Kathryn Travers, Prabha Khosla, and Suneeta Dhar (eds), *Gender and Essential Services in Low-income Communities: Report on the Findings of the Action Research Project Women's Rights and Access to Water and Sanitation in Asian Cities* (Women in Cities International, 2011).

[19] Examples include location and affordability. See Prabha Khosla and Suneeta Dhar, 'Safe Access to Basic Infrastructure: More than Pipes and

presence of men in the toilet complex, for instance, as caretakers of toilet complexes, and the use of community toilet complexes or public toilets by men and boys for various purposes including for rearing pigeons and playing cards makes it difficult for women to use them.[20] Further, the absence, or inadequacy, of community toilet complexes or public toilets disproportionately affects the realization of the right to sanitation of women, particularly, working women and homeless women. This is especially important in a context where a large number of women in rural and urban areas go out of their homes to earn a livelihood.

Overall, the existing law and policy framework neglects the fact that there is a greater need for toilets in public places for women than for men, from the perspective of privacy and dignity. At the same time, it needs to be underlined that the rural sanitation policy framework cannot continue to promote the construction of toilets primarily for women. This may lead to a scenario where toilets are used only by women, and men will continue to turn to open defecation, as is the case in many villages in Rajasthan. Further, the mere construction of toilets may not lead to the realization of the right to sanitation for women, if the social and cultural factors affecting the sanitation behaviour of women are not taken into consideration.

Menstrual Hygiene Management: From Neglect to Recognition and Beyond

Menstrual hygiene management is an important sanitation concern for women. Menstruation is a natural process, which is a part of their reproductive health. However, the cultural notion that equates or explains menstruation with a great deal of negativity and disgust has led to a discernible silence in respect of MHM in society. The use of terms such as 'dirty', 'smelly', 'unhygienic', and 'unclean' to describe

---

Taps', in Carolyn Whitzman et al. (eds), *Building Inclusive Cities: Women's Safety and the Right to the City* (Routledge, 2013).

[20] Khosla and Dhar (n 19).

menstruation is common.[21] Menstrual hygiene management is also difficult due to the lack of adequate mechanisms. The issues are multifaceted including the non-availability of sanitary napkins, economic inability to purchase them, and the lack of an environment friendly mechanism to dispose of the used napkins.[22]

Women and girls are expected (rather told or taught) to deal with menstruation silently and discreetly. As a result, they tend to 'hide' the biological fact of menstruation particularly from men. A teacher in a school in rural UP mentioned that even though dustbins are provided in schools, girl students do not use them to discard the used absorbents due to the fear of being seen by boys. The 'discreetness' associated with menstruation has implications for maintaining hygiene during the menstrual period. In rural areas, women and girls use (and reuse) cloth as absorbents. Cleaning and drying of this cloth or disposal of pads have been highlighted as a source of indignity, fear, and stress.[23] Women usually wash and dry the cloth inside the house. Sometimes the lack of water supply at home forces women and girls to walk to a pond to wash the cloth or to a field to bury/burn the used absorbents.[24]

The social and cultural factors make hygienic management of menstruation difficult, and this may also cause a number of health risks, for instance, the risk of reproductive tract infections.[25] This

[21] Vatsalya, *Women with Wings: Celebrating Womanhood: Menstrual Hygiene Management: Path to Better Health, Dignity, Opportunities and Empowerment* (Vatsalya, 2014), 5.

[22] Water Supply & Sanitation Collaborative Council and Indian Institute of Public Administration, 'Menstrual Hygiene Management: Training of Master Trainers' (Water Supply & Sanitation Collaborative Council and Indian Institute of Public Administration, 2013), 6.

[23] Vatsalya (n 21).

[24] Vatsalya (n 21). See also Zachary Burt, Kara Nelson, and Isha Ray, *Towards Gender Equality through Sanitation Access* (UN Women Discussion Paper, 2016), 22.

[25] Inga Winkler and Virginia Roaf, 'Taking the Bloody Linen Out of the Closet: Menstrual Hygiene as a Priority for Achieving Gender Equality', (2015) 21(1) *Cardozo Journal of Law & Gender* 1; Shamima Yasmin et al., 'Menstrual Hygiene among Adolescent School Students: An In-depth

may occur, for instance, when girl students do not change the absorbents at school due to the lack of facilities or due to the fear of being noticed by boys and male teachers.[26]

The social and cultural taboo around menstruation imposes several restrictions on access and movement of women and girls. Within the household, this includes a prohibition on entering the kitchen, sleeping on a bed, eating certain food, and touching holy books.[27] The restrictions are not limited to private spaces. Most Hindu temples, if not all, prohibit entry of women during the period of menstruation on the grounds of purity and pollution. Some temples prohibit the entry of women for the entire period from menarche to menopause. Thus, women are discriminated both in private spaces and public places on the ground of a basic bodily function. These restrictions have triggered a campaign on social media called 'Happy to Bleed', which challenges the cultural taboo around menstruation. Further, a case is pending before the Supreme Court of India that challenges the ban on women of a certain age group (after puberty and before menopause) from entering the Sabarimala temple situated in the state of Kerala.[28]

The issues and concerns relating to MHM have also received some recognition at the policy level.[29] The explicit recognition of MHM as

---

Cross-Sectional Study in an Urban Community of West Bengal, India', (2013) 5(6) *IOSR Journal of Dental and Medical Sciences* 22.

[26] Water Supply & Sanitation Collaborative Council and Freshwater Action Network, *Leave No One Behind: Voices of Women, Adolescent Girls, Elderly and Disabled People, and Sanitation Workers* (Water Supply & Sanitation Collaborative Council and Freshwater Action Network, 2016), 17–18; Burt, Nelson, and Ray (n 24), 23.

[27] Vatsalya (n 21), 8; Sowmyaa Bharadwaj and Archana Patkar, *Menstrual Hygiene Management in Developing Countries: Taking Stock* (Junction Social, 2004).

[28] *Indian Young Lawyers Association v State of Kerala*, Writ Petition (Civil) No. 373 of 2006 (Supreme Court of India). The Supreme Court of India completed the hearing on 1 August 2018 and reserved the case for judgment.

[29] For example, Government of India, Ministry of Drinking Water and Sanitation, Menstrual Hygiene Management: National Guidelines, December 2015; available at http://www.mdws.gov.in/sites/default/files/Menstrual%20Hygiene%20Management%20-%20Guidelines_0.pdf.

a sanitation issue is indeed a progressive step. However, its contribution to the actual realization of the right to sanitation depends on how the concern is translated into action. At the local level, there are very few interventions to facilitate MHM. This is mainly due to the overwhelming focus on toilets, as promoted by the law and policy framework. The implementing agencies at the local level generally hold the view that *other* sanitation concerns including MHM will be taken up after achieving open defecation free (ODF) status.

At the same time, there have been some modest efforts. For instance, the National Rural Health Mission (NRHM) has launched a Scheme for Promotion of Menstrual Hygiene among Adolescent Girls in Rural India. In 2015, the state of UP announced the target of 100 per cent menstrual hygiene, and sanitary napkin coverage by 2017 for all girls between the age group of 10 and 19 years, studying in class 6 to class 12 of government-run schools.[30] As a result, pilot projects were started in Barabanki, Mathura, and Mahoba Districts, where women's groups produce and sell low-cost sanitary napkins. Similar initiatives are also in the pipeline in the state of Kerala. Some panchayats have already constructed girl friendly toilets in public places (for example, Chirakkal in Kannur District) and the idea is being promoted in schools.

However, the evolving policy approach mainly focuses on the provisioning of toilet facilities, and access to sanitary napkins. While this approach is being promoted by international organizations, and the Central Government as well as state governments in India, it is contested on the ground that it is an imported concept that completely neglects the existing practices followed in India that are probably

---

[30] Kapil Dutta, 'UP State Govt to Provide Free Sanitary Napkins to School Girls', *Hindustan Times* (26 July 2015); available at http://www. hindustantimes.com/noida/up-state-govt-to-provide-free-sanitary-napkins-to-school-girls/story-4luvS2tF4Zl9aIbOMR3eaO.html. Similar initiatives have been announced in other states as well. See Rahi Gaikwad, 'Free Sanitary Napkins for Bihar Schoolgirls from April: Nitish', *The Hindu* (13 February 2014); available at http://www.thehindu.com/news/national/other-states/free-sanitary-napkins-for-bihar-schoolgirls-from-april-nitish/article5685534.ece.

more hygienic and affordable.[31] Further, the environment-friendly disposal of used sanitary napkins continues to be an unresolved and unattended issue.[32]

Participation and Agency of Women in the Policy Framework: Needle in a Haystack?

The participation and agency of right-holders is a basic element of rights including the right to sanitation. This section examines to what extent effective and equal participation and agency of women is ensured in the framework for rural sanitation. It focuses in particular on an important reason for the gender myopia of the framework, that is, its tendency to work within the existing patriarchal social structure.

Promoting Toilet Construction through Patriarchy

The dignity and privacy of women is a rallying point for the implementation of the rural sanitation policy framework. The awareness creation programme, which is known as the 'triggering' programme among implementing agencies and various developmental agencies, liberally uses the norms of dignity and privacy of women. While awareness creation programmes may be helpful to achieve sanitation goals, they are problematic when they reinforce social and cultural norms that are based on an artificial hierarchical relationship between men and women.

In particular, the implementing agencies have relied on women-specific narratives, and the dignity of women, to promote construction of household toilets. However, these efforts are counterproductive and regressive. The language employed by the implementing agencies is not couched in terms of the rights of women. Instead, awareness creation programmes mainly address men. For

---

[31] Sinu Joseph, 'Why India Doesn't Need the Sanitary Napkin Revolution', *Swarajya* (19 July 2015); available at https://swarajyamag.com/culture/why-india-doesnt-need-the-sanitary-napkin-revolution.

[32] Joseph (n 31).

instance, the implementing agencies in the state of Rajasthan use existing discriminatory and oppressive social practices including the purdah system,[33] which has been condemned and opposed by women's movements for several years, to invoke male prestige to achieve the goal of construction of individual household latrines (IHHLs). One of the questions posed to men with the objective of 'triggering' them to build toilets at home, was to know how they can let others see 'their' women defecating in the open while they do not let others even see the face of 'their' women.

The implementing agencies in the state of UP have also used similar narratives. For instance, a large number of public posters and paintings project toilets as essential infrastructure to ensure the dignity of women. In certain cases, the approach has gone to the extent of depicting a man declaring the need to protect the dignity of the women in his house by building a private toilet. The narratives generally convey the impression that toilets are to be built *for* women *by* men.

The use of these narratives is often justified by the implementing agencies on the ground of their perceived effectiveness and expediency. Thus, immediate results, that is, toilet construction, are prioritized, regardless of the objectification and stigmatization of women perpetrated and perpetuated by them. These narratives also reflect the element of male domination in the making and implementation of policies, because women have been made the target and the object of awareness creation programmes *by* men, although there is no data to show that women are the predominant open defecators. On the contrary, experience from fieldwork in rural areas in the states of Rajasthan and UP reveals that men are more reluctant to use toilets than women. This is probably because, as promoted by the awareness creation programmes, men generally view the construction of toilets as primarily for women.

---

[33] O'Reilly explain the purdah system in the following words: 'Regardless of their age, women living in their in-laws' homes practise purdah (literally "curtain"), which entails remaining inside the family compound, covering their faces (*ghunghat*), and speaking little or quietly in front of strangers, senior men, and senior women. Unmarried girls who live with their parents do not practise purdah or ghunghat.' See O'Reilly (n 15), 55.

The use of messages rooted in patriarchy is regressive because it undermines the basic principle of gender equality as enshrined in the Constitution of India. Further, it has not contributed significantly to the realization of the right to sanitation, as it does not target the sanitation-related habits of men. The Government of India has taken note of the implications of the use of patriarchy by the framework for rural sanitation. The Ministry of Drinking Water and Sanitation has instructed the implementing agencies not to use gender stereotyping messages and patriarchal norms in awareness creation programmes.[34] It is yet to be seen to what extent these new guidelines will change the approach of implementing agencies at the local level, especially when they view practices such as the purdah system as 'useful' and 'effective'.

Limited Role of Women in Policymaking and Implementation

There is little or no participation of women both at the level of policymaking as well as its implementation. An overwhelming majority of the policymakers at the level of the Central Government and the officials who constitute the implementation machinery at the state, District, and village levels are men. As a result, the basic nature of the framework, its priorities, and approaches, are largely informed by their understanding of sanitation. One may expect the scenario to be different in places where District collectors or the presidents of the gram panchayats are women. However, fieldwork reveals that even women District collectors are bound by the top-down approach of the sanitation framework, although they may be more sensitive to gender-specific concerns. Insofar as membership of the gram panchayat is concerned, in a majority of cases, the name of the woman member is mentioned only for official purposes, probably because the particular post was reserved for women. In practice, the male

[34] Government of India, Ministry of Drinking Water and Sanitation, Guidelines on Gender Issues in Sanitation, Doc. No. S-11018/2/2017-SBM, 3 April 2017. These Guidelines have been made an explicit part of the Guidelines for Swachh Bharat Mission (Gramin), 2017. See Government of India, Ministry of Drinking Water and Sanitation, Guidelines for Swachh Bharat Mission (Gramin), 2017, Annexure XI; available at http://ielrc.org/content/e1708.pdf.

members of the family of the female *sarpanch* (usually her husband or son) discharge her public duties. This was also the case in the village water and sanitation committees, where women were included as members according to the requirements of the administrative directions, but in practice, women members were sometimes not even aware of their membership.

The approach of overlooking the participation of women while implementing sanitation interventions is further clear from the fact that women are not consulted while taking decisions at the panchayat level as well as at the household level. For instance, a group of women in a village in UP stated that they were not consulted while building toilets. Similar observations have been noted in other studies as well. As mentioned earlier, a toilet at the front side of a house makes it difficult for women to use it because this is a space mostly occupied by men and guests.[35] This indicates the fact that non-participation of women while making and implementing the rural sanitation policy framework affects the realization of their right to sanitation as well as their right to participate.

Gender-Based Violence and Sanitation: Scope and Limitations of Law and Policy Responses

Gender-based violence is an important issue in the context of sanitation from a gender perspective. Open defecation is often cited as one of the factors that increase the vulnerability of women to sexual and other forms of violence. Women become 'prisoners of daylight' because they have to go for open defecation early in the morning or late at night.[36] Sometimes, they have to walk long distances to find isolated places such as open areas and vacant lots for defecation. These compromises arguably increase their vulnerability to verbal and/or sexual harassment, non-physical intimidation, threat of violence or

---

[35] O'Reilly (n 15).

[36] UNICEF, Gender and Water, Sanitation and Hygiene (WASH) (UNICEF, 2010); available at http://www.unicef.org/esaro/7310_Gender_and_WASH.html.

actual assault, abduction, and/or theft.[37] The reduction of vegetation/ tree/forest cover, and the conversion of open spaces reduce the availability of places for open defecation, and may further increase their vulnerability.

Safety and security concerns of women are usually discussed more in the context of urban sanitation, but similar concerns exist in rural areas as well.[38] A majority of the open defecators live in rural areas,[39] and there are a large number of reported cases (at the level of the high courts and the Supreme Court of India) concerning sexual violence against women in the context of open defecation, most of which are from rural areas.[40] In some reported cases, women went missing after

[37] JAGORI, *Women's Rights and Access to Water and Sanitation in Asian Cities* (JAGORI, 2011); Khanna and Das (n 1); UN HABITAT, *Navigating Gender in Development of Water and Sanitation in Urban Areas: A Rapid Gender Assessment of the Cities of Bhopal, Gwalior, Indore and Jabalpur in Madhya Pradesh, India* (UN HABITAT, 2006); Anupama Nallari, '"All We Want are Toilets inside Our Homes!" The Critical Role of Sanitation in the Lives of Urban Poor Adolescent Girls in Bengaluru, India', (2015) 27(1) *Environment & Urbanization* 73.

[38] For example, Madan Kumar, 'Rapists on Prowl in Loo-less Rural Bihar', *The Times of India* (Patna) (17 January 2013); available at http:// timesofindia.indiatimes.com/city/patna/Rapists-on-prowl-in-loo-less-rural-Bihar/articleshow/18055170.cms; Shailvee Sharda, 'Gender Crimes Haunt Women who Head to Field for Nature's Call', *The Times of India* (6 July 2013); available at http://timesofindia.indiatimes.com/india/Gender-crimes-haunt-women-who-head-to-field-for-natures-call/articleshow/20942886.cms.

[39] In India, 52.1 per cent of the rural population practices open defecation. See Government of India, Ministry of Statistics and Programme Implementation, National Sample Survey Office, Swachhta Status Report, 2016 (Ministry of Statistics and Programme Implementation, 2016), 47.

[40] For instance, *R Tamilarasi v The District Collector* 2010 (8) MLJ 662 (High Court of Madras, 2010); *Tasleem S/o Masoom v State of Uttar Pradesh* Jail Appeal Nos. 5728, 5729 and 5730 and Criminal Appeal No. 5844 of 2005 (High Court of Allahabad, Judgment dated 10 July 2006); *Devalla Raghavulu v State of Andhra Pradesh* 2005 CriLJ 1041 (High Court of Andhra Pradesh, 2004).

going to relieve themselves at night, and were later found raped and hung on a tree.[41] However, the issue in the rural context has received disproportionately little attention from policymakers and researchers working on sanitation.

Violence or the fear of violence while exercising basic biological needs like defecation or urination is incompatible with the idea of human rights generally, and the right to sanitation, particularly. A key question in this regard is to what extent this issue has been addressed in, and can be addressed effectively by, the law and policy framework relating to sanitation.

The law and policy responses to the issue of women's safety in the context of sanitation can be viewed from two different angles. First, the commission of certain forms of gender-based violence is a criminal offence, and becomes the subject matter of criminal law. Second, the construction of toilets is widely projected as a major policy intervention to address the issue. Thus, the law and policy framework for sanitation may arguably provide pre-emptive solutions.

Criminal Law: Limitations of Post Facto Interventions

Once an act involving gender-based violence occurs, and it satisfies the requirements of an 'offence' as defined in the Indian Penal Code, 1860,[42] the matter falls within the domain of the criminal justice system. It is the duty of the government to prosecute and punish the offenders as the crime is viewed as an offence against the state. The root cause of the offence is not the concern of the criminal justice system. Prosecuting and punishing the offender(s) arguably have a deterrent effect, and thus are expected to reduce the occurrence of such crimes in the future. However, several factors, including social, cultural, and economic factors, diminish the scope of the deterrent effect.

Violence against women, especially sexual violence, is viewed as a matter of shame and loss of honour, rather than as a crime. A number

---

[41] See Bindu Shajan Perapaddan, 'Lack of Toilets Proves a Serious Threat to Women's Safety', *The Hindu* (1 June 2014), 9.
[42] For example, Section 375 of the Indian Penal Code, 1860, which deals with the offence of rape.

of cases are not reported to the police due to the social stigma or taboo around sexual violence. In some parts of rural India, the community may get involved and try to 'settle' the matter.[43] The accused may confess his crime and offer to marry the woman, or he may be persuaded to marry her by the panchayat, or the matter may be settled through monetary payment. The woman's family may prefer this approach to 'protect the victim's honour' without seeking her opinion.[44] In such instances, a criminal case will be filed only after the negotiation to 'settle' the matter fails. Courts have acknowledged the existence of this practice while addressing the question of condonation of delay.[45]

Even when the crime is reported and prosecution is initiated, there are several challenges that affect the outcome of the criminal case. In a number of cases, the absence of injuries or the failure to raise an alarm have led to an adverse inference that the woman had in fact given her consent for the sexual act, and the court gave the benefit of doubt to the accused.[46] A review of cases highlights various situations in which there may be little or no resistance. One reason is the fear of reprisal or a threat to kill the woman or her family.[47] Besides the absence of struggle or resistance (and therefore,

[43] For example, Sanjay Pande, 'Panchayat Settles Rape Case with Fine', *Deccan Herald* (12 July 2014); available at http://www.deccanherald.com/content/419456/panchayat-settles-rape-case-fine.html.

[44] TNN, 'When Rape Becomes a Reason for Marriage', *The Times of India* (Mumbai) (29 August 2013) 11; Brinda Karat, 'When a Judge Suggests a Woman Marry Her Rapist', *NDTV* (1 July 2015); available at http://www.ndtv.com/opinion/jayalalithaa-this-rape-victim-needs-your-attention-777041.

[45] For example, *Rajiv S/o Naresh Chand Prajapati* v *State of Uttar Pradesh* MANU/UP/0485/2007 (High Court of Allahabad, 2007) ('*Rajiv*'); *Shyam Nayak* v *State of Jharkhand* MANU/JH/0661/2007 (High Court of Jharkhand, 2007).

[46] *Deva Nand Singh & Others* v *State of Bihar* 2010 CriLJ 1839 (High Court of Patna, 2009).

[47] *Satya Vir* v *State* Criminal Appeal No. 89 of 2004 (High Court of Uttarakhand, Judgment dated 17 September 2009) ('*Satya Vir*'); *Satish Kumar Sahu* v *State of Chhattisgarh* 2006 CriLJ 1467 (High Court of Chhattisgarh, 2006).

no injuries on the woman's person), this may explain her failure to make noise to attract attention.[48] In some cases, the perpetrators made death threats to victims[49] and their families,[50] if the victim disclosed the fact of the incident to her family, or reported it to the police. Another possibility is that the woman may be tied up or drugged and raped.

However, it is to be noted that the existing criminal law has disapproved the traditional legal presumption of consent against the woman in sexual violence cases. The proviso to Explanation 2 in the amended Section 375 of the Indian Penal Code provides that the fact that a woman did not physically resist penetration cannot be regarded as suggesting that she consented to the sexual activity. Courts have also repeatedly held that the absence of physical injuries does not mean that the woman consented to the sexual act.[51]

In any case, except for the limited deterrent effect of the criminal justice system, its capacity to address the problem of sexual violence against women in general, as well as in the context of access to sanitation facilities, is limited. The specific context of the lack of sanitation facilities that leads to violence against women is irrelevant from the point of view of the criminal justice system. Criminal law and criminal courts, per se, cannot prevent the occurrence of such incidents. It is in this context that the role of sanitation interventions becomes relevant.

[48] In some cases, the victim's attempt to raise an alarm/cry for help was stopped by a threat to kill her by a firearm or at gunpoint. See, for example, *Md. Khalil* v *State* Criminal Appeal (SJ) No. 81 of 1995 (High Court of Patna, Judgment dated 23 June 2011); *Rajiv* (n 45).

[49] For example, *Kabhaibhai Deshaibhai Rathod* v *State of Gujarat* MANU/GJ/7011/2007 (High Court of Gujarat, 2007).

[50] For example, *Sanjay Kumar* v *State (NCT of Delhi)* Criminal Appeal No. 20 of 2004 (High Court of Delhi, Judgment dated 8 February 2010); *Satya Vir* (n 47); *Harishchandra Sah & Another* v *State of Bihar* 2005 (3) BLJR 1886 (High Court of Patna, 2005).

[51] For example, *Kapoor Alias Rajkapoor* v *State of Madhya Pradesh* Criminal Appeal No. 813 of 1990 (High Court of Chhattisgarh, Judgment dated 2 March 2009).

Toilet Construction as a Solution: Overstatement and Eclipsing of Structural Reasons

The rural sanitation policy framework promises that increased safety of women will follow from the construction of IHHLs.[52] As a result, the construction of IHHLs is presented as a solution to gender-based violence. This approach is problematic as it fails to consider—much less engage with or address—the root cause of, or structural reasons for, violence against women, and therefore, this calls for the adoption of a cautious approach while gauging its actual contribution.

First, the policy framework mainly focuses on toilet construction, and presumes that IHHLs will ensure the safety of women. The availability of IHHLs may be an effective intervention to ensure safety of women from 'outsiders'. However, the framework's perception of safety and dignity of women apparently is limited to 'saving' women from 'outsiders'. This ignores the fact that in an overwhelming majority of cases, the offenders are not strangers but known to the victims.[53] Thus, the idea of toilets as a solution to address gender-based violence in the context of defecation may at best address one specific category of violence, that is, the risk of sexual violence by outsiders.[54]

Second, the social and cultural factors leading to gender-based oppression and violence are deeper, more complex, and multifarious. Many of these factors require a multi-pronged approach. In this context, the potential of an IHHL to address gender-based violence is very limited, and it may not be able to address its root causes. Further, women's safety as the rationale for the construction of IHHLs is problematic from the perspective of gender equality,

---

[52] For example, Ministry of Drinking Water and Sanitation (n 34).

[53] 'Out of 34,651 rape cases, in 33,098 cases the offenders were known to the victims accounting for 95.5% of total rape cases'. See Government of India, Ministry of Home Affairs, National Crime Records Bureau, Crime in India 2015: Statistics (National Crime Records Bureau, 2016), 85.

[54] Apoorva Jadhav, Abigail Weitzman, and Emily Smith-Greenaway, 'Household Sanitation Facilities and Women's Risk of Non-partner Sexual Violence in India', *BMC Public Health* (8 November 2016); available at https://bmcpublichealth.biomedcentral.com/articles/10.1186/s12889-016-3797-z.

because in effect, it restricts women's movements. This is relevant in a context where open defecation has been regarded as an opportunity for rural women to socialize.[55]

Third, the overwhelming focus on the construction of IHHLs as a solution to gender-based violence also fails to take into account the reality that toilets, particularly public or community toilets, or toilets in schools and hospitals, or at bus stands and railways stations, are also a site of gender-based violence.[56] This confirms the failure of the framework to acknowledge and engage with the structural reasons for gender-based violence, rather than using the safety of women as the rationale to meet project targets.

Thus, one needs to be cautious about the cumulative impact of law and policy interventions on the freedom and rights of women. Such interventions must not lead to the displacement of women completely from the so-called public spaces to private spaces. The idea of human rights will lose its significance if different implementation frameworks for different human rights systematically (and sometimes discreetly) perpetrate gender inequality and injustice.

* * *

Women's engagement with sanitation is framed by specific biological needs that cannot be eliminated, and socio-cultural notions that choose to pretend that these needs do not exist and do not raise sanitation-related concerns for women. In this context, the effectiveness of the right to sanitation will ultimately be measured, among other factors, by the extent to which it addresses the gender dimensions of sanitation. The realization of the right, however, depends on its incorporation into, and implementation as a part of, the existing law and policy framework.

This chapter examined some aspects of the rural sanitation framework to problematize its role as the perpetrator of gender inequality, and the implications for rights-talk. It reveals that the law and policy

---

[55] Assa Doron and Robin Jeffrey, 'Open Defecation in India', (2014) XLIX(49) *Economic & Political Weekly* 72, 76.

[56] For example, Express News Service, '42-year-old Woman Raped in Ahmedabad', *The Indian Express* (Ahmedabad) (7 December 2014), 5.

framework either pays lip service to the gender dimensions of the right to sanitation, or there is a discernible silence. At the same time, the policy framework has 'used' gender concerns such as the privacy and dignity of women, and the external threat of violence against women, to promote the construction of IHHLs by men. This reaffirms the central position of patriarchy, which is inimical to any conception of gender equality. Other gender dimensions of sanitation, such as MHM, are also largely side-lined. Further, women have a weak voice in the policymaking and implementation processes, which is restrained by the male-dominated social and policy spaces.

Each of the issues discussed in this chapter—and other issues relating to the gender dimensions of sanitation—merit further attention, both in qualitative and quantitative terms. In addition, the endorsement of extension of the 'essential' household chores of women to provide water for use in toilets and to clean the village streets must be challenged. It is also important to subject certain gender–technology linkages to closer scrutiny. This includes the employment of women as manual scavengers and of men as handlers of septage tankers and masons for construction of toilets (although there are some female masons). Further, while the government policy to promote sanitary-napkin-production marts run by women has the potential to empower women, further engagement is required with the issue of social and cultural construction of menstruation, particularly, the attitude of a majority of men towards menstruation.

Glossary

andolan	social movement
anganwadi	mother and child care centre in India
avatar	incarnation or embodiment of a person or idea
basti	slum
chowk	a market place at the junction of two roads
crore	1,00,00,000
Dalit	a member of a lower caste
gali	a lane
ghat	flight of steps leading down to a river
ghunghat	veil
gram panchayat	a body elected by members of the gram sabha of a village
gram sabha	meeting of all adults living in a village
Harijan	a member of a hereditary Hindu group of the lowest social and ritual status
Indira Awas Yojna	a housing scheme for rural areas (renamed Pradhan Mantri Awaas Yojna in 2016)
jhuggi	slum dwelling
kabristan	cemetery/graveyard

kaccha	as opposed to pucca
kshettra samiti	Block committee
lakh	1,00,000
maidan	an open area
nagar palika	municipality
nalla	a water course, river bed, or ravine
nigrani	surveillance
nirmal Bharat	clean India
Nirmal Bharat Abhiyan	Clean India Campaign
Nirmal Gram Puraskar	Clean Village Award
Nirmal Gram Yojna	Clean Village Plan
panchayat	elected village council in rural areas
panchayati raj	decentralized system of governance in rural areas
Panchayati Raj institutions	institutions of local governance at the panchayat, Block, and District level
panchayat samiti	Block panchayat
patta	title deed to a property
pucca	solid and permanent
purdah	veil
safai karamchari	sanitation worker
Safai Karmachari Andolan	a movement by sanitation workers
safai karmi	person in charge of sanitation in rural areas
sarpanch	president of a gram panchayat, the lowest administrative unit in the rural context.
swachh Bharat	clean India
Swachh Bharat Mission	Clean India Mission
Valmiki	a scheduled caste, often considered 'untouchable'
vyavasaya samiti	a committee of traders
yatra	journey
zila parishad	District council

Editors and Contributors

Editors

Philippe Cullet is professor of international and environmental law at SOAS University of London, UK, and a senior visiting fellow at the Centre for Policy Research, New Delhi, India. He received his doctoral degree in law from Stanford University, Stanford, California, an MA in development studies from SOAS University of London, an LLM in international law from King's College London, Strand, London, and his undergraduate law degree from the University of Geneva, Switzerland. His work and publications focus on environmental law, natural resources law, water and sanitation law and policy, human rights, and the socio-economic aspects of intellectual property. His latest books are *Water Law in India: An Introduction to Legal Instruments* (Oxford University Press, 2nd edition, 2017, co-edited with Sujith Koonan) and *Groundwater and Climate Change: Multi-level Law and Policy Perspectives*, 2019, co-edited with R.S. Stephan). He was a member of the River Development & Ganga Rejuvenation Committee, Ministry of Water Resources, Government of India, drafting the Draft National Water Framework Bill, 2016, and the Model Groundwater (Sustainable Management) Bill, 2017.

Sujith Koonan teaches at Campus Law Centre, Faculty of Law, University of Delhi, India. He completed his PhD from SOAS University of London, UK where he was a recipient of the SOAS Doctoral Research Scholarship (2013–16). He holds an MPhil in international law from Jawaharlal Nehru University, New Delhi and LLM in environmental law and human rights from Cochin University of Science and Technology, Kerala, India. He is a member of the editorial board of the Law, Environment and Development (LEAD) journal. Before joining the University of Delhi, he worked with the Environmental Law Research Society (ELRS), New Delhi as a law researcher and taught at various institutions in India and abroad including SOAS University of London, UK; National Law University Delhi, India, TERI School of Advanced Studies, India, Indian Society of International Law, India and Amity Law School, Noida, India. He also has the experience of contributing to law and policy making; he was part of the working group constituted by the Planning Commission of India on water governance for the 12th Five-Year Plan (2012–17) and in 2018, worked with an expert group constituted by the Karnataka Knowledge Commission, Government of Karnataka to frame a comprehensive State Water Policy. His main areas of interest are environmental law, water and sanitation, law and natural resources, human rights, international law and agro-biodiversity. He has co-edited *Water Law in India: An Introduction to Legal Instruments* (Oxford University Press, 2nd edition, 2017, co-edited with Philippe Cullet). His publications can be accessed at http://ielrc.org/about_koonan.php.

Lovleen Bhullar received her PhD in law from SOAS University of London, UK. She holds an undergraduate degree in law from the National Law School of India University, Bangalore, India, an LLM in environmental law from SOAS University of London, and an MSc in environmental policy and regulation from the London School of Economics and Political Science, UK. Bhullar is associated with the Law, Environment and Development (LEAD) journal published jointly by SOAS and the International Environmental Law Research Centre (IELRC), Geneva, as well as the Environmental Law Research Society (ELRS), a non-governmental organization based in New Delhi. Her research focuses on the rights to environment, water, and sanitation, generally and specifically in the context of water pollution, and the associated international and domestic (in India) law and policy frameworks. She has also written on aspects of climate change, forest, and water governance.

Contributors

Akshayaa Benjamin is an advocate practicing in the Madras High Court, and other courts in Tamil Nadu. She holds a bachelor's degree from the School of Excellence in Law, Chennai, Tamil Nadu, India and a master's degree from Queen Mary University of London, UK.

Catarina de Albuquerque is the executive chair of the global partnership Sanitation and Water for All since December 2014. From 2008 to 2014 she was the first UN Special Rapporteur on the right to safe drinking water and sanitation. Between 2004 and 2008, she presided over the negotiations for the Optional Protocol to the International Covenant on Economic, Social and Cultural Rights. For almost twenty years, Albuquerque was a professor at the law faculties of the Universities of Braga and Coimbra, Portugal and a senior legal adviser at the Office for Documentation and Comparative Law, an independent institution under the Portuguese Prosecutor General's Office. She was awarded the Human Rights Golden Medal by the Portuguese Parliament in 2009 for outstanding work in the area of human rights. The President of the Portuguese Republic honoured her work in human rights with the Order of Merit in October 2009. She holds a law degree from the Law Faculty of the University of Lisbon, Portugal and a diplôme d'études supérieures (DES) from the Graduate Institute, Geneva, and she received a doctor honoris causa degree from the University of North Carolina at Chapel Hill.

Renu Desai is a research fellow with the Centre for Urban Equity (CUE) at CEPT University, Ahmedabad, Gujarat. Renu's research examines urban informality and urban transformation in Indian cities, with a focus on questions of equitable development and urban citizenship. She has a PhD in architecture from the University of California, Berkeley. Her doctoral dissertation examined how the intersections of urban redevelopment and Hindutva politics were reshaping urban space in Ahmedabad, Gujarat. Renu has been with CUE since October 2011, and has led research on riverfront displacement and resettlement in Ahmedabad, rental housing in Guwahati, land/housing tenure in Nagpur and Nanded, and construction workers' housing in Ahmedabad. She was part of CUE's team on a three-year IDRC-funded research project which interrogated the linkages between urban violence and urban planning/governance, and led the Ahmedabad part of the research. Renu has published several book chapters and journal articles.

Jackie Dugard teaches at the University of the Witwatersrand, South Africa. In February 2014, she established the university's new Gender Equity Office (formerly called the Sexual Harassment Office), and she was appointed as its director in August 2014. Jackie became the chairperson of the board of directors of the Socio-Economic Rights Institute of South Africa (SERI) in June 2015. She previously sat on SERI's board of directors and was an honorary senior researcher. Jackie co-founded SERI in January 2010, and was executive director of the organization till December 2012. Prior to founding SERI, Jackie was a senior researcher at the Centre for Applied Legal Studies (CALS) at the University of the Witwatersrand in Johannesburg between 2004 and 2009. Jackie's areas of expertise are socio-economic rights, socio-legal studies, and access to basic services and justice for the poor. Jackie has a BA (Hons) in African politics and an LLB from the University of the Witwatersrand; an LLM in international human rights law from the University of Essex, and an MPhil in the sociology and politics of development and a PhD in social and political sciences from the University of Cambridge.

Stephen Graham is professor of cities and society at the Global Urban Research Unit in the School of Architecture, Planning and Landscape, Newcastle University, UK. He has a background in geography, planning, and the sociology of technology. His research centres, in particular, on vertical aspects of cities and urban life; links between cities, technology, and infrastructure; urban aspects of surveillance; the mediation of urban life by digital technologies; and links between security, militarization, and urban life. Writing, publishing, and lecturing across many countries, and a variety of disciplines, Graham has been a visiting professor at Massachusetts Institute of Technology, USA and New York University, USA, among other institutions. He is the author, editor, or co-author of seven major books, and his work has been translated into eighteen languages. He has a PhD in science and technology policy from the University of Manchester, UK, an MPhil in town and country planning from the Newcastle University, UK (where he was awarded the Royal Town Planning Institute Prize), and a BSc (Hons) in geography from the University of Southampton, UK.

Mathew John teaches and is an executive director at the Centre on Public Law and Jurisprudence, Jindal Global Law School, Haryana, India. Mathew has a graduate degree in law from the National Law School of India University, Bangalore, India, and an LLM from the University of Warwick, UK, and he completed his doctoral work at London School of Economics and Political Science, UK, on the impact of secularism on Indian constitutional practice. He has previously worked at the Alternative Law Forum, Bengaluru, India on social justice lawyering; he was a law and culture fellow at the Centre for the Study of Culture and Society, Bengaluru, India; and he has been a visiting fellow at the Centre for the Study of Law and Governance, Jawaharlal Nehru University, New Delhi, India. His research interests are public law, constitutionalism, governance, pluralism, and human rights.

Shomona Khanna is a lawyer practicing in the Supreme Court of India and High Court of Delhi. She has been associated with numerous civil and democratic rights issues since 1991, both as a lawyer and as a writer. Shomona continues to handle several human rights cases in the courts, and render legal advice to a variety of organizations including Campaign for Survival and Dignity (a federation of people's organizations of forest dwellers), Ministry of Tribal Affairs, Government of India, Ambedkar University, New Delhi, India, and Plachimada Solidarity Committee. She has written several books and monographs on indigenous peoples, the Constitution of India, and the law, and most recently edited a compendium of court decisions on the Scheduled Tribes and Other Traditional Forest Dwellers (Recognition of Forest Rights) Act, 2006.

Colin McFarlane is a professor in the department of geography in Durham University, UK. He is an urban geographer whose work focuses on the experience and politics of informal neighbourhoods. This has involved research into the relations between informality, infrastructure, and knowledge in urban India and elsewhere. A key part of the former research has been a focus on the experience and politics of sanitation in informal settlements in Mumbai, which was part of an ethnographic project on the everyday cultures and contested politics of sanitation and water in two informal settlements, supported by the Economic and Social Research Council, UK. His current work examines the politicization of informal neighbourhoods in a comparative perspective, including African and South Asian cities. In 2013, he was awarded the Leverhulme Prize for his research in urban geography. In 2010, he was awarded the Gill Memorial Award from the Royal Geographical Society for contributions to urban geography, and in 2009, a fellowship for his work on sanitation from Berlin's Irmgard Coninx Foundation in conjunction with Humboldt University of Berlin, Germany.

Lyla Mehta is a professorial research fellow at the Institute of Development Studies (IDS), UK, and a visiting professor at Noragric, Norwegian University of Life Sciences. She is a sociologist by training (University of Vienna) and has a PhD in Development Studies from the University of Sussex. Her work focuses on water and sanitation, forced displacement and resistance, scarcity, rights and access, resource grabbing, politics of environment/development, the politics of Integrated Water Resources Management (IWRM) in Africa, and uncertainty and climate change from below in India. She has conducted extensive field research in India studying the politics of water scarcity; the linkages between gender, displacement, and resistance; access to water in peri-urban areas; and climate change and uncertainty. She has also worked on water management issues in southern Africa, and studied the cultural and institutional aspects of sanitation in Ethiopia, Bangladesh, India, and Indonesia, and the scaling of community-led total sanitation (CLTS). She has published extensively on various issues including water, sanitation, and environment, and development-related issues. She is currently the water and sanitation domain convener of the STEPS Centre (Social, Technological and Environmental Pathways to Sustainability) at IDS.

M. Nirmalkumar is an advocate practicing in the courts at Chennai and Puducherry. He holds a bachelor's degree in law from the School of Excellence in Law, Chennai, Tamil Nadu, and a master's degree in labour and administrative laws from Dr Ambedkar Government Law College, Chennai, Tamil Nadu. He writes on law and politics in print and online media.

P. Sakthivel teaches human rights, international law, and environmental law at the Tamil Nadu Dr Ambedkar Law University (TNDALU), Chennai, India. He has a PhD from TNDALU, and his thesis focused on irrigation laws and farmers' rights. He studied law at the Government Law College, Coimbatore, India and University of Madras, Chennai, India. He holds an MA in history from Annamalai University, Tamil Nadu, India. He has been a water law consultant to international agencies and technical universities. In addition, he has an interest in law and society.

Ruchi Shree teaches political science at the Janki Devi Memorial College (JDMC), University of Delhi, India. She received her PhD in 2015 from the Centre for Political Studies (CPS), Jawaharlal Nehru University (JNU), New Delhi, India. She did her MA and MPhil from CPS, JNU. Since 2012, she is one of the coordinators of a short-term course titled 'Peace and Conflict Studies: A Gandhian Alternative'. She has worked as a co-investigator on an Innovation Project of the University of Delhi titled 'Creative Solutions to Water-logging through Rainwater Harvesting in South Delhi' (2013–14). Ruchi's main areas of interest include the politics of water, natural resources and development discourse, social movements, human rights, and comparative politics. She has published many research papers and book reviews in renowned national and international publications. She has reviewed books for journals like *Contemporary South Asia, Strategic Analysis, Gandhi Marg*, and *Social Change*. She has also written several popular articles in Hindi.

Bezwada Wilson is the national convener of the Safai Karmachari Andolan (SKA), a national movement committed to the total eradication of manual scavenging and the rehabilitation of all scavengers to dignified occupations in India. He has been leading this movement for over a decade. Bezwada and his organization have served as a watchdog, pushing for legal action to demolish dry toilets across India and preparing manual scavengers for new sources of employment. His goal is to detach manual scavenging and sanitary work from Dalits in the larger context of reforming the caste system by pushing government agencies to replace manual scavenging with mechanization. He was awarded the Ashoka Fellowship in 2009. He was honoured with the Ramon Magsaysay Award in 2016.

Index